Long Road to Liberty

Long Road to Liberty

The Odyssey of a German Regiment
in the Yankee Army

THE 15TH MISSOURI VOLUNTEER INFANTRY

Donald Allendorf

For Janet,
It's still a great photo!
Don

The Kent State University Press
KENT, OHIO

© 2006 by The Kent State University Press, Kent, Ohio 44242
ALL RIGHTS RESERVED
Library of Congress Catalog Card Number 2006011513
ISBN-10: 0-87338-871-2
ISBN-13: 978-0-87338-871-9
Manufactured in the United States of America

10 09 08 07 06   5 4 3 2 1

LIBRARY OF CONGRESS CATALOGING-IN-PUBLICATION DATA
Allendorf, Donald, 1934–
Long road to liberty : the odyssey of a German regiment in the Yankee army :
the 15th Missouri Volunteer Infantry / Donald Allendorf.
p.   cm.
Includes bibliographical references and index.
ISBN-13: 978-0-87338-871-9 (hardcover : alk. paper) ∞
ISBN-10: 0-87338-871-2 (hardcover : alk. paper) ∞
1. United States. Army. Missouri Infantry Regiment, 15th (1861–1865)
2. Missouri—History—Civil War, 1861–1865—Regimental histories.
3. United States—History—Civil War, 1861–1865—Regimental histories.
4. United States—History—Civil War, 1861–1865—Participation, German American.
5. United States—History—Civil War, 1861–1865—Participation, Immigrant.
6. German American soldiers—Missouri—History—19th century.
7. Immigrants—Missouri—History—19th century.
I. Title.
E517.515TH .A45 2006
973.7'47808931—DC22   2006011513

British Library Cataloging-in-Publication data are available.

For Thomas and Christopher,
Elizabeth, David, and Emily,
that they may know of one
who went before.

Contents

Illustrations and Maps

Preface and Acknowledgments

A century and a half ago, a family member, a German immigrant, was among the first volunteers to join the Union army. Why, one might ask, would a foreigner—with a wife and two children—choose to go to war for a nation whose language he could barely speak, if at all?

The answer is hard to come by. German immigrant soldiers held to an almost stoic silence compared to their native-born counterparts, writing almost nothing of their motives or their soldiering experiences during the Civil War. The paucity of firsthand material from these volunteers has been a perplexing problem for historians. It certainly has been so for this writer.

James McPherson notes the virtual absence of immigrant soldier papers in his Civil War study *For Cause and Comrades*, when compared to the letters, diaries, and reminiscences of the American-born soldier. The Missouri Historical Society in St. Louis, the state's largest repository for Civil War papers, lists more than a thousand collections of letters, diaries, and personal manuscripts. Some five hundred of these are by Missourians. Yet just fifteen of these are by German immigrant soldiers—archived now in a city that was predominantly German during the Civil War and whose Union volunteers were also predominantly German.

Another large repository, the Western Historical Manuscript Collection at the University of Missouri-Columbia, lists 155 individual letters and diaries by Missourians who fought in the Civil War. Only four are by Germans from Missouri, two letters and two diaries, less than 3 percent of the total—when about 20 percent of the hundred thousand or so Missourians who fought for the North were German or of German-born parents.

All told, we have to date the personal letters or diaries of no more than two dozen of these German men from Missouri. Just two letters, one only a brief note requesting leave, are by soldiers of the 15th Missouri Volunteer Infantry.

The scarcity seems to have had an effect even on the public press of the time: except for a couple of clippings, one appearing long after the war had ended, St. Louis newspapers of the period have revealed almost nothing about the 15th Missouri.

There does exist, fortunately, a single firsthand account of the 15th, an almost day-by-day chronicle of life in this regiment, written years after the war by one of its survivors. A regional historian has referred to it as a rare find. Without it, writing this book would have been far more difficult. At the least, this odyssey of a German regiment in the Civil War would have taken on a wholly different character.

The lone firsthand account, of course, is not the only primary source. The regiment's official records—correspondence files particularly—are rich with substantive and anecdotal information. I have scoured the National Archive's *Compiled Service Records* of the 15th's more than nine hundred officers and men and the regiment's correspondence folders at the Missouri State Information Center, the state's archives. The findings are augmented with after-action reports, telegrams, dispatches, and correspondence from the *Official Records of the Rebellion*. They are combined here to bring the regiment and many of its volunteers into focus. Other primary sources, of those who fought with and against them have added to the picture.

Their odyssey began with Lincoln's first call for volunteers. It would take them more than 800 miles from their home state, but they would travel on foot, by steamboat, and by rail, all told, more than 10,100 miles. Four and a half years later they would arrive home again. Of the six hundred or so German boys of 1861 who first set out to save the Union, their new fatherland, there would be fewer than a hundred who would return. Except for a marker or a monument here and there in Tennessee and Georgia, they left little for their descendants or their adopted country to remember them by. This book is an effort to rectify that.

Maurice Marcoot wrote the only known firsthand account of the 15th Missouri Volunteer Infantry more than a century ago. If the construction of this book were like the building of a ship, his manuscript would be the keel.

Marcoot all but ran away to join the Union army at the age of sixteen. With Adolph Faess, his "bunkie," as Marcoot referred to his friend and comrade in arms, he began a log of their wartime travels with the 15th Missouri. It became a diary of sorts that would span the beginning of the Civil War to almost nine months after the end of the war, when the regiment was finally allowed to pass into history. Except for six months when he was away because of illness (probably due to typhoid fever from drinking from swampy waters along the march), Marcoot was both participant and eye-witness in one of the Union's "fightingest" regiments according to a massive study by a U.S. Army authority after the war. Unfortunately, because of his illnesses, Marcoot missed four of the regiment's battles in which the 15th fought so desperately at Stones River, Spring Hill, and Franklin, Tennessee, and finally at Nashville.

Even so, when he was away from "his boys" recuperating, his bunkie took on the job maintaining the log. In more than twenty other battles, Marcoot was the primary log keeper. Among his entries are accounts of both his personal and the 15th's near annihilation at Chickamauga and, two months later, his sharp-eyed report as a participant in the Union's dramatic "charge without orders" up Missionary Ridge.

The log would form the basis of his later manuscript. A reunion with a befriended Confederate veteran twenty years after the war prompted Marcoot to revisit the log and return to the old battlefields to refresh his memories. In 1890 he published his manuscript of reminiscences and offered it to the public for one dollar. One cannot help feeling, however, that he had a much larger reason for wanting his remembrances to live again.

In its printing more than a hundred years ago, Maurice Marcoot's typeset manuscript is peppered with misspellings, slightly incorrect place names and the like, but most of a minor nature. Poor proofreading at the time was more likely the culprit than Marcoot's own spelling. I have left these as is unless the error was so glaring it demanded correction. Because his manuscript is quoted extensively throughout, the editorial "[*sic*]" is not used; it would appear too frequently and consequently be too interruptive to the text to do so. An error will likely be obvious in any event. The same holds for the regiment's correspondence, frequently written by those more familiar with the German language and less so with the spelling of English words.

I want to thank particularly Dennis Northcott of the Missouri Historical Society Library in St. Louis for pointing me in other important directions, to "see" the St. Louis Germans and their role during that time of our nation's greatest trauma. It is hard for me to imagine a person and an institution more deserving of gratitude and special commendation for sponsoring the translation of the papers of these newcomers to America. Mr. Northcott's massive effort to summarize and compile the Society's guide to the more than one thousand of its Civil War collections—including the recently translated papers of German immigrants to Missouri—now puts the words of this immigrant soldier within easy reach of the English-only historian.

There are others, of course, who deserve my thanks as well:

To Mary Beck, military records archivist of the Missouri State Information Center in Jefferson City, for bringing to my attention the 15th Missouri's regimental correspondence files in the state's archives.

To Jim West, historian of the Stones River National Battlefield Park, and to the park's staff for giving so generously of their time to dig through their files and discovering pertinent papers, and for the personal tour of the very ground on which the 15th Missouri took their stand, a stand that very nearly became their last.

To the staff of the State Historical Society of Missouri and the Western Historical Manuscript Collection at the University of Missouri-Columbia for making files and papers available that were relevant to the 15th Missouri—and especially to James Goodrich, executive director of those fine repositories, now retired, for taking the time to read portions of my manuscript, making valuable contributions, and saving me from some embarrassing errors. If errors remain, they are solely mine.

To Eric Wittenberg, Civil War authority and author, for his encouragement and good advice and Daniel Sutherland, historian and professor, at the University of Arkansas, whose suggestions contributed much to the final form of this book.

To James Harlan, project manager, and Dwayne Hemmer of the Geographic Resources Center at the University of Missouri-Columbia for their cartographic expertise, to be sure, but also for their insistence on accuracy and their pains to produce the detailed battle maps; to Dr. Lorie Thombs of the University's Statistical Resources Center and Yun Bao, Man-Hua Chen, Zhijian Chen, Nur Isa Diandalu, Xiaonan Guo, Peigin Lu, Xiaogian Sun, and Jiahui Yan of Dr. Thombs' STAT class, for their careful analysis to calculate the accuracy confidence levels of my data for the "Statistical Portrait of the 15th Missouri Soldier."

To Will Underwood and Joanna Hildebrand Craig of Kent State University Press for their confidence in this story and their patience to see it through; to copy editors Tara Lenington and Mary Tederstrom, who combed every line and flagged my discursions; and to Christine Brooks, who directed the design and managed the production.

To John Graham, family member and former educator, and daughter Tracey Mershon, consummate communications professional: both raised questions during the project's embryonic stage that gave a shape to this book that I had not envisioned.

To my son, Dr. Mark Allendorf, for his interest and ever-encouraging support.

Finally, to my trail buddy, my wife, June Allendorf: for listening to my ramblings to start with; for launching out with me on research expeditions that took us hundreds of miles in every direction, driving the roadways and tramping the ground where her great-grandfather and his 15th Missouri comrades marched and fought; for sitting for hours on library chairs and sifting through papers with me, without complaint; for reading and proofing countless iterations of pages and drafts; for encouraging and occasionally pushing; and for more times than I want to remember, for raising tough questions (and raising my hackles in the process). In the end, though, we both knew she was right.

Introduction

In the years leading up to the Civil War, a major political party advocated an end to immigration and a ban on the right to vote for U.S. citizens born in a foreign country—so discriminatory was the temperament of the times against newcomers to America. Perhaps in no other place in the United States was this more vivid than in the state of Missouri. How ironic this is, for were it not for one group of immigrants, Missouri very likely would have seceded from the Union.

They were also among the first in the state to answer Lincoln's call for volunteers. These immigrants were from the same European country but most would never have known each other but for the awfulness of war. They would come together as volunteers in one of the first Union regiments from Missouri, a regiment made up almost entirely of recent arrivals from Germany.

Theirs is a story that has been virtually ignored by Civil War historians. But these newcomers to America share a large part of the blame. Mysteriously, and unlike their American-born counterparts, German immigrant soldiers wrote little of the war to family or loved ones. They were better educated than most native-born soldiers. They made up about 10 percent of the entire Union army and an even larger part of the armies that served in the western theatre. Compared to their American-born counterparts, they left little to explain why they fought, what they saw, how they felt. One must look elsewhere to attempt to understand these newcomers to America.

Historians will probably forever argue the causes that led to the Civil War, but there is no mistaking why the German immigrant fought. The question of individual rights was the centerpiece. The German immigrant who made his home in Missouri was driven by it. He had collided with discrimination in America because he was not considered an American; he was a "Dutchman." His decision to volunteer at the very outbreak of the war made it plain that he would no longer bow to the discriminations he and his ancestors had endured for centuries in his mother country.

Discriminations born of rigid class distinctions pervaded German life for centuries, but with the end of the Thirty Years' War in 1648, a revolutionary zeal began to animate the average German. The war had strengthened the power of the princes and landed aristocracy at the expense of the lower classes, falling hardest in religious and economic matters; where one worked and worshipped resided more than ever with the resident prince or at the caprice of the local *Oberschichter,* the landed gentry. But attempts to acquire the most basic of individual freedoms crashed against the autocratic demand for obedience to authoritarian rule.[1]

Suppressions continued for almost two centuries. Even intellectual freedoms suffered a devastating blow; a decision in 1835 by the Diet of the German Confederation, fearful of challenges to moral and religious standards, banned the writings of a group of writers labeled the "Young Germany."[2] Thirteen years later, in 1848, unrest flared into revolution. Sparked by university students and supported by German military, the revolt quickly gathered support among journalists, lawyers, and other professional people. Germany's democratic revolution nevertheless failed, and a major exodus to America began.

A decade earlier, the first German immigrants to come to Missouri in substantial numbers immigrated for religious reasons. In the early 1850s came the defeated revolutionaries to escape imprisonment or worse. The decade leading up to the Civil War also saw another wave, mainly tradesmen and farmers immigrating for economic reasons.[3] They would be in search of personal freedoms as well. None could know then the terrible road they would have to follow to gain those liberties.

Within the year following the end of the War of the Rebellion, some two thousand regiments, just about the entire Union army, officially mustered out of service and passed into history. Except for units such as the 20th Maine, the 1st Minnesota, and others immortalized on now-hallowed ground such as Gettysburg and hundreds of other places, few words have ever been written about most of them. Even so, firsthand accounts and regimental histories by the participants were often written only years later, belatedly but for very human, very understandable reasons. Those who saw the war and lived through it would require a long time for their hearts and minds to heal enough to revisit it all and finally record it.

So awful were the conditions endured by Civil War soldiers and so terrible the casualties throughout the war, it is doubtful that public opinion today rendered of a television age would have supported the war for very long. Yet, even when given a chance to go home after having served three terrible years, many instead, as did the immigrants of the 15th Missouri, chose to reenlist and once again "lay it all on the line," as they would have said. For that devotion and a three-hundred-dollar bounty, their muster cards note the singular honor of "veteran," bestowed only upon those who elected to reenlist at the height of the war and see it through to the end. Many years later, it would occur to some that what they had done, and the dangers they had met and faced down, should not be lost to the ages.

The regiment was often the context for many of their writings. It was the unit of military organization that was the soldier's community. His company within the regiment was his army family. As one of up to eighty-two privates in his company,[4] he would live with these brothers side by side, day and night. He would get to know their names and where they were from. Together, they would sleep, eat, drill, forage for food and firewood, and march.

Together, they would gamble, drink, and share memories of home. They would stand picket duty, and when word came down that the enemy was near, they would talk of home and try not to think of the storm of leaden hail that might come on the morrow.

Out on the company skirmish line, he would partner up, one covering for the other, taking turns firing single-shot rifles so that they would not be caught with an empty weapon. In the line of battle, when the sound of war drowned out all others, he would know the man next to him who fell, sometimes never to rise again. When the terrible noise finally died away, except for the moans and groans of the wounded and the dying, the duty to place his companion's body under the earth would fall to him. He would forever remember his comrade's name and where he was from.

Ten such companies made up a Union regiment of about eight hundred men in the ranks although the numbers would vary widely during the course of the war. Four regiments customarily made up a brigade; three brigades made up a division; three divisions comprised a corps; and two or more corps usually made up an army, such as the Army of the Potomac or the Army of the Cumberland.

Not all of the two thousand or so regiments that served in the Union army shared equally in the combat and the sacrifice. A small number disbanded before filling their ranks with volunteers. Still others did not finish

the war because the men, having seen enough of the "elephant,"[5] decided not to renew their three-year enlistments. These too were disbanded,
their remnants folded into the veteran units that had committed to see it
through to the end of the war.

As is so often the case in war, a relatively small percentage of the whole
bore the brunt of the casualties. It was the fate of some regiments to be
all but literally killed on the battlefield. Most regiments would survive,
although often not under the names or with the numbers with which they
had set out to fight. A monumental study published twenty-four years after the war identified three hundred regiments, the "Fightingest Three
Hundred," from the more than two thousand that had made up the Union
army. The criterion was based on their numbers killed in battle.[6] These
regiments lost in combat at least 10 percent of those who had served with
the regiment. One might argue whether these were indeed the Union's
"fightingest" regiments; yet they very likely would be found among that
group whatever the criterion. The least that can be said of these regiments,
considering their battle records along with their casualties, is that they
were indeed where the action was.

Out west in Missouri, torn murderously by divided loyalties, thirty-nine
infantry regiments from that state served the Union. Of those thirty-nine,
five are listed among the select Three Hundred. Of these five, two regiments were among the first to go to war and the last to leave. But what made
these two regiments different from the others is that their volunteers were
made up of recruits born in another country. Most could hardly speak English or knew none at all. They would participate in all but a few of the major
battles fought in the western theatre of the war. The 15th Missouri would
serve the longest. For their service, they would endure the highest percentage of battlefield mortality of all the Union regiments from Missouri.

The 15th Missouri Volunteer Infantry served almost five years, most of
that time in almost daily contact with their Southern adversaries in Tennessee and Georgia. Their desperate combat alongside brother regiments
at Stones River in Tennessee has been called by some historians the most
determined stand of the war, at a cost of almost 40 percent killed, wounded,
or missing. Their division commander, Gen. Phil Sheridan, wrote later that
never again would he experience so high a rate of casualties in any of his
commands. His later commands would fight at such bloody places as the
Wilderness and Cold Harbor.

At Chickamauga the 15th Missouri "charged bayonets" before being
all but surrounded by Alabama divisions of Longstreet's Corps. Swept by
fire from three sides, they made a brief stand before giving way, leaving 40

percent of their comrades on the field—dead, wounded, or prisoners of war—some to die as captives at the prison at Andersonville. Less than two months later, without orders, they with others of the famed Fourth Corps would scramble up the boulder-strewn face of Missionary Ridge above Chattanooga, and with shouts of "Chickamauga! Chickamauga!" rush into the Confederate trenches in one of the war's most dramatic charges. When the war was finally over, one of every eight men of the 15th had given his life in combat. All told, more than half of the 904 officers and men who had ever served with the regiment had been either killed or wounded. Another 107 died of disease.

Politicians in and around Washington, D.C., during the war paid less attention to the western armies than those in the East. Their focus was on Gen. Robert E. Lee and his Army of Northern Virginia, which was far more threatening, as it could put a quick end to everything with one decisive attack on the capital. No Southern general west of the Appalachians could even contemplate such a possibility.

Lincoln's directive to keep the Union Army of the Potomac between Washington and the enemy, no matter what other distractions arose, gave a clear understanding to this danger. The first Battle at Bull Run, just beyond the suburbs of the capital, struck justifiable fear into the federal government and demonstrated the wisdom of that strategy. Consequently, as Northern ranks continued to grow and muskets, cannon, and ammunition swelled federal warehouses, Washington heeded first the calls for men and supplies from the armies in the East.

The West, as a result, was the place you were sent if you failed to measure up in the East according to the judgment of the War Department. If you were outnumbered, outflanked, and gave way in the face of almost certain death, the high command in the East would require a scapegoat, which would be reason enough to send you west at the first opportunity. An entire corps, largely of German immigrant regiments, learned that after Gettysburg.

Journalists of the day viewed the war in much the same way. As the North's political and military vortex, the nation's capital was the center for the new telegraph system: all wires led to Washington, D.C. Consequently, the city was also the nation's news center.[7] The eastern theatre of the war was much closer to Washington, which made the war in the East that much easier for the large and powerful newspapers in New York City to cover from the capital. Correspondents would eventually penetrate the western theatre, but as the war rounded out its first year, "Bobby" Lee in the East and a general nicknamed "Stonewall" made very good copy. Besides, the only thing one would learn "out West" was that there was a Union general out there who drank too much on occasion, and in this man's army, that was hardly news.

The western theatre nevertheless hardly lacked for battle action, in size or number. Outside of Virginia, more battles and skirmishes were fought in Tennessee than in any other state. Next in line, incidentally, was Missouri, as skirmishing took place almost every day somewhere in the state.[8] The battle with the highest percentage of casualties in the entire war was fought along the Stones River near Murfreesboro, Tennessee. Along the Chickamauga River in northern Georgia, more men were killed or wounded during the second day of fighting than in any of the three days' fighting at Gettysburg. At the Battle of Franklin in Tennessee, the Confederate general John B. Hood sent more men against the Union lines, in what some have claimed "the grandest charge of the war," than Pickett had at his disposal at Gettysburg and with greater losses in dead and wounded. Battles in Virginia may have been strategically more important, though one may argue that their outcomes were no more consequential than those in Georgia and Tennessee. Indeed, a number of respected historians today have concluded as much.[9]

When the war broke out, German immigrants were among the first to volunteer. Although a handful of militia units would challenge it, the German Turner Rifles in Washington claimed the distinction of being the first volunteer unit mustered into service for the Union in January 1861—four months before the surrender of Fort Sumter and Lincoln's first call for volunteers. They would form the honor guard for the new president's inauguration.[10]

Germans volunteered in such large numbers that it became an embarrassment for native-born Americans in the North. In heavily German-populated cities such as Cincinnati, Milwaukee, and St. Louis, politicians feared a backlash from the larger population about *too* much German visibility.[11] As if to counter the rush of immigrant volunteers in New York, which produced more German regiments than any other state, a newly formed regiment claimed to be a truly American unit—in which all of its members were actually native-born.[12]

As the opportunity arose, newspapers and magazines throughout the North disparaged foreigners to a ready readership. Words and phrases were coined to demean the customs of the newcomers. Their efforts to speak the English language were ridiculed. Attempts were even made to impugn their character as soldiers. One such effort even made its way into song. The press of the day took pleasure in picking up the ditty, and for a while it was even popular with the American public.[13]

If there was anything positive to be said about the German immigrant, it could be found in the German-language newspapers of the day—hardly standard fare, of course, for English-speaking Americans. Even then, except for casualty lists, the reporting on German regiments from St. Louis rarely appeared. The *Anzeiger des Westens*, the city's powerful German newspaper, relied on other newspapers for coverage of major battles, papers whose correspondents were closer to the action. A report of the Battle of Stones River by the *Cincinnati Commercial* appeared more than a week later in the *Anzeiger*, a typical delay for the biweekly throughout the war. Aside from a tribute to the German brigade commander from St. Louis who had been killed in the battle (inserted by the *Anzeiger*), the report focused on Ohio and Kentucky units. No information appeared about Missouri regiments. One paragraph carried the subhead *"Ein Ungloeckliches Regiment"* ("An unlucky regiment"), referring to one with a "15th" designation, a Kentucky regiment in this instance.[14] For the *Anzeiger*'s readers, the 15th from Missouri would have been far more newsworthy. In the number of casualties alone, the 15th Missouri had also been far more unlucky.

Almost 2.5 million men served in the Union army. Most authorities estimate that 200,000 were of German birth, possibly a little less than 10 percent of the Union armies.[15] That percentage would place at least 100,000 German immigrants among the 1.1 million men who served in the western theatre. Even so, one is hard-pressed to find an account written by a German immigrant, in letters or diaries, in English or German, in reference libraries or bibliographies.

There is an almost eerie silence when one searches for these foreign voices from the past. Why the silence? Perhaps it was because many of these young men, having only recently arrived from the old country, had no immediate families in America to write to. Perhaps many of these writings went back to families in Europe, all but out of reach of historians in the United States.

There is reason to suspect that many of these soldier-immigrants did not in fact write home to the old country. It is sad to note, as one reviews the 15th Missouri's records of those who had been killed, that their personal effects often were sent to friends in America and not to family, in either America or Germany. Many of the records of these men rarely list a family member as a nearest relative. Instead, in the space marked for "Nearest Relative," the name of a friend appears, often the name of another immigrant in America. Perhaps the new soldier, now so far from home, did not want to give a mother and father still more reason to worry.

James McPherson, in his study *For Cause and Comrades*, concluded that the immigrant soldier did not write about his experiences because he was less educated than his American-born counterpart. His reasoning is based on the fact that the foreign-born soldier often came from the working class.[16] This is true, but that conclusion alone does not fully explain the lack of written records. The observation may hold for immigrants in general, but the education factor is not accurate when applied to the German immigrant soldier.

The German immigrant was typically better educated in his homeland, where education was prized even among farm families. Many German-born volunteers had been university students and military officers involved in Germany's failed democratic revolution of 1848. It is recorded, for instance, in the classic study of the Northern soldier, Bell Wiley's *The Life of Billy Yank*, that "many Germans and especially the Forty-eighters, were men of good education and refined tastes whose influence improved the cultural tone of the units to which they belonged. . . . The German volunteer had a reputation for unusual diligence in reading as well as a preference for 'stronger meat' than native Americans"[17]—strong evidence of a better education.

Many German soldiers did indeed come from working-class occupations—"laborer" is found frequently on the enlistment papers of those who served in the 15th Missouri. That fact sometimes had little to do with education or a lack of it. In the America of those days, the immigrant typically could get work only as a laborer because, at least in St. Louis in the mid-nineteenth century, he was ostracized as a foreigner.

Three years into the war, the horrors of the battlefields had become all too real, and the well of volunteers had dried up. The federal government was compelled to resort to conscription. Population data suggesting underrepresentation of immigrants in the Union army has led to judgments that immigrants were prone to dodge the draft. Data for the 15th Missouri show otherwise; the large majority of conscripts were native born, and for good reason. Only American citizens could be called for the draft, and one had to have lived in America for five years to even qualify for citizenship.[18] Many immigrants, not yet citizens, consequently did not appear on the draft rolls. Indeed, more than a few in the 15th Missouri probably were not citizens as yet when they volunteered in 1861, 1862, or even 1863. Many were in their early twenties, even in their teens, arrivals in this country less than five years before the opening of the war—too new to even apply for citizenship, much less qualify.[19]

There is another reason why few German immigrants may be found among a regiment's conscripts. German immigrants did not wait to be drafted. They *volunteered*. They volunteered in such numbers during the first weeks after the attack on Fort Sumter that an embarrassed President Lincoln had to withdraw an agreement to form an all-German brigade; there were simply too many eager Germans wanting to join.[20]

German immigrants served many months and in many bloody battles before conscription became law. They became the veterans of their regiments. Like their tattered battle flags, their ranks torn by three years of war, they would become the remnants of their regiments, their ranks replenished by conscripts of native birth; by 1864, with most Germans who could serve having already volunteered, there were few German immigrants left in St. Louis of an age to go to war.

Bias of an official nature has also affected the historical reporting of German units in the Civil War. It infected government records and continues to color historical accounts of these immigrant units. One has only to look at the record of Henry Halleck, chief of the Union armies, a known anti-immigrationist who, before moving on to Washington, practiced his own brand of ethnic prejudice while in St. Louis in command of the army's Department of the Missouri. His record reflects a predisposition against foreigners in general and Germans in particular within the military itself, from the lowest American-born soldier to senior officers in command of armies, east and west. It would trail along with the 15th Missouri throughout the war.

This was a time when ethnic groups, of Anglo and German origin particularly, practiced a brand of "racial" prejudice that extended beyond what one might consider "racial" today. Anti-Germanism was pervasive, and the German immigrant had no small hand in abetting it. The roots of anti-Germanism lay deep, the German poet and philosopher Johann Goethe said. "The Germans make everything difficult," he wrote, "both for themselves and for everyone else." As a modern German scholar attempted to explain it, "Foreigners have periodically confessed their inability to understand German behavior, to say nothing of German philosophy and the German language."[21]

In the years leading up to the Civil War, Germans took a strong stand against slavery, but it was that stand expressed in traits of Teutonic *Sturm* that alienated and even frightened many Americans. As one who wrote of Germans in America in 1860 observed,

> Germans are famous for their intensity of feeling and their downrightness and outrightness of blunt speech. . . . This trait was enhanced mightily by their flooding memories of harsh and oppressive government in their homelands and by the many futile sacrifices they had made in the cause of

the promotion of liberty. . . . Death had come to many of the kith and kin and imprisonment and wrecked health to many of them. . . . Were they to witness in this land of freedom an extension of slavery? . . . [Their] leaders were in no mood for shilly-shally, for subterfuge or flimsy speech or pretentious performance.

They were, the writer professed, the thunderbolts of the gods for the storm to come.[22]

In the mid-nineteenth century, German immigrants were indeed disliked nationally but perhaps more so in St. Louis, even though the city's inhabitants were mostly of German stock. The minority, Anglo and native born for the most part, were in sympathy with the South. Those differences sparked discriminations of a daily kind that flamed into virtual class warfare by the start of the war.

The newcomers to Missouri had no small part in contributing to the class distinctions they had sought and even fought to eliminate in their homeland. Germans escaping their failed revolution of 1848 poured into the state and across the river into Illinois. The Forty-eighters, as they became known, were unlike the first Germans—mostly farmers—who had arrived a decade or so earlier. The later immigrants included a strong percentage of professionals, intellectuals, and journalists. Arriving in their new homeland, they hauled out of their idealistic baggage a revolutionary zeal to mold their adopted new country into the image they had sought for their old homeland. In time they became a powerful voice for keeping Missouri in the Union. But in the process, they did nothing to endear themselves to the native-born Americans or even the German farmers who preceded them.

They spoke out strongly against slavery, for both economic and social reasons, not the least of which because it reminded them of their late status in their old homeland. They were firm in their conviction for saving the Union. While many Missourians held no particular opinion on slavery (only one in twenty households owned a slave), their blood ties were to the South. Fighting for the North would mean fighting against kinfolk.

The newcomers did not stop with their attacks against slavery and secession. In their radical (for the time) German-language newspapers, they criticized cultural and educational standards. They sniffed at the tolerance for dirty cities and pork-barrel politics. They went so far as to ridicule Americans for what they ate and drank, and how they did both. It was not long before these new arrivals were assailed for their "ignorance . . . arrogance . . . insolence"—by the editor of a German-language newspaper![23]

Nor did their criticisms stop when they joined the army. Former officers in the German military, now in the Yankee army, complained that the Americans kept a dirty camp. They marched and drilled poorly. As if that were not enough, the Germans proclaimed that they would show the Americans what soldiering was really all about.[24]

When the war was over, the German immigrant soldier in Missouri eventually assimilated into American life. He became bilingual and in time folded into both local communities and the national scene. A few reentered civilian life as journalists, doctors, or mercantilists. Thanks in part to German-born educators and their influence, public education in St. Louis during the late nineteenth century became the standard of the time for the rest of the United States, the first kindergarten (literally "children garden") one of their enduring innovations. Some too served successfully in political or public office, often winning the recognition in peacetime that was denied them in war.

Most simply went home. In time they would raise families, mainly as tradesmen as part of the solid citizenry of their communities in and around St. Louis. Except for a marker or two in the far-off battlefields, they would leave almost nothing in their remaining years to their children or to the generations that followed that would serve as recognition, a memorial, or even a memory of the sacrifices they had made for their country, in this case, their country by choice and not merely by birth.

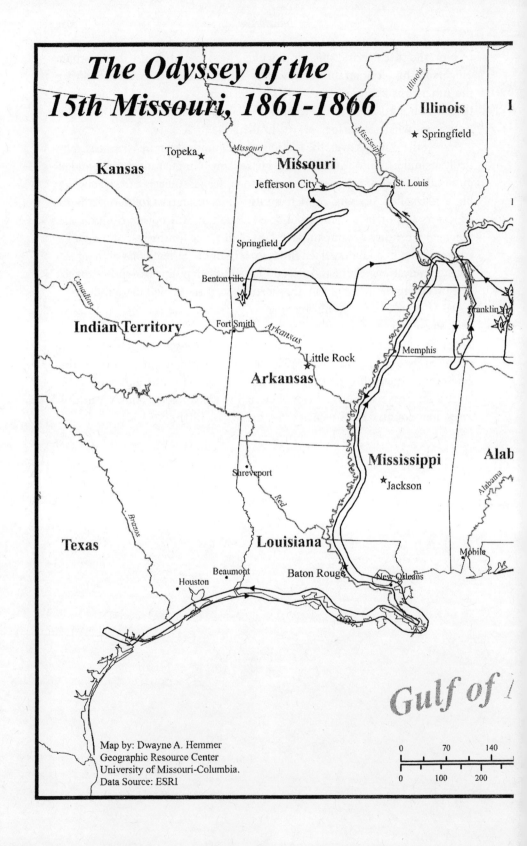

The Odyssey of the 15th Missouri, 1861-1866

Kansas

Topeka ★

Missouri

Springfield ★

Illinois

Jefferson City

St. Louis

Springfield

Bentonville

Indian Territory

Fort Smith

Arkansas

Little Rock

Arkansas

Memphis

Franklin

Mississippi

Jackson

Shreveport

Alab

Texas

Louisiana

Mobile

Beaumont

Baton Rouge

New Orleans

Houston

Gulf of

Map by: Dwayne A. Hemmer
Geographic Resource Center
University of Missouri-Columbia.
Data Source: ESRI

0   70   140

0   100   200

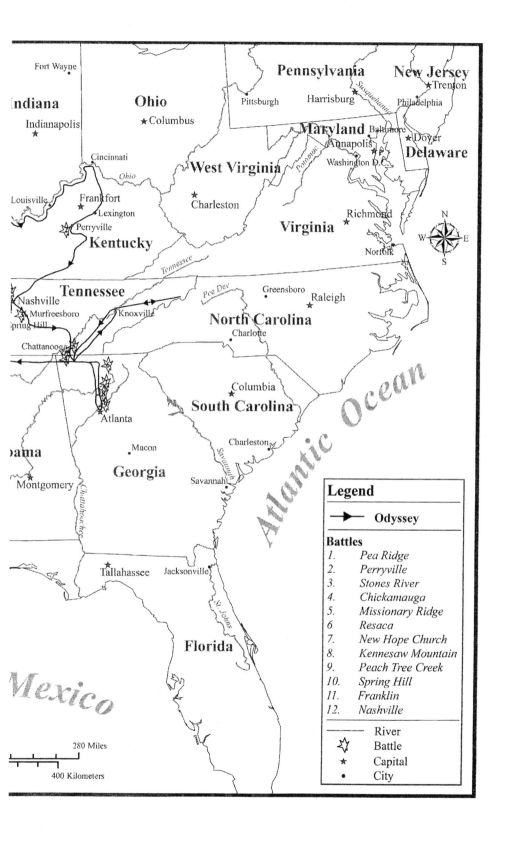

We received orders to charge on the enemy with the point of the bayonet. Nobly was this order carried out.
> —Col. Joseph Conrad, 15th Missouri Volunteer Infantry, Sunday morning, September 20, 1863, near Chickamauga Creek, northern Georgia

And some there be which have no memorial who are perished as though they had never been.
> —Ecclesiasticus XLIV

1861

At dead of night, at news from the south . . . a shock electric.

—Walt Whitman, "Drum Taps"

1

Black Dutch

President Lincoln's inaugural ceremonies in March had scarcely caused a ripple in Bond County, Illinois. Maurice Marcoot remembered that things had quieted down considerably since the election the previous fall.[1] It did not seem to matter that a string of Southern states had seceded from the Union, beginning with South Carolina the past December, or that just days after Christmas, South Carolinian troops had seized a federal arsenal with its 75,000 stand of arms, or that Georgia, Alabama, Florida, and Louisiana took over U.S. forts in their states. But if you got to travel outside of town, you could get the big picture.

Marcoot was sixteen and working in the general store of A. J. Gullick. One of his duties was to hitch up Mr. Gullick's team, load the wagon with produce, and drive to market in St. Louis. "I thus had opportunities frequently to see much of the excitement and stir."

St. Louis—161,000 people, 60 percent German and a minority from the South with about sixteen hundred slaves—was in turmoil.[2] Missouri had just inaugurated Southern Democrat Claiborne Jackson as governor little more than a week after South Carolina had seceded. But as Missouri voted for Democrat Stephen Douglas in the presidential election, St. Louis voted overwhelmingly for Lincoln and the new Republican Party.

Outside of St. Louis, Missourians generally cared little about political affairs. "It is hard to visualize the ignorance and political darkness," wrote a German state legislator, "that existed in the thinly settled counties at the time." In the "wild counties . . . where many lived . . . [they] knew the valley in which their fathers had settled but nothing else, not even their ABC's."[3]

Germans in their villages along the Missouri River west of St. Louis knew little more. "The great mass of those who were politically inexperienced to form an independent opinion were carried along by the firmness of their self-confident fellow Germans."[4] When talk did get around to whether Missouri should leave the Union, most Missourians preferred to steer a middle ground; only one in twenty or so families owned slaves, and that was counting those who had only one. Many had come from someplace in the South that they still called home, and that is what mattered most. The less said about it the better.

People in St. Louis saw things a lot differently. Southern sympathizers were in the minority. Even so, some on both sides of the issue were now past the talking stage, with words in the meeting halls giving way to rock throwing in the streets. Against this backdrop, Jackson, the governor-elect, barely won the election because he had done a good job of keeping a lid on his intentions when it came to secession. Jackson was from Kentucky, and in his inaugural speech on January 4, he made his views clear: "The destiny of all the slave-holding States of this Union is one and the same." Missouri, the governor said, should make "a timely declaration of her determination to stand by sister slave-holding States, in whose wrongs she participates, and with whose institutions and people she sympathizes."[5]

The legislature in Jefferson City felt about the same way. In just four days following the governor's remarks, a bill passed for a convention to consider relations "between the Government of the United States . . . and the government and people of the State of Missouri; and to adopt such measures for vindicating the sovereignty of the state and the protection of its institutions as shall appear to them to be demanded." In a word, secession.

That same day, January 9, the steamer *Star of the West*, with two hundred troops sent to reinforce Fort Sumter, was fired on by batteries manned by South Carolinian troops in Charleston harbor and driven back to sea. The first shots of the Civil War had been fired.

Days earlier, on New Year's Day, with groups in St. Louis taking to the streets, several hundred young Germans known as the Wide Awakes, an arm of the new Republican Party, approached the east door of the St. Louis Court House. "Negroes on hand and for sale at all times," read the notice on the door. A public auction of slaves was underway. Charging into the gathering, the young Germans called for a halt to the proceedings. The auctions would never resume. Germans, immigrants for the most part, had broken up the last public sale of slaves in St. Louis.[6]

The Wide Awakes were a countergroup to a Southern-sympathizing paramilitary unit called the Minute Men, which flew the Confederate flag from their downtown headquarters. Up until this time, the rivalry with the German Wide Awakes had amounted to little more than taunts and threats. But to Southern sympathizers in the city, the Germans in their attack on the auction now looked more like a small army, and the city's Democratic press was aroused to square off against the "Black Dutch."

The Germans, "the Dutch" as many native Missourians called them, first came to the state in noticeable numbers in the 1830s. Politically they were moderates. They were well-educated, many having attended universities. Some were doctors, lawyers, and other professionals. When it was too difficult for them as foreigners to practice their original livelihoods, they turned to farming. Locals in time referred to these newcomers as the "Latin Farmers," for their education and their knowledge of the classical languages. Many found a practice or a living in St. Louis, but just as many settled along the Missouri upriver from St. Charles; the country along its banks reminded them of their homeland.

The late 1830s saw a second wave of immigrants—three thousand German Catholics immigrated to St. Louis in just three years. They decided on Missouri as a destination based on what they had heard and read about from Germans already living there. By 1850, their numbers had grown to an estimated 24,000. At about the same time, a more organized religious migration began in Missouri. Some six hundred German Lutherans migrated from the province of Saxony. Some settled in St. Louis, while others headed a bit farther south. In time they would found the Lutheran Church–Missouri Synod. They too would keep to themselves and the old ways.

Around 1850, a new group began to arrive, distinctly different from the previous groups in just about every way. These newcomers would upset both native-born Americans and the Germans who had settled in and now called Missouri home.

The democratic revolutionary forces that had been brewing in Germany had boiled over into bloodshed in 1848. The revolt was mainly one of intellectuals, with beginnings in the universities, but it soon overflowed to every other level and institution, including the German army. The cause was against class oppression and for individual freedoms. But when the wave hit the German states, it crashed against the stern wall of Germanic will for order. The revolution failed. Those on the losing side had to run. To America—the New World and the new democracy—that was the place to go.

They began arriving as early as 1849, teachers, doctors, journalists, lawyers, merchants, and military men. The one thing these expatriates had in common was a zeal to upset every barrier against individual rights and freedoms—for *all* mankind, they said, the "Brotherhood of Man." That was radicalism even for much of America, and particularly for the state and the city where many of them would settle. Historians would refer to these Germans as the Forty-eighters for the year they had become survivors and escapees of the revolution that had failed in their homeland.

It took little time for the Forty-eighters to settle in and speak their minds on a variety of matters. Through their own German-language newspapers, they began to tangle with publications of the established and earlier new-comers from Germany. These confrontations started on common immi-grant issues, embroiling both newspapers favored by the first Germans to arrive and those of the newly arrived revolutionaries. The battles of their editors, laced with sermons from the pulpits, for a time enmeshed all of the original groups. But a new set of issues began to push the old polemics off their pages and those of the English-language papers as well. It would prompt a rage and a fury among the old adversaries, spilling over into hatred of a kind never before seen in the old city along the Mississippi.

The shove came in 1854 when Congress passed the Kansas-Nebraska Act. Its purpose was to create new federal land that could be turned over for railroad right-of-ways for westward expansion. But the devil was in the details; the act would also give the new territories the right to choose or reject slavery within their own borders. An unintended spark rekindled the smoldering issue older than the Constitution itself; once again, the issue of whether slavery should be permitted outside the original slaveholding states started a firestorm of national debate. Once again, Missouri was in the middle.[7]

Most Germans in the St. Louis area were dead set against slavery, but not entirely on moral grounds. The idea of one man owning another simply reminded them too much of the old tyrannies they had left behind. That memory united the squabbling Germans. They had a strong spokesman in Gustav Koerner, one of the original Latin Farmers, lawyer, publisher of the highly respected *Belleville Zeitung* across the river in Illinois, and soon a confidant of another young country lawyer by the name of Abraham Lin-coln. Almost from the time he had arrived, he had written that "slavery is the only rope by which the devil holds the American people." He predicted that "the Rupture between the Free and Slave States is inevitable."[8]

About this time a new group of Germans began to arrive, coming now in singles or in pairs, as brothers or as *Kameraden*. Occasionally a new hus-band and wife arrived with maybe a child or two. They were young people for the most part, the residue of the revolution, imbued with the ideals of

Gustav Koerner, 1830 émigré, publisher of the *Belleville Zeitung* (Illinois), and a leading voice against slavery, helped marshal St. Louis–area Germans to the Union cause. Koerner, one of Lincoln's inner circle at the 1860 Republican Convention, was instrumental in Lincoln's nomination. He also led the move against anti-immigrationists by expanding the "hostility to slavery" plank in the party's platform to embrace personal liberties for all Americans. (State Historical Society of Missouri, Columbia)

personal freedoms and fed up with the old institutional and class tyrannies of German life. They were also looking for something else. Not nearly as radical as the intellectuals who had preceded them—many were still from the well-educated ranks—but among them now were more tradesmen, artisans, and young farmers.[9]

Gustav Roehm came with his brother Christian from Thuringen in Wurtenburg. Gustav, barely twenty, was a shoemaker. Charles Delph, a musician, came from Holstein. Gotthardt Ruebsam, just twenty, and a brewmaster came from Fulda in Hesse. George Rau came with his two sisters from

Hesburghausen in Saxony. George was a cabinetmaker in his early twenties. George Mohrhardt and his brother Heinrich came and Engelbert Dreher from Baden, Peter Kleinmann, a shoemaker from Mainz, and Wilhelm Lorenz, a farmer from Prussia.[10] In time, they and about six hundred others like them would volunteer for the Union army. They would be assembled into a regiment to be numbered as the 15th Missouri Volunteer Infantry. For now, they were simply looking for a better place to work and live. They had heard that you could find both in America, in a place called Missouri.

Soon after they arrived, they found that Missouri was not quite what they thought it would be. For one thing, they had heard about slavery, but seeing it and how the black person was treated reminded them too much of what they had known and what they thought they had left behind. These new arrivals, unlike the Forty-eighters who had preceded them, kept to themselves and their mouths shut. But before long, they too would be labeled among the "arrogant, ignorant and insolent,"[11] a view that most Americans now held of all German immigrants, no matter who they were or when they arrived. Events soon would swirl over and around them, so that they would be compelled to take a stand, one way or another. In the end they would take hold of that "rope by which the devil holds the American people," as Gustav Koerner had called it. It was the rope that most Missourians refused to touch.

Native-born Americans saw in these latest arrivals a rising tide that might not ebb. If the waves of these foreigners kept up, what would happen to basic American values? To public temperance and crime? These foreigners would probably cheapen the cost of labor and take away jobs and vote differently. The voice of public concern continued to mount until it resulted in a new political group called the American Party and nicknamed the Know-Nothings because members were instructed to respond "I know nothing" to queries about the group.

The platform was not all that new. The Anglo-rooted Whig Party, going back to colonial times, fostered similar ideas: change naturalization laws and prevent immigrants from voting or holding office. Even Gustav Koerner of the *Belleville Zeitung* laid the blame for anti-German feelings and the revival of nativism on the Forty-eighters, for their "arrogance, imperious and domineering conduct."[12]

Virtually lost in the rising din were views expressed by the German clergy. Catholic priests generally opposed slavery but were more shocked by abolitionists who, in their opinion, were more of a threat to peace and order, a view not far removed from that of the rising Whig Party leader, Abraham Lincoln.[13] A lone dissenting voice came from C. W. Walther, a Lutheran cleric: scriptures taught nothing directly against slavery, he said, but rather supported it.[14] That stand would divide many of the newly arrived Germans.

The Southern-sympathizing *Daily Missouri Republican* turned its pages against immigrants. The paper had publicly worried back in 1851 that Missouri might become a new Germany. It openly sneered at almost everything German, their customs, their language, their beer, even their schools and churches.[15]

It was a scene repeated in Cincinnati, Milwaukee, and other cities with large German-born populations that unified German political leaders and editors. Turning toward the national level, they organized a German-American delegation to attend the national convention of the new Republican Party. The delegation as expected stood against the Kansas-Nebraska Act and Know-Nothingism. But it was the delegation's stand and rhetoric against slavery that rang like a fire bell in the night. The Germans recommended that the principles of the Republican Party be applied "most hostile to slavery." Lest America become another Germany, they insisted that "all rights of all classes of citizens" be protected.[16] It was a message that the Republican Party's candidate for president would echo little more than a year later before Congress.

It was unusually warm in Jefferson City for late February in 1861. The convention delegates to consider secession, after a day of meeting in close and crowded rooms, decided to move to more ample quarters in St. Louis. A more consensual setting for the business at hand had more to do with the move to St. Louis than with the weather. It was a masterstroke arranged by Hamilton Gamble, a former Missouri chief justice. Merchants and railroad men with talk of eastern markets were all around. Instead of the Southern intonations of the legislature heard in Jefferson City, Northern trade and capital were the sermons preached around the bar of the Planter's House.[17]

The delegates met in the Mercantile Library Hall on Locust Street. Here they were reminded that Missourians had blood ties to the South, but they also heard that railroads brought more powerful ties to the North and the East. If war came, Missouri, if it joined the Southern states, would still be bordered by Iowa, Illinois, and Kansas. And if the South survived the war as a separate Confederacy, Republicans would take control of the Union in the North, erect trade barriers, and ruin Missouri. A report was presented concluding that the state had no grounds to secede. The delegates voted to adopt the report and its conclusion with only one dissenting vote.[18] Missouri had decided to remain in the Union. Flowing capital was thicker than blood.

Five weeks later in the dark of a pre-dawn April morning, a thousand miles away, a lone, sparkling trail of light rose from the shoreline along Charleston Harbor, arched its way across the dark sky, and exploded with a brilliant red glare over Fort Sumter.

To the North, the firing on Fort Sumter was like a bang on a hornet's nest, and that was the real event. Walt Whitman captured the moment in "Drum Taps," one of his first Civil War poems:

At dead of night, at news from the south,
Incens'd struck with the clinch'd hand the pavement.

A shock electric, the night sustain'd it,
Till with ominous hum our hive at daybreak pour'd out
its myriads.

From the houses then and the workshops, and through all
the doorways,
Leapt they tumultuous.

The Union and the flag had been fired upon—and by rebs and secesh to boot. That is what stirred most native-born in the North to volunteer.

"The ominous clouds were broken," wrote Marcoot. "The storm was upon us."[19]

John Buegel left his room in St. Louis that April morning and headed for work. Arriving on the job site, he found all was quiet. No sound of hammering, no sawing, just a few men standing around as puzzled as he. One young German did mention how some Americans had hollered at him asking why he was not headed in the direction to join the Confederate army.

"The majority of ordinary folks did not know what it was all about, and what was the meaning of it all—neither did I."[20] By the end of the day, Buegel wrote, "all building operations had come to a standstill . . . and other work was not to be found . . . indeed all trade came to a sudden cessation. Moreover, one's very life was in danger." Southerners were recruiting soldiers, and "those who did not enlist voluntarily," Buegel said, "were beaten and had mud thrown at them. This happened to me myself. . . . Hovering between fear and hope we spent the days from April 14."[21]

Several days may have passed before he heard about Lincoln's proclamation of April 15 calling for "the militia of the several states of the Union, to the aggregate number of 75,000." In Jefferson City, Governor

Jackson had refused to meet Missouri's quota of 4,000, claiming Lincoln's call "illegal, unconstitutional and revolutionary." But in St. Louis, Congressman Frank Blair promptly offered the new Home Guards, German-born residents mainly including the old Wide Awakes of marching, singing Germans. Shortly after, they were sworn in as "Missouri Volunteers."[22]

Recruiting posters were now beginning to plaster storefronts, fences, and other surfaces in the German neighborhoods, similar possibly to those in other cities.[23]

Unabhangiges
Deutsches Regiment
fur Missouri!

"Independent German Regiment for Missouri!" An appeal to "all natural lovers of freedom and fighters for good causes" rounded out the bill, ending with a time and place to join up.

"On the morning of April 22, my friend H. Hinzman," Buegel wrote, "persuaded me to go with him to Washington Hall on Second and Elm Streets." Washington Hall and the St. Louis Turnverein were the major gathering places for young Germans. Bernhard Laiboldt, a former sergeant in the German military, was a proprietor of "one of the best amusement places, for dancing and other festivals."[24] Laiboldt would later join the Union army, earning the rank of colonel and the command of a brigade, which would include the 15th Missouri. Beugel and his friend "found to our great surprise that the large hall was full of young, sturdy Germans. Of course, a good lunch with fine beer was not lacking. Everything gratis."

If the rally followed a typical form, Buegel and his friend, as they ate and lifted their glasses, listened to the speakers' appeals in their native language. They may have been reminded why many of them had fled Germany. Germans unable to attain their ideals for freedom in the old country and having found them in America must now defend them, they were told. "Liberty is indivisible," ran one such speech in Cincinnati: "Germans should defend liberty wherever they find it. Disunion is a curse. Now that the South is threatening to divide America it must be opposed. Germans do not want the miseries of Europe reproduced in the New World."[25]

"Since we Germans at that time were looked upon (by) Americans, old and young, with contempt and disdain," Buegel went on, "we decided, after having listened to some speeches, to sell our skins as dearly as possible. . . . After three cheers for the Union . . . and 'Down with the traitors' . . . and having emptied a few more glasses, we marched through the streets of St. Louis to the Arsenal. Upon arriving there the guard (a regular soldier) allowed us to enter unhindered, but would not let us go out again. . . .

> That afternoon we were sworn in, and were issued rifles and shells. . . . In the evening we were served soldier fare—bean soup and crackers. . . . There were no uniforms available as yet. . . . That night we slept in tents, where we made ourselves as comfortable as possible.
>
> On the next morning at half past five the bugle roused us. At seven o'clock we had coffee and hardtack . . . at eight . . . drill. As we were placed in rank and file our regiment presented a very funny appearance. Every one was dressed as it suited him. Some wore caps, others straw hats and still others silk hats. . . . The majority had a certain amount of education and culture. The main thing, however, was that each one was eager to teach the German-haters a never-to-be-forgotten lesson.[26]

Governor Jackson was entertaining a similar idea. Jackson had been keeping in touch with Confederate president Jefferson Davis in Alabama. They agreed that St. Louis was the key to controlling Missouri and the West, and the key to controlling St. Louis was the federal arsenal. Taking the Confederate president's advice, Governor Jackson decided to seize the arsenal by a surprise attack. Unfortunately for the governor, Gen. Daniel Frost of the Missouri militia found the Union regulars already there. Frustrated, Frost set up his militia at Lindell Grove near the corner of Olive Street and Grand Avenue on the western edge of the city. He named it Camp Jackson.

The next day, May 10, "we received marching orders," Buegel wrote. At noon they too headed west. "By two o'clock in the afternoon," Buegel recorded, the federal troops surrounded the camp." A message was sent demanding an unconditional surrender of the camp with all weapons and material. "When the rebel saw that there was no escape, and that the Dutch really meant business, they surrendered and laid down their arms. . . . When the haughty young Americans were taken into custody . . . their rage knew no bounds . . . the Dutch, as we were generally called, were masters of the situation."[27]

As the Germans of the Missouri Volunteers began marching away with their prisoners, crowds gathered. Dirt clods and stones began to glance off the federal troops as they stood in the ranks.[28] "There was a moment of confusion, when the soldiers . . . began to fire over our heads. . . . I heard the balls cutting the leaves above our heads, and saw several men and women running in all directions, some of them wounded . . . a general stampede."

Then the troops marched away with their prisoners, remembered William Tecumseh Sherman, up from Louisiana with his young son.[29] Fifteen of the crowd of onlookers had been killed. Others were seriously wounded.

Bethiah Pyatt McKown had been living in St. Louis for more than twenty years. She and her husband had come from Maryland. Owners of a successful blacksmith bellows factory, they were, in her words, "comfortably situated." To her son in Marshall, Missouri, she wrote, "Our City is encompass'd with armed Goths and Vandels [*sic*], for they are Dutch and Poles that cannot speak our language and they search every carriage . . . every house in the environs of the City for arms and ammunition. . . . We are . . . in hourly peril of life and liberty, surrounded with Dutch bayonets employed by the Lincoln dynasty."[30]

Mrs. McKown was not alone in her opinion of what was taking place in her city. Stories began making the rounds that the Black Dutch were planning to murder citizens in their beds. Fear ran to panic. In some neighborhoods, families with friends in Illinois fled across the river where they figured it would be safe. It did not seem to matter that there were as many Germans there as in St. Louis.

Young Marcoot, on one of his wagon runs to St. Louis for Mr. Gullick, had found it all more exciting than he could bear. "Thrilling," he put it. Now back home in Millersburg, Mr. Marcoot's sixteen-year-old son was talking about going off to war to save the Union. The president had just followed his first call for 75,000 state militia with a new one for 42,034 volunteers to serve for three years. Older men around town counseled that it would all blow over in about ninety days. Still, some in Millersburg formed a company that was starting to drill on a regular basis. "I joined unsolicited"—but young Marcoot did not tell his parents. "I could have easily gone to father with my desires, but the pain I knew it would cause mother often caused me to hesitate."

Instead, Marcoot sought out his eldest brother, who was teaching school in Highland a few miles away. He persuaded him to come home to present the case to his father. After dinner, "for I preferred to risk it on a full stomach, I 'out with it.' I do not remember just what I said but I know I made it short. . . . Father, pushing his chair back from the table, surveyed me in cold surprise. 'You, only sixteen years old, your education not half finished, talking of going to war and throwing all your hopes and future away on a southern battlefield? No, I will not permit it; there are many who can better go than you, you are too young.' 'Yes father,' I replied, 'I know that I am young but . . . '" It required "a great deal of courageous pleading to overcome his persistent opposition and mother's tearful pleadings, but, by dint of perseverance, I at last succeeded so far as to win a sort of negative consent. . . .

"That night, I remained with my brother who was now more than ever my counselor. He told me that they were raising a company in Highland . . . it would be better for me to go with them as they were all old friends and acquaintances." Highland was also home to a good number of Swiss immigrants as were his parents. These men would probably make up the bulk of the new company. "I immediately . . . joined the Highland company." Searching now for a regiment in Illinois to join, the company sent letters to the governor "stating our readiness and anxiety to enter the field . . . but his answers uniformly informed us that his quota was already full. . . .

"We were not to be deterred, however, and after a short delay, at drill one Saturday afternoon in June, we decided to go to St. Louis, Missouri, where opportunities were more plentiful and the quota far from full."[31]

About a week later in the west Missouri town of Cole Camp, German recruits for the Union gathered into two barns for the night. Others went home as they waited for their first supply of arms. As they slept, a band with firearms crept up to one of the barns. Flinging open the barn doors and shouting, "No mercy for the Dutch!" they opened fire. Some fired their weapons through the walls. Those inside not killed outright struggled to get out through the barn doors. As they did, the men outside reloaded to shoot them down. In the dark nearby, Union men, recovering from the shock of the surprise attack, fired into the group of assailants, allowing some of the new recruits to escape.[32]

The dawn gave light to the scene: dead and wounded littered the farmyard. Those who were able struggled to a grassy area and fell near the farmhouse. Word spread fast to the little village and the surrounding farms. Fifteen had been killed, and fifty-seven more had been wounded.[33] Soon families in wagons began arriving to bear the wounded and the bodies of their sons and husbands back home. News of the massacre echoed across the rolling hills and down the Missouri River valley. Shock struck first in Rhineland, Hermann, and other towns along the valley. In St. Louis, the news bore through the German neighborhoods, streets, work sites, beer gardens, and the churches. And shock turned to rage.[34]

2

A Crowded Arsenal

Maurice Marcoot's father turned stubborn. His son had just informed him that he would leave with the Highland company the following Tuesday. They were going to St. Louis to join a regiment. Marcoot's father "insisted that I should not go . . . further, if I did, being under eighteen years of age, he would take steps to compel me to return." Young Maurice fired back that if that happened, he would run away and enlist "where he [Maurice's father] could never find me."[1]

At the St. Louis arsenal in June, dozens of military units, cavalry, artillery, infantry regiments, and a variety of support organizations were beginning to fill ranks. Two were the 12th and 15th Missouri Volunteer infantries.[2] Both would in time be considered German regiments for their heavy makeup of these volunteers.

Outwardly, there was little difference between the German immigrants and their American counterparts. Both groups averaged in age in their midtwenties, though the 15th's Germans appear to have been slightly older. Both groups ranged from boys in their teens—sixteen-year-olds in the 15th probably numbered a couple dozen—to gray-haired men well into their forties and even older. One man in the 15th from Switzerland admitted to being fifty-six. The men and boys in the 15th Missouri that volunteered the summer of 1861 stood on average, 5 feet 5 inches, probably typical for the Civil War soldier, who also averaged 140 pounds. A six-footer would have stood out noticeably in either group.[3]

For the 15th's Germans, brown hair and blue or gray eyes appear to have been the rule.[4] The occupations of tradesman and laborer dominated among the Germans while native Missourians and Illinoisans likely included more farmers. For the immigrant, though, the distinguishing characteristic surfaced when he stood before a record-taking clerk. Responding to the usual battery of questions, the German volunteer, his palms pointing upward, was likely to answer, "*Nicht forstehen*" ("I don't understand").

Following the signing-in formalities, "We were assigned tent quarters and were soon experiencing our first pleasures of inactive army life," Marcoot wrote. "We were bountifully supplied with quilts and other bedding, but could not discover for some time which, the right or the left side, was the softest to lie upon with mother earth as our bed, and sore hips and ribs were the general complaint for several days."[5]

A day or two later, because of the crowded conditions at the arsenal, the recruits were marched to the nearby Marine Hospital grounds. Along the city streets, column after column of infantry marched while throngs of artillery and cavalry rattled past, John Buegel noted in his diary, "all agitated, recruited and drilled."[6]

Civilians in the city were every bit as agitated. Bethiah Pyatt McKown wrote on July 14 to her son, "We hope that the independent Missourians will rise in their majesty & might to crush out these Vandal Lincoln hoards [*sic*]. . . . We expect soon to hear of hot work from the points where they are gone to, we do not believe the Missourians will permit them to cross their State but will acquit themselves like brave men and drive them with great slaughter from the soil of Missouri."[7] As if by premonition, a day later the new 8th Missouri Infantry ran into a guerilla ambush near Wentzville, about fifty miles west of St. Louis, and in the skirmish saw seven of their men killed. They were possibly the first of the Union volunteers in the new Missouri regiments to die in combat.[8]

A day later, on July 16, the men and boys from Highland were mustered into service as part of Company B of the new 15th Missouri Volunteer Infantry. "At first the regiment was to be named the 'Swiss Regiment,'" Marcoot wrote, then "Frémont's Body Guards." (John Frémont, the "Pathfinder," was extremely popular as a major general and was the new commander of the Western Department of the Army headquartered in St. Louis.) Finally, the new regiment, "settled down to the plain '15th Missouri.'"[9]

At best, Marcoot was only partly right regarding the early naming of the regiment. The first two were nicknames and nothing more. Reflecting the romantic notions about what life would be like in the army, many at the start of the war attempted to append equally romantic names to their new regiments. The idea of naming the 15th the "Swiss Regiment" ("Swiss Rifles" also shows up on some early reports) came from the Swiss immigrants from Highland; they were among the first to enlist in the first two companies of the ten that would eventually make up the 15th Missouri Volunteer Infantry.

Swiss immigrants and descendants made up only a small share, in fact, of the first two companies and eventually the regiment. Of the eighty-one men and boys who enlisted that summer and were assigned to Company B, the company to which Marcoot and the majority of his Highland comrades were assigned, only twenty-four are known to have been of Swiss origin. At least thirty-nine others were Germans, most likely from the St. Louis area. Of the remaining eighteen, all but one carried a Germanic surname. In sum, possibly as high as 70 percent of the volunteers assigned that summer of 1861 to Company B, the so-called Swiss Company of the regiment, were German immigrants or of German stock. In addition to the Swiss in the company, there was Engelbert Dreher, twenty-two, a laborer from Baden, Germany; William Lorenz, twenty-four, a farmer from Kreuznach, in Prussia; Christian Reber, eighteen, a laborer from Hanover; Fridolin Rommel, thirty-seven, a stonemason from Wurzburg, Bavaria; Gotthardt Ruebsam, twenty-four, a brewer from Fulda, in Hesse; Phillip Schuh, thirty-nine, a cooper from Baden; William Wilke, thirty-one, a miner from Mulhausen in Prussia; and Gustav Roehm, twenty-three, the shoemaker from Thuringen in Saxony.[10] Eventually, as volunteers filled the remaining companies to complete the regiment, the number of Germans making up the 15th was closer to 75 percent.[11]

Before the men and boys from Highland had marched off from home, the women of the town presented them with a battle flag resembling the Stars and Stripes, with the usual stars against a blue field but without the stripes; in place of the red and white stripes was a white cross sewn against a red field: the flag, in effect, of Switzerland.[12] Possibly for that reason alone, the regiment would be referred to in the field, at least for a brief time, as the "Swiss Regiment." The final time the 15th was so called in official communications was in the report following the Battle of Pea Ridge in March 1862, filed by its division commander, a Hungarian and former Austrian army officer. As far as the army was concerned, the regiment from the beginning was officially the 15th Missouri Volunteer Infantry, as enlistment papers of those who first mustered in on July 16, 1861, show.[13]

Once mustered in for duty, the first five companies were moved from the Marine Hospital grounds near the arsenal and into the city to a vacant block then named Camp Frémont. "It was but a short time until the strictest military discipline was put in practice," Marcoot wrote, and we were confined within the boundaries of the camp by guards of our own men. . . . Our guards were very strict, there was no such thing as getting a pass and no getting out without one. But this did not last long. It was soon observed that the company cook and his camp kettles were not included upon the restricted list, although he was frequently searched for fear that he might attempt to [smuggle] whisky into camp. . . . The large camp kettles, however, were never inspected, and it was not long before they served the double purpose of passing the boys out and the whisky in. . . .

During all this time of inactivity we experienced little further than the routine. We were frequently ordered to change our quarters, how-ever, and at last found ourselves lodged in a new brick building just opposite the arsenal, where the organization of our—Co. B—was at last completed. Mr. John Weber, [was] elected as its captain. . . . We now commenced drilling in earnest and were put under strict discipline. The skirmish drill was a specialty with Capt. Weber, and he devoted much time to its instruction, so much so, and so proficient did we become that Co. B was known as the skirmish company of the regiment . . . we were furnished with the short Enfield rifles with sword bayonets [imports from England on which both the North and South relied heavily the first two years of the war], while the other companies were armed with those known as the "long" Enfields. For this reason also Company B was assigned position at the head of the regiment, which distinction over Company A caused much feeling for a time. . . .

On the 26th of July, I received a letter from home announcing the death of my sister, Catharine, and while greatly desiring to obtain a fur-lough for a few days to return home, I was unable to procure one, and thereby experienced my first real distress and disappointment during the service.[14]

Outstate, things had not gone well either for the new Union regiments that had left St. Louis in pursuit of Governor Jackson and Gen. Sterling Price and his men. Near Carthage in the southwest part of Missouri, Col. Franz Sigel had run into a Confederate force with apparently more num-bers, but before anything got too serious, Sigel made one of his celebrated retreats.

Capt. Joseph Conrad was also *mit* Sigel. Conrad eventually would command the 15th Missouri, but his first command of a company would hardly demonstrate an auspicious career for an officer entertaining higher ambitions, and higher command was definitely in Conrad's mind. Conrad's company was spared Sigel's Carthage affair, having been detached to Neosho, Missouri, "for the protection of the Union-loving people," as Sigel put it, "against bands of secessionists."[15] Conrad and his command of ninety-four had hardly settled into town when, Conrad reported, "1,200 to 1,500 men known as the Arkansas Rangers came pouring in from all directions." Conrad was ordered to surrender, unconditionally: "I concluded it would be best to make the surrender." Conrad and his men were placed in the courthouse, where they were required to sign a "parole of honor not to serve any more against the Confederate States of America." With that, Conrad and his men were allowed to leave under escort—"for our security and protection, the people of Neosho and farmers of that vicinity ["Union-loving people" as Sigel had put it] having threatened to kill us in the streets."[16]

Pvt. John Buegel, having signed up with the ninety-day 3d Missouri, had just returned to St. Louis after marching with Sigel down to Carthage, followed by the withdrawal to Springfield. Outside of town near Wilson's Creek, Union forces were defeated in the first major battle in the West, less than three weeks after the Union defeat at Bull Run in the East. The Federals, little more than a rabble with arms, made their way back to St. Louis. "The rebels were masters in Missouri."[17]

Now back at the arsenal, Buegel and his regiment, their three-month service obligations having expired, were mustered out on September 3, and the men discharged. On his own now, Buegel headed back into the city. "The excitement," Buegel noted, was "greater than when I had left. . . . There were many differences of opinion and points of view. Indeed, there were families in which some were for the Union and others for the confederacy. . . . One feared the other . . . under such conditions all work and undertakings came to a stop. It was impossible to find employment of any kind."

His first decision "as a free man again" was to look up his old friends. "When I passed a wine shop at Second and Market I saw some of my old comrades. Of course, I had to go in. We ordered a couple of bottles and refreshed memories. . . . We all agreed to meet in the same place that afternoon between three and four o'clock."

His next visit was to a friend named Uhlrich at his pharmacy on Franklin Avenue and Twelfth Street. "Our meeting was extremely cool . . . but I did not say anything about it. Soon after that, teacher Uhlrich also came into the drug store. His greeting was also forced. However, he invited me to dinner. . . . During the meal, it immediately became clear to me that the Saxon [Lutheran] congregations, for the most part, were on the side of the rebels. The congregations were told by the professors and preachers that the south was in the right, and attempted to prove by the Bible that slavery was a just institution."

Buegel's next stop was to visit a friend who had a job working a wood lathe at Tenth and Washington Avenue; he "turned out table legs at seventy-five cents a day [less than the amount calculated to keep a slave]. He, too, was dissatisfied with the situation. But what could be done." Buegel is not clear about what he meant by being "dissatisfied with the situation," whether it had to do with the course the war was taking, the lack of jobs, the "slave" pay that added to feelings of being "cheated by the German-haters," in this case, almost anyone who ran a business in St. Louis. It was probably all those things.

That afternoon, Buegel returned to the wine hall. There he found that his old companions had reenlisted, this time for three years. "As I reflected on all that I had seen and heard, my decision was quickly made. . . . I went immediately to headquarters and had myself sworn in for a period of three years. I was therefore on one and the same day a soldier, a free man, and again a soldier."[18]

His volunteering had little to do, he said, with freeing slaves. Fighting to end slavery—that was important. But fighting to free *slaves* was "*nebensaech-lich*"—unimportant, incidental.[19] For the German, ending slavery would put an end to the kind of life he knew, abhorred, and thought he had left behind in his old homeland. It was a life he could understand and empathize with as far as the slave was concerned. That is as far as his understanding or even compassion for slaves in America went.

The German immigrant's reason for wanting an end to slavery was primarily pragmatic; abolishing slavery, he thought, would have the effect of bettering his economic footing—the immigrant felt he was competing for jobs for which the institution of slavery kept the wages absurdly low. A better income, the German immigrant felt, would somehow put him on the same social level as most other white Americans.

On that score, Germans held similar opinions to those of other Northerners. They were not going to war, they said, to set blacks free. The preponderance of immigrants and Americans volunteering for the Union had no interest in that. But here attitudes parted. Many Northerners were in fact against a war to free slaves and said so. While Germans appeared indifferent toward blacks, many native-born in the army expressed opinions on the subject in words and terms that most Americans today would find objectionable and even ugly.[20]

The issues probably boiled down pretty clear for George Rau. He had come to America as a Saxon Lutheran eight years before. Now he was married with a three-year-old daughter and another just five months old. As a cabinetmaker, with construction and every other trade and business in St. Louis at a standstill, he had a serious worry about how he was going to feed his family. The army at least offered regular pay and a hundred dollar bounty just for signing up. His two sisters were probably against his joining. They were members of the Saxon church, "Old Trinity" as the Lutherans referred to it. George too had probably been told that the Bible did not say anything against slavery. Indeed, it was common to find families in which some were for the Union and others who were not.

On the first day of September, George Rau went down to the arsenal to sign up. Enlisting that day also were John Beisel and Christian Graus. Charles Herbert, eighteen years old and a musician, enlisted thirteen days later. Beisel and Graus may have been musicians too, because one became a bugler in the regiment and the other a drummer. George Rau was known to have played the violin, so perhaps through music they had known each other before they enlisted. It is a fact that all four were assigned to the same company, Company F, a practice common among friends who wanted to stay together. Maybe in civilian life they had known each other while playing music in one of the neighborhood *rathskellars*. Perhaps, not too many days before, they had decided to join up together that day in September. After all, there was not much call for musicians during those days.

But it would be a mistake to think that young Germans new to America chose to volunteer simply because they needed work. The German volunteers in 1861 did not, perhaps could not, articulate all the reasons why they and their comrades crowded into the arsenal that summer. Unlike the naive and adventuring young patriot from Millersburg, the German volunteers were his antithesis. Realistic and pragmatic, they had lived with tyranny all of their lives, but in another place. Now they were living with it where it was not supposed to be. They had seen the bloodshed of conflict in their old homeland, and in that they learned there was no adventure and no glory. They had seen again the past, and for that they held back. Now they caught a glimpse of the future, and for that they could hold back no longer.

A few months later, the *Anzeiger des Westens* may have spoken for this soldier best: "For us Germans, emancipation is a matter of life and death. If Missouri remains a slave state, then we will not remain here any longer." Now, without the passion that characterized its pages in the past, the *Anzeiger* went on to declare if slavery survives, Germans "will always be seen as dangerous, incendiary . . . inevitable that we would always be outvoted . . . looked at askance, defeated in all matters, and cheated . . . it would then be best for us to leave." But if Missouri became a free state, the *Anzeiger* continued, "we would be saviors, not only in war but also in peace. . . . They would look upon us with respect."

Then with extraordinary insight into what lay ahead, the *Anzeiger* projected its vision for the time when the fighting would be over: "German immigration would then not simply rise but increase twofold and tenfold . . . prosperity would flow . . . for [all] people . . . the government, settled with emancipation . . . [could] proceed to the building of our railroads . . . and make a stride toward the great Pacific Ocean . . . Congress and the administration could show the faith they have in the free, proud future of this country . . . a great future for Missouri and the whole nation could be created."[21]

A noted historian wrote more than a hundred years later, "The binding thread was the great dream of 1848, now translated into an American idiom, even if still written *auf Deutsch*. The Union was worth dying for precisely because the American republic was bound up with the survival of . . . liberty itself."[22]

All those things, if they were there, were buried too deep now within their subconscious knapsacks as the German boys of 1861 marched off down the road.

3

We Are to Meet the Enemy

In September, the regiment was finally assigned a colonel. He was Francis J. Joliat, commissioned on July 16. Joliat was an appointee from Chicago, probably the beneficiary of a commission less for military qualifications than for connections in high places. His was typical of the appointments being made for many field-grade commanders at the outset of the war.

Washington, D.C., and the state governors in particular were taking the spoils of war to a new level. Although only the president could grant commissions for generals, it was given to the governors to appoint colonels to head the volunteer regiments. But the spoils did not stop with officer commissions. Both Lincoln and the governors were overwhelmed with requests and pleadings from constituents to authorize new regiments; the agenda behind these requests all too often was to create officer positions that could be filled by friends, relatives, political supporters, and not least of all, by the author of a request himself.

The German contingent too was not shy about banging on doors and desks for a share of the new ranks. Carl Schurz, possibly the most influential German politician at the time and a future Missouri senator, even persuaded Lincoln to create an all-German brigade. When the president learned that more Germans were volunteering than a brigade would have room for, an embarrassed Lincoln had to withdraw the authorization. The waves of Germans volunteering in cities such as Cincinnati, Milwaukee, and St. Louis were becoming a national embarrassment for the larger society in the North.[1]

Too much German visibility in the army was becoming a concern. In St. Louis, where anti-German feelings were running higher possibly than anywhere else in the country, German leaders came up with a model that many other cities would follow in filling regimental commands, while at the same time diminishing the sense of an overwhelming Teutonic presence. For the 15th Missouri, it would get them Colonel Joliat.

In Illinois, Chicago and downstate political leaders were flooding Gov. Richard Yates's office with pleas seeking favors and appointments.[2] So many demands were pouring in from German constituents and political leaders that Yates hired a German-speaking secretary to handle the correspondence.[3]

Passing out commissions was one thing, but finding a place for them was something else altogether. Relief for one prospective new colonel turned out to be across the river in St. Louis, where politicians were looking for anybody but another German to command a regiment. And so, on July 22, Francis J. Joliat of Chicago became a colonel without a regiment, at least not just yet.[4]

The record does not show whether the commission came from Illinois or Missouri, nor is there any indication that Joliat brought along any military experience to his new commission.[5] Exactly two months later, Joliat, a thirty-six-year-old Swiss immigrant with apparently strong connections in Chicago, was given command of the newly formed 15th Missouri Volunteer Infantry. The fact that the new regiment was promoting itself around the drill field as the Swiss Rifles, at least by those handful of Swiss immigrants who had been among the first to join the unit, and with a Swiss flag to show for it, and from Illinois to top it off, may have had something to do with his being assigned the job. The Swiss connection, as far as the St. Louis politicians were concerned, may have been enough. Never mind that the new regiment's company commanders, as well as the men being added daily to its ranks, were almost all German immigrants—Joliat was *not* German. If Joliat brought along any military experience, and no record shows that he had any to bring, that too very likely was not German. Non-German or no military experience at all—either fact would not have gone unnoticed in a regiment that boasted officers with vast experience in the German army. The Germans in the 15th would likely have proclaimed their ridicule, and loud enough for Joliat to hear it.

On September 24, two days after Joliat's appointment to the 15th, the regiment was ordered "to tack baggage," or to get ready to move out. "The nights were becoming cold," Marcoot wrote, "and our knapsacks proved too small to accommodate the effects we thought indispensibly necessary to take with us . . . but we shouldered our saratogas, as it were, and marching down to the levee[,] boarded the steamers 'John Warner' and 'White Cloud' and were, four days later, landed at Jefferson City.

Here we expected to see some service for it was understood that Jefferson City was threatened by the army of General Price, then jubilant over its dearly bought victory at Lexington [Missouri]. But the enemy came not, and on the fifth day of October we again broke camp and started on our campaign under Gen's Fremont and Sigel, marching eighteen miles [west from Jefferson City] to Lookout Station. . . . Oh, how we groaned under our heavily loaded knapsacks. All along the line of that, our first day's march, bed clothing was scattered in endless profusion, ample in quantity to have equipped royally several veteran regiments a few years later. I was obstinate, as usual, and had no intention to enrich the citizens along the line of march, so I held to my property manfully. We were not yet provided with tents and night closed in upon us camped out upon the commons near the depot. Our comfort was not materially enhanced during the night when it began to rain. Every available shelter was sought, but still it poured down in torrents. Together with a number of our boys, I crawled under the depot platform, but as the hogs had occupied it previously and rooted up the earth forming big holes, it soon became most horrible. The water poured in and about us. What a night, and what a sight we presented the next morning. Can we ever forget Lookout Station.

"I pulled out my baggage, and, with the assistance of a comrade, wrung the quilts and blankets dry, for I still proposed to keep them company. It did not take us many days, however, to realize our mistake and reduce our baggage to a minimum quantity." The regiment continued its march, arriving at Warsaw on the 17, where they were detailed building a bridge over the Osage River. "During this time our rations ran short and we suffered much from hunger."[6]

Marcoot apparently never learned that the reason for their suffering lay at the feet of their new colonel. Joliat had ordered ten days of rations drawn by the regiment's quartermaster to be shipped to St. Louis and *sold* on the open market.[7] In spite of hunger, compounded by the labor of building a bridge, the men completed the construction, and less than a week after starting on the bridge, the regiment again took up the march, arriving at Springfield on October 27.

"We remained in Springfield until November 8th, when General Fremont [was] relieved by General Hunter." David Hunter, a major general respected for his experience and sagacity, had spent a good part of his army career in the Western Department. Lincoln, hoping to head off problems he was beginning to encounter with Frémont, had asked Hunter to go to St. Louis to try to advise "the Pathfinder" on the ways of political realities. Headstrong Frémont would have none of it. The final straw came when Frémont issued a proclamation to free all slaves in the Western Department. Lincoln, fearing that Frémont's proclamation might drive such border states as Missouri to secede, relieved him and placed Hunter in temporary command.

"We did not at this time appreciate the change of commanders," Marcoot recorded. "General Fremont was dearly loved by all," so much so that German immigrants in the army for a while even threatened to mutiny over Frémont's firing. Nevertheless, "We were in the best of spirits," Marcoot continued, "and although we now firmly believed that we were to meet the enemy we had been seeking for two months, we had no doubt of our ability to whip him."[8]

The 15th marched off in search of Price's army, but they discovered they had to retrace their steps to Springfield where, in Marcoot's words, "we found that the opposing army had broken up camp and was marching rapidly toward Rolla" near the center of the state. "Our division, Sigel's, moved in the opposite direction for the purpose of deceiving the enemy in regard to the real movements of the army."[9] On the march, Colonel Joliat had his first recorded run-in with one of his officers, Capt. Francis Mohrhardt of Company F. The issue was over a horse. Mohrhardt was commissioned back on June 2 and assigned to recruit volunteers and ultimately command a company in the newly forming 15th Missouri. He likely was German, because the bulk of his company was made up of German immigrants whom he had recruited, including George Rau and the three musicians. Mohrhardt was no slouch as an officer. Later in the war, he would be promoted to major in the 15th and eventually selected to serve on Gen. Phil Sheridan's staff. He was or would become an exemplary officer, an officer unlikely to lose command of a situation or his emotions. But on the march to Rolla, something happened that caused Mohrhardt to snap.

Mohrhardt was approached by the officer of the day, a Lieutenant Wilson of Company B. Wilson held an order for Mohrhardt to give up his horse. The order was signed by the division commander, General Asboth, but given circumstances that would show up months later, one can almost sense the influence of Colonel Joliat lurking in the background.

Mohrhardt refused to give up the horse. Further, Mohrhardt "took a revolver from the Officer of the Day and threatened to shoot the first man to attempt to take the horse from him."[10] The matter came to a quick halt. Mohrhardt kept the horse, no one was shot, and the Officer of the Day may have even gotten his pistol back. The lieutenant withdrew but dutifully filled out the charges and specifications form against Captain Mohrhardt. Even so, and incredibly, nothing came of the incident or the charges. At least for the moment.

The reason may have had something to do with an ongoing trade in stolen horses, a racket that was being run by officers and men in the army itself. A young captain by the name of Philip H. Sheridan serving as chief quartermaster for the army in Missouri spotted the scheme: "Certain officers and men more devoted to gain than to the performance of duty," he later wrote, "began a regular system of stealing horses from the people of the country and proffering them to me for purchase [for the army]. It took but a little time to discover this roguery, and when I became satisfied of their knavery I brought it to a sudden close by seizing the horses as captured property, branding them U.S. and refusing to pay for them."[11] Events later would show that Sheridan was not as successful at stopping the trade as he thought.

For the moment, however, for Captain Mohrhardt, or for any officer for that matter, disobeying an order, and from a general at that, combined with an assault with a weapon on an officer, were serious charges to say the least. Nevertheless, Mohrhardt heard nothing for his part in the incident. Joliat probably never felt that a subordinate officer would, upon a direct order from a general, fail to give up the horse; the colonel no doubt was stunned to learn otherwise. But for Joliat to pursue charges against the captain might risk an unraveling of a profitable trade and possibly reveal his own complicity.

While most of the 15th was marching and countermarching, amid rumblings probably beginning to circulate about the new colonel, new recruits began to arrive in Rolla. George Rau and the three musicians were among the new arrivals. On the last day of October, the four young men, Rau being the oldest at twenty-seven, mustered in together into Company F. Three weeks later, the rest of the regiment arrived in camp, covering fifty-six miles in ten days, a leisurely pace considering the enemy was thought to be out in front. As the men began to unload their gear for what looked to be an extended stay, Marcoot expressed "a vague feeling that we would have to return home without having ever seen a battle."[12]

The regiment began to settle in to winter camp in Rolla. The men were supplied with tents that would pass for home and shelter from the winter blasts to come. The tents were wedge-shaped canvas constructions, designed to house about a dozen men. For warmth, each was usually equipped with a stove and pipe that passed through an opening at the top, although Marcoot's reminiscences suggest that theirs were not so equipped; the men simply built a fire on the ground in the center of the tent.[13]

In good weather the canvas was raised for ventilation, but with rain, cold, or snow, the canvas edges were lowered and the entry flap drawn tight, producing, as one Yank in another part of the army reminisced, an accumulation of "exhalations from the bodies of twelve men . . . an experience which no old soldier has ever been known to recall with any great enthusiasm."[14]

This first camp was a time for the companies and the regiment to organize. Judging from the muster cards of the regiment, the 15th was probably ahead of the other volunteer units in the state in terms of organization, thanks no doubt to the company commanders with German military experience. The first companies to fill out their ranks probably got themselves well in order during the summer back at the arsenal. But the newer companies, with many of their recruits just arriving and mustering in, had the organizational details to go through for the first time.

Election of sergeants and corporals by the men in the ranks was a common practice. The men did elect at least some of their sergeants and corporals during the summer at the arsenal and later that autumn in Rolla. Thereafter, men would have to earn their stripes on the battlefield. But for now, the privates picked others from among their tentmates who, for whatever reasons, had earned the confidence that they could be trusted to rule over them. Gustav Roehm, the twenty-three-year-old shoemaker from Saxony, was promoted that September to corporal and then to sergeant in Company B, all in one month. His performance on the march may have had much to do with the rapid-fire promotions.

That same set of promotions fell to George Rau, another *Landsman* from Saxony. Rau barely had time to put on his uniform before he got his corporal stripes. Then, inside of a month, he too had to sew on a new set of three stripes. In a daguerreotype that probably was made soon after his last promotion, Rau with evident satisfaction thrusts a sleeve forward to display the stripes of his impressive new rank. His countenance shows a determination that may have convinced his comrades that here was a man who would show no fear taking them into battle when the time came, even if he knew less about soldiering than about making cabinets and playing the violin.

Election of captains and lieutenants by the men in the ranks sometimes also took place.[15] John Weber, in fact, had been elected captain of Company B that past summer at the arsenal in St. Louis.

George Rau sat for his photograph during the 15th Missouri's first winter camp at Rolla, Missouri. An air of determination may have influenced men in Company F to elect him to the rank of sergeant. Rau wears the brimmed black hat identified with Union troops from Midwestern states. (Janet Walton)

It does appear that some of the regiment's first set of officers came directly by way of appointments from Gov. Hamilton Gamble (either way, final appointments had to go through him), with no input from the men in the ranks or the regiment's senior officers. More than a few of the 15th's newly commissioned officers arriving on a direct line from the governor had no military qualifications. A year later, the adjutant general of Missouri would receive a complaint from the 15th's lieutenant colonel about officers being "sent to the regiment with commissions from the governor" but with no qualifications whatsoever,[16] but the problem was not limited to the 15th Missouri.

Serious discipline problems confronted the new chief of the Department of the Missouri. Maj. Gen. Henry W. Halleck had just arrived in St. Louis to take command. Halleck would eventually move on to Washington as general of the army to carry out the president's directives in prosecuting the war. He was an officer who managed to leave a bad impression on just about everyone who came to know him. A cabinet member once wrote, Halleck "originates nothing . . . plans nothing, suggests nothing, is good for nothing."[17] A nativist at heart, Halleck also left no illusions about his dislike of foreigners.[18]

Many of the officers in his department ridiculed drills as simply "playing soldier."[19] Discipline was weak at best and, in some cases, nonexistent. Halleck's letter zeroed in on those he considered the culprits. Not surprisingly, they were, for him, "foreigners, officered in many cases by foreign adventurers or perhaps refugees from justice and having been tampered with by political partisans for political purposes." They "constitute," he ranted, "a very dangerous element in society as well as in the army." Lincoln got wind of the letter, and he knew that "foreign" meant Germans to Halleck. Writing to the general, the president came to the defense of the Germans in Missouri: "The Germans are true and patriotic, and so far as they have got cross in Missouri it is upon mistake and misunderstanding."[20]

Halleck tarred with a broad brush. In his "very dangerous element to society" dispatch, he reported that he was mustering out seven "illegal organizations." All of these "illegal organizations" were German units. One indeed—Frémont's Body Guards—was hardly illegal. It had been officially mustered into the Union army on August 1. A week before Halleck had them disbanded, the Guards had charged and routed two thousand Confederates at Springfield, killing and wounding a number equal to their own entire force.[21] The Guards had been fiercely loyal to Frémont and likely were among those units that threatened mutiny when the general was fired. That circumstance probably played no small role in their official disbandment. Illegality and accusations of thievery likely had nothing to do with it.

The number of Halleck's units accused of theft, in fact, represented a small share of the total. When thievery did occur, it crossed all lines. Hunger and deprivation on the march and in the camps sometimes forced soldiers in all of the Civil War armies, North and South, to steal to stay alive. Officially it was called foraging, the practice the armies used to sustain themselves on the march. Payment officially required nothing more than an IOU from the government, scratched out on a scrap of paper by a junior officer or sergeant whose signature no one could probably read anyhow. In reality, foraging was an official license to steal. Too often it gave way to plunder and wanton destruction.[22]

As far as Halleck's army in the West was concerned, lack of discipline lay at the bottom of the problems. Within the four-state Department of

Missouri, a comprehensive report, possibly one as balanced as any a commander was going to get on the subject, was issued by the Union army's inspector general a month after Halleck wrote his report. Regiments of native-born volunteers came in for more blistering in the inspector general's report than did the German units.[23]

Halleck, however, made it clear that he was talking about Germans. "Union men in Southwestern Missouri have begged me not to permit General Sigel's command [the ninety-day German volunteers] to return to that part of the country, as they robbed and plundered wherever they went, friends and enemies alike." Halleck was likely also influenced by reports from officers in the field such as Brig. Gen. John Schofield, another West Pointer, most recently a professor of physics at Washington University in St. Louis. Schofield, chasing Rebel bands between St. Charles and Mexico, Missouri, reported that the only cavalry force at his disposal was "a battalion of Germans, utterly worthless for this kind of service. If I trust them out of my sight for a moment they will plunder and rob friends and foes alike. I have arrested two of the officers and have five of the men in irons."[24]

While Schofield may well have been accurate in his assessment of his newly appointed cavalry, there was another set of circumstances in Missouri. Halleck may have failed to recognize it. Having just arrived from the East, he likely was not even aware of it. Within Missouri's borders lived an explosive mixture possibly unlike anything anywhere else, North or South. Living in the same towns, sometimes just next door or perhaps the next farm over, were Southern sympathizers and Unionists, seceshes and Black Dutch, foreigners and German haters, each living almost side by side, and neither at all pleased about it. The combinations were sometimes different from one town to the next. They lived together, but they were hardly neighbors.

Unionists, native born and German alike, straying too far beyond St. Louis, "often found themselves in dangerous predicaments."[25] A German immigrant in St. Louis, a Missouri state legislator and later a correspondent for the German-language *Westliche Post*, spoke of a secret organization that developed among Unionists for self-protection. The organization soon stretched throughout the state. Strangers "who met on the street were reserved and distrustful of one another. They observed each other so attentively that very often they forgot to greet . . . the slightest sign of recognition was not overlooked. . . . As soon as a member of this league noticed [the] sign from a stranger and had answered with another sign, they shook hands, and in this greeting and in addressing each other the strangers had to legitimize themselves" as members. "If the tests proved satisfactory, they made known to each other without reserve everything that might be of importance to the other."[26] Mutual disrespect born in the 1840s had grown to mutual hatred in the 1850s. Now in the 1860s, the result was vengeance. Both Unionist and secessionist practiced it to settle old scores. It was at times literally murderous.[27]

As the German regiments marched into the interior of Missouri, the memories of killings in Cole Camp; the cursings, rock throwings, and shootings back in St. Louis; and the threats to kill them in the streets in Neosho were all probably part of the emotional baggage that was impossible to leave behind. Missourians, clustered along the country lanes as they watched Union regiments march by, saw only foreigners and Dutchmen. The German immigrant soldier as he marched along saw no friends and few allies.

Numbing cold settled in on the 15th Missouri's first winter camp. "The winter was a hard one," Marcoot wrote, men taking sick, dying, others breaking down and being discharged for disabilities.[28] Gambling filled the men's free time, an activity that was to grow into a chronic problem. An enterprising young lieutenant in the 15th Missouri, Samuel Rexinger, to add to his income offered a clandestine game of poker to the men, with liquid refreshment on the side. From St. Joseph, Missouri, with family ties to the South in Georgia, he joined the 15th as a second lieutenant in September 1861. If he had one strong point, it was that he was very close to his men. Too close sometimes, perhaps too much of an entrepreneur as well. Settled now into winter camp, he started up his little recreation for the men, but his enterprise was soon discovered; charges were brought against him for running a "gambling house" in one of the tents and, further, for selling liquor to the men (at $2.50 a gallon, one-fourth of a soldier's monthly pay). But nothing came of the charges against Rexinger.[29]

A more serious claim against Joliat was beginning to unfold in the officers' tents. New grumblings could be heard about the colonel. There was now reason to believe that he had something to do with the short rations and the terrible hunger the men had suffered back in October. The boys of 1861 were coming to realize that they had other enemies than just those they would meet on the battlefield.

1862

Silent cannons, soon to cease your silence,
Soon unlimber'd to begin the red business

—Walt Whitman, "Drum Taps"

4

A Home Not Made with Hands

The company captains found out about Joliat's selling of the rations back in October. With still no lieutenant colonel to fill the second-in-command vacancy, the regimental captains took on their colonel. On January 8, six company captains and the quartermaster filed a charge and specification letter addressed to the brigade commander, Brig. Gen. Alexander S. Asboth: "Specification: . . . said Colonel F. J. Joliat ordered the sale of the ten days rations drawn by the Quartermaster of the 15th Regiment at Tipton from thence shipped to Sedalia and from thence taken to St. Louis and stored at Grous & Sons for which Company commanders of said 15th Regiment never made requisitions."[1] Signing for the group was Francis Mohrhardt, the captain of Company F who had refused to give up his horse.

A day later another charge and specification letter was filed against the colonel. The second, signed this time by three-fourths of the regiment's officers, brought general charges that in the main supported a Major Landry who apparently was dismissed—unfairly the letter charged—by Colonel Joliat. He did have one defender; the chaplain wrote to Asboth that he considered the colonel upstanding in every regard and that "Major Landry [was] morally and intellectually unfit for the high command" in which he had been placed.[2] The record is incomplete in every other aspect about the charge, including its disposition. In substance and detail, the letter was composed as if all who might read it would know all there was to know about the matter. Lacking hard facts, the letter may never have made it past the brigade adjutant. Besides, it was probably common knowledge by now that the 15th's officers had no use for their colonel.

But selling government property—*that* was a charge that could not be dismissed so easily. Colonel Joliat was placed under arrest. Mohrhardt's charge and specification letter made its way up the line, the officers in the chain of command adding their perfunctory endorsements as required before the letter finally landed on General Asboth's camp desk. Asboth, a native of Hungary and a former Austrian army officer, apparently ordered Joliat to his tent to hear the colonel's side of the story. Standing before the general, "a grim son of war, rigid and stern as an iron statue," as one Illinois soldier described Asboth,[3] Joliat confirmed the essential facts of the charge. Soon after, Asboth set down his decision on the back of the charge and specification letter: "The officer explains the rations drawn could not be hauled with the troop and was supposed to be regimental property. They were therefore sent to St. Louis. The colonel subsequently had them sold for the benefit of the Regiment. It was all wrong but I think it all proceeds from ignorance of the law. The Col. may deserve summary reprimand but the trial for such charges would not result in any this month. I concur with others in giving instructions and reprimand to the Colonel. Arrest suspended."[4]

It is not clear what Asboth meant by "the trial for such charges would not result in any this month." Perhaps Asboth's new commander had everything to do with it. Gen. Samuel R. Curtis made it clear that he did not want to see any more courts-martial of officers. "The arrest and trial of officers by courts-martial embarrass the command," Curtis wrote to Halleck. "The bickerings . . . employ too much time, which they should devote to the enemy."[5] Twelve days later, Halleck notified Curtis, "Your dissolution of the general court-martial [is] contrary to law," but Halleck gave no further directive.[6] In any case, there would be no courts-martial papers from Asboth's command, at least for the moment.

As the regiment's officers were doing battle with Joliat, the men in the ranks were fighting another kind of war. Life itself was draining from the command. "Language cannot be found too strong to describe the condition of many of the regimental and some of the post hospitals. They were sickening to behold." The comment came from a report to Halleck by the president of the United States Sanitary Commission.[7] The commission was a volunteer organization appointed by Congress to report on the condition of the army's camps and hospitals. "Could you witness the sufferings which I to-day witnessed," the report concluded, "to-morrow's sun would not go down without an order correcting it." The report spanned every aspect of the army's medical resources in Missouri, from the inadequacy of civilians employed as nurses to an inability to identify diseases and their causes. Given the ignorance of the times about bacteria and sanitation necessities, the commission was not always correct when devising remedies. Nevertheless, the report was specific enough to be damning:

> From a recent examination of the camps and hospitals at Rolla . . . we find there are at that post 1,542 sick out of the aggregate strength of 14,762. . . . At the various posts along the line of the main stem of the Pacific Railroad there were found over 1,300 sick in hospitals alone. . . . The source of most of the sickness in this division can be traced to the crowded condition of some of the tents and barracks, especially the Wedge tent, which averages five and a half persons to a tent of 8 by 7½. Bad as this tent is, the close and crowded barracks are even worse. . . . The air is most foul and breeds disease and death. . . . The regulations allow 225 square feet for 6 men . . . there is but 60 feet for 6 men, which is entirely inadequate. The small-pox has made its appearance . . . to arrest and mitigate the horrors of this dreaded disease it is necessary that some obligatory order be issued to colonels of regiments, holding them responsible for the prompt execution of the same.

If an "obligatory order" was issued, there is no record of it. There is in fact no record of any response to the commission's report from General Halleck.

A month later, the inspector general filed his report with Washington on the general condition and readiness of Halleck's Department of the Missouri. "The troops generally are in physical appearance all that could desired—fine specimens of manhood." However, "A large portion has been stationed near Rolla, which well deserves the name it has, of being one of the most unhealthy places in the state. . . . The percentage of deaths here is high, about 7 per cent."[8]

That would not have come as news to the men of the 15th. Of the camp at Rolla, Marcoot wrote, "Many of our comrades were called to 'that home not made with hands,' . . . others became badly broken down in health."[9]

Their muster cards tell the story: in Company B, Marcoot's company, Pvt. John Bauer was one of many to go into the hospital. Seven months later, Bauer was discharged for disability. John Bernhart, one of Marcoot's friends from Highland, was recorded as "sick at Rolla Hospital"; a year later he would be discharged for disability. Christoph Duerr, twenty-eight years old, from Germany and a butcher in civilian life, entered the hospital; six months later he would be discharged with "rheumatism." John Luhm, another of the Swiss volunteers was discharged with "Profuse Diarrhoea." For Anton Eschger, Jacob Kircher, and John Krauchy, their muster cards read, "Died, disease."[10]

In Company F, one of the four musicians, Christian Graus, entered the hospital, as did Frank Beni, Christian Kirch, Adam Kraus, William Leiber, Nicholas Lenver, Charles Lenz, and Louis Niederhauser, 10 percent of the company. "Chronic diarrhea" shows up again and again on the muster cards. They would be released but discharged from the army within the year. Christian Graus would be released to go home almost immediately after entering the hospital, leaving his three musical friends to carry on without him.

Others were discharged because soldiering was simply too hard, or they were unfit for soldiering and should not have volunteered in the first place, as was the case for John Miltenberger from Baden, Germany: "Asthma, almost continually on sick list," his record reads, "he will never be fit for military service . . . should never have enlisted"; and for Sebastian Bucher, Lucerne, Switzerland, his record indicates that he was "never fit for a soldier . . . used to haul wood and water."

Of the 1,685 men in Asboth's brigade, which included the 15th, one in five could not be reported as "present for duty."[11] Most were sick or in the hospital. Others, seeing no future in staying, simply walked away and deserted.

Halleck nevertheless was getting ready to meet the enemy. Pressure had been mounting from those in the southwest corner of Missouri for him to do something about getting rid of the Rebels in that part of the state. But attacking the enemy was not really Halleck's idea. His marching orders to Curtis showed where the pressure was really coming from: "the authorities at Washington are exceedingly urgent." The president had been urging Halleck for some time to make an attack in western Kentucky.[12] He was also getting pressure to send some of his regiments back east: "On to Richmond" was the cry. But Halleck was not about to give away any part of his command and risk diminishing his importance. Initiating an attack here in Missouri would give him an excuse for not letting go any of his troops.

Not that Halleck was expecting a fight in Missouri. "I do not believe that Price will fight you," he finished to Curtis, believing apparently that Price would choose instead to withdraw into Arkansas when faced with an approaching Union army, joining up with other Confederate forces.

Curtis was skeptical of just about everything Halleck was telling him, including the judgment that Price was disinclined to do battle. Following orders and writing to Franz Sigel to prepare his brigade to march, Curtis added that Price's Rebel army "always will be underrated by our friends [in

Southwest Missouri] who are over-anxious for us to come to their relief. . . . Besides, his force is never in camp except when a battle is anticipated, when they come in from all the hills and hollows of the surrounding country."[13] Curtis then informed his brigade commanders to break camp.

"It was a warm pretty day," Marcoot wrote as they began the march, "but as the frost had but just left the ground the mud was nearly knee deep." The regiment marched only eight miles, accompanied by a large wagon train. "Owing to the impassable condition of the roads the train failed to reach camp . . . we were compelled to put in the night without rations or the shelter of our tents. We were not long however in turning in upon a temporary bed made of fence rails covered with old corn stocks with our blankets and our coats as coverings; while a portion of the boys made a night of it about the fires. During the night it turned colder and snowed heavily. It was at this time that our comrade, Wendolin Trapp, deserted us."[14]

The men arose the next morning to the reality that the wagon train with food and supplies had not kept up.

A little squad was formed to look it up. Retracing our steps we found it stuck—frozen fast in the mud some four miles back. By the use of the ax the frozen ground was soon trenched out and in a short time the train was in camp. The boys at once set about preparing breakfast, but before many had succeeded the morning having already well advanced, the command was given to "fall in." . . . The boys were considerably disgruntled over the failure to secure breakfast and a good strong cup of coffee after the fast the evening before and the bitter cold. . . . It was not to occur again . . . hereafter our marching speed should not prove faster than the ability of the train to follow.

The regiment covered only four miles the second day, camping on the banks of the Gasconade River.

It remained fearfully cold. . . . We struck our tents, but as the ground was so frozen, we were unable to drive a peg and were compelled to place rocks, chucks of wood &c., upon the edges to hold them up and out. Fires were soon burning in the center of every tent. . . . Had it not been for the melting of the snow and frost in the ground we would soon have been most comfortably housed. But horror of horrors what mud. The tramping of so many feet about the enclosure together with the warmth of the fire soon worked it up until it was a perfect mire and we were compelled to go to the woods in quest of brush &c., for flooring and

beds. When we had thus at last completed our quarters were rewarded
with a most pleasant night's sleep.

The march continued the next day, the weather moderating and the
snow finally melting. "But not so with the mud . . . every evening the same
difficulty arose relative to our beds. . . . Our troubles did not end here for
when we left Rolla each was provided with a new pair of shoes and nearly
every pair proved worthless. The soles ripped from the uppers and we were
compelled to tie them to our feet with strings to hold them in position.
The mud, sand and water worked into them and our feet soon presented a
horrible condition. . . . Finally on the 6th arrived at Lebanon."[15]

On February 11, the 15th again took up the march, returning to
Springfield on the 13th, the troops occupying the barracks Confederate
troops had evacuated only the night before. "This was the beginning of
an excited chase," Marcoot wrote, "with our regiment continually in the
advance . . . reaching Camp Halleck, Benton County, Arkansas, on the
18th where the pursuit was abandoned and a few days' rest granted us. We
had been on a forced march for four consecutive days during which time
the weather was most galling, storm after storm of snow and rain fell, and
skirmishes with the enemy were an everyday occurrence."

The 15th "remained in Camp Halleck until March 3rd," Marcoot continued,

> when we were moved to Bentonville, where on the 4th Captain Weber
> with his company was detailed for an expedition, the object of which
> was to intercept a company of rebel recruits. . . . The regiment made
> a forced march of about eighty miles in two days. . . . We were fortu-
> nate enough in securing the services of a "native" guide, but our line of
> march was not strewn with roses. Foot paths and by-ways were rough,
> rocky and broken and the country mountainous. Our feet were soon
> badly blistered and many suffered sorely. In fact some thirteen of our
> comrades who were unable to keep up with the command were com-
> pelled to suffer themselves to be captured by the enemy . . . while the
> main portion of the company who withstood the ordeal reached our
> army in safety.[16]

Reports began to come in to Brig. Gen. Franz Sigel: "The main force of
the enemy is . . . gathering re-enforcements . . . burned the mills and cotton factories at Cane Hill." A spy reported that "Price was moving . . . his
artillery passed through Fayetteville yesterday." Two days later, Curtis sent

another dispatch to Sigel: "A deserter, apparently a very reliable man, has arrived . . . left Price's army at Fayetteville this morning at 8 o'clock. They are coming sure."[17]

Sigel concluded that his army should unite at Sugar Creek near a travelers' wilderness inn known as Elkhorn Tavern. That night, the 15th with the Second Division under Asboth crossed the border into Arkansas and halted to set up camp on the McKissick farm three and a half miles southwest of Bentonville. At eleven that night, Asboth received orders to march to Bentonville starting at two the next morning and to wait there for further orders. Arriving just before daylight, the command was overtaken by General Curtis and ordered to continue to Sugar Creek, about ten miles to the northeast.

Asboth and his division arrived a little after ten and were making arrangements to encamp when a courier dashed up to report that Curtis was under attack and surrounded by a "vastly superior force at Bentonville."[18] Asboth again set his men in motion and hurried back to the southwest where he found Curtis engaged about five miles along the Sugar Creek–Bentonville road. The attack was repulsed, and Curtis, expecting a second attack, ordered Asboth to draw his force into line along the road. The attack failed to materialize, and Curtis closed up his line with the main body on the Telegraph road.

The next day, Friday, March 7, began with word that the Confederates were advancing. It appeared that they intended to cut off the roads back to Missouri and encircle the Union force. Curtis detached the First Brigade under Col. Frederick Schaefer, which included the 15th, "to take position upon the heights" above the Sugar Creek–Bentonville road.

"The battle speedily opened both in the direction of Leesville and Keetsville, at Pea Ridge, and raged furiously," Asboth reported, "without involving the First Brigade or the 15th Missouri." Marcoot recalled, "A few skirmishers from the heights on the opposite side of the valley and several wounded horses of the rebels without riders were all that we saw."

Two companies of the 15th (not identified in Asboth's report) had previously been detached with other units to guard the rear. Four miles from Sugar Creek, along the Bentonville road, they "encountered the enemy," according to Asboth, "and exchanged fire with them with shell and spherical case shot until dark." Rifle shots fired by the two unknown companies likely were the first fired in combat by the 15th Missouri.

At seven the next morning, the Union forces opened fire followed by a "sharp and continuous return from the enemy," Asboth wrote. "So severe was their fire as to imperil our camp" before additional support arrived, "and the whole force moved from position to position like an immense machine." The end for the Confederate troops came quickly.

From the outset of the battle, the 15th had been designated as reserves. In his report, Asboth added a final paragraph: "I have to regret that the efficient Swiss regiment, Fifteenth Missouri Volunteers, whose beautiful flag floated so picturesquely throughout the battlefield, had not the opportunity they so ardently longed for of following their energetic commander, Colonel Joliat, to the heart of the conflict, and of attesting by their blood their devotion to the cause."[19]

Marcoot and his comrades saw it all in a somewhat different light. Aside possibly from a skirmish or two, they had just witnessed their first full-scale battle. It would take only this first for Marcoot to conclude later that all battles are horrible to behold, their aftermaths particularly, reinforced in this case by an incident that would not happen again during the Civil War: "One of the most horrible features of the battle—and all battles are horrible," said Marcoot, "was that many of our comrades who fell dead and wounded upon the field were found to have been scalped by the Indians under the command of the rebel General Pike. This discovery aroused the most bitter feelings in the ranks and loud and determined were the expressions for retaliation."[20] The Confederate force had in fact numbered in their ranks two regiments of Cherokees, Choctaws, and Creeks from the reservation in Indian Territory. The South would not so involve tribal units again.

There would be a more enduring memory for Marcoot and the 15th, as well, which would become imbedded in their minds as part of a litany to be repeated after every battle: "We buried the dead," Marcoot remembered, "the Grey as well as the Blue, and cared for the wounded and prisoners as best we could."

The reports coming in from Pea Ridge were garbled, the *Anzeiger des Westens* reported. "Information on the great battle in Arkansas has been maddeningly slow in coming in, and this has caused great anxiety, both because of the large mass of St. Louisans involved, which leads virtually everyone to fear the loss of a relative or friend among the heavy casualties."[21]

In Washington, in spite of the victory at Pea Ridge, there was little to celebrate. Although there had been no recent defeats, there had been no real progress in getting Gen. George McClellan and the Army of the Potomac to move on Richmond. In addition, immense grief draped the White House for much more personal reasons. Following a brief illness of "bilious fever," probably typhoid, the Lincoln's young son Willie had died just two weeks earlier. Mary Lincoln had taken to her bed and would remain there for three weeks, so desolate that she would not attend the funeral. For nearly a year all social activities and celebrations at the Executive Mansion (it would not be called the White House until seventy years later) were suspended.[22]

At Pea Ridge, the Union suffered 1,384 casualties, compared to the loss of an estimated 2,000 Confederate troops.[23] It was the price paid to preserve Missouri for the North.

To the east in western Tennessee the firing had finally stopped around the little log cabin that served as the Shiloh Methodist Church near Pittsburg Landing. Early in the morning the day before, the Confederate Army of Tennessee under Gen. Albert Sidney Johnston had launched waves of savage attacks against the Union Army of the Tennessee of 62,000, commanded by Maj. Gen. Ulysses S. Grant—by the end of day, driving the backs of the blue-coated masses against the Tennessee River. The next day, April 7, Grant, with the larger force, pushed Johnston's army back in another daylong battle, ending finally with both armies at about the same place they had started. Ultimately, more than 24,000 men on both sides fell in just two days of fighting, the largest number of casualties in one battle that America to this point had ever known.

The shock at the magnitude of the bloodshed resonated across the North and the South. In St. Louis, along the levies, people watched in stunned silence as steamboats began the slow and careful unloading of the wounded, stretcher after stretcher intermingled with the bandaged and the hobbling, moving dreamlike down the gangplanks and up the stoned levee in files that seemed to have no end.

The day the firing had begun around the little church in Tennessee, the dogwoods and redbuds were beginning to bloom in Arkansas as the 15th formed up and joined a column of about five thousand infantry and cavalry marching away from Pea Ridge. "We retraced our steps through Keetsville," Marcoot said, "camping on the banks of the Flat River" in Missouri. On April 10, the 15th reached Galena, north of Springfield. Crossing the James River the next day on a bridge made of wagons, the regiment reached the banks of Bull Creek. On the 12th, they arrived at Forsyth on the White River.[24]

In the column with the 15th was the 36th Illinois. Two men of the 36th described the march as they left Forsyth: "The march was resumed in the midst of a rain storm, the column headed eastward . . . to West Plains in Howell County. Day after day the rain came pouring down in unmeasured quantities. The country was deluged, the streams filled to overflowing, rendering a detour necessary, far up among the hills toward their sources, to enable the army to cross the roaring torrents. The passing of men, horses and vehicles over the execrable roads soon mixed the spongy soil into mortar, through which plashed [sic] the slow moving columns of mud-encased horses and men at the rate of less than a mile an hour."[25]

Leaning into the driving rain day after day, physically drained, their spirit gone, some would decide they could go no farther. Horse and man would fall, some never to rise again. "While on the march, winding through the deep valleys and traversing the pine clad hills, universally prevalent in this poverty stricken country, a private of Company I, named Martin Rinehart, sickened and died, and was buried by the road in the depths of the gloomy forest, away from the sight of man, with nothing but the wailing pine to stand guard and watch his lonely forest grave."[26]

The column continued on, "something like a hundred miles into Arkansas," Marcoot wrote. Following the torrents, "the sun poured down its fiercest rays, raising the temperature to fever heat . . . the column pushed bravely on, amidst clouds of dust. . . . Not a third of the troops were able to keep up with the marching column. They fell out of ranks by scores, and each shady nook by the wayside was monopolized by squads of exhausted, dust covered men, who all day long wearily dragged their way to camp."[27]

At Hicks Ferry on the Current River, "one of the saddest accidents yet experienced occurred," Marcoot recalled. "The river was crossed on a flat boat ferry which was operated by a rope attached from bank to bank, securely fastened. The current was very swift and it happened as one of the crews was making the passage, all those placed to handle the rope let loose at the same time and before they could recover their hold the rope was beyond their reach. In their effort to regain the lost rope the boat was capsized and five of our boys were drowned. . . . Two were brothers, who, together with their father, were serving in the same regiment, and the distress of that father was most pitiable to behold. He had schooled himself to the thought of possibly losing them in battle, but to see them drowned without the power of aiding them, seemed almost to unman him and the pall hovered over him for many days."[28]

The men in the 36th Illinois remembered the tragedy as well. "Efforts to resuscitate them were unavailing. . . . Their death and burial on the banks of the stream caused a chill of sadness." The column started up again, passing through a "country-side deserted, houses empty, a few terror-stricken women and children peering from behind the darkness."[29]

On April 22, they arrived in Cape Girardeau, Missouri. An Illinois soldier remembered,

On entering . . . many men were barefooted, their feet so lacerated and swollen as scarcely to be able to hobble along. The soles of the shoes . . . were largely composed of oak-wood, chips, and fragments of felt colored on the outside, or covered with thin pieces of leather. . . . A few days' marching served to use up these shoes . . . the furnishings of these shoes was one of the many gigantic frauds perpetrated by the contractors upon the Quarter-Master's Department [and] the common soldiers. . . . The next morning a supply of clothing was obtained, and the persons and wardrobe of the men were thoroughly renovated.[30]

The Illinois men recalled, "The camps were thronged with peddling . . . dirty-faced girls, ugly old woman, dilapidated men and thieving boys, with their ceaseless importunities to buy their peanuts, fruit. . . . The soldiers were liberal patrons of the pie and cake venders. . . . Rank smelling haversacks, that for months had been receptacles of only foul-looking slices of . . . hog, [were] suddenly plethoric with gingerbread and turnovers."[31]

For some in the 15th Missouri, what may have come close to overpowering was the fact that they were standing again on the banks of the Mississippi. It had been eight months almost to the day that they had left St. Louis. They had crossed Missouri and crossed it again, now to stand at the river that rolled past the place most of them could call home, a place now little more than a hundred miles away. It was, and many of them may have sensed it, as close as they were going to get to home for a long time to come.

On May 23, 1862, the 15th Missouri Volunteer Infantry crossed over the river. "We boarded the steamer 'Denmark' and proceeded down the Mississippi to Cairo," Marcoot logged in his journal, "thence up the Ohio and Tennessee rivers."[32] Veterans of the 36th Illinois, one of the four brigade regiments with the 15th Missouri, recorded, "The trip up the river to Paducah was almost a continuous ovation. Steamers thickly crowded the Ohio in passing to and fro, and from each, cheer upon cheer went up when it became known that the troops thronging . . . from pilot-house to deck, were the heroes of Pea Ridge."[33] Disembarking at Hamburg Landing on the Tennessee, the brigade "took up its line of march. . . . The afternoon was oppressively warm, and wearily the column plodded on, over roads that were mere forest trails."

"Passing over a portion of the battle-field of Shiloh, every tree, field and building, attested [to] the severity of the conflict. Trees pierced by shot and shattered by shell; fields were plowed by cannon balls, and the ground everywhere littered with broken muskets, fragments of knapsacks,

cartridge boxes and articles of clothing, while the stench arising from the
festering carcasses of horses poisoned the air and sickened the passing soldiers. . . . Now and then the sound of distant cannonading in the direction
of Corinth fell upon the ears of the soldiers."[34]

"The day following," Marcoot wrote,

> we marched up to within supporting distance of the main army, then
> besieging Corinth, Mississippi. Three days later we were formed in line
> of battle and moved forward some two miles to Farrington [Farming-
> ton], where we laid on arms all night, expecting orders to charge every
> moment. It was evident that the rebels were evacuating Corinth. . . . On
> the 12th day of June we returned to Rienzi, Mississippi, and went into
> camp . . . [where] our duties were severe. While one half of our number
> were on picket duty the other half were put to work on the fortifications
> . . . constantly harassed by the enemy as well. The Country . . . was
> swampy and the weather at the time was sultry, so much so that many of
> our boys sickened.[35]

Many, as Marcoot had written, "passed to that home not made with hands."

Swamps and sultry weather had little to do with it. It was yet to be discovered how bacteria transmitted disease, and countermeasures for anti-
sepsis were still several years away. Ignorance ruled in matters of personal
and camp hygiene. Sanitary regulations, what few existed in the camps,
were largely ignored. The combination killed as surely as a bullet.

Contaminated water sent thousands of men to the hospitals. Troops
regularly drank water from the Ohio and Mississippi rivers and from other
waters wherever they were found—creeks, ponds, shallow wells, even rain
puddles. Purification procedures were unknown.

Ignorance of water contamination even in supposedly informed circles
was displayed in an inspection report by the president of the United States
Sanitary Commission:

> The Mississippi water has a general reputation for wholesomeness. The
> Missouri mud . . . in settling carries down whatever vegetable or ani-
> mal substance may exist in the water and leaves it, though still colored,
> comparatively pure. The Ohio water, being more conveniently reached,
> is, however, chiefly used by the troops. They had all suffered diarrhoea
> from the use of this water, or from change. It took about a fortnight
> to accustom them to it. The surgeons were doubting the expediency

of going into the use of the Mississippi water from fear that another change might produce another access of the same complaint.[36]

Pitching camps on swampy land with poor drainage and crowding together in the tents were common for the armies campaigning in the South. Far more dangerous to their health was the filth, especially in the early days of the war. Latrines, or "sinks" as they were called, were shallow trenches left uncovered for long periods of time and located so near the tents as to blanket the occupants with nauseous odors.[37]

Personal cleanliness, or rather the lack of it, added to the appalling conditions. Regulations prescribed daily washing of hands and faces and complete baths once a week. But few companies complied. Exposure to the elements, inadequate clothing, and bad food compounded the deprivations, ending sometimes in death. When sickness struck, some men did as much as possible to avoid going to the regimental surgeon to get a cure. "Jackass," "fool," and "sawbones" were typical of the figurative shingles soldiers hung on the army doctors. "The Doctors are no account," wrote one Illinois soldier in 1861. His comrade added, "Our Doctor knows about as much as a ten year old boy."[38] True or not, those were the soldiers' impressions.

"It was while camped at Rienzi that I first suffered indisposition," Marcoot remembered, "but my dread of the army surgeon and hospital, materially assisted [me] in keeping out of their hands and I never failed to respond for duty on call."[39]

"During our stay at Rienzi, George Flach deserted us," Marcoot recorded. So did a number of their other comrades. The men in the ranks were not alone in choosing to walk away. Officers and privates alike picked up and left. Most intended to return, and when they did, they were rarely punished for being absent without leave.[40]

Probably truly ill himself, Colonel Joliat got a twenty-day sick leave on June 22 and left with a Lieutenant Raconi for St. Louis. July 20 came and went, but Joliat failed to return to the regiment's camp in Mississippi. (Raconi was arrested for being absent without leave and mustered out of the service inside of a month.) When Joliat was two days overdue, Captain Elliott of the regiment telegraphed the brigade commander, General Asboth, in Corinth: "Col. Joliat had a 20-day leave but nothing has been heard of him since . . . if absent without leave he has no right to give orders to his regt. and should be ordered to rejoin his reg't." Asboth responded immediately with an order to "send an ambulance for Colonel Joliat" to return him to Corinth.[41]

Ironically, as things turned out, the order to send a conveyance for the colonel to return to his command was addressed to Lt. Col. Joseph Conrad, then in charge of paroled prisoners awaiting exchange in St. Louis. Conrad was the captain who a year earlier had gotten himself and his company captured at Neosho. For the moment he was serving his parole and awaiting a prisoner exchange that would free him to find a regimental command. That command eventually would be the 15th Missouri.

Conrad was able to quickly locate Joliat. The colonel responded to Asboth the next day, explaining the reason for his absence was "to recover from sickness." Apparently Joliat did return to the regiment in Mississippi, because his muster card shows "present" for July and August.

Others had their reasons for leaving, at least temporarily, for some would also return. For George Rau, perhaps it was the sight of all the sick and the dying he had seen in the camps, those going into the hospital tents and never coming back. Or maybe it was seeing the Mississippi back at Cape Girardeau. After what Rau had seen and been through the past eight months, the sight of that rolling river may have reminded him that his wife and his two young children were only about a hundred miles away. The way things were going, he may have felt that this was probably as close as he was going to get to see them for a long time.

Perhaps he decided a bit farther down the river at Cairo. Or at Paducah. That is where Pvt. Christian Heyer from Rau's company decided to leave the regiment. Heyer left for St. Louis on May 25.[42] Rau may have gone with him. He may have contrived passage on one of the troop and supply steamers plying up and down the river. In any event, the evidence suggests that Rau went home. (A leave request three years later alludes to an "unfaithfulness" in his service at this time.)

In July, Heyer came back on his own. There is no record that the thirty-eight-year-old private was punished for his absence. Rau may have come back at the same time and on his own too, but Rau was less fortunate than Heyer; on July 3, although the record does not show why, Rau was "reduced to the ranks," the army euphemism for being demoted to private.[43] His captain may have wanted to make an example of a man who once held rank. In any event, the impressive sergeant stripes that Rau had so proudly displayed in the photograph six months ago were no more.

5

Generals, Slavery, and Slurs

"Brigadiers scarce. Good ones scarce. Asboth goes on the month's leave you gave him ten months since. . . . The undersigned respectfully beg that you will obtain the promotion of Sheridan. He is worth his weight in gold." The addressee of the telegram was Major General Halleck, now in Washington, D.C., and the undersigned included generals Rosecrans and Granger, as well as Asboth.[1]

Phil Sheridan, the young captain who had spotted the racket of selling stolen horses to the government back in Missouri, was making a name for himself. Now a colonel in command of two cavalry regiments, he had recently held off a Confederate force more than five times the size of his regiments at Booneville, Mississippi, refusing to withdraw in the face of a far stronger enemy even when his superiors were urging him to do so.[2] In addition, the telegram added, he and his horsemen had just captured letters and prisoners "showing the rebels' plans and dispositions." Halleck, ensconcing himself in his new headquarters back east as commander in chief of all the Union armies, and burdened now with much larger concerns than the backwaters of Missouri and Mississippi, failed to respond.

In the meantime, the colonel judged by his superiors to be worth his weight in gold wrote, "I among others was ordered to conduct . . . to Louisville or Cincinnati, as subsequent developments might demand—my regiment, Hescock's battery, the Second and Fifteenth Missouri, and the Thirty-sixth and Forty-fourth Illinois regiments of infantry, known as the

'Pea Ridge Brigade.'"[3] With this column, Col. Philip H. Sheridan marched to Corinth, Mississippi, on September 6, for the purpose of getting railroad transportation to Kentucky. "We started that night."

"We marched thirteen miles to Corinth on the 7th day of September," Marcoot recorded. "The day was very hot and water was such a scarcity enroute that when we reached our camp in the evening we were almost wild with thirst. Ere long numerous impromptu wells, two feet deep, which rapidly filled with swamp water, were provided. Our thirst was thus relieved, but the evil results of drinking the vile stuff harassed many of us for some days afterwards. I was seriously affected with it, and was unable to secure medical attention for several days."[4] The reason Marcoot was unable to get medical attention may have had something to do with, once again, Colonel Joliat.

Neglect, mainly through ignorance but sometimes by flagrant dereliction, has been cited as one reason early in the war for troops suffering in camp and on the march.[5] One of the more blatant examples of neglect occurred in the 15th, and once again, the guilt was laid at the foot of the colonel. Fifteen officers of the regiment would later make a formal accusation that "through the negligence of the col. the sick were left out in the woods and open air all night without medical aid which caused great excitement in the Regiment, and one of them died from the effects, the Col rode in a buggy accompanyed by the surgeon of the Regiment at the head leaving the sick entirely unprovided for." Riding in a buggy at the head of the regiment, Joliat again had taken command, though apparently still too ill to take his customary position astride a horse. It was probably at this time, in September, that the colonel once again took unauthorized leave from his regiment, this time going to his home in Chicago. On October 1, the regiment would mark Joliat "Absent Without Leave."[6] Marcoot, although he did not know it at the time, was probably suffering the first stages of typhoid fever.

The regiment traveled by rail on September 15 to Columbus, Kentucky, where they boarded a steamer for Cairo, Illinois. "It was our first return to Illinois soil since our enlistment," Marcoot remembered,

> and we became very jubilant . . . when we took passage via the Illinois Central [Railroad] for the north and east . . . this was probably the happiest experience of our service. At every station we were surrounded by crowds of enthusiastic people, men, women, and children greeted [us] most heartily with cheers and song. They provided us bountifully with the best the country afforded, and our cars were literally loaded down

with choice eatables, fruits and confectionery. The small boys also played an important role, for they would call for our canteens and return them bountifully filled with "mountain dew" while cigars were never so abundant afterward. This enthusiasm and hospitality was even surpassed, if such could be, as we neared Cincinnati. . . . Oh, how I regretted my inability to enjoy the feast, for I had not as yet recovered from the effects of too much swamp water—in fact, I was gradually growing worse.

"Upon our arrival at Sandoval where we changed cars . . . many of the boys cast longing glances toward the northwest." They were no doubt thinking that possibly some of them might never get so near to home and friends again. Aboard the cars again, the regiment was soon "journeying rapidly eastward, amid the continued plaudits and cheering of the people all along our route. Nor was the enthusiasm less expressive as we neared Cincinnati; . . . it seemed to increase, for when we reached that city it seemed as if the very heavens resounded so great was the joy expressed."[7]

"Never was there such a . . . feeling experienced by the citizens of Cincinnati," the men of the 36th Illinois recalled, "at the arrival of the 'Pea Ridge Brigade.' They could not too warmly testify their . . . gratitude. Stores were thrown open, and such of their wares as the soldiers wanted were at their command without remuneration. Cheers followed their march through the city, flags floated from house-tops, and the streets presented the appearance of a vast laundry from the handkerchiefs which fluttered from every window."[8]

"We were hailed the veterans of Pea Ridge," remembered Marcoot, "while confidence was expressed on every hand in our ability to defend their city from the destruction threatened. We were royally banqueted at the market place and later surrounded and almost literally carried to their private homes. Their best rooms and parlors were opened unto us and every comfort freely tendered.

"The result was what might easily have been forseen. The commands became separated . . . the officers found it no easy task to gather their respective commands together the next morning. As fast as they were corralled, however, they were sent over the river to Covington, Ky.; while, and I regret to be compelled to state it, some were never secured but took the opportunity to desert; among them were John Wanner, U. Hochuhel and Scheible and John Huser of our company."

The 15th and the brigade remained in the Covington area until September 17, "when it became known that the Enemy had withdrawn from our front and was moving down upon Louisville." The brigade boarded a steamer headed for that city. "To my great discomfort I was not one of them," Marcoot noted, "for I had become so much debilitated that I had been sent to the hospital. . . . I truly dreaded becoming a charge in one of them. The doctors here proved coarse and almost inhuman while the nurses were even worse, and it was not long before I resolved to risk it with the boys to escape the institution again, rather than to suffer in bondage. Accordingly a few days later I managed to escape the institution and securing passage down the river, joined my command at Louisville."[9]

Others were not so fortunate. The swamps and sinks around Reinzi and the march to Corinth had commanded a deadly price. Before leaving Reinzi and Corinth, possibly as many as 10 percent of the regiment had to be left, too sick to travel on—25 percent in Marcoot's Company B alone: these were John Krauchy, John Lenherr, Joseph Loyd, John Luhm, Phelix Marbeth, John Morgenthaler, William Schaedler, Charles Schoemacher, Emil Siegrist, and Charles Walter. Most were transported to hospitals in Nashville and St. Louis. Many of them would die by year's end.[10]

Departing Covington, Sheridan's column switched to rail to reach Columbus, Kentucky, where they embarked on a waiting fleet of five steamboats. Sheridan appointed one as his flagship and directed the rest to follow, transporting the brigade. A Union gunboat patrolling the river informed him that a strong enemy force was at Caseyville. "Accepting the information as correct, I concluded to capture the place. . . . Pushing in to the bank as we neared the town, I got the troops ashore and moved on Caseyville, in the expectation of a bloody fight, but was agreeably surprised upon by an outpouring of its inhabitants—men, women, and children—carrying the Stars and Stripes, and making the most loyal professions."

The small task force continued up the Ohio. About three miles below Cincinnati, Sheridan received instructions to halt and go no further. "I was ordered . . . to take my troops back to Louisville, and there assume [formal] command of the Pea Ridge Brigade."[11]

But Sheridan remained a colonel. No doubt exasperated with Halleck for his inaction on the matter, Sheridan's commanders again fired off a telegram to the general in chief on September 12, repeating the request of six weeks earlier: "We have no good generals here and are badly in want of them. Sheridan is worth his weight in gold. Will you not try and have him made a brigadier at once? It will put us in good shape."[12]

The next day, Halleck responded: "Brigadier-General Sheridan has been reappointed, with his original date."[13] (Halleck's "reappointed" wording is a puzzle; had Sheridan been appointed earlier? There is no record of it, and Sheridan made no such reference to it in his memoirs. Had Lincoln turned down an earlier recommendation? There is a hint that Lincoln may have considered the thirty-one-year-old Sheridan too young for senior rank.[14] Or was Halleck shifting blame away from himself for his earlier inaction?)

The day the 15th Missouri boarded the steamboat for Louisville, on September 17, the Army of the Potomac was fighting one of the bloodiest battles of the war on the outskirts of Sharpsburg, Maryland—rolling farm country planted mostly in corn and marked by a creek called Antietam. By day's end, the South's first serious invasion attempt of the North was turned away. Calling the battle a victory for the North stretched the point, but for Lincoln, it was enough to signal the political moment he was waiting for: he declared that on January 1, 1863, the federal government would proclaim all slaves as free, but only in those states that had seceded. That meant that slaves in Missouri, Kentucky, Maryland, and Delaware were not included, because Lincoln feared that their emancipation might cause those border slave states to leave the Union for the Confederacy.[15]

It is curious that Marcoot makes no mention of the declaration or the feelings his comrades may have had about it at the time; throughout the North, the announcement created a storm of opposition. Many Union soldiers vowed not to reenlist with news of the proclamation. The Illinois legislature even considered recalling its regiments. Irish troops took particular affront; no new Irish regiments from New York could be raised following the proclamation.[16] In all but the abolitionist northeast, northern newspapers and prominent journalists protested or advised against the proclamation. Overseas, British journals predicted Negro uprisings, the London *Times* turning particularly "hysterical" (but public opinion there trumped the scribes).[17] In both the western armies and the Army of the Potomac, mutiny seemed a possibility.[18]

Seeing an end to slavery ranked high for German immigrants fighting in the western theatre, but not so with many native-born Americans. Perhaps such was also the case for Marcoot, one of only a handful of native-born soldiers among the Germans in the 15th Missouri. Marcoot had written that his reason for volunteering was "patriotism alone."

Of the Civil War generation, racism and nativism penetrated the thinking of most Americans on both deep and pervasive levels. Racism was not simply white versus black; "race" applied also to national groups such as Germans, Scots, French, and Irish.[19] As another Illinois soldier, a sergeant-major in the 13th Illinois, wrote at the time, "Everyone in the whole command had hoped that those 'animals,' the G-d-d-d dutch would go in one direction, and the white men in another. I used to think any white man was better than a negro, but I had rather sleep or eat with a negro than a dutchman."[20]

The 13th Illinois, a regiment of native-born Americans, at one time served in the division of Brig. Gen. Peter Osterhaus, a German immigrant. In their brigade were the 3d, 12th, and 17th Missouri, German regiments all. Perhaps it was all too much for the Illinois sergeant-major. Those who thought of themselves as Americans because they were native-born considered themselves different from all the rest. Not just different, but better. In that regard, the American and the German were alike. "That prejudice and favoritism existed" among both, one authority has stated, "was beyond doubt." American-born soldiers serving in German or Irish regiments "often complained that they felt out of place and mistreated."

Other factors added to the mix: differences in religious beliefs, politics, drinking habits, and in a German unit, the often rigid discipline of the German officers.[21] There is some evidence of a favoritism charge against Colonel Conrad by one and possibly more of the handful of Americans that found themselves in the 15th Missouri.[22] Unfortunately, the source providing the evidence, Conrad's diary, once in the possession of the state of Missouri, can no longer be accounted for.

American and German hubris showed up especially when regiments of the two marched alongside the other. Slurs shot both ways. Sometime before the march to Cape Girardeau, the 36th Illinois, the lone American regiment trooping along with German regiments under General Osterhaus, found the barbs coming from the German regiments more than they could take. The Illinois colonel asked for his regiment to be transferred to another command. The German regiments, he declared, were "united in charging all pecadillos [sic] of the division upon the 36th, a proceeding which all were beginning to be heartily tired of [from] the lager beer Germans."[23]

The 36th was eventually transferred from Osterhaus's division to that of General Asboth, but the reason may have had little to do with Teutonic peccadillos. The transfer likely had more to do with a need for the three German regiments to divert from the column and head south to join an expedition to hunt Confederates deeper into Arkansas,[24] consequently calling for the Illinoisans to be assigned to another command. But in the command change, the 36th Illinois failed to escape their lager-beer nemeses. Instead of finding themselves in an "all-American" outfit to their particular liking and specifications, they were hitched to the nearly all German brigade of the 2d and 15th Missouri.

Once again, the new set of "Dutch" march-mates may have proved too much for the boys from Illinois. Or maybe a new general simply wanted to add their veteran experience to a new brigade of green regiments. In any event, soon after the column's arrival in Louisville, Gen. Don Carlos Buell reorganized his army, realigning many regiments with new brigades. In the reorganization, the 36th Illinois was allowed to escape the Germans a second time. But, with an almost diabolical twist for the 2d and the 15th Missouri, another American outfit took its place. The new regiment, another Illinois unit, could hardly have been more different from the Germans from Missouri.

The 73d Illinois, while not exactly a new regiment, having formed about the same time as the 2d and 15th, had yet to see any real battle action. The regiment was made up of men from prominent families in and around Chicago. Further, nine of the 73d officers were ordained Methodist ministers. Prayer meetings were as regular to the camp routine as drill.[25] The Methodists—a stern bunch in those times, with a special abhorrence for alcoholic spirits and for anyone who imbibed in them—were hardly a match made in heaven for the likes of the *gemutliche* Bavarian or even the iron Prussian.

Nevertheless, the "Preacher Regiment," as they were to become known, was put with the Germans of the 15th and the 2d Missouri, plus the 44th Illinois—the old Pea Ridge Brigade sans the sensitive 36th. They formed the new Thirty-fifth Brigade of the Eleventh Division of the Army of the Ohio. Lt. Col. Bernard Laiboldt, a German immigrant from St. Louis, the proprietor of the Washington Hall at Second and Elm streets and a former noncommissioned officer in the German military, was appointed the brigade's commanding officer.

In command of their new division was Brig. Gen. Philip H. Sheridan. For better and for worse, they were to remain together for many months to come.

6

War Means Killing

On October 1, "orders were issued," Sheridan wrote, "for an advance upon the enemy, with the purpose of attacking and the hope of destroying him within the limits of the 'blue grass' region, and, failing in that, to drive him from Kentucky."[1]

In the 15th, with Joliat ill and marked absent without leave once again, Maj. John Weber took command and led the regiment forward. In the ranks, Marcoot was unable to walk "or assume my duties . . . but [I] could not be persuaded to be left behind. The ambulances were over-crowded and my only alternative lay in taking passage aboard the old rough six-mule army wagon."[2]

Buell had ordered his columns to converge on Perryville, southwest of Lexington, where Gen. Braxton Bragg was reported to have concentrated his Confederate troops. "Much time was consumed" in the march, too much time as far as the impatient Sheridan was concerned. On the evening of October 7, Sheridan's division finally neared Perryville, where the Confederate army was "in strong force on the opposite side of a small stream called Doctor's Creek."[3] The weather in Kentucky was hot and dry, a drought having dried many of the creeks to little more than a trickle. "The troops were suffering so for water," Sheridan recorded, "that it became absolutely necessary that we should gain possession of Doctor's Creek." The 15th made only five miles on the march that day, probably due to the lack of water.[4]

Night brought long, dark hours of thirst. In the hour before dawn, "my division was brought up," Sheridan recorded, "and passed to the front."[5]

Across the creek loomed the prospect of going into battle for the first time for the men and boys of the 15th Missouri.

Marcoot gave little detail when describing battles, declaring that all the battles in which he had taken part simply were too terrible to talk about. It may also be fair to say that normal descriptive powers fail in the suffocating fear at the prospect of being killed. In the Civil War, it fell to the infantry-man to bear the brunt of battle, although artillery and cavalry usually were in view in close support.

As Sheridan's men waited in the line of battle early that morning of October 8, the enemy visible out beyond the creek, a soldier in the 73d Illinois wrote, "Feelings stole over us that can be better imagined than described. . . . Who will fall? For whom, and for how many, will this day be the last on earth?"[6]

Laiboldt's brigade moved off the road leading to Perryville and formed into line of battle, the 2d and 15th Missouri in front, with the 44th and 73d Illinois to the rear in support. Marcoot wrote, "The skirmishing began while the moon was yet casting her soft pale light upon the fields about us."[7] At daylight, the four regiments of about twelve hundred men and horse-drawn cannons and caissons splashed across the creek to hold it for water supply for the troops. But, "with some slight skirmishing," Sheridan found "that we could not hold the ground unless we carried and occupied a range of hills, called Chaplin Heights, in front of Chaplin River."[8]

For about two hours, the men remained in line while some took turns returning to the creek to fill canteens. About midmorning, through a heavy line of timber to the east, "the enemy advanced in considerable force. . . . I then directed Colonel Laiboldt to advance two of his old regiments and drive the enemy from the timber."[9] The two "old regiments"—"old" pos-sibly because of their slight battle experience as compared to the two Illi-nois regiments, which had no battle experience—were the 2d and 15th Missouri. After more than a year of service, the German-Missourians were about to get their first, true test of battle.

"At about 11 o'clock, the 2d and 15th Missouri Regiments became hotly engaged," the historians of the 73d remembered. "The 44th Illinois and our own regiment were lying in easy supporting distance while the fighting was going on."[10]

The men of the 36th Illinois in the brigade to the left probably had the best view. Resting on their arms in some woods, they could see diagonally across the creek and up the slope on the other side and what lay ahead for the two Missouri regiments. The Illinoisans saw "few indications of a hostile force" except for "thin clouds of smoke . . . rising lazily above the tree-tops,

followed by a shrieking shell which the enemy now and then tossed over
to our position." From their vantage point, they saw a brigade "under Col
Leibold [Laiboldt] move forward out of line, the 2nd Missouri in the lead,"
the 15th Missouri and the 44th and 73d Illinois in close support,

> our skirmishers moving slowly from tree to tree . . . now halting as if to
> select a particular object at which to fire, then crouching and delivering
> their shots deliberately as target practice. They gradually pushed up the
> hill in the face of a withering fire towards the summit where every rock,
> tree and clump of bushes concealed a Rebel sharpshooter. . . . The rattle
> of musketry grew louder and more continuous. . . . The line, a mile in
> extent . . . [Laiboldt's] Brigade, the gallant 2nd Missouri in the lead . . .
> never wavering. . . . The air was filled with shrieking lead . . . cheers and
> yells of the opposing forces and the continuous roll of musketry. . . . Little
> by little the Rebel line wavered . . . broke . . . then retreated in disorder.[11]

The men in the 36th were undoubtedly correct in describing the 2d Missouri in the lead ahead of the 15th, for the 2d suffered the severest casualties
by far in taking the lead, losing seventy men dead and wounded, about 20
percent of the regiment, in the assault that lasted less than an hour.[12]

"After taking [Chaplin] Heights," Sheridan wrote, "I brought up the rest
of my division and intrenched [sic], without much difficulty, by a throw-up
of a strong line of rifle-pits, although the enemy's sharpshooters annoyed
us enough to make me order Laiboldt's brigade to drive them in on the
main body. This was successfully done in a few minutes, but in pushing
them back to Chaplin River, we discovered the Confederates forming a
line of battle on the opposite bank, with the apparent purpose of an attack
in force, so I withdrew the brigade to our intrenchments [sic] on the crest
and there awaited the assault."[13] But not without some confusion, maybe
with even a bit of panic; the colonel of the 73d Illinois misconstrued the
order to take position in the front line, and "the regiment was mistakenly
conducted several yards to the rear [and] . . . the two Missouri regiments
interpreted the hasty move as evidence that the 73d was panic-stricken.
The mistake was soon rectified; the 73d quickly found and filled its proper
place, much to the surprise and gratification of the Missourians," according to the 73d's historians.[14]

"Soon after returning to the crest [at about 3:00 P.M.] and getting snugly
fixed in the rifle-pits," Sheridan said, "my attention was called to our left,
the high ground we occupied affording me in that direction an unob-
structed view." A column of Union troops was advancing toward Chaplin

River. They were unaware that they were about to be attacked by a Confederate force from across the creek. "The fury of the Confederate assault soon halted this advance force, and in a short time threw it into confusion, [and] pushed it back a considerable distance."[15]

The Confederates then placed two batteries on Sheridan's right flank and began massing troops behind them, apparently intending to make an attack. It was not long before the Confederate "legions," as Marcoot referred to them, "moved upon us in formidable columns, presented a most inspiring appearance. They advanced down the hill from a bit of timber upon its summit in full view, and their long lines of gleaming bayonets were only interspersed by their battle flags." In the line just ahead of the 15th, the Methodist boys in the 73d Illinois were now hearing the precautions administered by their preacher colonel: "Aim low, aim low; war means killing."[16]

"As soon as they came within reach of our artillery we opened a deadly fire," Marcoot wrote, the men in the line "following suit in quick succession with our muskets. The division bravely held its ground, although over one-third of their number fell dead and wounded about them, until compelled to break their front from the heat of a large barn in their very midst filled with burning hay. This caused them to waver, permitting the enemy to turn their left flank and gain the rear of the left center. . . . The rebels, swinging a large force further to the rear, at once attacked [Sheridan's] division, then constituting the right and left center. For a while it seemed as if all was lost." The Confederates advanced "almost to my intrenchments [*sic*]," Sheridan said, even though "a large part of the ground over which they had to move was swept by a heavy fire of canister from both my batteries." They "charged up the hill apparently greatly elated over their success." But they were "woefully unprepared for the deadly reception."[17]

A Confederate soldier in the 1st Tennessee recalled that reception: "Our line was fairly hurled back by the leaden hail that was poured into our very face. The iron storm passed through our ranks, mangling and tearing men to pieces. The very air seemed full of stifling smoke and fire which seemed the very pit of hell, peopled by contending demons . . . the sun was poised above us, a great red ball sinking slowly in the west, yet the scene of battle and carnage continued. I cannot describe it."[18]

"Our other divisions having by this time again reformed," Marcoot later wrote, "the battle continued to wage all along the line lasting until sundown. Again and again did the rebels attempt to dislodge us." For the Southerners, "it was a veritable blood-bath . . . halting, they were soon routed—greatly demoralized . . . darkness alone terminated the dreadful scene of blood and carnage. We slept on arms that dreadful night."[19]

On the Confederate side, a little more than 3,100 lay dead or wounded. Twenty years later, Sam Watkins reflected that he "was in every battle, skirmish and march that was made by the First Tennessee . . . and I do not remember of a harder battle than that of Perryville. If it had been two men wrestling, it would have been called a 'dog fall.' Both sides claim the victory—both whipped."[20]

For the Union, almost 3,700 had fallen. Seventy in the 2d Missouri, almost 20 percent of the regiment, had been killed or wounded in that "gallant charge" that the men of the 36th Illinois described. Fifty-five more in Laiboldt's brigade fell, eight in the 15th Missouri in support of the 2d Missouri on their fateful charge that morning. In the 15th, Anton Seiss, thirty-two years old, a private from St. Louis, was among those killed, the first in the regiment to die on the battlefield.[21]

The 73d suffered slight losses compared to the casualties of the 2d Missouri. They nevertheless were inspired to help themselves to a bit of self-adulation: "The conduct of the [73d] regiment in the battle was heartily applauded by the 'old soldiers' of our brigade, especially by the Missourians," their historians said.[22]

Perhaps. Both the 2d Missouri and the 15th, in line behind the 73d the afternoon of the Confederate charge, were in position to see how the Illinoisans fought. The Missourians may have been more relieved that these newcomers had stayed to fight. They had seen them head for the rear at first, albeit perhaps mistakenly, before the real firing had started.

Praise in their direction may have come from someone, but not likely from the "Dutchmen." The two regiments, the 15th and the 73d, would never come to like each other. Years later, in their regimental reminiscences, the preacher boys from the good families in Chicago would even hurl a slur or two at these immigrants from along the rivers down in Missouri.

For the German Missourians to hand out praise would have been out of character in any event. These Germans were never so charitable. If they granted credit to anyone, it would go to no regiment but their own, least of all to a regiment of Americans.

The day's events bore too heavily on the Germans for anything as supercilious as a round of backslapping. More likely, the 2d and 15th Missouri were for the first time feeling the wages of *das Arbeit*, the work, in this case, the work of killing. Mingled with the "dreadful scene of blood and carnage," as Marcoot described it, welled up the sorrow over the loss of so many in the 2d whom they had known, or had gotten to know, back in St. Louis.

More likely, they shared the sentiments of another who fought next to them that day. "We had a terrible loss[,] a slaughter[,] whatever you are a mind to call it," a man in the 44th Illinois would write to his sister a week later: "Men went down by the hundreds in a few minutes. . . . We, when we could, fought like deamons [*sic*]. For my part I felt determined to die before I would surrender but thanks to Him who rules the Heavens I escaped either. . . . This battle is the one that tried men's souls. Men in whom I had but little confidence raised themselves in my estimation while others lowered themselves just as much. If any man is hateful to a soldier it is a Coward."[23]

For the wounded, being alive was the only thing that could be said for their situation; many a man probably wished he had died for what was to follow. The Union commander, Maj. Gen. Don Carlos Buell, had chosen to leave most of the army's medical supplies and hospital wagons behind "for the sake of speed," he said, to pursue the Confederates into Kentucky. The results were disastrous.

"Since there were no hospital tents, the 2,800 wounded occupied every house in the village of Perryville and every farmhouse for ten miles around, making it difficult to attend them properly. With no more medical supplies than the surgeons could carry on their persons, many wounds were not dressed for days. Since all the wells in Perryville were dry, the patients were dirty. The only foods available were . . . hardtack and salt pork, virtually inedible to invalids." Eventually medical department and Sanitary Commission supply trains arrived with relief, but not before a good number of men had been added to the list of "battlefield deaths" who otherwise would have survived.[24]

Marcoot found himself "more dead than alive . . . my exposure to the chill and cold of the night following affected me most seriously. Upon our army resuming the march I was again compelled to resort to the army wagon for passage. I was perched way up on top of all the other baggage and never once enjoyed the comforts of the ambulance. [Marcoot did not know it, but there were no ambulances.] My comrades were very anxious about me and would come to the train every evening for me."[25]

The 15th Missouri faced about, returning through the Kentucky hamlets to Bowling Green with diminished numbers. Sheridan later wrote, "I reached Bowling Green with a force much reduced by the losses sustained in the battle . . . and by sickness . . . many poor fellows, overcome by fatigue, and diseases induced by the heat, dust, and drought of the season, had to be left at roadside hospitals."[26]

Marcoot was one of those left behind.

By this time I was so badly affected that I was placed in the hospital. . . . We had no beds, no bed clothing and no fires. We were compelled to lie upon the floor [and] . . . many of my comrades called and bid me good bye. . . . My captain volunteered the unnecessary admonition that I must not attempt to follow them again or they would be forced to bury me by the roadside. The Orderly Sergeant said, stay here quietly, don't fret, and you will soon get well, while my 'bunkie,' Adolph Faess, brought me a new woolen blanket and an army overcoat and told me to see to it that I got home or I would surely die. Thus they all shook hands and bid me farewell. . . .

The doctor in charge of the hospital . . . was a civilian and was paid a stated sum for each inmate per diem by the government. He was unquestionably very poorly supplied with medicine, and our rations were the same as those we had always drawn from the government—salt pork and crackers. . . . Suffice it to say that it was necessary that I be carried out at least once an hour, day and night, cold as it was.

"I wrote home stating my condition [and] . . . it was not long before my dear old mother was by my side. The meeting I will not attempt to describe." Arranging for lodging in a home nearby, Mrs. Marcoot was able to cook for her son, "expressing the belief that proper diet alone was the all-important medicine." When her appeal for a sick furlough for her teenage son was rejected, she asked to move him to a private home where she could attend to her son herself. The doctor consented, and Marcoot began to rally.

"My mother had now been away from home for some time and had been put to considerable expense." Fearing that a return to the hospital would bring on a relapse, she displayed a citizen's suit of clothes. She informed her son that she intended to take him home with her, but "I insisted that I could not leave without a furlough." Marcoot admitted to "a strong desire to return [home] for a time, but I had entered the service with only one motive, that of patriotism, and I very positively told her that I would not consent to thus leave the service . . . however, I made every effort to secure a furlough." After several tries, Marcoot, with no small amount of chicanery, succeeded in getting a pass. "The next train found mother and me aboard, bound for Louisville and home. . . . Arriving finally at the old home, I was most joyfully received by my father, brother and sisters, but I missed one face from the little circle, sister Catherine, who had died the preceding year. . . . I was in no condition to enjoy my reception, however, for I was very ill. . . . Often during this time it took four of them to hold me in my bed, so intense was the pain and so delirious had I become."[27]

With Marcoot gone, Pvt. Adolph Faess, Marcoot's "bunkie," took up the duty full-time to document the day-to-day movements of the 15th.

Unfortunately, Faess apparently treated the diary more like a travel log; consequently, for the events to come, a participant and eyewitness to some of the regiment's most dramatic hours chose not to record much other than to note that the 15th Missouri took part.

At Bowling Green, Buell was relieved by Maj. Gen. William S. Rosecrans. The army did not show much regret at the change, according to Sheridan, "for the campaign from Louisville . . . was looked upon generally as a lamentable failure. . . . Had a skillful and energetic advance of the Union troops been made, instead of wasting precious time in slow and unnecessary tactical maneuvers, the enemy could have been destroyed before he quit the State of Kentucky."[28] Adolph Faess meanwhile logged that the 15th Missouri left Bowling Green on November 4, taking up a line of march toward Nashville.

7

A New Colonel

It had been in their minds for some time. The march into Kentucky and the battle near Perryville, followed by the long march back into Tennessee, delayed it, but within a week after their arrival in camp near Nashville, the officers of the 15th Missouri finally found time to compose a letter of charges against Colonel Joliat. The charges ranged from selling government property to abject neglect of regimental duties.[1]

While his regiment had been engaged and bloodied in battle for the first time, Joliat was at home in Chicago. That he was ill at the time appears true enough; an affidavit signed by a Cook County justice of the peace testified that the colonel "has been under treatment for bilious and intermittent fever with chronic diarrhea contracted in Mississippi and Tennessee."[2]

Now, almost a month later, Joliat may have heard of the planned attempt by his company officers to remove him from the regiment and maybe even from the army. Perhaps Joliat sensed the hounds getting close, or perhaps it was coincidental that, on November 3, before the officers of the regiment had a chance to formulate and set down their charges, Joliat sent a letter of resignation to headquarters in St. Louis. Hundreds of miles away, the officers of the 15th were probably unaware that Joliat had stolen a march on their efforts. Nevertheless, on November 13, they issued their letter of charges and specifications against their colonel:

To the Assistant Adjutant General of Missouri.

Dear Sir—I would submit to your consideration the following charges, against the Col. F. J. Joliat of the 15th Regt. Mo. Vol. wich I the undersigned formaly Capt of Comp G. 15th Regt Mo Vol would bring to your military superiority and wich is of the greatest importance for the welfare and efficiency of the entire Regt, now sir the charges I lay before are the following to wit

First that we deem Col Joliat unfit as commander of a Regiment. . . .

Second that through the negligence of the Col, the sick were left out in the woods and open air all night without medical aid which caused great excitement in the Regiment, and one of them died from the effects, the Col rode in a buggy accompanyed by the surgeon of the Regiment at the head leaving the sick entirely unprovided for.

Third that the Col, at Camp Fremont St. Louis in September 1861. ordered 2 Captains out of Camp [the letter doesn't specify the exact reason except to point out that one Captain Ehner "was ordered back to the Regt by Major Gen. Halleck."]

Fourth that the Col went to St. Louis in the month of December 1861 and there sold ten days['] rations belonging to the Regiment and never acounted for the same Fifth that on the second day of the battle of Pea Ridge there was captured from the enimy three horses two of said Horses were turned over to the government authorities and the third horse Col Joliat retained and sold to Capt Richter of Comp. I for the sum of two hundred and fifty Dollars and retained said mony he has never accounted to the government for the same.

Sixth that at Camp near Rienze Missisippe Col Joliat sold two horses branded U.S. to Capt Nelson formaly Comp. K. said horses were a short time afterwards taken from him by the quartermaster at Rienze Miss. they being property of the government said horses were sold for one Hundred and Seventy five Dollars to Capt Nelson.

Seventh that Col Joliat sold two horses at Camp Rienze Miss to Capt Jaklin formaly Comp K. said horses were branded U.S. said horses were taken from him at Columbus Ky by the quartermaster of that post for the same reason.

Eight that the Col in the month of July came to St Louis in company
with Lieutenant Raconi said Leut being absent without leave Leut Col
Conrad reported said fact and said Raconi was mustered out of service
that afternoon in the month of August Col Joliat retained said Raconi and
mustered him for pay after having been duly notified from Col Schaefer
commanding Brigade to discharge said Raconi from the Regiment.

I respectfully beg leave to refer you to the following officers to substan-
tiate the forgoing charges and will at any time you may deem it proper
procure the attendance of said officers before you at your office or at any
place you may desire.[3]

The letter was signed by George Birg, captain, Company G, followed
by the names of fourteen other officers who could be called on to substan-
tiate the specifications, each probably having put in some effort as to what
the letter said and how it said it.

They had no way of knowing that they could have saved themselves the
trouble. The army could not get rid of Joliat fast enough. In fewer than
five days from the time Joliat had dated his letter, the army accepted his
resignation with no further inquiry. For the officers and men of the 15th
Missouri, Joliat at last was out of their lives.

On November 8, just five days after Joliat's letter, the 15th's brigade commander in Nashville, Col. Friederick Schaefer, sent a personal letter to Governor Gamble in Missouri recommending the name of an officer to take
command of the regiment. The letter cited the candidate as "a most gallant
and efficient officer and a perfect gentleman," one Col. Joseph Conrad.

Two days later, another letter arrived from Nashville:

To his Excellency H. R. Gamble, Governor of the State of Missouri.
    We the undersigned Officers of the 15th Regiment Missouri Vol-
unteers, most respectfully ask of you the promotion of Lieut. Col. Jos.
Conrad as Colonel of our Regiment. . . . Lieut. Col. Jos. Conrad is
generously beloved and respected in the Regiment by both Officers and
Men and by promoting him, your Excellency would confer a great favor
on the Regiment. We would further present to your kind notice the
conduct of our brave, and worthy *Major John Weber*, who has virtually
commanded the Regiment for the last three Months, he was the only
Field Officer with the Regiment in the late severe Campaign in Kentucky, and in the bloody Battle of [Chaplin Hills]; he proved, both by
his bravery and coolness, that he was able to command a Regiment; he

has the love and respect of every Officer, and Soldier in the Regiment, and the sincerest wish of the whole Regiment is to see him promoted to Lieutenant Colonel of our Regiment.

Confidentially laying this matter in your Excellency's hands; trusting to your impartiality and justice in rewarding true merit wherever you find it, thus encouraging and firing on to new deeds of honour your brave *Sons of Missouri*.

The letter was signed by twenty-eight officers, captains, and lieutenants representing each company of the regiment, plus the surgeon.[4] Schaefer endorsed the letter and the recommendation, taking note that he had already sent a personal letter to the governor recommending Conrad.

Unaware of Schaefer's effort on his behalf, but knowing of the letter from the regiment's officers, Conrad sent his own letter on November 18 to the adjutant general of Missouri to "respectfully apply" to fill the vacancy in the 15th. But Conrad's request was incidental; endorsements from Schaefer and General Sheridan, appended to the officers' letter, had already gone through and were on their way to the governor for approval. A little more than a week later, on November 29, the officers' requests to promote both Conrad and Weber were approved. The former captain who had gotten his career off to a poor beginning by getting himself and his small command captured back in Missouri was now the colonel of a veteran regiment.

But Conrad was still under the conditions of the parole resulting from his capture. He could only continue in his assigned duty in charge of paroled men at Benton Barracks back in St. Louis. He would have to wait to be officially exchanged as a prisoner of war before taking command of his new regiment. In the meantime, Weber would have to continue to lead the 15th, but now with his new rank of lieutenant colonel and in the official capacity of second in command of the regiment.

Joseph Conrad was one of the first German immigrants to volunteer at the start of the war. Within a week of the fall of Fort Sumter, Conrad, at age thirty-four, was sworn in as a captain of the ninety-day German 3d Missouri Infantry. That he had been a German army officer before coming to the United States no doubt got him his commission. There is no evidence of any political connection.

Conrad was born in Wied-Selters, Nassau, Germany, and at age twenty entered the Hesse-Darmstadt State Military School in 1848, the year of the failed democratic revolution.[5] The outbreak of the rebellion in Germany probably rushed his being granted an officer's commission, but what role he took in the revolution is unknown; he probably was among those in the military who sided for democratic reform—ultimately the losing side—because with the failure of the revolution, he, like many insurgent German officers, soon left his homeland for the United States.

The exact date that Conrad arrived in Missouri is unknown. He likely was among the Forty-eighters—educated, idealistic, and generally associated with the intellectual groups that characterized the tidal wave of Germans that reached the American shore by 1850. There is little doubt that Conrad also brought along his dream of a military career. The fact that he volunteered immediately on the side of the North suggests that he also carried with him the ideals of the democratic and personal freedoms that he had fought for in the old country. Given his education, his former commission in the German military, plus other observable qualities that granted status among the class-conscious Germans, Conrad was probably assigned to the "higher class" by his fellow expatriates living in Missouri. In time, more than one officer, German and native born alike, also took note of him as a man of exceptional character and integrity, a gentleman with uncommonly good sense, all of which served to enhance his military qualifications and reputation.

Beyond that, almost nothing is known about Conrad as a civilian in St. Louis before the war. The city directory of 1860 lists a number of Joseph Conrads as bartenders, butchers, and other tradesmen or laborers, except one, who is listed as a notary public. If he were any of those, the last would appear to be the more likely, possibly holding a clerical position. The mysteries surrounding his life before the war appear in keeping with an observation from an adjutant who said, in admiration of his colonel during the war, that Conrad was a man of few words.

Even less is known about John Weber. He, like Conrad, lived in St. Louis, but with the fall of Fort Sumter was not among the first to volunteer. Not until four months later, in August 1861, did Weber enter the army, but he did so with a commission as a captain. The men elected him to the position, but his new rank likely had something to do with previous military experience. Based on what Marcoot had said about Weber's drilling the men relentlessly back at the arsenal, it is likely that knowledge may have come from experience in the German military. Or perhaps he was a member of the Wide Awakes, who were known to drill before volunteering. Judging by his regimental correspondence, in which he expressed disdain for men with political commissions and no military experience, it is likely that Weber himself had known some life in the army, most likely German, which suggests, as does his name, that he too was German.

Weber was not as fortunate as Conrad in peer assignation. Perhaps attributed to the German proclivity to sniff at others considered of a lower social class, the new lieutenant colonel found himself on the receiving end of backhanded treatment from one of the regiment's own officers, and one junior in rank at that.

Lt. Adolphus Erdmann, assistant adjutant at the time, must have held a high opinion of himself, for he took the liberty to offer an uninvited opinion of Weber to Major General Curtis in St. Louis. In a letter marked "private communication," Erdmann urged the general to expedite Conrad's exchange, noting that "by the shameful mismanagement of its late commander, Col. Joliat, the Regiment has been neglected in a manner disgraceful to the honor of our gallant state." Erdmann chose to ignore the fact that Weber had been in command for the past two months and had effectively led the regiment through its first battle. Even so, Erdmann went on to say, "Major John Weber . . . by profession a Saddler—although a good soldier and of an honest character, does not possess by any means those high *military* and *social* qualities indispensable for a Commander of a Rgmt. and consequently must fail to use the desired beneficial influence upon his command."[6]

There is no record that Curtis acknowledged Erdmann's letter. The general in fact had ignored correspondence from the lieutenant on the subject three weeks earlier. Nor is there any evidence that Weber ever learned about the lieutenant violating the chain of command by writing directly to a general without the lieutenant colonel knowing about it—much less offering an opinion about the commander himself. That no doubt was very fortunate for Lieutenant Erdmann.

Despite the importations of the earnest lieutenant, neither the Union army nor the Confederates saw fit to expedite Conrad's exchange. Consequently, Weber, soon to wear the silver oak leaf braid of a lieutenant colonel, continued to fill the role as the 15th's commanding officer.

While in camp, the army was once again reorganized. "My division," Sheridan wrote, "became . . . the Third Division, Right Wing, Fourteenth Army Corps, its three brigades of four regiments each being respectively commanded by General [Joshua W.] Sill, Colonel Frederick Schaefer and . . . Colonel George W. Roberts. . . .

"General Sill was a classmate of mine at the Military Academy," Sheridan wrote, taking particular note of Sill's modesty, courage, and capacity for command. In Colonel Roberts of the 42d Illinois, Sheridan saw "an ideal soldier both in mind and body . . . young, tall, handsome, brave, and dashing, and possessed [of] a balance-wheel of such good judgment that in his sphere of action no occasion could arise from which he would not reap the best results."

"Colonel Schaefer, of the Second Missouri Infantry," Sheridan continued,

> had been absent on sick-leave during the Kentucky campaign, but about this date he returned to duty, and by seniority fell in command of the second brigade [replacing Colonel Laiboldt]. He was of German birth, having come from Baden, where, prior to 1848, he had been a non-commissioned officer in the service of his State. He took part as an insurgent in the . . . revolution . . . and, compelled to emigrate on the suppression of the insurrection, made his way to this country and settled in St. Louis. Here the breaking out of the war found him, and through the personal interest which General Sigel took in him he was commissioned a colonel of volunteers. He had had a pretty fair education, a taste for the military profession, and was of tall and slender build, all of which gave him a student-like appearance. He was extremely excitable and nervous when anticipating a crisis, but always calmed down to cool deliberation when the critical moment came. With such a man I could not be less than well satisfied, although the officer whom he replaced—Colonel Laiboldt— had performed efficient service and shown much capacity in the recent campaign. . . . I was fortunate in having such brigade commanders.[7]

Sheridan also felt favored in his regimental commanders. "They all were not only patriots, but soldiers, and knowing that discipline must be one of the most potent factors in bringing to a successful termination the mighty contest in which our nation was struggling for existence, they studied and practiced its methods ceaselessly inspiring with the same spirit that pervaded themselves and the loyal hearts of their subordinate officers and men. All worked unremittingly in the camp at Mill Creek in preparing for the storm, which so plainly indicated its speedy coming."[8]

Adolph Faess took a smaller and more immediate view of things in the 15th Missouri. "On the 14th . . . the regiment was ordered to guard a large train back to Mitchelville, returning on the 18th. . . . On November 22, we broke camp and marched through Nashville to Mill Creek," where they arranged a "fine camp and held a dress parade."[9]

The 15th was quickly assigned to picket duty, while its brother regiment in the brigade, the 2d Missouri, was sent on a reconnoitering expedition and suffered one man killed and two wounded.

The sutler was soon to arrive, Marcoot wrote, and "made glad the hearts of the boys." "John Barleycorn" no doubt had come along. Just a day or two earlier, the regiment had mustered to receive two months' pay. "No wonder the sutler had come," Marcoot said. "He had smelt the mouse."[10]

Several days later, the 15th, out on patrol, were relieved by the 73d Illinois, the Preacher Regiment, which, Marcoot wrote, "soon afterward, were driven in by the enemy. The 15th turned out immediately, and skirmishing all over the fields, failed to see or discover a trace of the boys in Gray."[11] Marcoot's insinuation—that the 73d had returned to camp under a suspicion of cowardice—may have had its roots in the ethnic disdain that the Germans and the Americans held for each other.

Bad blood between the two regiments probably broke out almost from the day the two met a couple of months earlier in the camps around Louisville. It may have begun with what they poured from a bottle into their tin cups; what each drank for liquid refreshments, beer, whiskey, or neither, was often cause for dispute between German and American units. While the sutler with his liquid wares made glad the hearts of the 15th, there would be no welcome for "John Barleycorn" from the Methodist boys of the 73d.

Each preserved their differences, even long after the war. Forty-four years later, a veteran of the 73d in a paper presented at a reunion took the opportunity to accuse Germans of the 15th of rifling their tents of canteens, blankets, "and other movable property" when the members of the 73d were attending their evening prayer meetings. "Within a month," claimed the elder veteran of the Preacher Regiment, "it was magnanimously admitted by the veteran Germans who had profited at our expense."[12]

That the incident took place is not hard to believe, though the Germans may have been motivated more by spite or retribution than larceny. That the "veteran Germans" admitted to it is another matter. Given the bad blood between these two regiments, it is difficult to believe that any of the 15th would have owned up to it—perhaps years later but not "within a month." The 73d's own history, written just ten years after the war and remarkable for its breadth and detail, makes no mention of the incident. (In a related item, the paper's author also referred to the 36th Illinois as a "Regiment of German Veterans," a glaring error, particularly for one who served in the same brigade with the 36th. The 36th Illinois was a distinctly American regiment, having had its own run-ins with the German regiments from Missouri.)

The author's final note on the matter suggests that the passing of the years may have reflected a failing memory or even an embellished tale. The "veteran Germans," the author wrote in 1906, "admitted" the thefts by writing "dot pious Sheventy-dirt fellers, he pray like der preacher, und shteal like der shail birt, und fight like der teffel,"[13] continuing the ridicule of the German immigrant's effort to speak English, common among the American public during the Civil War period and long after. If indeed a German veteran did say this, he had also paid the "Sheventy-dirt"—the 73d—a compliment from the German's point of view: that the 73d fought like the devil, a tribute that the old Illinois veteran apparently missed almost a half-century later.

In the 15th's headquarters tent, Lieutenant Colonel Weber attended to the paperwork that Joliat had "neglected in a manner disgraceful," as the assistant adjutant had put it a month earlier. One neglected item, Weber learned, was that a good number of officers in the regiment had been serving as long as five months without pay. Joliat had used the technicality that the officers had not been officially commissioned, and on that technicality, by Joliat's order, they would collect no pay. They were awaiting only the paperwork to formalize the promotions. (Joliat had not troubled with technicalities in the past. Did this officer, albeit Swiss born, harbor a bias against his German officers? Was it retribution for the resentments his German staff almost certainly held against him?)

Early in November, Weber had addressed the matter of the paperwork to the assistant adjutant general of Missouri but received no reply; the assistant adjutant had written to another officer that he preferred to wait for the 15th's new colonel to take over before forwarding the commissions. Weber tried again on December 21. He also took a shot at educating the officer-bureaucrat: "Allow me, Colonel, to observe that this is unjust . . . as is the custom in all the volunteer regiments, forthwith instated in their positions [as officers], they have since that time a period of five months, done all the duties, went through all the hardships, assumed all the responsibility . . . without receiving a cent of pay . . . for they cannot procure their pay as Officers before they have their commissions." One can almost sense the heat rising:

"I further learn that there are several persons commissioned or about to be commissioned in this regiment who are unknown to the regiment and have probably never been in the army before. I am well aware that his Excellency, the Governor has the right to commission whoever he pleases, yet I must observe that it has a damning influence on the discipline and efficiency of the old troops to send to them men as Officers: as is very often the case; that understand nothing about the duties of an Officer, consequently they cannot enforce the respect and obedience of their subordinates, and are therefore, a nuisance in the Army."

That said, the lieutenant colonel got to the heart of the matter:

We have in the regiment men . . . who have gone through all the hardships and dangers that is likely to fall to the lot of a soldier, and who are in every way qualified to make good officers. It is my opinion that these men are justly entitled to promotion when vacancies occur. This would encourage others to do their duties promptly and cheerfully, thinking that promotion may sometime or other be there [*sic*] reward. I therewith give you a list of those that are to be commissioned. I recommend them to you as men that I have seen in action as well as in other severe trials where it required courage, patience and ability and I never found them wanting in those qualities; there are some of them that have commanded companies before the enemy without a commission, and done it well, and I have not the least doubt that they could do it again and do it with more cheerfullness and pride if they had their commissions.[14]

There followed a list of eleven names deemed deserving of their commissions, followed by those they had replaced.

Good work for a "mere" saddler. The lieutenant colonel was clearly a literate man with more than a hint of the Germanic in syntax and directness, to speak up in the face of injustice when he saw it, even when it meant confronting a superior.

Eight days later, on December 29, the commissions were issued.[15]

Two days after sending his letter on the commissions, Weber received a personal letter from St. Louis. The letter prompted another official request, this one on his own behalf. He wrote: "I respectfully submit to you a request that a furlough of twenty days may be granted me to attend to a family matter of the gravest importance. . . . I have this day been informed of the death of my only child and that the mother, my wife, who has been sick for some time has through this catastrophe been so much reduced, that her Physician has given up all hopes of her final recovery."[16]

The request was denied. Weber may not have even gotten a response—there is no record of one if he did, for regulations at the time forbade a furlough request based on personal reasons. His muster card indeed shows him present for all of December. Weber did not know, and was not in a position to know, that the army would soon move against Gen. Braxton Bragg and his Confederate Army of Tennessee. As the commanding officer of the 15th, and the only regimental officer with field grade rank to take the Missourians into battle, Weber was not about to be spared.

"You will advance with your corps to a good military position and camping ground in the vicinity of Nolensville." So began the order to Maj. Gen. Alexander McD. McCook on the day before Christmas 1862.[17] He was to put his corps, which included Sheridan's division, on the march south.

Rosecrans at last was ready to move. But there was a hitch; Rosecrans's lead corps under Maj. Gen. Thomas L. Crittenden was not quite ready, and so the whole business was delayed.[18] No one knew for sure when the army was to move. Certainly Lieutenant Colonel Weber of the 15th did not. "Early on the morning of Christmas Eve," Private Marcoot noted, "the tents were taken down and camp broke up" only to be "again placed in position" on Christmas Day, only to be ordered taken down again.[19]

That night, December 25, Rosecrans invited his three corps commanders to his headquarters for a drink. For a while he was the genial host. Then, he abruptly banged a glass down on a table and announced, "We move tomorrow, gentlemen! We shall begin to skirmish probably as soon as we pass the outposts. Press them hard! Drive them out of their nests! Make them fight or run! Strike hard and fast! Give them no rest! Fight them, fight them, I say!" As his commanders prepared to go, he gripped each man's hand and repeated, "Fight! Keep fighting! They will not stand it!"[20]

"Early on the morning of December 26, 1862, in a heavy rain," Sheridan recorded, "the army marched, the movement being directed on Murfreesboro."[21]

8

Fighting Retreat, Bloodiest Day

The day after Christmas, in a steady downpour, the 15th advanced ten miles, all the while skirmishing and driving Confederates before them. On December 27, the regiment advanced another six miles before stopping finally near the town of Triune.

"It continued to rain and sleet night and day and being baggageless the boys suffered much from cold," Marcoot wrote. "The [28th] was spent in camp, and the guns were ordered shot off and cleaned up for inspection. On the 29th, [we] moved forward again, some ten miles, or within five miles of Murfreesboro, where camp was struck but no fires permitted. All were wet, cold, tired and hungry, and but very little rest was obtained during the night."[1]

A private in the 24th Wisconsin remembered the march: "It was nothing but a continual rain day and night, so that we were wet through. The roads were full of mud and slush . . . my feet were soaking wet all the time . . . all that was left of my shoes gave way, so that I had to go it barefooted."[2]

On December 30, Sheridan's division led the advance of McCook's corps before swinging left onto the Wilkinson pike, which ran east and west north of Murfreesboro. About three miles from the town, slight skirmishing took place, Sheridan reported, but "the enemy's pickets grew serious, and a little further on so strong that I had to put in two regiments to push them back. . . . By sundown I had taken up my prescribed position, facing almost east, my left [Roberts's brigade] resting on the Wilkinson pike, the right [Sill's brigade] in the timber . . . and the reserve brigade [Schaefer's, which included the 15th Missouri] to the rear of my centre."[3]

The 15th was assigned a position near the Harding house, close to a brick kiln. They were about a half mile south of the Wilkinson pike, in reserve with the 44th Illinois, about three hundred yards behind the main line. On a slight rise in front were the six-gun batteries of Hescock's 1st Missouri and Houghtaling's 1st Illinois artillery.

On the line in their front was the 24th Wisconsin, formed just four months earlier. Here the barefooted private was told to go back to the wagons to try to find some shoes. On his way, he stopped by the camp of the 15th Missouri. He figured that by "hanging around . . . I could get a pair of shoes, and a new gun, for my gun had the misfortune of having the tube [barrel] broken off." ("Tube"? A veteran would have said "barrel.")[4] Green were the Wisconsin boys. The barefooted private had more than a little larceny in his heart. A soldier would be charged six dollars out of his thirteen dollars monthly pay if he lost his musket, so losing it was the same as losing almost a half month's pay. Being the veterans they now were, the boys in the 15th were not about to take their eyes off of their muskets. The Wisconsin boy would not "pick up" a new gun there.

Darkness of the late December day gradually enveloped both armies. Sheridan's three brigades of 4,100 men, soaked and chilled to the bone from marching and skirmishing in the hard rain, wrapped themselves in their blankets as the wet cold of the winter night came on. Back around the 15th's camp, numbering little more than three hundred, Marcoot wrote that "the boys were permitted to stand around small fires."[5] The regiment was far enough from the main line, and behind a rise, that the general order of no fires could be set aside. Somehow the men were able to light fires with wood collected from the dripping timber. Soon, but for the crackling of burning twigs and branches, low voices, and an occasional stomping of feet, all was still.

Somewhere off in the distance a regimental band struck up a few notes. They began to play the army's favorite tunes, sad and melancholy songs about sweet Lorena, Aura Lee, and home. From across the fields and through the cedar thickets soon drifted the sounds of a Confederate band. "The still winter night carried their strains to a great distance," wrote a private in the 1st Tennessee. It was not long before the playing began to grow into something of a contest. "Yankee Doodle" was answered by "Dixie," and "The Bonnie Blue Flag" prompted a rousing "Hail Columbia." Finally, when the musicians had played all the tunes they had to offer, a federal band struck up the familiar "Home Sweet Home." "A Confederate band picked up the strain," a captain in the 19th Tennessee wrote, "and then one after another until all the bands of each army were playing *Home Sweet Home*. And after our bands had ceased playing, we could hear the sweet refrain as it died away on the cool frosty air on the Federal side."[6] Once again, all was still.

Sheridan inspected the length of his line, "to let the men see that I was alive to their interests and advantages." He then went to the rear, about four hundred yards from the camp of the 15th, where he set up his headquarters behind the trunk of a fallen tree as shelter from the wind, lying down finally beside a small campfire for the night.

At about two in the morning, Brig. Gen. Joshua Sill, commanding Sheridan's First Brigade, came to him to report sounds of moving infantry and artillery coming from across the way. He said it had been going on all night. Sill was convinced that the Confederates were massing for an attack in the morning. Sheridan thought Maj. Gen. Alexander McCook, his corps commander, should be made aware of what apparently was going on, "so Sill and I went back to see him at his headquarters, not far from the Griscom House [Gresham] where we found him sleeping on some straw in the angle of a worm fence." They talked it over for "some little time" but McCook concluded that no further dispositions were needed and went back to sleep.[7]

Sheridan and Sill returned to the campfire behind the log. As they continued to talk, Sill grew more anxious. He was convinced more than ever that an attack was coming in the morning. To calm him down, Sheridan told him he would move the 15th Missouri and the 44th Illinois to within a short supporting distance of Sill's brigade.

At four o'clock, long before dawn, the 15th was wakened with the rest of the division. Sheridan came along by himself, on foot, visiting each of his regiments one by one. He called for the major. Arouse the men quietly, the general said, and have them get their breakfast. Probably a hardtack cracker, some cold bacon, or whatever else a soldier could find in his pocket or knapsack, washed down with coffee, that is if he had any coffee beans left. That done, the men were ordered "to form in line of battle at once with cannoneers directed to stand to their guns."[8]

While all of this was quietly going on, as quiet as four thousand men can be along the half-mile front that Sheridan was covering, "all the recent signs of activity in the enemy's camp were hushed, a death-like stillness prevailing in the cedars to our front."[9] Finally into line with muskets and with artillerymen at their cannon, they stood and waited. They waited for about an hour in the cold and dark.

A wind came up about daylight, blowing away the fog drifting up from the river, and the sky began to clear. Shortly after first light, the 15th and the 44th Illinois received orders to support Sill's brigade just ahead. Lt. Col. John Weber was put in command of the battalion of the two regiments. In the ghostly half-light, they heard the thump and bang of artillery about a mile off to the right. Sounds of musketry followed like strings of firecrackers going off. The attack Sill had predicted had begun.[10]

Weber's battalion slogged across about two hundred yards of sodden field and into a strip of trees. Emerging from the woods, Weber was ordered to place the 15th next to the trees, about thirty yards behind the green 24th Wisconsin, who were just behind the veteran 36th Illinois on the front line—veterans to the front and veterans to the rear—just in case the new fellows from Wisconsin decided to run "when the ball opened." The 44th Illinois moved into line next to the Missourians.[11]

As the light began to filter through the treetops, to the right the sound of firing grew louder with each minute. Shortly after seven, in the dim predawn light, Sheridan, standing with Sill behind the lines, with the 15th in close support, spotted gray skirmishers darting through the cedar thickets across a cotton field in their front. Behind them, advancing out of the cedar timber and into the field came a battle line of massed Confederate infantry. "Very soon our skirmishers were falling back," recalled Maj. Silas Miller of the 36th Illinois. "The enemy advanced in splendid style, their first lines coming up closely upon each other, until within range of our boys." Immediately, the division's three batteries of eighteen guns opened fire from the rear and the left. "An awful roar shook the earth; a crash rent the atmosphere. The foremost lines of the rebel host were literally swept from the field, and seemed to melt away like snowflakes before a flame."[12]

The effect was terrible, Sheridan wrote, but the Confederate column "continued on till it reached the edge of the timber where Sill's right lay . . . my infantry opened at a range of not over fifty yards." An Illinois soldier recalled, "A dazzling sheet of flame burst from the ranks." Some said that the men in butternut and gray fell in windrows.[13] One man in that charge recalled, "The crest occupied by the Yankees was belching loud with fire and smoke . . . [we] were falling like leaves of autumn in a hurricane."[14]

Just after the first volley, "Lt. Col. Weber received orders to advance in double-quick," Brigade Commander Laiboldt reported. "The order was promptly executed, and Lt. Col. Weber found himself in front of the enemy, the artillery previously stationed there [the 8th Wisconsin] having retreated leaving one Parrott gun." Ordering his men to lie down, Weber directed the regiment to "fire at the advancing gray line."[15]

"For a short time the Confederates withstood the fire," Sheridan recorded, "but then wavered, broke, and fell back." Sill's brigade, with the 15th Missouri and 44th Illinois rising up and joining in, "followed in a spirited charge, driving them back across the open ground." Twenty-one-year-old Henry Drake was caught up in the charge as his 24th Wisconsin was pulling back: the "men of the 15th Missouri . . . passed through [the 24th] at the double quick, bayonets slanted and gleaming. . . . I was so excited," Drake said, "that I and a handful of boys . . . turned upon the enemy with the Missouri men."[16] Killed in the charge was brigade commander Joshua Sill, shot in the face while trying to rally a regiment that broke.

A break in the action followed. Sheridan took advantage of the lull to regroup. In place of the dead Sill, Col. Nicholas Greusel of the 36th Illinois was put in charge of the brigade. Then, noticing a new gray column beginning to move in their direction again, Sheridan ordered the colonel to recall the brigade. Joining in the withdrawal, Weber's men hurried back to the rest of their comrades in Schaefer's brigade.

The Confederate columns were coming on once more, aiming again at the center of Sheridan's line, but adding now a new threat. Gray columns were also advancing toward the right, at Woodruff's brigade of Davis's division. To cover the right, Sheridan ordered Schaefer to post his brigade to form a right angle to the front line and Greusel to take position to the right of Schaefer. Just ahead were twelve cannons of Hescock's, Houghtaling's, and Bush's batteries.[17]

Once again, artillery on both sides opened up. Rapid volleys of musketry joined in, creating a horror of ear-splitting sound. For a moment or two, a new kind of confusion reigned in the regiments to the right—scores of rabbits exploded from a thicket and burst into the ranks of Greusel's men, the 15th Missouri next to them, "nestling under their coats and creeping under their legs in a state of utter confusion. They hopped over the field like toads, and as perfectly tamed by fright as household pets."[18]

But there was no time for distractions. Firing from Greusel's and Schaefer's brigades began again, the two regiments halting and breaking the gray lines for a second time. After the third attack, Woodruff's brigade on the right began to crumble, men drifting back in singles, in clusters, then giving way completely, with two of Greusel's regiments joining in the dash for the rear. Other regiments in support rushed forward to take their places, but not for long. "When it was absolutely impossible to do so longer, they fell back," Maj. Silas Miller of the 36th Illinois recalled.[19]

With the two regiments on their right breaking for the rear, Weber's battalion of the 15th and the 44th Illinois held their ground, firing, biting off paper cartridges, loading, plunging ramrods down the muzzles, and firing again—when another regiment broke, this time on the left. Still Weber's battalion refused to leave. "They kept up a steady firing, even when . . . [the green 24th Wisconsin] broke on their left and ran." Now they were an island in the line, regiments on both sides now gone.[20]

Ignoring that both flanks were now exposed, the two regiments "held their position until attacked from both the flank and front at once. Lt. Col. Weber gave the order to withdraw. Slowly the men pulled back, keeping up a constant firing, all the while pressed by the enemy." When they reached a cornfield, Weber ordered a halt. The withdrawal had been orderly, Weber keeping the men together.[21]

They were back again near the brick kiln where sections of Hescock's and Houghtaling's batteries had been banging away all morning. But Weber's Missourians would not stand here for very long: "Soon afterward our troops on the left advanced again on the enemy, when Lt. Col. Weber also rapidly advanced to a place about fifty yards in advance of this previous position and formed in line of battle. He had the gun [the Parrott of the 8th Wisconsin] dragged by his men to the rear of his column, from where it afterward was removed to a safer place."[22]

They had been fighting continuously for almost three hours. Still there was no respite. Near ten o'clock, Confederates under Lt. Gen. W. J. Hardee began advancing, once again to the left. At the same time, Cheatham's division of Southerners began moving to the right, threatening to envelop Sheridan's regiments on the left. Once more, hands fumbled for the paper cartridges.

It was getting hot again for the 15th. "Lt. Col. Weber contested his ground admirably until the enemy advanced six columns deep." After firing volley after volley, someone in the 15th noticed that the 44th Illinois was withdrawing, probably low on ammunition. Soon after, their own ammunition gave out. The after-action report by their brigade commander reads, "Only then was the order to retreat given."[23]

It would be a fighting retreat. While Sheridan's regiments were pulling back, the 15th was sent scurrying to the rear in search of ammunition. Across the Wilkinson pike they rushed, back through a stand of cedars, perhaps as far as a quarter mile to the rear, where they finally found an ammunition wagon at the edge of an old cotton field. Here they also found the .58 caliber cartridges they needed for their Enfields. Darting again back through the timber, they broke into the clearing of the cornfields just in time to support a charge covering the division's pullback to the rail fences along the Wilkinson pike.[24]

The 15th Missouri rallied behind this rail fence (reconstructed) with other regiments along the Wilkinson Pike at Stones River. They soon withdrew on the run across the field to the woods in the background, which would later be known as the Slaughter Pen. A Confederate veteran wrote, "I cannot remember now or ever seeing more dead men and horses and captured cannon . . . all jumbled together, than that scene of blood and carnage and battle on the Wilkerson [*sic*] turnpike. The ground was literally covered with blue coats." (Stones River, rail fence. Jim West, National Park Service)

What followed was a kind of reverse leap-frog of brigades, two brigades taking turns pulling back while another charged to hold the Confederates at bay. After Sill's brigade, now under Greusel, charged, Sheridan "hastily withdrew Sill's brigade, and the reserve regiments [the 15th and the 44th] supporting it, and ordered Roberts' brigade . . . to cover the withdrawal by a charge on the Confederates as they came into the timber where my right had originally rested." The retreat was carried out "without improper haste," until "the pressure by the enemy was so hard that it became necessary to resort to the double-quick." Reaching the Wilkinson turnpike, the men paused to get off a quick volley from behind the rail fences along the roadway. It was but a moment before the order to retreat was given once again. This time, Schaefer ordered his brigade "to retreat across the pike toward a piece of cedar woods." It was to be, Sheridan reported, "one of the bitterest and most sanguinary contests of the day."[25]

Private Watkins of the 1st Tennessee reflected another set of emotions: his brigade of Confederate infantry, with a "whoop and yell, swooped down on those Yankees like a whirl-a-gust of woodpeckers in a hail storm."[26] The 15th Missouri pulled back with the others from the rail fences along the pike. Deliberately at first, they drifted back slowly, some probably stopping to reload and fire off yet another round. The Confederate wave surged closer, the men in gray themselves stopping to fire before charging on—until the Missourians, intermingled with the larger blue mass of three thousand mounted officers and horse-drawn cannon and caissons, joined in a dash for the cedars a hundred yards or so away.

George Rau in Company F made it, but Henry Fuhrer and Schwab did not. Company lieutenant George Mohrhardt went down with a bullet in his leg and was captured. In Company B, Capt. George Ernst was hit in the shoulder but was able to keep going. Sgt. Frederick Grundlihner, who was carrying the colors, was shot down and killed. So was Lt. Christian Quinzius.[27]

The private from Tennessee wrote of the scene in the cornfields along the Wilkinson pike, "I cannot remember now or ever seeing more dead men and horses and captured cannon, all jumbled together, than that scene of blood and carnage and battle on the Wilkerson [sic] turnpike. The ground was literally covered with blue coats."[28]

Sheridan's regiments raced into the woods. To hold off the charging Southerners close behind, two companies of the 2nd Missouri, no more than sixty men, Col. Bernard Laiboldt reported, "found cover behind "huge and deeply cut rocks, opened a brisk fire on the enemy, which kept him at bay for a considerable length of time."[29]

"We fell back slowly through the thick cedars," a 73d Illinois soldier wrote years later, "without orders, purpose or a ray of knowledge as to what was transpiring outside the limits of our short line of sight. Under us the surface was piled with rocks and rent with caverns; above us the thick, green foliage intercepted the sunlight. Around us, at every point of the compass seemingly, the roar of battle was deafening . . . as far as we could see, the woods were filled with disorganized masses of troops [the broken regiments from the right wing] flying they knew not whence or whither, but utterly panic-stricken and uncontrollable . . . a yelling mob; officers weeping or swearing, soldiers demoralized and shivering."[30]

Since daylight, with the beginning of the Confederate attack, the right wing of the Union line had been bent like a jackknife, swung back at the end of a radius about five miles. "It was now only ten o'clock in the forenoon, so rapidly had events proceeded."[31]

In the center, Sheridan's men had been driven back about a half mile since the fighting had started three hours earlier. Sheridan now began reforming his line for the next onslaught. The brigade was the hinge of the jackknifed Union line. Schaefer's and Greusel's brigades were now formed into a line in the fringe of the cedar wood, facing west. The 15th again found itself on the right of Schaefer's brigade, next to Greusel's brigade. To their left in line were the 44th Illinois, the 73d Illinois, and the 2d Missouri. Bending back to the left and facing southeast was Robert's brigade. "My position was strong," Sheridan said, "located in the edge of a dense cedar thicket and commanding a slight depression of open ground that lay in my front. My men were in good spirits . . . notwithstanding they had been a good deal hustled around since daylight, with losses that had told considerably on their numbers."[32]

Just behind them were about four acres of tall cedars with a lesser mix of hickory and other hardwoods. These stood on a floor of low limestone slabs and outcroppings forming shallow hollows two and three feet deep, with a low ravine or two about shoulder high, just shallow enough to make natural rifle pits, running through a portion of the woods. These depressions would also serve as refuges for men to hunker down in when ricocheting bullets and shrapnel rang off the limestone, many striking trees and bodies. In time, these woods would become known as the Slaughter Pen.

Sheridan had barely gotten his line formed in the edge of these woods when Cheatham's division, in spite of the staggering blows dealt them earlier, moved forward again toward Sheridan's right. Just in front, a wheeling movement by General Hardee's gray columns was aiming in. "At the same time," Sheridan wrote, "the enemy opened artillery fire from his intrenchments [*sic*] in front of Murfreesboro . . . it seemed that he was present on every side. . . .

"Only a short distance now separated the contending lines . . . as the batteries on each side were not much more than two hundred yards apart when the enemy made his assault, the artillery fire was fearful in its effect on the ranks of both . . . the enemy's heavy masses staggering under the torrent of shell and canister from our batteries, while our lines were thinned by his ricocheting projectiles, that rebounded again and again over the thinly covered limestone formation."

As the Confederates were recoiling, "repulse after repulse," Sheridan said, "I received a message from Rosecrans telling me that he was making new dispositions, and directing me to hold on where I was until they were completed." The implication of the message probably sent Sheridan's stomach into a free fall:

Confederate artillery fired shot into the tall cedars, shattering trees and rifling wooden splinters through the timber and ricocheting killing iron off the limestone outcroppings. How many died in the bombardment, Gen. Phil Sheridan wrote years later, would never be known. (Stones River, the slaughter pen. Jim West, National Park Service)

From this I judged that the existing conditions of the battle would probably require a sacrifice of my command. . . .

I informed Roberts and Schaefer that we must be prepared to meet the demand on us by withstanding the assault of the enemy, no matter what the outcome. . . . As ammunition was getting scarce, instructions were given throughout the command to have it reserve its fire till the most effective moment. . . .

In a little while came a second and a third assault . . . in each case the Confederates were repulsed, driven back in confusion . . . but not without deadly loss to us.[33]

Within minutes of the last attack, Col. George W. Roberts was hit, three bullets in his body, and he fell from the saddle. "Boys, put me on my horse again." They lifted him up, but he was gone before he reached the saddle, Sheridan's second brigade commander to die in the fighting thus far.[34] Minutes later, Col. F. A. Harrington was killed, a shell tearing away his jaw. "The loss of subordinate officers and men was appalling."

Sheridan reported. Still, "there was no sign of faltering with the men, the only cry being for more ammunition, which unfortunately could not be supplied."[35]

After the third assault, and probably no more than an hour since they had last darted through the cedars looking for cartridges, the 15th ran out of ammunition for the second time. The men in the other three regiments too dug into their cartridge boxes only to come up empty. Schaefer's entire brigade had now run completely out of ammunition.

The other two brigades were in no better shape. "A lull followed the third fierce assault, and an investigation showed that, with the exception of a few rounds . . . our ammunition was entirely exhausted." Sheridan calculated that while Hardee and Cheatham were reluctant to try another assault, he could not hold out much longer without the danger of capture and "so I prepared to withdraw."[36] Roberts's four regiments, now commanded by Col. Luther Bradley, withdrew first and were given a chance to get away. They had a few rounds of ammunition left, which might have been enough to protect themselves in the retreat.

Schaefer's regiments had not a cartridge among them. By that default, circumstance required the 15th Missouri to take its stand among the three other regiments in Schaefer's brigade, to be sacrificed if it came to that. "I directed them to fix bayonets," Sheridan said, "and await the enemy."[37] Bradley's brigade, offering such resistance as its small quantity of ammunition would permit, pulled slowly back toward the Nashville pike.

"Eighty of the horses of Houghtaling's battery having been killed, an attempt was made to bring his guns back by hand over the rocky ground, but it could not be done, and we had to abandon them. . . . Thus far the bloody duel had cost me heavily, one-third of my division being killed or wounded. I had already three brigade commanders killed," recalled Sheridan.[38]

The heavy firing of the Confederate artillery continued to send shot and canister screaming over the cedars and into the woods, shattering trees and rifling deadly iron and wooden splinters through the timber now heavy with smoke so thick that a man could not make out his own regiment. "Dozens of horses were torn to shreds," said one eyewitness. Wounded men lay in pools of blood frozen to the ground.[39] How many died in the bombardment of those cedars will never be known.

Slowly, those who could began to lift themselves from the limestone floor of the cedar woods. "Retiring sullenly under a heavy fire," Sheridan said, they made an effort to reform and withdraw. The choking smoke and the irregular footing of the limestone outcroppings caused two regiments of Sill's brigade to get separated from the rest. Still, at about eleven o'clock, about an hour after they had fallen back across the Wilkinson pike, the cornfield, and into the woods, "the division came out of the cedars with unbroken ranks, thinned by only its killed and wounded and but few missing."[40]

As gray troops entered the cedars, those in blue emerged on the other side. A captain in the 1st Tennessee remembered what he saw: "Stretched before and behind us, in every crevice in the rocks . . . the Federal wounded had crept for shelter. Mangled masses of human forms, torn in every conceivable way, lay scattered in all directions."[41]

On the other side of those woods, from across a cotton field, Union troops about a quarter mile away began to see something else: columns of men, to be sure, but columns of a walking debris of blue drifting toward them. Like the smoke rising from the cedars, men emerged from the woods in singles and in pairs, one helping the other; men with guns, men without guns; a caisson, dragged by hand; here and there a galloping riderless horse; men limping, faces blackened with powder and smoke, others blood-soaked.[42]

They had taken a stand in those woods, as one historian wrote more than a century later, equaled a few times but "possibly never surpassed," even at Chickamauga, Cold Harbor, or the Peach Orchard at Gettysburg. Others would say "it was the most determined stand of the entire war."[43]

For the 15th and the rest of Sheridan's regiments, the battle was still not over. The Missourians had no sooner refilled their cartridge boxes, the first thing they did after coming out of the cedars, when General Rosecrans ordered Sheridan to take the 15th and another of Schaefer's regiments and "immediately" place them "in front to resist the enemy," as Sheridan put it. They were ordered to hurry to a slight rise of about four heavily wooded acres. "The two regiments went in very gallantly, driving the enemy from the cedar timber and some distance to the front."[44] Locals called it the Round Forest. The men who fought there would call it Hell's Half Acre.

Rosecrans had posted artillery in those woods, and throughout the day a Union brigade threw back charge after charge of Confederate infantry. It was the only place on the battlefield the Union had been able to hold. Now, at midafternoon, Bragg was beginning to bring up still more columns to storm the woods, to drive the Union gunners out, and give him the higher ground for his own artillery.

"Under a storm of shot and shell that came in torrents," Sheridan's troops took up the new ground, advancing through a clump of open timber. "Lt. Col. Schaefer ordered the 15th Missouri Volunteers to deploy in a cornfield" to the left of the railroad in front of the Round Forest, "while the balance of the brigade held the railroad and kept up such a galling and well-aimed fire the enemy, though of a strength to which our force was hardly comparable, and fighting with the utmost desperation, was again and again repulsed." But pressure was mounting on the Union regiments to the right. They started to fall back. "The 15th Missouri Volunteers, being in danger of being outflanked, retreated toward the position of the brigade." Schaefer galloped forward to meet Weber to give him further orders, when he was struck and toppled from his horse, dead.[45]

"Our good Schaefer fell," wrote Lieutenant Fuelle to his friend in St. Louis, "so many of the 2nd regiment owed their lives to him on this hot day, he gave us good covered positions and made sure to protect the 2nd regiment for a wonderful deed, a bayonet attack, when it came to the extreme. . . . He died a beautiful death! A hero's death for the father land!" It was, however, no longer for the Teutonic lands of his fathers.[46] All three of Sheridan's brigade commanders who had started out that morning had been killed—plus a fourth who had replaced another moments before he too was killed.

Schaefer's brigade, now in command of Lt. Col. Bernard Laiboldt, held their position in front of the Round Forest until, once again, "it had expended its ammunition." Sheridan then withdrew the brigade "to the rear of this timber, where it was again supplied [the 15th for the third time] and joined by the 36th Illinois." Laiboldt was ordered "to make a charge should the enemy again assault us."[47]

"The expected attack never came," Sheridan reported,

however the shot and shell of a furious cannonade told with fatal effect upon men and officers as they lay on their faces hugging the ground. . . . This gallant brigade remained in close column of regiments and under the fire of the enemy's batteries which killed about 20 of the men by round shot. The torments of this trying situation were almost unbearable . . . [but] a silent determination to stay seemed to take hold of each individual soldier. . . . Nor was this grim silence interrupted throughout the cannonade, except when one of the regiments broke out in a lusty cheer as a startled rabbit in search of a new hiding-place safely ran the whole length of the line.[48]

Hearsay has it that one old soldier was heard to sing out, "Go it cottontail, I'd run too if it wasn't for my reputation."[49]

"While the troops were still lying there, Rosecrans with a part of his staff and a few orderlies rode out on the re-arranged line to supervise its formation and encourage the men . . . within range of the batteries that were shelling us so viciously." Sheridan joined him, "when a solid shot carried away the head of Colonel Garesche, the chief-of-staff. . . . Garesche's appalling death stunned us all, and a momentary expression of horror spread over Rosecrans' face, but at such a time the importance of self-control was vital, and he pursued his course with an appearance of indifference."⁵⁰

"No other attacks were made on us to the east of the railroad for the rest of the afternoon," Sheridan ended, "and just before dark I was directed to withdraw and take up a position along the west side of the Nashville pike, on the extreme right of our new line."⁵¹ Here night closed in, and the bloody day finally ended.

After dark, parties of men from both armies, some with stretchers, moved among the dead and the moaning bodies, others stumbled through the cedar woods someone years later would call the Slaughter Pen, black now in a deathlike stillness. A Tennessee officer making his rounds on picket duty heard "halloahing and moaning" coming from within the woods. Following the mournful sounds, he came upon a Union soldier lying in one of the small, limestone ravines, badly wounded. "Nearly frozen to death, he asked me to make a fire at his feet. He begged so pitifully, and as he was down in a ravine," the Southerner wrote in his diary, "I made him a fire and gave him some water, placed his head on his knapsack and made him as comfortable as possible . . . the poor fellow had bled and laid on the ground until life was nearly gone. . . . I went back in about two hours, but he had crossed over. . . . I could do no more for him."⁵² Farther behind the Confederate lines, Gen. Braxton Bragg wired Richmond: "God has given us a happy New Year."

In Washington, the telegraph in the War Department on New Year's Eve began to ticker. The message read that one of the bloodiest days of the war had been waged at Murfreesboro, Tennessee. Earlier that month, almost thirteen thousand men in blue had fallen at Fredericksburg, Virginia. Now in the West, thirteen thousand more had fallen. Once again, the president went to bed with the news of men marching, fighting through the rain and the mud, and dying.

The news trickled into St. Louis. Eight days after the battle, the *Missouri Republican*, in the tombstone headline style of the time, reported on its front page,

> Great Battle at Murfreesboro!
> 2000 Men Killed
> 5000 Wounded
> Gen. Sills and Many Officers Killed
> Rosecrans the Hero

Lt. Col. Garesche of St. Louis
Chief of Gen Rosecrans Staff Killed
The Cannonading heard at Nashville,
Twenty-eight miles

The correspondent got only some of it right but, his emotions getting the better of him, concluded his news story possibly as well as any reporter could have at the time: "How can I find words to express the life and strife of this terrible battle."[53]

Sheridan's effective force in the battle was 4,154 officers and men; of those, 1,633 had been killed, wounded, or reported missing, nearly 40 percent. "In the remaining years of the war, though often engaged in most severe contests," Sheridan said that he "never experienced in any of my commands so high a rate of casualties."[54] His commands would include such bloody battles as The Wilderness and Cold Harbor.

The 15th Missouri suffered the highest loss among the brigade's regimental officers. Among those killed in the 15th were Capt. Melchoir Zimmerman and lieutenants Christian Quintzuis, Charles Kellner, and Martin Schroeder. Quintzuis and Kellner never learned that, two days earlier, Halleck's army bureaucrats in St. Louis, in response to Lt. Col. Weber's letter, had finally granted their commissions.[55]

The next day was the first day of the new year. Marcoot wrote of it years later. "Such a New Years day may none ever live to see again. . . . The dead and wounded were legion in every direction."[56] Those living around Murfreesboro remembered that the land for years bore the scars of the great battle: splintered and mangled cedars, bleached bones of dead horses, and rows of depressions that marked disinterred graves where hastily buried bodies had once been.

The Union took into battle some 44,000 troops, the Confederates variously reported as 34,000 to 37,000. Together, the armies lost 23,515 in killed and wounded—more than the 23,110 at Antietam, the bloodiest one-day battle of the war.[57] Stones River, fought essentially on that last day of the year, but officially a three-day battle because of a minor engagement two days later, would but for that technicality, deserve the tragic honor of the bloodiest one-day battle of the Civil War. All told, roughly a third of the total number engaged at Stones River became a casualty, the highest percentage of any battle in the Civil War, including not only Antietam but Gettysburg as well.

Leaders in the North regarded Stones River as an important victory. The president telegraphed Rosecrans: "God bless you and all with you! Please

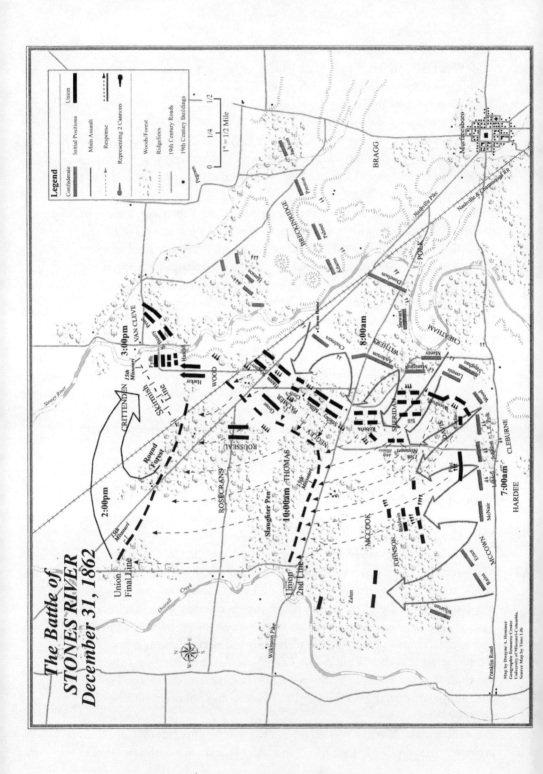

The Battle of STONES RIVER December 31, 1862

Legend

Confederate — Union

Initial Positions	
Main Assault	
Response	
Representing 2 Cannons	
Woods/Forest	
Ridgelines	
19th Century Roads	
19th Century Buildings	

0   1/4   1/2 Mile
1" = 1/2 Mile

CRITTENDEN

VAN CLEVE

3:00pm

15th Missouri

Fyffe

Harker

Hazen

WOOD

Stones River

Round Forest

2:00pm

Union Final Line

15th Missouri

ROSECRANS

ROUSSEAU

Slaughter Pen

THOMAS

NEGLEY

10:00am

58th Missouri

Union 2nd Line

Zahn

JOHNSON

Baldwin

Willich

McCOOK

Post

Kirk

McNair

Liddell

Johnson

L.E. Polk

CLEBURNE

HARDEE

7:00am

Chalmers

Anderson

Maney

Stewart

Vaughan

Manigault

Loomis

Wood

Woodruff

SHERIDAN

Sill

Roberts

44th Illinois

15th Missouri

DAVIS

Rains

8:00am

WITHERS

CHEATHAM

Cox House

Loomis

POLK

Donelson

Stewart

BRECKINRIDGE

Palmer

Adams

Hanson

Jackson

Preston

Pegram

BRAGG

Murfreesboro

Nashville Pike

Nashville & Chattanooga RR

Overall Creek

Wilkinson Pike

Franklin Road

Map by Dwayne A. Hommer
Geographic Resources Center
University of Missouri–Columbia
Source Map by Time-Life

tender to all, and accept for yourself, the nation's gratitude for your and their skill, endurance, and dauntless courage." In a letter later to Rosecrans, Lincoln expressed the feeling that had Stones River "been a defeat, the nation could scarcely have lived over."[58]

From a military standpoint, Sheridan saw it as a strategic though "negative victory. The enemy came near destroying us. Had he done so, Nashville would probably have fallen . . . Kentucky would have been opened again to his incursions . . . and the theatre of war very likely transferred once more to the Ohio River. As the case now stood," he wrote, Bragg had been "thrown on the defensive, was compelled to give his thoughts to the protection of the interior of the Confederacy . . . rather than indulge in schemes of conquest north."[59]

In the South, the editor of the *Richmond Examiner* concluded, "The battle of Murfreesboro' [*sic*] may be accounted a Confederate success . . . the Yankees, although their claims to the victory of Murfreesboro' are questionable, had great reasons to congratulate themselves that an army which, in the first day's battle, had its right wing broken and one-third of its artillery lost, should have escaped destruction and extricated itself in a manner to assure its further safety."[60]

The St. Louis Board of Common Council passed a resolution expressing the city's gratitude to "the Second and Fifteenth Regiments of Mo. Vol. Infantry, and Captain Hescock's Battery, of the First Regiment of Artillery, Mo. Vols., from St. Louis" for having "taken a signal part in the bloody contest." The resolution would honor them for their "heroic gallantry."[61]

Camped now two miles south of the battlefield, 1st Lt. Charles Fuelle, an adjutant of the 2d Missouri, wrote his father of a bitter aftertaste. "Oh how I long to see our army perjed and made clear of all those rotten sneaking scoundrals who pretend to be Union men, while they are the worst & most dangerous traitors with whom we have to deal. . . . We [were] well nigh losing all here, in consequence of having a traitor to command a part of our forces on the right wing. . . . It is true I may not know it all, but I think some."[62] (The "traitor" in Fuelle's opinion was Brig. Gen. Richard W. Johnson, who commanded a division that broke at the beginning of the battle. Johnson, a West Pointer from Kentucky, had that summer surrendered a command to a smaller force, was captured himself and was exchanged; nevertheless, he was given a division on his return, to the disgust of many in the army. Johnson went on to have a distinguished army career and later a career as an author and educator, including as professor of military science at the University of Missouri.)[63]

RESOLUTIONS

Expressing the THANKS of the City

To Officers and Soldiers engaged in the late battle of Murfreesboro'.

WHEREAS, a brilliant victory has recently been achieved by the brave Army of the Cumberland, under command of Major General Rosencrans, over the enemies of the Union and Constitution, at Murfreesboro', Tenn.;

AND, WHEREAS, the Second and Fifteenth Regiments of Mo. Vol. Infantry, and Captain Hescock's Battery, of the First Regiment of Artillery, Mo. Vols., from St. Louis, have taken a signal part in the bloody contest, and have displayed heroic gallantry on the said battle field ;

Be it therefore resolved, by the Common Council, that the thanks of the city of St. Louis are due, and are hereby tendered, to her sons engaged in the battle aforesaid for their bravery and patriotism, which have shed new lustre over the annals of the city of their nativity or adoption.

Resolved, That the memory of Colonels FREDERICK SCHAEFER, JULIUS P. GARESCHE, and other gallant men who fell to rise no more, will be revered by their fellow-citizens of St. Louis, and forever honored by their country, and that our sympathies are hereby extended to their widows and bereaved orphans.

Resolved, That a copy of the foregoing resolutions shall be transmitted to Colonel Laibold, and to the other officers in command of the St. Louis Regiments and Companies that have been engaged in battle at Murfreesboro'.

Board of Common Council,

To Charles Fella
1st Lieut: & Regt. Adjutant   St. Louis, January 23, 1863.
Sir: 2d Infty. Regt. of Mo. Vols.

In accordance with instructions, I have the pleasure to transmit you the above copy of the resolutions adopted at a meeting of the Board, of this date, tendering the thanks of this City to the officers and soldiers engaged in the late battle of Murfreesboro'.

Respectfully, your Obedient Servant,

J G Woerner
President Board Common Council

Attest. A. R. Burma, Clerk

For their "heroic gallantry" at the Battle of Stones River, the St. Louis Board of Common Council passed a resolution "Expressing the thanks of the City" to the three German regiments: the 2nd and 15th Missouri infantries and the 1st Missouri Artillery. (Fuelle Papers. Stones River National Battlefield Park)

On a more hopeful note, the German lieutenant from Missouri wrote his father of a time to come, "that we may meet again in peace to enjoy the blessings of liberty. Yet I fear that the time is to be prolonged beyond this coming spring."[64]

A Confederate soldier, "sick and tired" of fighting, was not so optimistic. "I see no peace for a long time to come. . . . The Yankees can't whip us and we can never whip them."[65]

1863

Rank after rank falls, while over them
   Silently droops the flag,
Baptized that day in many a young man's
   Bloody wounds

    —Walt Whitman, "Drum Taps"

9

"Those cowardly Dutch"

A "deafening thunder of cannonading" aroused the men of the 15th Missouri. Ordered into a skirmish line, they moved across the Nashville pike, the railroad tracks, and then toward the river where gray columns of infantry were moving down a hill and heading for the Union left. Ahead of the 15th, blue columns were wading through the frigid, muddy, and rain-swollen water, muskets held high to keep from fouling the mechanisms where the percussion caps would go. Struggling out onto the slippery banks, they charged up the hill and gradually forced the Confederates back. Desultory charges and firing continued until dusk when the noise of battle finally died away.

"The night was not one of comfort and rest," Marcoot wrote, "for our troops were put to work upon the breast works and the early dawn of Saturday morning [January 3] found these nearly complete. The rain continued to fall in torrents and cannonading was renewed, but very little real fighting was done.... The day's work ... of burying the dead, was not only gloomy but distressing, and the suffering of the wounded pitiable."[1]

On January 5, the army moved across the river to take possession of Murfreesboro. After marching three miles beyond town, the 15th struck tents for the first time since the beginning of the Stones River battle almost two weeks before. Two days later, the wagon train with the men's baggage arrived, and "the old Sutler now put in an appearance ... the boys begin to live again."

Back in St. Louis, Col. Joseph Conrad had at last been exchanged the day before Christmas. On the second day of the new year he was given a

97

pass, "with servant and horse," to travel to Louisville and head south. He was on his way at last to take command of his new regiment.[2]

The two armies again sat facing each other. The Union Army of the Cumberland dug in just south of Murfreesboro. To the south, about forty miles away, the main body of Bragg's Army of Tennessee gathered itself around Shelbyville and Tullahoma and set up winter quarters.

About this time, Sheridan ordered the division to form into a great hollow square. Into the center were marched four officers. Sheridan recorded that these officers were among the "very few who had shirked their duty" in the great battle of New Year's Eve. "An example was necessary," he declared. "Telling them that I would not humiliate any officer or soldier by requiring him to touch their disgraced swords, I compelled them to deliver theirs up to my colored servant, who also cut from the coats every insignia of rank. Then, after there had been read to the command an order from army headquarters dismissing the four from the service, the scene was brought to a close by drumming the cowards out of camp."[3]

None of the drummed-out officers were of the 15th. The adjutant general's *1863 Annual Report to the State of Missouri* lists no officer of the regiment being dismissed at that time. That the 15th had held its ground at a critical point early in the battle, while three other regiments of Sheridan's command next to them broke and ran, adds weight that no German-Missourian was among the dismissed.

When the matter of handing out punishment came up, the Union army was generally guilty of allowing officers to get off easier than the men in the ranks.[4] That probably had much to do with a prevailing attitude among officers that enlisted men, being from the "lower classes," required harsher punishments as an example for the rest of the rank and file. Much the same could be said of Sheridan, a stern disciplinarian from the outset, in an army early in the war known all too well for its laxness. He would brook no wavering in what he considered "appropriate military behavior," particularly in the face of the enemy. The difference was that a man from the ranks sentenced for deserting could expect to pay with his life. As for the four officers who were marched that January day into the center of Sheridan's massed division, the general recorded, "It was a mortifying spectacle, but from that day no officer in that division ever abandoned his colors."[5]

In St. Louis, aboard the steamer *Science*, Colonel Conrad began to make his way down the Mississippi and then up the Ohio River on his way to take command of 15th Missouri. Somewhere past Louisville, the steamer was fired on "by Rebels from the shore," a bullet striking Conrad in the face. Lieutenant Colonel Weber so informed the adjutant general in St.

Louis. Seriously wounded, Conrad was taken to the army hospital in Nashville. Conrad's muster card for January–February 1863 notes his absence as "Sick at Nashville, Tenn. January 17, '63."[6]

South of Murfreesboro, "my division," Sheridan wrote, "settled quietly down in its camp. . . . Its exhausted condition after the terrible experiences of the preceding week required attention. It needed recuperation, reinforcement, and reorganization." Sheridan also used the time to plunge into every area to sharpen the regiments with drills, parades, reconnaissance, and foraging expeditions.[7]

At the end of January, the men were mustered to sign the rolls to collect fifty-two dollars for four months' pay. It came in a military currency that the men called "shin plasters," worth about as much in their opinion as the name implied. "It was not gold," Marcoot wrote, "nor its equivalent, not silver nor the interest bearing greenback. . . . Neither did it have the purchasing power of gold, as many a soldier's little family at home realized to their sorrow. But it was received in good faith," Marcoot wrote, "for they knew it was the best their government could do, and the sentiment to defend that government at all hazards was universal."[8]

Contrary to Marcoot's sentiments, the feeling was hardly universal. During most of the war, privates received thirteen dollars a month, and eventually sixteen dollars with the last raise in 1864. They were supposed to be paid every two months, but most of the time the government was tardy, sometimes more than six months. Consequently, as one Yank put it, "a paymaster's arrival will produce more joy in camp than is said to have been produced in heaven over the one sinner that repenteth."[9]

The weather began to settle down in March, and the entire division was issued five days' rations and sent on an expedition, passing through Eagleville, where they "heard considerable cannonading in [our] front."

Sending his regiments on expeditions had a more practical purpose. "The feeding of our army from the base at Louisville," Sheridan wrote, "was attended with a great many difficulties, as the enemy's cavalry was constantly breaking the railroad and intercepting our communications on the Cumberland River." Accumulating rations was unpredictable, "and to get forage ahead a few days was well nigh impossible." But corn was abundant around Murfreesboro. "I employed a brigade about once a week in the duty of collecting and bringing in forage, sending out sometimes as many as [a] hundred and fifty wagons to haul the grain which my scouts had previous[ly] located."[10]

Sheridan did not say how he paid for the grain. The local farmers were more than sympathetic to the Confederacy, so whether Sheridan's men paid, as regulations required them to do, in local scrip or the federal IOU "shin-plasters," they understood better than anyone that they were in "Reb Country." With a thousand Billy Yanks shepherding a hundred empty wagons heading their way, the locals no doubt figured out why bluecoats were in their neighborhood. They were not tabbed as bill-paying customers. Sheridan did add, "In nearly every one of these expeditions, the enemy was encountered, and the wagons to haul the grain were usually loaded while the skirmishers kept up a running fire."[11] Officers were not about to take much time tallying up their take with the local farmer while gray cavalry and bullets were whizzing around. One of these expeditions took the 15th Missouri and its brigade on a sixty-mile march in three days. "Overall for the expedition," Marcoot recorded, the regiment "had been on the road ten days, in an almost cold and constant rain, on five days' rations."[12]

"Routine duties followed," Marcoot wrote, "followed by work on the fortifications and vice versa, with frequent drills interspersed . . . inspections, dress parades and reviews. Gen. Rosecrans reviewed his entire army here on the 23rd on which occasion the 15th, by request, executed a number of flank movements in his presence."[13] The 15th's growing reputation for drilling by now had probably reached the general himself. It is probable there was less appreciation from the other regiments who had to post, stand, and watch those Germans drilling out in front.

With the winter's battle casualties, the number of men in the ranks had been greatly reduced in many regiments. Desperate for fresh blood in the ranks, the War Department got Congress to push a conscription act through the legislative mill, only to see it botched with the provision that a man could buy his way out of the draft by paying three hundred dollars for another to take his place. "I believe that a poor man's life is as dear as a rich man's," one Yank angrily wrote.[14]

Taking another approach, and as if to prod a dozing and out-of-touch administration, the Democratic governor of Ohio bypassed the Republican president with a letter to Secretary of War Stanton. Curt for its tone, the letter advised "that you grant an amnesty to all soldiers who are now absent without leave, on condition that they voluntarily surrender themselves to the commanding officer of the nearest post within thirty days, with forfeiture of pay during their absence, announcing at the same time your fixed determination to punish all with the extreme penalty of the law who do not thus return." The letter ended tersely, "David Tod, Governor."[15]

Stanton obviously passed it up the line. Four days later, Lincoln himself responded. Possibly chagrined for having been caught in an oversight, the president acknowledged, "I think your advice, with that of others, would be valuable." He ended with a reference to "the selection of provost-marshals,"[16] but with no further acknowledgment of the question of amnesty for deserters. That must have left the Ohio governor puzzled if not totally baffled. But like wrestling in the prairie towns, knocking your adversary off balance was part of politics, and Lincoln played that game as well as anybody.

Nevertheless, an amnesty proclamation was issued the next day, March 10. From the Executive Mansion, it read: "A Proclamation. Respecting soldiers absent without leave." "I do hereby declare and proclaim that all soldiers now absent from their respective regiments without leave, who shall, on or before the first day of April . . . report themselves at any rendezvous designated [by the War Department] . . . may be restored to their respective regiments without punishment, except the forfeiture of pay and allowances during their absence; and all who do not return within the time above specified shall be arrested as deserters and punished as the law provides."[17] It was signed, "Abraham Lincoln."

Back in Millersburg, the words may have fallen hard on the young Marcoot. "I recovered," he wrote, "but very slowly. . . . As I became stronger I took to horseback riding. My father was anxious also that I should attend school and I finally consented. . . . My term was a short one, however, only a few weeks. I had been in correspondence with my regiment all the time and still carried on the company's roll as 'sick in the hospital at Bowling Green,' as they had no other official report of me. . . .

"Dr. Rutz, my brother and my officers constantly advised me to remain at home until I had permanently recovered, but I was not satisfied thus, and about the first of April I took advantage of President Lincoln's proclamation, relative to soldiers absent from their commands without leave, though I did not need it." That may have been wishful thinking.

Nevertheless, the young private gathered up his things, said his goodbyes, and left home once again. "I reported at Benton Barracks, St. Louis." But on the following day, Marcoot was transferred to the Hickory Street hospital, "sick with diarrhea. I was much dissatisfied with the turn things had taken and wanted to get back to my regiment, but the officers in charge would not permit me to leave."[18]

April brought a return of the rain and cold but no end to the expeditions of Sheridan's men looking for Tennessee corn. "The 9th was pay day," Faess recorded, "[and] the boys receipted for two months' pay, $26, in 'shin plasters.' It was very good in quality as far as it went but it did not go very far—especially at the Sutler's tent, and change smaller than a twenty-five cent piece was not in demand here at this time. No article on the entire list sold for a less figure, while chewing tobaccas rated at $2.50 per pound, a small package of limberger cheese $1, small cans of condensed milk $1, whiskey $5 a quart, etc., while even at home in the North the same conditions were experienced."[19]

The next day, Col. Joseph Conrad reported for duty and took command of the 15th Missouri.[20] With Marcoot absent from the regiment, Adoph Faess continued to maintain the log but neglected to make any mention of the arrival of their new colonel.

On the 17th, the regiment was marched to Sheridan's headquarters, where they were permitted to view "the beautiful sword that had been presented to that gallant officer."[21] The sword was a presentation for the general's role at Stones River.

Sometime after Conrad's arrival, the 15th was sent out on one of Sheridan's expeditions. "The officer in direct command always reported to me personally," the general wrote, "whatever had happened during the time he was out." On this occasion,

> the colonel in command, Colonel Conrad of the Fifteenth Missouri, informed me that he got through without much difficulty; in fact, that everything had gone all right and been eminently satisfactory, except that in returning he had been mortified greatly by the conduct of *two females belonging to the detachment and division train at my headquarters*. These women, he said, had given much annoyance by getting drunk, and to some extent demoralizing his men. To say that I was astonished at his statement would be a mild way of putting it, and had I not known him to be a most upright man and of sound sense, I should have doubted not only his veracity, but his sanity. Inquiring who they were and for further details, I was informed that there certainly were in the command two females, that in some mysterious manner had attached themselves to the service as soldiers; that one, an East Tennessee woman, was a teamster in the division wagon-train and the other a private soldier in a cavalry company temporarily attached to my headquarters for escort duty. While out on the foraging expedition these Amazons had secured a supply of "apply-jack" by some means, got very drunk, and on the return had fallen into Stone River and been nearly drowned. After they had been fished from the water, in the process of resuscitation their sex was disclosed. *Gott im Himmel!*

Determining that "the story was straight and the circumstance clear," the general continued, and "convinced of Conrad's continued sanity, I directed the provost-marshal to arrest and bring in to my headquarters the disturbers of Conrad's peace of mind. After some little search the East Tennessee woman was found in camp, somewhat the worse for the experiences of the day before, but awaiting her fate contentedly smoking a cob-pipe." Sheridan went on to relate how she had been "refugeed" from East Tennessee and, taking on men's clothing, got the job as a teamster in the quartermaster's department. "Her features were very large, and so coarse and masculine was her general appearance that she would readily have passed as man."

The next day, the other impersonator, the "she dragoon," as Sheridan called her, "was caught, and proved to be a rather prepossessing young woman, and though necessarily bronzed and hardened by exposure, I doubt if, even with these marks of campaigning, she could have deceived as readily as did her companion. . . . They both were forwarded to army headquarters, and, when provided with clothing suited to their sex, sent back to Nashville, and thence beyond our lines."[22]

Faess noted that the regiment exchanged the large wall tents for the so-called pup tents. Writing about it years later, Marcoot described the "comical appearance . . . as we had so long been used to those of the larger pattern. . . . The camp presented an appearance of a prairie dog town and the boys played the prairie dog bark for several days. In fact, some of them became very proficient in their imitations of that little animal's bark."

"The month of May was passed so nearly like that of April" except for "one incident that no doubt is still fresh in the minds of all the boys then present with the command." The historians of the 73d Illinois recalled the same incident. Marcoot recounted,

A rebel spy had found his way successfully into camp and had succeeded in very cleverly passing himself off as a friend of the soldiers, one simply jaunting around the country to satisfy his own natural curiosity. He was a jolly fellow, and the boys without exception, soon learned to enjoy his company and put every confidence in him. He would visit from company to company, and being a clever talker, was soon a welcomed guest at all of their campfires. He became very popular for his quaint singing of patriotic songs, a number of which he claimed to be composed by himself, and it was not an infrequent occurrence to see him mounted upon a stump thus entertaining his listeners. . . .

He was also very observing and was frequently noted jotting down memorandums. It was not long, however, before the authorities became suspicious and put detectives on his track. . . . At last one dark night he eluded the detectives and succeeded in reaching the picket. He had planned it well and so arranged it that the guard would be a personal acquaintance. . . . Coming upon him he seemed to be in a most jolly mood, just out on a lark simply on his way to the farmhouse just beyond, where he expected to secure something extra for breakfast the next morning. The guard, however, was not so satisfied and promptly refused to let him pass, but his refusal was lightly treated, as if it were a joke, and walking on he replied in a very [confident] manner that that was all right. The guard warned him again and ordered him to halt, but he continued in his course and doggedly refusing to obey was fired upon and killed.

It was discovered that he wore . . . new boots. . . . They contained a double hollow sole in which was found a series of papers containing full descriptions, illustrations and specifications of our works and forts, and the number and positions of our infantry, cavalry and artillery.[23]

In Tennessee, Rosecrans remained mired around Murfreesboro, finding the muddy roads impassable and ignoring Lincoln's observation that the Confederates were dealing out more damage over the same roads. The only word the president heard from the general in reply was a complaint that Grant's new commission as a major general was given an earlier date of rank than his own, and Grant therefore outranked him. Responding, his patience and charitable humor now abandoning him, the president told Rosecrans that he "didn't give a fig" about who ranks who.

On April 28, Maj. Gen. "Fighting" Joe Hooker began moving seventy thousand of his men south across the Rappahannock River. Once across, his plan was to turn left toward Fredericksburg to strike Lee's army. The Army of the Potomac executed the maneuver in a crisp fashion and headed east. Seeing the danger, Lee rushed his Army of Northern Virginia west toward the tiny wilderness crossroads of Chancellorsville.

The news of fighting in the Virginia woods trickled in. Successes during the first day prompted almost giddy optimism, but as bad reports began to arrive to start the second day, the mood in the telegraph office in the War Department turned somber. Lincoln spent most of the time there, across the street from the Executive Mansion. He held onto a shred of hope but feared that Hooker had been licked. By midafternoon on May 6, three days after the fighting had stopped, Lincoln's worst fears had been realized; the telegraph clattered that Hooker had retreated north across the river.

Returning from the War Department, he held out a telegram to a visiting friend, his voice trembling: "Read it—news from the Army." As the visitor read of the defeat, Lincoln paced back and forth, all the while crying out, "My God! My God! What will the country say! What will the country say!"[24]

In some ways, Chancellorsville was a mirror of the Stones River battle. Stonewall Jackson struck an outnumbered corps on the Union right, the gray columns stealing through a dense wilderness, then rushing through the heavy underbrush and bursting into the open, literally into the faces of the troops in blue. Shocked and in panic, Union troops sprinted for the rear.

At Stones River, regiments of native-born troops did the running; of the nineteen regiments on the Union right that collapsed and ran that morning in Tennessee, only two were German.[25] In the center of the line, held by Sheridan's twelve regiments, American units broke in the early hours of the Confederate attack while Sheridan's two German regiments, the 2d and 15th Missouri, stood their ground as frightened Americans next to them abandoned the line. There were no criticisms of ethnic fighting abilities following the battle along the Stones River.

At Chancellorsville, the ones doing the running were mostly Germans of the Eleventh Corps. Newspapers wrote of the "cowardly Dutch."[26] It did not matter that nine—a third of the corps' twenty-six regiments—were made up of native-born troops.[27] To Hooker, the press, and just about everyone else who was not German, the national feeling was that the "Dutchmen" of the Eleventh Corps were to blame.[28]

The command of the Eleventh Corps believed that Hooker's headquarters inspired the finger-pointing. Brig. Gen. Alexander Schimmelfennig angrily complained that Hooker's own staff had spread "the most infamous falsehoods" to newspaper correspondents. Speaking for the German units, Maj. Gen. Carl Schurz appealed to the War Department: "We have been overwhelmed by the army and the press with abuse and insult beyond measure. We have borne as much as human nature can endure."[29]

If the general thought he was going to get any sympathy from Halleck, he would be disappointed. Halleck's antiforeign bias was now well-known.[30] Ever since their experiences with Halleck back in Missouri, German troops, spread now throughout the western theatre, could have told their comrades in the Eleventh Corps all about the general now ensconced in Washington, D.C.

Washington and the generals in the Army of the Potomac had much more important matters to attend to than to listen to some comic-sounding immigrant general, even if in the doing the morale of one bloodied corps might get a needed boost. More important was what to do about Hooker. The Germans' complaints were nothing compared to the backbiting that was going on in the Army of the Potomac following the defeat at Chancellorsville.[31]

In the final analysis, bad generalship at the highest levels proved to be the great equalizer for both Germans and Americans. At Chancellorsville and Stones River, Union commanders were caught napping. Smug and self-assured, they had left their men poorly positioned and unprepared for the havoc that daring enemy leadership could wreak. As a consequence, the men in the ranks, immigrant and native born alike, paid with their lives. To disbelieving Americans, it was something even birthplace could not overcome. In the long lists of the dead and wounded, there was no discrimination.

Among Germans, anger at the accusations spread beyond the men in the army to their countrymen throughout the North. German-American political leaders called for public protests, sensing once again the odors of Know-Nothingism. Faced with insults both in the military and at home, German recruitment dropped. Some officers even resigned their commissions.[32]

The bad air blanketing the Germans may have even infected the 15th Missouri. One officer in the 15th resigned his commission a week after the battle.[33] Since late in 1861, when Lieutenant Colonel Weber seems to have had some effect in flushing out incompetent officers, the regiment had not seen any resignations. The resignation, coming as it did at this particular time, appears too coincidental. For the remainder of the war, the accusations that followed Chancellorsville, and soon after at Gettysburg, would have an effect on every German regiment in the Union army. Lincoln apparently offered no rebuttal or attempt to assuage the feelings of the Germans, in spite of the pleas coming from German senior officers, including Carl Shurz. There is no record if he did. Perhaps the torrents of political opposition and public criticism now flooding over him drowned out everything else, including the noise growing out of Chancellorsville. Lincoln nevertheless retained the Germans' support, at least on the issues of fighting for the Union and ending slavery. But for many, he no longer had their enthusiasm.[34]

In the camp of the 15th Missouri, Capt. George Ernst, recovering from a shoulder wound suffered at Stones River, had just learned of the death of one of his daughters. A letter from St. Louis told him further of the serious illness of another and that his wife was "at the point of death." If he could come home to see her, the letter said, she might live. On April 23, the captain requested fifteen days' leave to go home to his family. "I couldn't hesitate a moment," Conrad wrote, endorsing the request as it went up the line. The request was approved. The regiment's military records do not record, of course, whether Ernst's family survived. The captain returned in May to take command of the brigade's battalion of sharpshooters.[35] He would finish the war as one of the heroes of the regiment.

10

A Question of Will

Early in June, after almost six months away from his regiment, Private Marcoot rejoined the 15th at Murfreesboro, his muster cards all the while reporting him as "Sick in hospital at Bowling Green, Kentucky." Within days of his return, he witnessed an event that may have struck him with more than a normal amount of revulsion, and even terror, given his own late and long absence: "On the 20th we, for the first time, witnessed the execution of a deserter who was shot to death as a penalty for his act."[1]

Marcoot gives no further detail, but what he witnessed may have been the army's ritual for an execution calculated to make a deep and lasting impression on the men in the ranks. In advance of the gruesome spectacle, the prisoner's division or brigade was ordered to form a rectangle open at one end. After the troops had completed the formation, the prisoner was marched out, escorted by the provost marshal on horseback, followed by a band playing a tune called the "Dead March." This procession was followed by an armed guard of twelve men, which was deployed across the open end of the formation. Next came four soldiers bearing a coffin and then the condemned man accompanied by a chaplain flanked by armed guards. Last came the firing party, usually composed of twelve men, one of whom unknowingly carried a musket with a blank charge so that a rifleman could rationalize that his bullet may not have killed a comrade. The prisoner was then seated on the coffin placed near a grave in the open end of the rectangle. Following the chaplain's last words, the provost marshal blindfolded the prisoner and read the official order of execution. He then directed the firing party to carry out the order. Silence followed momentarily except for the clicking sound of muskets being cocked. Then came the fateful command "Fire!"[2]

Following a surgeon's pronouncement that the execution had been carried out, the soldiers making up the formation may have been required to march by the corpse for a close-up reinforcement of a deserter's fate.

Sheridan went into some detail describing how he marshaled his division to witness officers about to be drummed out of the army. But he made no mention of this particular execution, even though the ritual was to be performed at least two more times while he was in command of a division in the West. Perhaps he thought the public would find the business too shocking or impolitic to include in his memoirs more than once. Then too the general appears to have been more appalled by cowardice of an officer than by a soldier from the ranks. That reaction would have been consistent with an attitude not untypical among the officer class of the time, namely, that more was expected of men with rank, whom they inherently counted for more, than a man who had none.

As Marcoot was reporting in at Murfreesboro, Rosecrans's chief of staff, who one day would be president, was expressing mortification "almost akin to shame" to fellow Ohioan, treasury secretary Salmon P. Chase. Brig. Gen. James A. Garfield wrote that the Army of the Cumberland was probably the best army the country ever had, but it lacked the "live and earnest determination to . . . make its power felt."[3]

Some in Washington had also been feeling that way. Back in January, Rosecrans's army had staggered into Murfreesboro torn and bleeding after the battle along the Stones River. The Confederate army stumbled away in the same condition, neither able to pick up the fight in any serious manner. In truth, the two had fought each other almost to the death. It did not seem to matter to the critics back east that the westerners had taken just as many casualties holding off the gray legions in the mud and mists in Tennessee as the Army of the Potomac had suffered at Fredericksburg, but with less than half the men.

For the next five months, Rosecrans all but stood still, with no more than a division occasionally taking to the road for a momentary probe of Bragg's forces. That, Lincoln and Halleck felt, was just too long without a single effort to do serious damage to the enemy.[4] Finally, late in June, Rosecrans began to move. Sheridan's division in McCook's corps broke camp and started their advance along the Shelbyville pike toward Liberty Gap. In the line of march was a new set of brigade commanders to replace the three killed at Stones River. Col. Bernard Laiboldt, the former commander of the 2d Missouri, now succeeded the slain Col. Friedrich Schaefer. Laiboldt was a former sergeant in the German army who had immigrated to St. Louis. All of the new commanders were still in their early thirties. The growing appetite of war was now beginning to demand colonels and generals from among the young.

The 15th began its march from Murfreesboro on June 23, a day on which "it commenced to rain again," Marcoot recorded, "and kept it up almost constantly for seventeen consecutive days. . . . Our beds at night consisted almost invariably of two rails or polls, one end of which was placed upon logs or stumps to keep us out of the water and mud. On these rails we bunked very comfortably with our cartridge boxes for pillows and a rubber blanket for a covering. The patter of the rain during the nights acting most soothingly to the weary, sleeping troops."[5]

On the first day of July, Laiboldt's brigade broke camp about seven miles north of Tullahoma, and at two in the afternoon the four regiments, which included the 15th Missouri, took up the march again and headed south.

Marcoot remembered, "We pushed on through Winchester, and early the next morning celebrated the 4th with an artillery salute. We, however, indulged in no barbecue or picnic, nor were we fortunate enough to have time to tarry for our orators to address us. We did not learn of the fall of Vicksburg or of the great battle of Gettysburg until the 7th. The victories proved a source of much pleasure to our army and enthusiasm ran high for sometime thereafter."[6]

By this time it was clear to Rosecrans and his generals that Bragg intended to fall back behind the Tennessee River at Chattanooga. "Middle Tennessee was once more in the possession of the National troops, and Rosecrans, though strongly urged from Washington to continue on, resisted the pressure until he could repair the Nashville and Chattanooga railroad, which was of vital importance in supplying the army from its secondary base at Nashville. . . . The enemy," Sheridan learned, "had meanwhile concentrated most of his forces at Chattanooga for the twofold purpose of holding this gateway of the Cumberland Mountains, and to assume a defensive attitude."[7]

As Bragg gathered his army in and around Chattanooga, Rosecrans brought his to a halt fifty miles off to the northwest. To those in Washington, this was not at all what they had in mind. On July 7, Secretary of War Stanton telegraphed Rosecrans: "Lee's army overthrown, Grant victorious [at Vicksburg]. You and your noble army now have the chance to give the finishing blow to the rebellion. Will you neglect the chance?"[8]

Lee's army was hardly overthrown. Beaten and withdrawing, yes, but a long way from finished. Neither Stanton nor Rosecrans could know that for sure; nevertheless, Rosecrans resented the admonition and quickly struck back with one of his own: "Just received your cheering dispatch. . . . You do not appear to observe the fact that this noble army has driven the rebels from Middle Tennessee. . . . I beg in behalf of this army that the War Department may not overlook so great an event because it is not written in letters of blood."[9] If Washington had had the intelligence that Rosecrans received that same day from two of his generals, Stanton's prod may have been considerably sharper; Sheridan reported that Bragg in his retreat had left several bridges over the Tennessee River "uninjured." Further, "his losses from desertion are very numerous among the Tennessee troops and others. Many of the companies have lost as many as 20 men. They are coming in in small squads, a number having come in this morning, and I hear of large numbers in the mountains who are making their way home, avoiding our army." Maj. Gen. George Thomas, commanding the Fourteenth Army Corps of the Army of the Cumberland, confirmed Sheridan's assessment; Bragg's "loss is as great in number as if he had fought a grand battle, in addition to which his army is in a completely demoralized condition."[10] Bragg's army appeared ripe for the taking.

"On the 11th the 2nd and the 15th Mo. regiments received orders to march," Marcoot wrote. "Proceeding southward on the line of the railroad, they passed through the tunnel—over a half mile in length—and camped in the Cumberlin [sic] mountains. The next day we proceeded just beyond Anderson Station, Ala., where we remained until the 18th, when the first railroad train reached us [with food and other supplies]. We then advanced as far as Stevenson" in Alabama, thirty miles or so southwest of Chattanooga.

"While here on the 26th, our paymaster again appeared," and the men of the 15th "signed the roll for another $52 installment of 'shin plasters,'" Marcoot wrote. "We had not seen our knapsacks since our departure from Murfreesboro until this time, nearly five weeks before, and were badly in need of a change of clothing. A general clean-up followed and we were soon more like ourselves again. A strong spring of water high up in the mountain side furnished ample of the purest water. . . . We were splendidly quartered here and although you might say it was midsummer, two woolen blankets proved very comfortable during the nights."[11]

A day earlier, on the July 25, Rosecrans, after receiving Halleck's blunt demand to outline his army's positions, Rosecrans responded the same day with a cryptic telegram of his own. A day later, his veiled insolence got Rosecrans another demand from Halleck: "You . . . must move forward immediately." Before Rosecrans had a chance to reply, Halleck followed up the next day with another message, this one marked "PRIVATE AND CONFIDENTIAL":

GENERAL: . . . I have deemed it absolutely necessary, not only for the country but also for your own reputation, that your army should remain no longer inactive. The patience of the authorities here has been completely exhausted, and if I had not repeatedly promised to urge you forward, and begged for delay, you would have been removed from the command. It has been said that you are as inactive as was General Buell, and the pressure for your removal has been almost as strong. . . . I am well aware that people at a distance do not appreciate the obstacles and difficulties which they would see if nearer by; but whether well founded or without any foundation at all, the dissatisfaction really exists, and I deem it my duty, as a friend, to represent it to you truly and fairly.[12]

There followed a series of dispatches from Rosecrans to Washington, starting with one on the evening of August 1 that began, "Assure the President." (Rosecrans knew with certainty where the heat was coming from.) Rosecrans's apparent intent was to keep Lincoln at arm's length, while he, Rosecrans, worked to repair railroads and bridges and build up his supplies for an advance. The general, in fact, built a strong case in his August 1 dispatch to Halleck for not moving precipitously.

> 1st. Our base at Louisville is 264 miles distant from our present position.
> 2d. We are 83 miles from our principal depot—Nashville.
> 3d. We must transport all our subsistence, our clothing, camp and garrison equipage, wagons, animals, ammunition, and most of our forage over these distances by raft.
> 4th. We have before us 60 or 70 miles of barren mountain country, destitute of forage and subsistence, traversed by few difficult roads.
> 5th. We have to cross the difficult defile of the Tennessee, a river from 600 to 1,000 yards wide, in the face of a powerful enemy, and maneuver or fight him from an entrenched position.[13]

Halleck turned a deaf ear and fired back another ultimatum, but Rosecrans continued to bob and weave with more rhetoric. Fed up with Rosecrans's less than artful dodging, Halleck sent still another ultimatum on August 9, this time adding a challenge to his subordinate's veracity: "It is said that you do not draw straight in the traces, but are continually kicking out or getting one leg over."[14] Rosecrans's assessment that the president was paying close attention was correct; there was only one person in Washington who could turn such a phrase.

A week passed before Rosecrans finally began to move. On August 16, 63,000 men of the Army of the Cumberland struck their tents and filed onto the roads heading south. The objective was Chattanooga, a sleepy town of low frame buildings and 2,500 people, but strategically important because it lay astride railways through the Appalachians into Virginia and south into Georgia and the heart of the Confederacy. Taking the town would also pressure Southern forces to back out of eastern Tennessee, which was home to many loyal to the Union. Seeing that event come about was ever close to the heart of the man who occupied the Executive Mansion.

Facing Rosecrans was more than Bragg and his Army of Tennessee. The country was another tough and dangerous obstacle. First came the Cumberland Mountains, a lofty barrier that the enemy could man to block the way. Assaulting an entrenched enemy in the hollows and on the heights could command a dear price in casualties. Next was the river, the Tennessee, a barrier of another kind that coiled around Chattanooga.

Sheridan's division moved ahead of the main body to Bridgeport on the Tennessee River, west of Chattanooga, one of four places at which the army would attempt to cross. Sheridan was assigned to build two pontoon bridges, the retreating Confederates having burned the railroad trestle that had spanned the river at this point. "As there were not with the army enough pontoons . . . I was expected to build one of them of trestles." What emerged was a rickety-looking contraption barely wide enough to hold the width and weight of wagons, cannon, and caissons and marching men two abreast.[15]

On September 2, Sheridan received orders to cross. The plan now was to make a sweeping left wheel and move against Chattanooga and the Rebels from the southwest. Five days later, Bragg concluded that a heavy force of Federals, maybe even the main body, had gotten across the Tennessee. His left was now definitely threatened. With his supply line now in danger, Bragg ordered his army to evacuate Chattanooga and march south. Reports began to trickle in, confirming that Southern regiments were indeed vacating the town. The prize—the vital rail hub along the river—now belonged to Rosecrans. He had outmaneuvered his adversary with hardly a shot. Further, all of Tennessee was now free of a major Confederate army, which, as Halleck put it a few days later, also made Kentucky "perfectly safe."[16]

Rosecrans lost no time in deciding to pursue. There was to be nothing deliberate about the chase. "This corps is ordered in pursuit," read the directive to Sheridan late that night. "General McCook directs that you break camp by daybreak in the morning and move directly to Winston's [Gap]. . . . When you get to Winston's your troops will move up the mountain, leaving the trains behind, except your ammunition train." so as "not to be impeded."[17] Laiboldt's brigade was to move southeast from Bridge-port, up over Raccoon Mountain, down along Lookout Creek to Trenton, turning southwest to Winston's Gap and up again to Lookout Mountain, a march of more than forty miles.

The next day, September 10, the brigade "was up at three, ready to march at five A.M.," wrote the historians of the 73d Illinois. "Did not get off until seven. The 3d Division all moved out, our 2d Brigade in the rear."[18] The weather had turned hot and sultry, and the division of four thousand infantry and artillery ahead soon tromped and ground the road into ankle-deep, choking dust. Laiboldt's men got the worst of it. Bringing up the rear, they literally ate the dust trailing from those up ahead.

"The rate of speed for three miles was not rapid, but on making this distance and after a short halt, orders came to push forward as hurriedly as possible. The roadside soon became lined with soldiers, from all the regiments, who were unable to keep up. . . . The heat of the sun was severe, as reflected from the gravel and rocks, and one man of the 42nd Illinois who had been prostrated by sunstroke, did not recover."[19]

The men, Marcoot recalled, "were compelled to aid our artillery in crossing the mountains[.] [A]s the road was very rocky in many places the guns had to actually be lifted over some of them, and the grade was very steep for several miles. . . . We crossed Lookout Valley on [September] 10th and camped on the top of Lookout mountain."[20]

McCook and his division commanders were getting nervous. They were now separated by more than forty miles from the other two corps off to the east—in a mountainous country dense with forests, thick wiry undergrowth, and a few roads, which were often nothing more than trails. "The scattered condition of the army began to alarm us all," said Sheridan.[21] Bragg, his whereabouts and the size of his army unknown and his army possibly concentrated, could fall on Rosecrans' divided forces and destroy the separated elements piecemeal, with little possibility that one Union corps would be able to come to the aid of the other in time to prevent their destruction.

Rosecrans, meanwhile, was getting reports of encounters with Confederates in considerable force along Chickamauga Creek in the valley south of Missionary Ridge. By the morning of September 11, Rosecrans had become "satisfied . . . that the main body of the rebel army was in the vicinity of La Fayette."[22] Bragg had not retreated pell-mell for Atlanta, as some of Rosecrans's staff had said he would. He had stopped and turned about. Furthermore, he was close, and that knowledge was chilling.

At midnight on September 12, McCook received orders to "draw in toward Chattanooga." Sheridan immediately issued orders to move at daybreak, back over the mountain from where they had just come, a forced march this time to join up with Thomas's corps more than forty miles to the east.[23] Once again it was to be up over the rocks and boulders, in the heat and through the dust.

Back in Washington, Halleck was getting nervous. But for a different reason than the worries Rosecrans and his staff were having in Tennessee. A day earlier, Halleck had telegraphed Rosecrans, "It is reported here by deserters that a part of Bragg's army is re-enforcing Lee. It is important that the truth of this should be ascertained as early as possible."[24] If there was one thing that could set nerves on edge in Washington, it was the possibility of Lee taking the offensive again. The thought blinded Halleck to another offensive possibility in the west.

As Sheridan's men were filing once again onto a dusty road in Tennessee the morning of September 13, in Virginia, "trains of cars had been heard running all the time, day and night, for the last thirty-six hours, on the Petersburg and Richmond road, evidently indicating a movement of troops in some direction." So read a telegraphed message that night received in Washington from Fort Monroe, Virginia.[25] Some in Washington thought Lee was sending a force to Petersburg, others, "to make an attempt to capture Norfolk," Halleck later reported to Stanton.[26]

The trains in fact were headed *away* from the Army of the Potomac and away from Virginia. Halleck had gotten it all wrong. Bragg was not reinforcing Lee. It was the other way around—Lee was sending Longstreet's corps to Bragg, a reinforcement by rail of more than ten thousand troops. Traveling day and night, chugging and clanking for almost two thousand miles in a giant "U" through the South, on a variety of rail gauges that would require Longstreet and his men to change trains seven times, they would first point south, then west, before turning north to join Bragg's Army of Tennessee.

Mary Chesnut caught a glimpse of Longstreet's Corps stopped momentarily on a siding in South Carolina. In her diary she noted the "strange sight—miles, apparently, of platform cars—soldiers rolled in their blankets, lying in rows, heads and all covered, fast asleep. In their gray blankets, packed in regular order, they looked like swathed mummies. . . . A feeling of awful depression laid hold of me," she continued. "All these fine fellows going to kill or be killed." A phrase started beating about her head, she wrote, "like an old song—'the unreturning brave.'"[27]

It would prove to be a fitting lament, but not just for those for whom she envisioned it.

11

The River of Death

It would be called one of the epic marches of the war.[1] It was made "with all possible celerity," Sheridan wrote, "for the situation was critical and demanded every exertion. The ascent and descent of the mountains was extremely exhausting, the steep grades often rendering it necessary to drag up and let down by hand both the transportation and artillery."[2]

Captain Kyger of the 73d Illinois recorded in his diary that Laiboldt's brigade was "up and under arms at four o'clock."

We drew three days' rations. . . . At eight A.M. we were hurried into line . . . made slow progress in getting up the mountain . . . [and] called to help a battery up the hill. . . . By 6.30 P.M. we had arrived . . . on top of Lookout Mountain . . . moved on two and one-half miles and bivouacked for the night . . . last jaunt was made through dust and darkness.

Monday, September 14th . . . up at 3.30 A.M. descent of the western slope of the mountain began. . . . We tarried not . . . by one o'clock P.M. the entire regiment, almost, had dropped out and joined the long line of stragglers in the rear. . . . We reached a spring of water in Lookout Valley, and General Sheridan ordered a halt. . . . This halt enabled many who had dropped behind to catch up . . . marched seven miles by 2.30 P.M., when another halt was called . . . soon on the way again, but we moved slowly and rested often. . . . By six P.M. we were bivouacked for the night . . . marched twenty-four miles, a long and fatiguing march, considering the heat and dust. . . .

On the morning of the 15th . . . again started on the march. The road followed was an obscure one and little used . . . [with] fallen timber . . . marched steadily and arrived at Johnson's Cove at 5.15 P.M., and bivouacked for the night. The train kept passing . . . until it became too dark to see how to drive. . . . The medical wagon . . . turned over and much damage was done to the contents.

September 16th . . . started up the mountain, leaving eight men with each wagon to help the mules up the steep road. . . . It required the putting forth of the utmost strength of the mules and men to get the train over the most difficult places.

The captain took time to note that "half-way up . . . we came to a small field . . . and an old log hut. In the hut was a poor, helpless woman, suffering from intermittent fever. She was lying on a very scant and rickety bed . . . an army blanket for her covering . . . a part box of army crackers, some coffee and sugar had been left by the passing soldiers, for the woman and her two small children. . . . The husband and father had been killed in the rebel army . . . the suffering and poverty within, made the picture a sad one to contemplate." The captain and his men moved on and "made the descent to the valley—two miles— . . . bivouacked at the foot of the mountain in McLamore's [McLemore's] Cove."[3]

Thus ended a four-day march of forty-six miles in choking dust and heat for the second time in little more than a week, up and over two mountains, steep climbs of about two miles each, pushing and heaving loaded wagons, cannon, and caissons, which the mules alone could not pull, shuffling and slipping finally down a long descent into a broad plain bordered by deep woods with thick underbrush—woods, a man in the Confederate army later wrote, that had an evil-looking appearance. Somewhere through those woods curled a creek the Cherokee Indians had named Chickamauga, "the river of death."

The next day, the "report came in that the enemy was approaching," Conrad wrote. "I was ordered with my regiment to hold Stevens' Gap at all circumstances." The 15th was stationed there until the next day, when at nine in the morning, "we moved about 5 miles farther on to McLemore's Cove. Moved again that night at 10 P.M. to Pond Spring, 18 miles south of Chattanooga, where we arrived at 2 A.M."[4]

Early in the morning on September 18, Conrad's men "formed in line of battle on the crest of the hill, from where [the brigade] was ordered to take position near Gordon's Mills, and to guard a ford of Chickamauga Creek." From corps headquarters, Maj. Gen. Alexander McCook reported, "I have

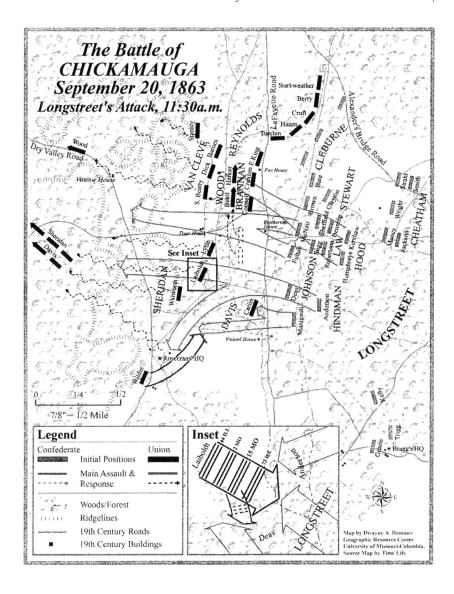

The Battle of CHICKAMAUGA
September 20, 1863
Longstreet's Attack, 11:30a.m.

Legend

Confederate		Union
	Initial Positions	
	Main Assault & Response	

Woods/Forest
Ridgelines
19th Century Roads
19th Century Buildings

Inset

Map by Dwayne A. Hemmer
Geographic Resource Center
University of Missouri-Columbia.
Source Map by Time Life

the honor to state for the information of the General commanding that all is perfectly quiet on the right this morning."[5]

At nine in the morning the next day, Conrad reported "heavy cannonading to our left. The battle had commenced." A Union division had stumbled into Confederate cavalry about four miles off to the left. For the rest of the day, both armies fed reinforcements into the fighting along a four-mile front of thick forest occasionally broken by a few small farms. Muskets and cannon flashed almost continuously from the deep woods. Units on both sides found it impossible to maintain formations in the dark and tangled timber, men getting separated and lost from their companies in the confusion.

On the far right of the Union line, the 15th left camp at eleven o'clock, marched to the left at the double-quick to Crawfish Spring, then the double-quick again, this time to Gordon's Mill, Conrad reported, "where we took position in line of battle. . . . Here we lay for an hour, but the firing on the right of our line getting heavier, and two brigades under General Wood being in confusion, we moved again at double-quick to the battle-field, where the Second and Fifteenth Missouri were drawn up in line of battle at the edge of timber . . . under a most appalling fire of the enemy."[6] "Just before dark," Marcoot remembered, the Rebels "made a desperate attempt to turn our right. The muskets fell with a ringing sound on every hand and the dead and wounded lay in great numbers in our midst." Lytle's Third Brigade of Sheridan's division "had repulsed and driven the enemy fully a half a mile, but night came on and we were compelled to desist."[7]

With the darkness, the fighting died down and federal forces contin-ued to hold the original line along the LaFayette road. The left, however, under Maj. Gen. George H. Thomas and the Fourteenth Corps, had been pushed back to the Kelly farm, putting them too on the country lane with the rest of the Union troops. Conrad reported that the 15th remained in line of battle at the edge of the timber, lying on their arms "all night in much discomfort, as the cold was very severe and fires were not allowed."

Behind the regiment, division headquarters were set up for the night, with extra guards drawn from the 73d Illinois and posted near Sheridan's tent. Light came from the entrance, and a corporal stationed himself close by in an effort to pick up whatever scrap of information he might overhear. The corporal thought he detected "a feeling of anxiety, extra seriousness . . . from the general down to orderlies." Maj. Gen. Alexander McCook and two or three other officers arrived at the tent and went in. They had just come from a meeting of corps commanders at Rosecrans's headquarters at the Widow Glenn's house, where "reports of the positions and condition of their commands [were] heard, and orders given for the disposition of the troops for the following day."[8]

Inside the tent, McCook passed on the orders he had gotten from Rose-crans. The corporal said, "An animated and somewhat protracted consul-tation was held. . . . General Sheridan grew more restless and uneasy. He was greatly displeased at the rough usage his 3d [Bradley's] Brigade had received" in the fight early that evening. Bradley had received two severe wounds while leading the brigade, and his assistant adjutant general lay mortally wounded. The corporal said that Sheridan "was apprehensive that there would be more of the same . . . for his two remaining brigades next morning." The meeting finally came to an end, and McCook and the other officers departed.

Sheridan, the corporal recalled, "paced back and forth in his tent, and bewailed the situation . . . using language more emphatic than elegant, as General Sheridan only could do." Ominously, the corporal added, "We were aware of the fact that our . . . brigade [Laiboldt's] had not been engaged during the day."[9]

Rosecrans was also aware of the fact. He recorded, "We had present but two brigades which had not been opportunely and squarely in action."[10] The two brigades Rosecrans had in mind were in Sheridan's division. One of those brigades was Laiboldt's, the brigade of the 15th Missouri. The eavesdropping corporal concluded, "We could feel pretty thoroughly assured that we should have a chance to 'see the elephant' in the morning. . . . The regiment and the brigade were reconciled to the inevitable, prepared to take things as they came."[11]

Earlier that afternoon, the chugging locomotives slowed as they passed the rust-colored sandstone rail station at Ringgold in northern Georgia, before finally bumping and jerking to a stop. Unraveling slowly from their blankets, the men began to jump down from the cars, one and two from each car at first, then whole groups at a time, the rattle and clatter of muskets, bayonets, and canteens now mingling with the sound of the clanking and hissing steam engines. Forming into companies, regiments, and finally moving into line as divisions, Longstreet's men marched off toward the sound of booming cannon to the northwest.

Before daylight on the 20th, the 15th Missouri with the rest of the brigade "was marched about a mile to the rear and right," Conrad recorded in his after-action report, "General Sheridan's division holding the extreme right and our brigade the extreme right of General Sheridan's division. Companies I and K of my regiment were thrown out as skirmishers." The rest of the regiment rested on their arms.

Marcoot recalled, "The morning of the 20th dawned bright and clear and the sun came up in all its splendor."[12] Four miles to the left across from the Union line, Sam Watkins remembered that Sunday morning much the same way. He wrote that the sun rose over the hills "clear and beautiful. The day itself seemed to have a Sabbath-day look about it." He also noted that the country, rough and broken, with trees and undergrowth that had never been disturbed by the ax, "looked wild, weird, and uncivilized."[13]

The battle opened again about nine o'clock and raged away to the left. The 15th Missouri with the other brigade regiments, the 2d Missouri, and the 44th and 73d Illinois, were moved to the left in direction of the firing. Near the Widow Glenn's house, General Rosecrans's headquarters, they were halted at the top of a slight ridge. Sheridan directed Laiboldt to form the brigade into column of regiments facing toward an open field to the east. The positioning and the formation of the brigade were for the purpose of protecting the right flank of two small brigades down the slope in a belt of woods a quarter mile ahead—clearly a defensive tactic on Sheridan's part.[14] "We were stationed on a hill," Marcoot wrote, "about half a mile from the woods in our front where the rebels lay. We were formed three columns deep with our artillery in line also."[15]

In columns of regiments, as Sheridan directed, the brigade of four regiments was arranged in lateral lines, the men standing almost shoulder to shoulder, presenting a front line of a hundred men or so across the top of the slope, the lines stacked one behind the other. Ahead was an open field, to the rear, a stretch of woods. Each regiment formed into three lines, "three columns deep," as Marcoot said, which meant they were closed up tight, each line behind the other. A small interval of two strides separated each regiment. Each probably formed into the same number of lines as the regiment in front, so that the brigade of four regiments, perhaps twelve hundred men, was a compact mass of twelve lines, each of the regiments separated by no more than a couple of yards.[16]

This formation was a good defensive one, on "a very strong ridge," according to Sheridan.[17] Stairstepped in lines down the slope, the formation would allow the front line to fire a volley, reload, followed in turn by volley firing by each successive line. It meant that the brigade of four regiments could possibly get off a volley of a hundred muskets or so every few seconds if ordered to do so. Indeed, a strong defensive formation, but not one for an attack or charge. In that case, only the front line would be able to fire; the eleven lines behind would each be blocked by the line ahead. In a compact and massed body, they would also be easy targets.

"It was a position without fortifications," Marcoot said, "but one which we thought we could hold until dooms day against all attacks from the front."[18]

The 73d Illinois formed the first of the four massed regiments. The 73d's first line was positioned behind a loose barricade of fallen timber, followed by three of the 15th Missouri, then the 44th Illinois, and finally the 2d Missouri. Directly behind was a six-gun battery of the 1st Illinois Artillery. With the brigade formed the way he wanted it, Sheridan left and marched his other two brigades to the left as ordered, to fill what Rosecrans and headquarters thought was a gap in the Union line.

But there was no gap. In his leaving, Sheridan unwittingly created a very real one. Now the 15th Missouri and the other three regiments were alone, a tactical island, with no immediate support to the right or left.

Peering down the open slope, Laiboldt's men could now turn their attention to the stretch of woods about a quarter mile away. The two Union brigades under Brig. Gen. Jefferson C. Davis (no relation to the Confederate president) were in there somewhere, some behind barricades, others firing occasionally in the tangled underbrush at an unseen enemy.

About a quarter mile further on, beyond the woods and along the edge of another strip of woods, General Longstreet galloped down a lane with a number of his staff and drew up before Brig. Gen. Zacharia Deas and his Alabama brigade. The sun was near its zenith for this late summer day. Col. J. G. Coltart of the 50th Alabama noted the time: eleven o'clock. The Southerners had been waiting most of the morning. Deas's men were the first in line of three large brigades totaling sixteen regiments, plus artillery—almost half of Longstreet's corps, five thousand men. Formed into line of battle, they waited, five lines deep, the first stretching along the edge of woods for more than a half mile, their battle flags flapping in an occasional breeze as if impatient to get on with it.[19]

Ahead in a strip of woods, unseen, lay Davis's two blue-coated brigades, each numbering barely a thousand. Some lay behind low barricades of hastily thrown-up timber, themselves virtually blind in the woods and tangled brush.

After the introductions, Longstreet pointed to the woods ahead and said that the enemy was somewhere in there. Turning back to Deas, he gave the order to advance. A lieutenant in one of the Alabama regiments took note of the time: 11:20 A.M. The long lines began to move forward.[20]

Deas's brigade moved across the field and into the woods without skirmishers to give away their coming. Pushing through the thick underbrush, the Confederates were on top of Davis's men before the Union troops knew it. Some stayed to get off a round or two, "and in some instances the musket was used" as a club against the wave beginning to flood over and around them.[21] Some ducked their heads behind the log barricades. Others got up and bolted. "They scattered to the four winds," wrote the lieutenant from Alabama.

"Nothing but precipitate flight could save my command from annihilation or capture," Davis later reported. Dashing through the timber on horseback, Davis was among the first to emerge from the woods, his fleeing men close behind. Desperate for help, Davis galloped up the hill, heading for the brigade formed at the head of the slope. "I rode up to Colonel Laiboldt . . . and informed him that if he was there for the purpose of supporting my troops it must be done immediately."

A staff officer galloping alongside Davis concurred. But the practiced battle eye of an experienced field officer would have instantly discerned that Longstreet's Corps, a wave of thousands of Confederate troops a half mile wide, line after line stretching far beyond Laiboldt's left and right flanks, would quickly envelop and overwhelm the brigade's front of a hundred men.

Davis claimed that Laiboldt "at once commenced deploying his troops."[22] Laiboldt did no such thing: He balked.[23] For Colonel Laiboldt, the staff officer off to his side was easy to ignore. Simply, Laiboldt outranked him. Further, the staff officer carried no written orders from McCook requiring him to charge. General Davis was another matter. Not only did he outrank Laiboldt, Davis had gained a reputation for a temper with a hair trigger. In a sensational confrontation a year earlier, Davis had drawn a pistol and shot and killed another general in the lobby of a Louisville hotel. One impartial witness called it cold-blooded murder. The general got off without a trial, thanks to the powerful help of the governor of Indiana.

Laiboldt was no milksop himself. A former sergeant in the German army, he was not about to be bullied. Certainly not by an American officer, even if he was a general. German officers typically harbored little respect for their native-born counterparts, and this one from Missouri was no different. (That he had more than his share of courage, and no patience for anyone who tried to intimidate him, he would prove again a year later. Commanding only the 2d Missouri at that time, Laiboldt would find himself outnumbered, probably by as much as ten to one, by Fighting Joe Wheeler's gray cavalry. Confronted with a demand to surrender, Laiboldt replied, "You'll have to take me first." Laiboldt and his Missourians held off the Rebel force for nine hours before the Southerners gave up and withdrew.[24])

At the top of the slope, while General Davis continued to argue with Laiboldt, Major General McCook, the corps commander himself, rode up. Another general who knew him well, himself a highly regarded division officer, once labeled McCook a blockhead ("chucklehead" according to one source), unfit to command even a squad of men.[25] McCook was about to demonstrate why.

Hearing the discussion between Davis and Laiboldt, McCook settled the matter. Laiboldt later reported, "After a short interval, when General Davis' division was already routed, Major-General McCook ordered the brigade to charge."[26] That Davis's division *was already routed* was a fact Laiboldt pointedly put in his report. Laiboldt apparently wanted the record clear: McCook had, in effect, ordered him to give up his prime defensive position, to "support" units that had already been broken up and defeated and to charge into an enemy that outnumbered his men by an enormous factor. The order was the height of folly: army postmortems would so judge, Sheridan's among them.

Men in the 73d, some likely overhearing the intense words passing between the officers just in front of them, questioned the order among themselves: "We were in fine position at the crest of a hill, in heavy timber, and with our battery well located." A captain on Laiboldt's staff remembered that the colonel suggested that he first be allowed to redeploy the brigade, in order to protect his flanks; "McCook replied with a preemptory order to charge as we were."[27] Laiboldt knew then he had no choice but to obey the direct order. He gave the order to charge.

For the 15th, Colonel Conrad recorded, "we received orders to charge on the enemy with the point of the bayonet." Marcoot too remembered the order: "Charge bayonets, forward, double-quick, march!"[28]

Continuing in his after-action report, Conrad wrote, "Nobly was this order carried out. The men went in good order in the woods in column of regiments wheeling on the march to the right." Conrad apparently gave the command to "wheel to the right" in order to get the regiment beyond the 73d, so that the 15th would have a clear field of fire without hitting the Illinoisans.

Writing twenty-seven years later, Marcoot recalled, "The command was obeyed to the letter amid such yelling as I never had heard before. You would have thought to have heard it, that all the demons of the infernal regions had broken loose. . . . Down the slope we went, over the fence and into the very woods where the enemy lay."

The columns of the 73d Illinois had gone in first with the 15th on their heels. At the bottom of the slope, where a small brook ran through bordered by tall brush, they ran into Davis's panicked troops heading for their ranks, Longstreet's brigades right behind. The 73d could not fire for fear of shooting into Davis's men, but the first line got off one ragged volley before Longstreet's men were into them.

General W. P. Carlin, one of Davis's brigade commanders retreating with his men, saw what happened next. "There was a hand-to-hand struggle for a few minutes; then more volleys of musketry on the right and left flanks, as well as the front."[29] Pushed back by the overwhelming numbers, the front ranks of the 73d fell like dominoes into the trailing 15th. Conrad's men got off one ragged volley with only time then to turn their muskets into stabbing bayonets and swinging clubs. Like a great train wreck, Laiboldt's regiments behind began to crash into the columns in front. The 44th Illinois, following the 15th, veered off track, also to the right, to get into position to fire. Instead, they found themselves being fired on from front and both sides. "The Second Missouri, in the rear of the brigade, had no chance whatever to return the fire of the enemy without running the risk of killing our own men."[30]

General Carlin "saw the poor fellows struggling to deploy into line, in order to use their arms against the enemy. But the enemy was too close. . . . A volley poured into Laiboldt's compact, almost solid, mass of men, at only a few steps distant." The 2d Missouri's color bearers and all of the color guard were shot down at once. Others trying to take their places were immediately hit. Men went down all around. "The loss of men was very great." All "organization was broken, and the brigade melted away."[31]

"We were nearly surrounded," Conrad wrote, "and the alternative was either to get killed or be taken prisoners. . . . The men retreated, but still fighting." Marcoot recalled,

> The fight now became a desperate hand to hand encounter with bayonets and clubbed muskets, and heroic blood flowed, as it were, in streams. Being so largely outnumbered it was but a short time until the enemy swept over and through our band on all sides. . . . Many of us soon found ourselves surrounded and greeted with "surrender you Yankee _____."
>
> . . . We fought our way backwards and finally had a fair foot race with our jubilant opponents in reaching our artillery, which had all this time remained almost inactive for fear of doing more harm to our own forces than to the enemy with whom we were battling so desperately. It was no stampede, for the boys retained their composure and fought desperately every foot of the bloody pathway.[32]

"In going up the hill again," Conrad continued, "the rebels had an excellent opportunity to do us much harm. . . . Their bullets swept the hill from three sides, and many of our brave men fell there, or were wounded and taken prisoners."[33]

On reaching the top of the slope, "Some of the boys actually shed tears (Engelbert Dreher for instance)," Marcoot wrote.

> So greatly were they chagrined at our ill success, not to speak of the number of companions who had fallen. . . . When we reached our artil-

lery every horse was dead and barely men enough left to handle the guns but these few poured grape and canister hot and fast into the very face of the advancing foe as soon as they could safely do so. The booming of our artillery soon brought a murderous, concentrated fire . . . from the enemy's guns and we [the firing by the 1st Illinois battery] were compelled to cease. We now again began to fall back, but the Captain of the artillery, nicknamed "Leather Breeches," begged us to save his guns. We retraced our steps, and taking hold pulled manfully. Their weight and the galling fire to which we were exposed soon compelled us to desist however, although the brave Captain and several of his gallant men stubbornly refused to leave them and they were lost. We never saw or heard of them afterwards and know naught of the fate that befell them.[34]

Sheridan's remaining two brigades had been passing to the rear of the ground where the disaster struck. "McCook directed me," Sheridan wrote, "to throw in Lytle's and Bradley's brigades. This was hastily done, they being formed to the front under a terrible fire. Scarcely were they aligned when the same horde of Confederates . . . poured in upon them a deadly fire and shivered the two brigades to pieces. We succeeded in rallying them, however, and by a counter attack regained the ridge that Laiboldt had been driven from." Years later, an Illinoisan in the 73d recalled, "to that alone most of us who escaped death or imprisonment, are indebted . . . while Sheridan was not there to put us in, he was there to help us out."[35]

Reaching the top of the hill, a man in the 36th Illinois recalled, "The sight was truly appalling." The dead and wounded of Laiboldt's brigade lay everywhere down the slope. "The ground was covered with dry grass and old logs which the bursting shells had set on fire. A thick cloud of smoke had risen about as high as our heads and seemed hanging like a funeral pall in the air. Under this we could see, away down the slope of the hill and across the little valley just as far as the eye could reach, moving masses of men hurrying toward us." The hurrying masses of men moving toward them were still more of Longstreet's regiments. "We could not hold the ridge," Sheridan wrote.[36]

Marcoot remembered that "a few brave officers now made strenuous efforts to stop our fleeing commands, but at this very moment . . . Sheridan, came dashing along the line [on] his huge black charger and shouting . . . 'Let them go! Let them go for their lives, and rally beyond the hill where they are safe from this murderous fire.'"[37]

The collapse of the Union right and center was all but complete, with more than thirty thousand now in flight to the rear—Rosecrans, McCook,

The order to "Charge bayonets" sent the 15th Missouri in Laiboldt's brigade down this slope at Chickamauga before being overwhelmed by Longstreet's Corps. Twenty-eight years later, the brigade's veterans returned to mark the farthest advance of the four regiments for the nation's first military park at the Chattanooga-Chickamauga National Battlefield Park. The second postlike marker behind the larger one for the 73rd Illinois locates the farthest advance of the 15th Missouri. (from the author's collection)

and a number of generals fleeing with them—leaving fifteen thousand more lying dead or wounded in the fields and woods behind them.

Shortly after his division "rallied on the low hills" less than a quarter mile behind the slope where Laiboldt's dead and wounded lay, Sheridan discovered that "the enemy, instead of attacking me in front, was wedging in between my division and the balance of the army; in short, endeavoring to cut me off from Chattanooga."[38] Longstreet was in fact making a right-hand turn, focusing his attention now on what was left of Rosecrans's army still in line under George Thomas on Snodgrass Hill a half mile away. Starting about midafternoon and continuing until dark put a halt to the firing, Thomas and his Fourteenth Corps would put up a tremendous fight and repulse the Confederates, earning for Thomas the immortal sobriquet, "The Rock of Chickamauga."

Sheridan moved his badly crippled division onto the Dry Valley road, which ran along the east slope of Missionary Ridge. Sheridan's idea was to hook up with Thomas on Snodgrass Hill. Along the way, he met and joined up with General Carlin and what was left of his brigade. Stragglers from other broken units clogged the road in confusion. An officer on Rosecrans's staff, trying to wedge his way through but forced to ride through the deep brush alongside the road, had to weather the derision coming from the ranks shuffling along with him. "See Phil?" "See Jeff?" "Some old trudger in the ranks called out, 'We'll talk to you, my son, when we get to the Ohio River.'"

The officer eventually came upon the two generals "with the remnants of their five brigades. General Phil was furious . . . he was swearing mad, and no wonder . . . the truest and bravest had fallen in vain resistance around him . . . his splendid fighting qualities and his fine soldiers had not half a chance. He had lost faith. . . . I offered to ascertain the situation with Thomas, and report as soon as possible. I hurried off."[39]

Sheridan, thinking he could still hook up with Thomas, "rode some distance . . . to look for a way out, but found that the enemy had intervened" to isolate his division. "I then determined to march directly to Rossville, and from there effect a junction with Thomas by the Lafayette road. I reached Rossville about 5 o'clock in the afternoon, bringing with me eight guns, forty-six caissons, and a long ammunition train."[40]

By this time, Rosecrans had made it safely to Chattanooga. At 5:00 P.M., his telegraph to Halleck said, "We have met with a serious disaster."[41]

For the 15th, "The night was a frightfully dark one," Marcoot wrote,

but we succeeded in reaching our new position and entrenching ourselves in a very respectable manner. Our lines were then reformed and we awaited the coming of the enemy, but in vain for they came not. . . . Our only great sorrow was the fact that we were compelled to leave our dead and wounded, comrades we loved so well, in the hands of the enemy . . . the first roll call after the battle was the saddest I ever attended.

Many strong men were moved to tears as our Sergeant (our orderly had lost a leg and an arm[42]) with quivering voice called one familiar name after another without receiving the prompt answer of "here," and if I am not mistaken only thirteen of Co. B responded on that memorable day, while not one ever turned up afterwards as a straggler, all not present being either killed, wounded or captured. Of the number [of Co. B] who were captured [and confined in a Southern prison] only one (Henry Rutz . . . of Highland) ever returned, and he was held prisoner until the spring of 1865. He escaped twice but was on both occasions recaptured, and his sufferings were liken unto the many who endured the same fate.[43]

Whatever occurred after the fury on the slope barely managed to regis-
ter with Laiboldt and Conrad. Both were able to single out Conrad's adjutant, Lt. Friedrick Lipps, "for true courage and valor" on that slope. Lipps
was a twenty-five-year-old Swiss immigrant who had enlisted as a private
back in July 1861, and one of the lucky ones who had survived this particular Sunday. There were, no doubt, many others of true courage and valor.
Trouble was, they were left lying back on the slope. Neither Laiboldt nor
Conrad could bring himself to write or comment much more in his report
about what happened afterward, except to say that they marched that night
to Rossville, arriving about eleven o'clock. They were now about ten miles
from where nearly half of their men lay, dead, dying, or taken captive. For
the 15th Missouri, Conrad concluded his report: "I am in much uncer-
tainty as to the fate of many of my men."[44]

McCook, along with several others, was blamed for the disaster. A
number of officers, including Sheridan, called for his dismissal. Indicted,
McCook requested a board of inquiry be held first, in hopes of being
absolved of any culpability in the debacle. After a lengthy hearing with
numerous depositions, McCook was officially exonerated, some even testi-
fying that he had handled his men satisfactorily and in a professional manner. The board concluded that only his decision to flee the field with a
number of other generals was to be questioned. In spite of an official assessment that Laiboldt's brigade had been ordered to charge an overwhelming
"superior force, under every conceivable disadvantage"—a judgment made
by McCook's own inspector general[45]—the inquiry did not address his
order that led to the near destruction of Laiboldt's brigade, if not Sheridan's
entire division. Even so, the army's trust in McCook had been shattered.
Never again would he hold a command of troops in the field.[46]

"Be of good cheer." So began the telegraph coming in to Rosecrans's headquarters early the morning after the disaster. The message had been sent
from Washington shortly after midnight. It was signed, "A. Lincoln."[47]
There is no record of Rosecrans's reaction, if he was able to react at all. He
was probably too brainsick in any event to give the words much weight,
an army chaplain even now at his side trying to steady the shaken general.
Words, any words, put forth to conciliate likely rang lame and hollow,
for the enormity of the situation was beyond Rosecrans's or anyone else's
comprehension. This he knew, and it was all that mattered: his army at
this moment was beyond his or anyone else's control. Thirteen miles away,
along a stretch of a good four miles, thousands of his men lay dead or
wounded, bodies strewn across the fields and deep into the surrounding

woods. He could only imagine the rest: thousands more lost somewhere in the dark, strung out along the narrow lanes the locals called roads, some trudging in a direction thought to be north, others wandering and straggling aimlessly in the night. The enemy, his whereabouts unknown and possibly close, might even now be closing in for the kill.

During the night, "a frightfully dark one," Marcoot had written, the 15th went to work entrenching. The work finished, as much as time would allow, they waited. But, as Marcoot noted, "they came not."

With the coming daylight, the 15th, with the rest of Sheridan's division, was "drawn up in line of battle," Conrad reported, "a renewal of the fight again expected." But there was no sign of the enemy. Bragg's army too had been badly hurt. "His inaction," Sheridan later wrote, "gave us the opportunity for getting the broken and disorganized army into shape. It took a large part of the day to accomplish this. . . . The army moved back from Rossville, and my division, as the rear-guard of [McCook's] Corps, got within our lines at Chattanooga about 8 o'clock the morning of the 22nd."[48] A day later, the 15th Missouri, "having daily heavy picket duty to do," Conrad reported, "are all in good spirits; they all know that the enemy failed in accomplishing his object, and are willing and anxious to try the enemy again."[49]

In headquarters tents throughout Chattanooga and the surrounding countryside, officers began the writing of their grim reports. Most began with the customary, "I have the honor to respectfully report." Near the close of most of these reports, a phrase such as the following, or something similar, introduced a lengthy paragraph: "The following officers and men were especially distinguished." General Sheridan cited "Colonel Laiboldt, commanding my Second Brigade, [who] behaved with conspicuous gallantry." Sheridan also recommended his German brigade commander from Missouri for promotion, which would place Laiboldt in line for brigadier general. (Laiboldt would never get his promotion. He would be transferred back to Missouri. His stand less than a year later at Dalton, Georgia, stood for naught as far as a higher rank was concerned. Perhaps the stand he took contesting the order to charge down the slope that Sunday morning labeled him too independent for the army establishment. Whether the fact that Laiboldt was German had anything to do it will never be known. Halleck would be general in chief to the end, and all recommendations for promotion to general would have to go through him. Lincoln too likely was feeling no further need for German generals to appeal for the support of German Americans. By war's end, Germans still made up at least 10 percent of the Union army, yet less than half that share was represented among those with the rank of brigadier general or above.[50])

Among his regimental commanders, Sheridan cited Col. Joseph Conrad and Lt. Col. John Weber "for skill exhibited and great personal courage." Weber was also listed among the wounded, his horse having fallen and nearly crushing him: "severe contusion of entire right side of the body, unable to travel with his regiment without endangering his life."[51]

For the 15th, Conrad mentioned "especially his adjutant, First Lieut. Friedrich Lipps."[52] Laiboldt included Conrad among his regimental commanders for "unflinching courage and gallant behavior," recommending "the highest commendations."[53]

Commanders then tolled their losses. Sheridan reported the mournful numbers: "The total casualties—officers and men—in this division are as follows: Killed, 152; wounded, 1037; captured, 328. Total 1,517," of "4,000 bayonets" he would later write, which made the loss almost forty percent.[54]

Sheridan's report made the casualty list almost as long as the one for Stones River. It meant that the division had taken almost 80 percent in casualties in less than a year. Many who had been wounded would return. They would indeed be veterans now. When it came finally to compile the lists of the dead and wounded of the regiments that had charged down the slope that Sunday morning, the 15th Missouri turned out to have suffered the most.[55]

The 15th Missouri's casualty report begins simply enough. The word *List* appears alone at the top of the page, written in pen and ink by a fine hand on lined, light-gray foolscap, legal-size in length. It is followed by a brief paragraph that summarizes the contents:

> of killed, wounded and missing commissioned
> Officers and enlisted men of the 15th Regiment
> of Infantry Mo. Vols. Commanded by Colonel
> Joseph Conrad at the battle on Chikamauga [sic] Creek
> Tenn. on the 19th and 20th of Septbr. 1863.

The heading is followed by four pages of almost artistic yet orderly penmanship, names carefully written in a column down the lined paper. The first listed after *Staff* is "Hospital Steward Adolph Schrader." Next to his name is written the word, "missing." Next in the column is "Company A," followed by "Private Frank Wueppermann, missing; Private Henry Mangelsdorf, missing; Private Max Gintner, missing," each succeeding company adding their names: "1st Sergt. Jacob Wagner, Killed; Private George C. Thornburg, Killed; Private William Rieser, Killed; Private Urban Rufeuer,

Killed; Private Christian Frank, Killed." The pages proceed through the ten companies, ending finally with Company K, the last entry, "Private Balthasar Gruenfelder, wounded present." One hundred names on four pages, each page having been carefully removed from a once-bound journal. They rest today in the Missouri state archives in Jefferson City.

In mid-October, the 15th departed the camp at Rossville and returned to Chattanooga. It had been almost a month since the charge down the slope and the battle they now called Chickamauga. Marcoot went to visit a wounded comrade. Gustav Roehm, Company B's first sergeant, was twenty-five years old and unmarried. Born in Thuringen, Germany, Roehm was a shoemaker in St. Louis when he volunteered. Now he lay in an army hospital, far from any place he might call home. A musket ball had shattered his left arm. Left on the field with the other wounded as Longstreet's divisions swept away the brigade, Roehm was taken prisoner. Six days later, the Confederates under a flag of truce returned him with the other severely wounded who were then taken to Chattanooga, where they were placed in the U.S. Army General Hospital.

"I visited him at the hospital," Marcoot wrote, "where he lay pale and emaciated with his shattered arm resting upon an oil cloth. He had laid thus for many long weary days waiting for strength without which he could not withstand the amputation necessary. After a few moments' conversation, for I was greatly affected at his pitiable condition, I asked him if he would answer me one question truly, and readily assenting, I said: 'Suppose you were at home, and in good health, just as you were before this terrible war, and you knew all this would come to you if you enlisted in the service, would you enlist? Looking me squarely in the eye, he responded promptly: 'Yes sir,' and in a whisper he continued, 'I would in a minute.'" Many years later, Marcoot would add, "This was patriotism, as we boys of '61 understood it."[56]

Roehm recovered his strength sufficiently in the opinion of the doctors to undergo the amputation. Not long after, two months to the day after he fell on the field in Georgia, the young shoemaker from Thuringen died.[57]

12

The Buzzards Hold All the Cards

"Be of good cheer," the telegraph from Washington had begun. "We have unabated confidence in you and in your soldiers and officers." The president was not being quite truthful. Within hours of sending the message, Lincoln sat himself down on his secretary's bed, and before the young John Hay had even a chance to rise up, the words spilled forth: "Well, Rosecrans has been whipped, as I feared. I have feared it for several days."[1]

Three weeks later, Grant, then at Cairo, Illinois, received a letter from the general in chief in Washington. It began, "You will receive herewith the orders of the President of the United States placing you in command of the Departments of the Ohio, Cumberland and Tennessee."[2]

Almost from the day the Battle of Chickamauga had ended, the War Department had seen several generals coming and going, the president too occasionally, meeting with Secretary of War Stanton and sometimes other cabinet members. Reinforcements from the Army of the Potomac—the Eleventh and Twelfth corps—had been rushed west to Chattanooga.

Grant knew something was up. A week earlier he had been ordered with his staff to proceed from Vicksburg to Louisville, "for immediate operations in the field." He was to wait there for an officer of the War Department. Now at Indianapolis, his train was about to pull out for Louisville when the secretary of war himself, just off a train from Washington, came aboard. The two sat down, and Stanton began to outline a new organizational structure in the West. In substance, Grant would now command everything this side of the Alleghenies (except for Louisiana). He was then handed two orders. Stanton said he could take his choice: "The two were identical in all but one particular. . . . One left the department commanders as they were, while the other relieved Rosecrans and assigned Thomas to his place. I accepted the latter." Grant was to go immediately to Chattanooga and relieve Rosecrans.[3]

Grant ordered the War Department announcement and the change of command telegraphed at once to Chattanooga. Separately to Thomas, he wired, "Hold Chattanooga at all hazards. I will be there as soon as possible." Grant also asked Thomas how long his supplies would last. Thomas wired back three days later that he had rations to feed the men for five days, with supplies for two days more on the way. He then signed off, "I will hold the town till we starve."[4]

"A retreat would have been a terrible disaster," Grant wrote. "It would not only have been the loss of a most important strategic position to us, but it would have been attended with the loss of all the artillery still left with the Army of the Cumberland and the annihilation of that army itself, either by capture or demoralization."[5]

On October 20, Grant started by train for Chattanooga, reaching Bridgeport, Alabama, two days later. "From here we took horses and made our way" east to Chattanooga. "There had been much rain, and the roads were almost impassable from mud, knee-deep in places." Grant's chief of staff recalled the "valley [as] the muddiest and the mountain road the steepest . . . ever crossed by army wagons and mules." Someone riding over it, he said, "if he hadn't seen it with his own eyes, would not believe it possible" to get over it on horseback. For wagon teams, the feat was even more incredible. At one time, five hundred teams of wagons got hung up on the mountain part, unable to move in any direction.[6]

The experience made an indelible mark on Grant's memory.

The roads were strewn with the debris of broken wagons and the carcasses of thousands of starved mules and horses . . . the country afforded but little food for [the] animals, nearly ten thousand of which had already starved, and not enough were left to draw a single piece of artillery or even the ambulances to convey the sick. The men had been on half rations of hard bread for a considerable time, with but few other supplies except beef driven from Nashville across the country. The region became so exhausted of food for the cattle that by the time they reached Chattanooga they were much in the condition of the few animals left alive. . . . Indeed, the beef was so poor that the soldiers were in the habit of saying, with a faint facetiousness, that they were living on "half rations of hard bread and *beef dried on the hoof.*"

"All supplies had to be brought from Nashville," Grant continued. Bragg's army held the mountains west of Chattanooga, commanding the railroad, the river, and the best wagon roads. All supplies had to be "hauled by a circuitous route north of the river and over a mountainous country, increasing the distance to over sixty miles. . . . Nothing could be transported but food, and the troops were without sufficient shoes or other clothing."[7]

"Luckily for my division," Sheridan wrote, a company of cavalry attached itself to the general's headquarters, which in turn was used "for the purpose of collecting supplies for my troops . . . by paying for everything it took from the people, in a few days was enabled to send me large quantities of corn for my animals and food for the officers and men, which greatly supplemented the scanty supplies we were getting from the sub-depot at Bridgeport. In this way I carried men and animals through our beleaguerment in pretty fair condition, and of the turkeys, chickens, ducks, and eggs sent in for the messes of my officers we often had enough to divide liberally among those at different headquarters."[8]

The men of the 15th Missouri remembered it somewhat differently. First of all, "The rebel cavalry . . . often captured and destroyed [the wagon trains]," Marcoot wrote,

and we were, as a natural consequence, compelled to subsist on less than a quarter of our usual rations. . . . For nearly a whole month we were thus kept on "short" rations and many of our horses and mules actually died of starvation. What little provision we received over three small crackers a day consisted of beef that had been driven from Nashville over a country that furnished them no subsistence. They would be on the "left" [starving] almost from the commencement of their journey until they reached us and we would kill each day only those which we thought would not live until the morrow. The boys used to say that our commander was playing seven up with the buzzards to see which should have the beef, and that the latter held "high, low and jack, and that he was pretty sure of getting the game." Indeed, the beef was so poor that we often called it beef dried on the hoof.

Sheridan and Marcoot could at least agree on the last part.

The men "were also out of shoes, literally barefooted, and almost destitute of clothing with the cold season fast advancing. Fuel also began to be quite an item. There was none within our lines on our side of the river and even the very stumps had disappeared. Expeditions were organized, and as we had no teams to do our hauling we would proceed up the river, cut the trees from the north bank, form them into rafts and float them down to our lines, and carry them into camp on our shoulders.

"When the officers fed their horses[,] usually a pint of shelled corn on the ground [corn fallen to the ground], they were forced to stand by and watch until it was eaten, or the boys would invariably steal it so ravenously hungry were they becoming." "Gloomy times" was how Marcoot summed up the days back in Chattanooga.[9]

The 15th was now holed up in Chattanooga with the rest of the Army of the Cumberland while Bragg's Army of Tennessee took possession of the heights to the south. Bragg's plan was to starve the Union force into submission. "The rebs . . . made a few successful attempts to drive in our pickets," Marcoot wrote, but then

firing ceased, and the brass band of the Rebs and the Yanks would take their positions frequently on their respective picket lines and alternately render their national airs. But the several batteries of artillery on both sides never did evince much friendliness. . . .

During all this time we had been kept hard at work building forts, &c., and our artillery kept up an almost constant fire on the enemy. Shells were frequently thrown to the top of Lookout Mountain. . . . The rebs on the other hand played their artillery upon our lines at the same time but did not succeed in doing us much harm.[10]

Sheridan took special note of that. "It is strange to see how readily soldiers can become accustomed to the sound of dangerous missiles under circumstances of familiarity, and this case was no exception. . . . The shelling from Lookout was kept up, the screeching shots inquisitively asking in their well-known way, 'Where are you? Where are you?' . . . Few casualties occurred, and soon contempt took the place of nervousness, and as we could not reply in kind on account of the elevation required for our guns the men responded by jeers and imprecation whenever a shell fell into their camp."[11]

One can almost see the picture. Men with shovels and axes, in the mud, some digging, others swinging long handles with sharpened iron blades, thunking into the logs and the mud, a drizzle all the while coming down to

lay a cold blanket on all of it. One or two men pause every so often to look
up: a whistle, a screech, then the THUMP-BANG of an incoming iron ball
exploding its black powder, its iron bits whining and whirring in every direction. A curse mocks the disruption. A shiver in the chill, and then a reach for
the handle. Another swing into a log, another shovel into the mud.

Corp. Conrad Herrmann of Company F had come from Baden, Germany. He had been a laborer in St. Louis before volunteering following
the attack on Fort Sumter. Now in Chattanooga, he had taken sick. He
was transported to the hospital in Nashville: chronic diarrhea, the list said.
On October 6, Conrad Herrmann died. His last possessions were listed
as "Knapsack, canteen, wool blanket, haversack, rubber blanket, two wool
shirts, one pr. socks, one pr. wool mittens, one hat, one cap, pr. shoes, port-
folio, one testament, hymn book, one half shelter tent, pocket book, cotton
handkerchief, jack knife." He was twenty-five.[12]

Near the end of the month, soldiers heard cheering down at the mouth
of the valley where the road crossed Raccoon Mountain and went out to
the pontoon bridge. It sounded like the kind of cheering soldiers make
when a popular general comes on the scene. Grant was due to show up
and inspect things, but so far he was only a name. A private was sent down
to find out what the noise was all about. Reaching the landing and finding
men standing all about, he asked, "Has Grant come?" "Grant be damned,"
monotoned one. "A boatload of rations has come."[13]
     Steamboats, with the railroad to follow, had opened what the troops
would call "the cracker line" for the delivery of boxes of the army basic, the
hardtack cracker. Two steamboats—one left behind by Bragg's retreating
army and another built on the banks of the Tennessee, mainly from lum-
ber dismantled from the area's buildings and looking more like a floating
wagon shed—transported the supplies up from Bridgeport, cutting more
than fifty miles off the treacherous trail over the mountain. The arrival
of these two boats, plus a railroad track that was being slowly repaired,
delivering thirty freight cars a day, sometimes more, were beginning to
have an effect. The big problem, though, was getting enough forage for
the mules. Grant reported "the capacity of the railroad and steam-boats
was not sufficient, however, to supply all the wants of the army, but actual
suffering was prevented."[14] Others would disagree.
     Writing his memoirs twenty years later, Grant stuck to his story: a
week after "my arrival in Chattanooga . . . the troops were receiving full
rations."[15] By the general's accounting, that would have meant that the men

were starting to eat regularly during the first week of November. This was not the story Grant would have gotten from the men swinging the shovels and axes, Marcoot wrote, on little more than "three army crackers a day." Or even from the army's quartermaster-general. As late as November 16, Gen. Montgomery C. Meigs, down from Washington to see for himself, could report only modest progress on the supply situation: "Ten days' rations on hand, but animals still suffering and breaking down for want of forage. Capacity of the railroad still under fifty cars per day. Track bad . . . Two steam-boats have enabled us to accumulate rations at Chattanooga and get up a small supply of forage. . . . Our present great difficulty is to procure forage to relieve our starving animals."[16] Without forage to fuel the starving animals, no wagons with rations could be pulled to feed the starving men.

Near the end of November, Marcoot wrote that the 15th Missouri was still in serious straits. On the 19th, the paymaster appeared in camp. But as Marcoot recorded, "We did not have much use for wealth here. We had no means of forwarding it home to be placed to our bank account, and no opportunity of spending it for any good purpose for ourselves, although we were seriously in want."[17]

That day, in Gettysburg, Pennsylvania, the president was dedicating a cemetery there for those who had fallen in the great battle back in July, "for which they gave their last full measure of devotion," he said.

The business of war was too much for some. Desertion once again became the avenue for a way out. Sheridan referred to one case, calling it a "sad incident": "Three men of my division had deserted their colors. . . . They were soon arrested, and were brought back to stand trial for the worst offense that can be committed by a soldier [and] convicted. . . . To make the example effective, I paraded the whole division for the execution, and on the 13th of November, in the presence of their former comrades, the culprits were sent . . . to render their account to the Almighty . . . there could be no evasion, no mitigation of the full letter of the law; its timely enforcement was but justice to the brave spirits who had yet to fight the rebellion to the end."[18]

Marcoot and the 15th remembered the incident as well. "On the 13th of November the whole division was mustered and marched out, forming a huge hollow square, to witness another execution for desertion. These were painful experiences, and on this occasion, two soldier boys, who had thus fallen from grace, one from the 44th and the other from the 88th Illinois, were shot to death."[19]

13

"Chickamauga, God damn you!"

Grant and the Army of the Cumberland never shared a mutual admiration. Marcoot reflected the broadly held suspicion that "Gen. Grant was slow to trust the old Cumberland army, because of the feeling that they had been so badly whipped at Chickamauga, and that the old 11th corps [transferred from the East] had been spoilt at Chancellorsville, and that for his main dependence, he was compelled to fall back upon only the army of [the] Tennessee," his army that took Vicksburg.[1]

Further, Grant did not care much for Rosecrans, a feeling that was mutual, whereas "Ol' Rosy," as the men referred to their former general, had been immensely popular. Even Sheridan may have betrayed a certain amount of affection: "When his departure became known deep and almost universal regret was expressed, for he was enthusiastically esteemed and loved by the Army of the Cumberland, from the day he assumed command of it until he left it."[2] Perhaps those feelings between Grant and now *his* Cumberlanders rubbed both ways. But Grant did nothing to alleviate those feelings; in the days to come, his actions and those of his staff would in fact serve to reinforce them.

It began with a reorganization shortly after he arrived in Chattanooga. The old Twentieth Corps was dissolved into the new Fourth Army Corps, Maj. Gen. Gordon Granger replacing the dismissed Alexander McCook. Sheridan prospered; the number of regiments assigned to his new division more than doubled. Commanding the brigade in which the 15th was assigned with seven other regiments was Col. Francis T. Sherman, formerly commander of the 88th Illinois.

Colonel Laiboldt was one of those losing out in the shuffle. A new "demi-brigade" classification was added to the organization, "an awkward invention of Granger's," Sheridan said, "but at this time it was necessitated—perhaps by the depleted condition of our regiments." For all intents, the demi-brigade was little more than a full regiment made up of two battle-thinned regiments. Instead of continuing in command of a brigade of four regiments, Laiboldt now commanded only two, and those little more than half their mustering-in size. He now commanded the demi-brigade of the 2d and 15th Missouri, little more than shadows of themselves from their original complement. He also reported to new brigade commander Francis T. Sherman (no relation to William Tecumseh) instead of directly to Sheridan.

In his new command, Grant soon saw he was hung up on the proverbial horns. He could not attack the Confederates up on Missionary Ridge, and he could not retreat. He and his army were stuck below in Chattanooga. "The artillery horses and mules had become so reduced by starvation," Grant concluded, "that they could not have been relied on for moving anything." If an attempt at retreat were to be made, it would have to be with the men alone, with only the supplies each man could carry on his back. But, "A retreat would have been almost certain annihilation, for the enemy, occupying positions within gunshot of and overlooking our very fortifications, would unquestionably have pursued our retreating forces."[3] All those things considered, Grant dispatched William Tecumseh Sherman at Vicksburg to hurry his corps to Chattanooga.

Shortly after taking possession of the heights above Chattanooga, Bragg sent Longstreet and his corps down into Lookout Valley. The move blocked boat traffic, forcing Union wagon trains to traverse the sixty-mile horror over the mountain to supply the troops entrenched around the city. To break the hold, Grant approved a plan developed by Gen. William "Baldy" Smith, his chief of engineers. It called for troops to converge from three directions on the Confederates at Brown's Ferry. One brigade would have to float downstream on pontoon boats under cover of darkness. In the early morning of October 27, the Federals surprised a small rebel contingent and took control. Two days later, Longstreet counterattacked shortly after midnight, one of the few night battles of the war, but a brigade of Brig. Gen. Adolph von Steinwehr's division of the Eleventh Corps, troops known "for their want of steadiness," Longstreet had said contemptuously, struck the Southerners in a wild bayonet charge in the dark and broke up the Rebel

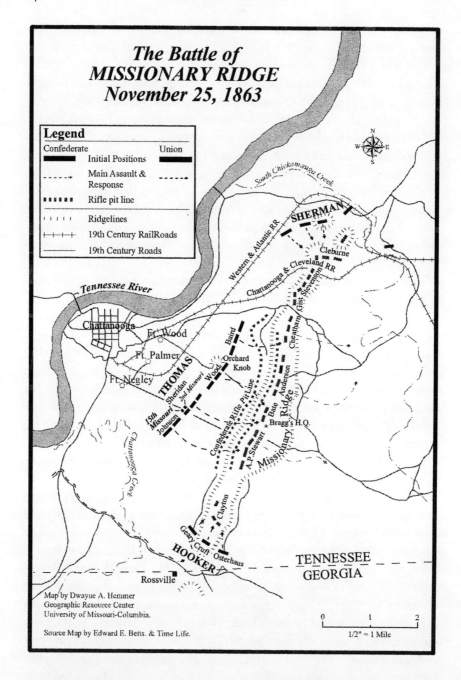

The Battle of
MISSIONARY RIDGE
November 25, 1863

Legend

Confederate	Union
Initial Positions	
Main Assault & Response	
Rifle pit line	
Ridgelines	
19th Century RailRoads	
19th Century Roads	

Map by Dwayne A. Hemmer
Geographic Resource Center
University of Missouri-Columbia.

Source Map by Edward E. Betts. & Time Life.

0   1   2
1/2" = 1 Mile

attack. Before daybreak, Longstreet and his men withdrew back up Lookout Mountain, leaving the river crossing at Moccasin Point in Grant's hands and allowing the German brigade to reopen the "cracker line."[4]

By the end of October, no one—not Grant or anyone else—expected or even thought of an attack by Bragg's army. "Missionary Ridge, summit, side, and base, was furrowed with [Confederate] rifle-pits and studded with batteries," wrote Brig. Gen. Joseph S. Fullerton of Maj. Gen. Gordon Granger's staff.

> Lookout Mountain, now a mighty fortress, lifted to the low hanging clouds its threatening head crowned with siege-guns. The two lines of pickets were not more than three hundred yards apart; but, by common consent, there was no picket firing. On a still night, standing on the picket line, one could hear the old negro song "Dixie," adopted by the Confederates as their national music; while from our line came, in swelling response, "Hail Columbia" and "The Star-spangled Banner." With a glass [telescope] Bragg's headquarters on Missionary Ridge, even the movement of his officers and orderlies, could be seen; while from the ridge or Lookout Mountain our whole camp was clearly in view. By daylight our troops could be counted, our reveille heard, our roll-call noted, our scanty meals of half rations seen . . . .
>
> The fall rains were beginning, and hauling was becoming each day more difficult. Ten thousand dead mules walled the sides of the road from Bridgeport to Chattanooga . . . the men were on less than half rations. Guards stood at the troughs of artillery horses to keep the soldiers from taking the scant supply of corn allowed these starving animals. . . . They followed the wagons as they came over the river, picking up the grains of corn and bits of crackers that fell to the ground.[5]

Grant had no plan for breaking out of Chattanooga. His ongoing priority was to rebuild his wagon and rail systems, and that was coming hard. Then, on November 8, a messenger with a Confederate deserter in tow arrived at Maj. Gen. O. O. Howard's Eleventh Corps headquarters: Longstreet had moved north past Grant two nights before, marching for Knoxville a hundred miles to the northeast.[6]

Longstreet was preparing to attack the Union force under Maj. Gen. Ambrose Burnside. It was general knowledge that Lincoln had a particular fondness for holding that part of the state. In spite of secession, most in eastern Tennessee had remained loyal to the Union. The president even held to a hope that eastern Tennessee might yet secede from the Confederacy through elections and return to the Union.[7] The harder reality was logistical and military; vital railroads ran through Knoxville into Confederate Virginia. Knoxville therefore was vital for strategic reasons: if Burnside

A wartime view of Missionary Ridge after the battle. Sheridan's division formed in this area for the assault that would be known as "the charge without orders." Though starting in the last column of Sheridan's twenty-six regiments, the 15th Missouri was one of the first into the Confederate trenches atop the ridge. (Library of Congress)

gave way, East Tennessee would be lost. Grant would have to turn and fight, or maybe even retreat all the way back to Nashville.

The move forced Grant's hand. To take the pressure off Burnside, Grant, "feeling strongly the necessity of some move that would compel [Bragg] to retain all his forces and recall those he had detached, directions were given for a movement against Missionary Ridge, with a view to carrying it, and threatening the enemy's communication with Longstreet . . . however, it was deemed utterly impracticable to make the move until Sherman could get up."[8]

On November 15, General Sherman reached Chattanooga ahead of his troops. General Grant's plan, in brief, was to turn Bragg's right. He selected his old army, the Army of the Tennessee, now under Sherman, to open the battle, make the grand attack, and carry Missionary Ridge as far as Tunnel Hill (the railroad between Knoxville and northern Georgia, cutting off Longstreet from Bragg).[9]

Three days later, Grant issued an order to Maj. Gen. George Thomas and the Army of the Cumberland: "All preparations should be made for attacking the enemy's position on Missionary Ridge by Saturday at daylight. . . . The general plan, you understand, is for Sherman, with the force brought with him, strengthened by a division from your command . . . to secure the heights from the northern extremity to about the railroad tunnel before the enemy can concentrate against him. You will co-operate with Sherman." The division to support Sherman "should show itself as threateningly as possible on the most practicable line for making an attack up the valley. Your effort then will be to form a junction with Sherman, making your advance well toward the northern end of Missionary Ridge, and moving as near simultaneously with [Sherman] as possible."[10]

In other words, Grant was calculating that Sherman would be able to take control of the north end of the ridge, where the railroad tunnel was, because Bragg would hesitate to move quickly enough against Sherman on his right. Grant figured Bragg would hesitate, for down in the valley, the Confederate would see the Army of the Cumberland marshalling for a possible attack on his front. By the time Bragg might decide to attack Sherman, the latter would have taken the northern point of the ridge. Thomas then was to move to the left—not up the ridge to his front. Grant apparently was thinking that Thomas would then face a reduced number of the opposition in moving up the ridge closer to Sherman, because Bragg would be occupied with the larger threat from Sherman.

To succeed, a good number of assumptions would have to fall into place, not the least of which was Grant being able to second-guess his adversary at several key moments. Further, for Thomas to effectively "cooperate" or support Sherman, communications would have to be precise, even though Sherman at the time of his attack would be at least four miles away. That would be a healthy distance for couriers to dash between in order to coordinate the assaults, assaults that were to be "as near simultaneously as possible," Grant said.[11] As far as Thomas was concerned, about all he could do was get his army into position and then wait.

Late on the night of November 22, a Confederate picket who had deserted was brought to General Sheridan. The deserter said that Bragg was about to fall back. When the information was passed to Grant, he ordered Thomas to throw one division forward in the direction of Orchard Knob to find out if the Rebels were still nearby.

"Orchard Knob is a rough, steep hill," wrote Brig. Gen. Joseph Fullerton, Granger's assistant adjutant general, "one hundred feet high, covered with a growth of small timber, rising abruptly from the Chattanooga Valley." Rebel rifle pits extended for a mile on both the north and south sides of the hill, hidden in part by a heavy belt of timber that covered about a quarter mile from the foot of the hill into the plain. "Between this belt of timber and our lines were open fields . . . not a tree, fence, or other obstruction, save the bed of the East Tennessee Railroad. On the plain were hundreds of little mounds, thrown up by our and the enemy's pickets, giving it the appearance of an overgrown prairie-dog village."

At noon on the 23d, Grant, with major generals Thomas, Granger, Howard, and Hooker, and Assistant Secretary of War Dana, stood on a parapet facing Orchard Knob. Thirty minutes later, "Wood's division, supported by Sheridan, marched out on the plain in front," Fullerton reported.

> Flags were flying; the quick, earnest steps of thousands beat equal time. The sharp commands of hundreds of company officers, the sound of the drums, the ringing notes of the bugle, companies wheeling and counter-marching and regiments getting into line, the bright sun lighting up ten thousand polished bayonets till they glistened and flashed like a flying shower of electric sparks,—all looked like preparations for a peaceful pageant, rather than for the bloody work of death. . . .
>
> [The] enemy's pickets, but a few hundred yards away, came out of their pits and stood idly looking on, unconcernedly viewing what they supposed to be preparations for a grand review . . . the advance was sounded." Wood's division started forward. "Not a straggler or laggard was on the field . . . drummers were marching with their companies, beating the charge. Now the enemy realized, for the first time, that it was not a review. His pickets fell back to their reserves. . . . Firing opened from the enemy's advanced rifle-pits, followed by a tremendous roll of musketry and roar of artillery. Men were seen on the ground, dotting the field over which the line of battle had passed. Ambulances came hurrying back with the first of the wounded. Columns of puffy smoke arose from the Orchard Knob woods. A cheer, faint . . . indicated that the boys in blue were carrying the breastworks on the Knob! A sharp, short struggle, and the hill was ours.[12]

The 15th Missouri marched out onto the field about 2:00 P.M. and took position on Bushy Knob to the right, all the while driving the enemy's picket line before them. After Orchard Knob was taken, the division moved closer to Wood's division, "taking up a line where I remained inactive," Sheridan said, "but suffering some inconvenience from the enemy's shells."[13] Here, about two miles from the base of the ridge, the men bedded down for the night.

The next morning there was silence over on the right near Lookout Mountain. But the Stars and Stripes could be seen flying at its crest— before daylight eight adventurers of Hooker's men in the 8th Kentucky had scaled the palisades and run up the flag. "The enemy had stolen away in the night."[14] Early in the afternoon, blue-coated formations, their regimental flags whipping in the breeze, could be seen rounding the front of the mountain, the roar of battle echoing in the plain below.

Capt. Johann Osterhorn of the 31st Missouri, a German regiment from St. Louis, took part in the charge on Lookout Mountain. "None of us expected that happy result. We saw the rebels,—so many and so small, like ants swarming on the mountain and also at the top of the mountain. We marched forth, stormed, and took, the rock mountain. The first victory was ours, and indeed none of us hoped,—each of us believed that it would end up being our grave.—before we reached the top of the mountain."[15]

The men in the 15th Missouri below would remember "the famous Battle Above The Clouds: As our division was not engaged at this time we had a splendid view," Marcoot wrote.

> It was a magnificent sight and was observed with breathless interest by all. Not infrequently during the progress a low flying cloud would appear and screen the scene like a veil, completely hiding the combatants from our sight. Then again we could observe our lines advance step by step from rock to rock. Once we plainly saw a squad of "Johnnies" with their stars and bars above them perched upon a huge flat elevated rock, while a little below were likewise situated a squad of our boys in blue, with the star spangled banner floating above them. It was an exciting encounter as each tried to probe the other with their bayonets and thus dislodge them. But they could not. It was an exciting scene but the efforts of "our boys" failed as did the efforts of the "Johnnies" in every instance until the latter, not observing the forward movements of our scattered line which had passed them on the right and left had been cut off from their comrades. Retreat was now impossible, they were surrounded and thus forced to surrender. As the climax of this little incident came we could see the hats of our boys fly in the air and could almost persuade ourselves that we heard their hearty hurrahs. It was a memorable scene to us all and one never to be forgotten.[16]

Meanwhile on the left, Grant had been informed that Sherman had gained the top of Missionary Ridge at the north end. The report would turn out to be erroneous; Sherman had made it to the top all right "with only slight skirmishing," but he was not where he thought he was—because of a faulty job of reconnaissance, he learned he was still one hill away from the mount of Missionary Ridge. Nevertheless, with the information in hand, Grant figured all was in readiness to spring the final assault on the summit. At midnight he began issuing the orders. To Sherman went the order "to advance as soon as it is light in the morning." To Thomas, "your attack, which will be simultaneous . . . in co-operation. . . . Your command will either carry the rifle-pits and ridge directly in front of them or move to the left, as the presence of the enemy may require."[17]

Thomas never acknowledged the order. He ignored it in his official report. Did he receive it? If he did, he apparently failed to relay the order to at least one of his corps commanders. So began a series of confusions and contradictions that Grant and his generals would have to deal with on the crucial day ahead.

Early in the morning of November 25, Grant and Thomas, with their staffs, took position on Orchard Knob. The morning "opened clear and bright," Grant wrote, "and the whole field was in full view. . . . Bragg's headquarters [at the top of the ridge, directly in front a mile and a half away] were in full view, and officers—presumably staff officers—could be seen coming and going constantly."

"Sherman was directed to attack at daylight," Grant wrote. "Hooker was ordered to move at the same hour. . . . Thomas was *not to move*, until Hooker had reached Missionary Ridge" (emphasis mine).[18]

Here was the first contradiction. Fewer than twelve hours earlier, Grant had ordered Thomas to attack simultaneously with Sherman. The order made no mention of waiting on Hooker to reach the ridge. Further, "As I was with [Thomas] on Orchard Knob," Grant said, "he would not move without further orders from me."[19]

At sunrise, General Sherman began his attack on Tunnel Hill at the north end of Missionary Ridge. Hours passed. On the plain below, Grant with his generals on Orchard Knob continued to wait, the Army of the Cumberland in broad battle lines stretching before them, motionless, the glare of the midmorning sun now full in their faces. The din of battle four or five miles off to the left was the dominant sound, and the only one that mattered.

At noon, Sheridan's division was moved forward some three hundred yards. Francis Sherman's brigade was ordered to the right and to re-form into four lines of battle. Into the first line filed the 44th, 36th, and 73d Illinois. The 88th Illinois and 24th Wisconsin joined to form the second line. The third was the 22d Indiana. Into the fourth went the 2d and 15th Missouri with the 74th Illinois, Colonel Laiboldt commanding this demi-brigade making up the last line. With a front of three regiments, close to fifteen hundred men, the brigade presented a force a half-mile wide, forming the right wing of Sheridan's division of three brigades, six thousand men all told.

Into the afternoon, the men waited. By this time they had been allowed to get off their feet and rest in whatever way they chose. Some lay down and dozed, others simply sat, thoughts probably of places far away. Still others, "while thus waiting in line with our muskets stacked . . . groups of boys could be seen gambling formed as they lay in line, along the entire length." Gambling, Marcoot recalled, had become "frightfully frequent, and cards and dice held full sway."[20]

Miles to the left, assault followed assault throughout the morning, but Sherman's Army of the Tennessee had made little headway. The Confederate division under Gen. Patrick Cleburne continued to hold the works on the hill. By midafternoon, all hope of meeting the objective faded, and further attacks were called to a halt.

Meanwhile, Hooker, with the Eleventh and Twelfth corps, on the south flank had fought his way to the southern end of the ridge but too late and, six miles away, too far to take pressure off of Sherman's men. With the twilight of the late November day coming on, all operations ceased. "Bragg's right had not been turned. Success had not followed Sherman's movement," Fullerton wrote. "The battle as planned had not been won."[21]

On Orchard Knob, Grant was off to himself, others of his staff standing about nearby. "It was now past 3 o'clock," Granger's adjutant noted. "The day was dying, and Bragg still held the ridge. If any movement to dislodge him was to be made that day, it must be made at once. At half-past three o'clock an attack was ordered by General Grant." Grant himself wrote, "I now directed Thomas to order the charge at once."[22]

Grant's generals later would not agree on what exactly the man himself had ordered them to do. Grant wrote in his official report that Thomas was to "carry the rifle-pits at the foot of Missionary Ridge, and when carried to reform his lines on the rifle-pits with a view *to carrying the top of the ridge*" (emphasis mine).[23]

That is not how the generals on Orchard Knob remembered it. Charles A. Dana, assistant secretary of war, was on the knob with Grant, Thomas, Granger, and the others. Dana was a newspaperman and former managing editor of Horace Greeley's *New York Tribune*. He had been given his appointment to keep an eye on the army in the West and to keep Secretary of War Stanton informed. For a journalist, Dana's dispatches back to Washington occasionally contained surprising inaccuracies, with observations peppered from time to time with more conjecture than fact.

Even so, Dana claimed that "Grant gave orders at 2 P.M. for an assault upon [the Confederate] lines in front of Thomas"—nothing about assaulting the ridge—"but owing to the fault of Granger, who devoted himself to firing a battery instead of commanding his corps [an observation supported by others], Grant's order was not transmitted to the division commanders until he repeated it an hour later."[24] Did Grant bypass Thomas, as Dana implies, and give the order directly to Granger, one of Thomas's corps commanders, thereby violating the inviolable chain of command?

It may explain why Thomas made no mention of an assault order of any kind in his official report. In fact, but for a reference to an order he received from Grant two days earlier, Thomas makes no reference in his report to Grant whatsoever. The Rock of Chickamauga would remain forever silent on what actually took place that afternoon on Orchard Knob. Whatever took place, the assault's objective from Grant's order was not clear to Thomas's corps commanders.[25]

In outlining his plan a week earlier, Grant had directed Thomas "to cooperate with Sherman . . . with one division [to] show itself . . . for making an attack *up the valley*" (emphasis mine).[26] There is nothing in Grant's order on November 18 about attacking *up the ridge*, an order that officers at the time would likely have considered suicidal.

The advance was to be made at a signal of the firing of six cannons, one shot after another. Ahead of Sheridan's front was a heavy line of skirmishers. On the right, Francis Sherman's brigade was posted, the 15th Missouri in the last line. The center of the division was opposite Bragg's headquarters on the summit of Missionary Ridge. At the foot of the ridge was the enemy's first line of rifle pits; midway up its face, there was another line; on the crest was a third, where Bragg had massed his artillery.

"The enemy saw we were making dispositions for an attack," Sheridan wrote, "and in plain view of my whole division he prepared himself for resistance, marching regiments from his left flank with flying colors, and filling up the spaces not already occupied in his intrenchments [*sic*]. . . . It was plain that we would have to act quickly if we expected to accomplish much, and I already began to doubt the feasibility of our remaining in the first line of rifle-pits [if we] carried them."[27]

Sheridan was not clear on what his orders were, and he discussed the situation with his three brigade commanders. They concurred on the predicament they could be getting into, "so while anxiously awaiting the signal I sent Captain Ransom of my staff to Granger . . . to ascertain if we were to carry the first line or the ridge beyond." At 3:40 P.M., the signal guns were fired. "I told my brigade commanders to go for the ridge." At least that is what Sheridan claimed.[28]

Grant made no provision for what was to happen after the rifle pits at the base of the ridge had been taken. The clear, tactical reality was that men left there, motionless, out in the open and in clear view of Bragg and his Confederates, would be sitting ducks, to be shelled from above with every ordinance of iron the Confederate troops had available. That Thomas or his corps commanders did not ask for some kind of clarification seems equally incredible. Perhaps bad feelings that had been festering against Grant blocked any impulse to try to communicate with the commanding general.

The booming of the six signal cannons was a moment that Marcoot would not forget. "The orders came at last, and we were commanded to move forward." Colonel Conrad moved to the head of the regiment. Second in command, in place of the injured Weber who had been left behind to recover from the near crushing by his horse, was Capt. Samuel Rexinger, the young officer originally from Georgia and more recently from St. Joseph, Missouri, who two years earlier had been charged for running a poker game and selling liquor to the men. With Conrad in the lead and the enterprising Rexinger close behind, the 15th stepped out. "We marched at common time through the woods," Marcoot wrote,

> until we reached the edge of the plain, when double-quick was ordered. . . .
>
> The distance from Orchard Knob, where our corps had formed, to the foot of Mission Ridge was one and a half miles, interspersed with small strips of timber, through an open but rough valley, every foot of the route of which was well guarded by the enemy. And when we finally reached the foot of the ridge, what then?
>
> A strong line of works was well manned by the enemy [Marcoot is referring to the entrenchments further up the ridge, about halfway up]. If we succeeded in taking that line of works, capturing the forces or putting them to flight, what then? A hill fully four hundred feet high, the crest of which was similarly protected and likewise strongly manned, from which they could pour forth such a shower of grape, canister and musketry that it would prove exceedingly difficult for us even to hold the first. But if we should be successful in also capturing the second, what then?
>
> Another, a third, some four hundred feet further up the mountain was in perfect readiness to make our reception highly interesting. Between the second and third line of fortifications the mountainside was broken, and further possessed many huge rocks. Large trees had also been felled so as to obstruct rapid passage and an advancing army would be thus compelled to move slowly amid most deadly fire. But passing the third successfully and thence up to the very top of Mission Ridge itself, what then? The main army itself would have to be encountered. The outlook surely was not an inviting one.

"All this and more was in plain view before us," Marcoot said, "when the command 'forward' was given, and even the most bold and careless of our number could not help but feel the gravity of our situation."[29]

Sheridan, mounted on his black charger, took his place in the center, in front of the middle brigade (Harker's), between his men in long lines of battle behind him and the skirmishers up ahead. Leveling his sword toward the ridge ahead, accompanied by only an orderly so as not to attract the enemy's fire any more than necessary, Sheridan and his division of six thousand moved forward.

A mile back, on Orchard Knob, Grant and his generals watched. They saw a panorama of four divisions of twenty thousand men, with more than a mile to go, advancing four lines deep across a front two miles wide, a double line of skirmishers out front, giant siege guns in the Chattanooga forts in support from behind, roaring above the light artillery and musketry in the valley.[30]

A young Confederate from Florida looked down from Breckinridge's division lining the top of the ridge. What he saw looked to him like a magnificent dress parade. Most of their own uniforms had long worn out, he and the men around him wearing a motley combination of clothing, some of it taken off dead and wounded Northerners at Chickamauga. It all made for a double impression on those watching the scene below: "The officers, all superbly dressed, pranced out on their high-mettled chargers; the bands played, and to the music came the most wonderful array of splendidly equipped soldiers I ever saw. The old flag waved beautifully at the head of each regiment and the smaller flags were in their places with the brigade and division commanders."[31]

The long blue lines had a mile to go to reach the foot of the mountain where, Granger's adjutant recalled, "The enemy's rifle-pits were ablaze, and the whole ridge in our front had broken out like another Aetna."[32]

"Under a terrible storm of shot and shell," Sheridan reported, his lines "pressed forward steadily through the timber, and as [they] emerged on the plain took the double-quick and with fixed bayonets rushed at the enemy's first line. Not a shot was fired from our line of battle and as it gained on my skirmishers they melted into and became one with it, and all three of my brigades went over the rifle-pits simultaneously."[33]

Brigadier General Fullerton had a good view of it all. "The distance to the foot of Mission Ridge [was] made in about thirty minutes, and not a single soldier wavered, while we left many dead and wounded in our trail. . . . By a bold and desperate push they broke through the works in several places and opened flank and reverse fires. The enemy was thrown into confusion, and took precipitate flight up the ridge."[34]

Sheridan's men "then lay down on the face of the ridge, for a breathing-spell and for protection from the terrible fire of canister and musketry pouring over us. . . . There had been little use for the bayonet," Sheridan said, "for most of the Confederate troops, disconcerted by the sudden rush, lay close in the ditch and surrendered, though some few fled up the slope to the next line. The prisoners were directed to move out to our rear, and as their intrenchments had now come under fire from the crest, they went with alacrity, and without guard or escort, toward Chattanooga."[35]

After a pause, "to get breath" and to "drive out a few skulkers who were hiding" in the trenches, as Sheridan described it, "I was joined by Captain Ransom, who having returned from Granger, told me that we were to carry only the line at the base and that . . . [Ransom] in his capacity as an aide-de-camp had directed Wagner [Sheridan's brigade on the left], who was up on the face of the ridge, to return, and that in consequence Wagner was recalling his men to the base."[36] That decision was to have tragic consequences. Who on Orchard Knob had ordered the lines to stop at the first line of rifle pits, and who was now ordering the recall? None of the generals on that hill ever laid claim to either.

It likely was not Thomas, who, with Grant taking command, was remaining his silent self. It is doubtful that the order came from the corps commander; Sheridan's aide reported on his return that Granger had suggested that the ridge be taken if deemed possible. Orders coming off the knob that afternoon were coming from only one general, and that certainly was not Granger.

As soon as Grant saw the first movement out of the rifle pits, the men now heading up the ridge, he, according to Granger's adjutant, "quickly turned to Thomas . . . I heard him say angrily: 'Thomas, who ordered those men up the ridge?'" Thomas replied in his usual slow manner: "'I don't know; I did not.'" Thomas then turned to Granger: "'Did you order them up, Granger?' 'No, they started up without orders. When those fellows get started all hell can't stop them.' General Grant said something to the effect that somebody would suffer if it did not turn out well, and then, turning, stoically watched the ridge. He gave no further orders.[37]

Granger, possibly feeling heat radiating from Grant, the cigar now clamped tightly in his teeth, turned to the aide, and maybe in a voice meant for Grant to hear, ordered, "Ride at once to Wood [the division in the center], and then to Sheridan, and ask them if they ordered their men up the ridge." Then Granger, the general who had marched with his corps to the sound of the guns to aid Thomas at Chickamauga, said in a lower voice, "Tell them, if they can take it, to push ahead.'"[38]

History will never know for certain who issued the orders. It was all academic anyway. Most men had already started up. Once they had taken the first line of rifle pits, what then? Marcoot had asked.

A mile off, Sheridan overruled whatever communication there was to stop at the base. "I could not bear to order the recall of troops now so gallantly climbing the hill step by step, and believing we could take it, I immediately rode to Wagner's brigade and directed it to resume the attack." Wagner's men "again advanced under a terrific fire."[39]

But not before the brigade had started to withdraw down the hill. With Sheridan's order to turn around and start back up the ridge, Wagner's men had to fight their way back, over the old ground where the Confederate fire was the most killing. In the process, Wagner probably lost most of the four hundred he would lose in the assault all together.

By the time Sheridan rode back toward the right of his line, the men in Francis Sherman's brigade were already on their way up. The orderly riding along behind Sheridan recorded the picture: "The troops having rested, started to climb the steep sides of the ridge. An aide having been sent to Genl. Granger for further orders, came back with a suggestion that the troops be recalled if it was judged expedient." It was too late for that. "By this time they were half way up the ridge. Every regiment had lost its organization, and were all massed in a sort of triangle with the point upwards. About every flag of our division was struggling to reach the top first, every man for himself. Now and then a flag would fall, its bearer being shot, but it appeared in an instant held by the next soldier. The General said, 'Let them go, they will be over in five minutes.'"[40]

The 15th Missouri, having reached the entrenchments at the foot of the ridge, paused, and then began to make their way up. "Here our line became broken on account of the obstacles," Captain Rexinger reported, "and we struggled up the hill as best we could under such a fire, each man for himself, our officers taking the lead." Rexinger made no mention in his official report of being ordered up the ridge.[41]

Watching the Missourians come up the mountain, Charles Hemming, the young Confederate who earlier had thought he was watching the start of a dress parade, lay waiting with the others as the 15th and the rest of Sherman's brigade approached. "We did not fire a gun until they got within two hundred yards. . . . When the order was given to fire, it seemed to us that hundreds fell, and at first their line wavered, but brave officers held them to the work and, cheering wildly, they came at us again."[42]

The brigade was now approaching the line of works midway up the ridge. Pvt. William Willie, the 15th's eighteen-year-old bugler from St. Louis, led the way for the Missourians, "continually in front sounding his bugle to advance." Right behind were the regiment's color-bearer, Sgt. Michael Kicke, an "unruly but brave lad" from Trenton, Missouri; St. Louisan Ulrich Frei, a thirty-two-year-old corporal, one of the color guard; 1st Sgt. John Droste of St. Charles; and Sgt. Henry Frillman of Hermann, Missouri—all would be cited for bravery and gallantry in going up the ridge. "In our ascent," Rexinger reported, the Confederates "charged their cannon with double shot and canister and bags of bullets . . . but for the shelter afforded by stumps and logs," would have "swept away every man from the hill."[43]

A captain in the 36th Illinois recalled that this part of the climb "was our hardest time; we had to pass a more exposed point. From tree to tree, from stump to stump, and from log to log, we went until we came to a point where the slope was greater, the ascent steeper, perhaps about forty degrees elevation." They were within reach of the second line of rifle pits, and the Confederates, seeing them coming, abandoned the works.[44]

"The second line of fortifications," Marcoot recorded, "[was] soon in our possession. We were now almost completely fagged out from our exertions and were compelled to take a short rest. . . . We were truly a sad lot of half starved Yankees . . . we were fighting now for our 'cracker line,' almost our very life itself."[45]

Perhaps it was about this time—the record is uncertain—that Captain Avery from Granger's staff on Orchard Knob caught up with Sheridan with the message he was ordered to deliver: Sir, I am instructed to ask who ordered the men to charge up the ridge. It was of course much too late for that—Sheridan's men had made the decision long before any of the generals back on the knob had even thought of the question. "I didn't order them up," Sheridan purportedly replied, "but we are going to take the ridge!"[46] They were now looking up at the toughest part of the ridge. The steepest incline to the top began here, with about another hundred yards to the crest, and all of it up.

After reorganizing their line, the 15th again began "struggling forward and upward. . . . Huge rock boulders were loosened," Marcoot remembered, "and rolled down upon us amid most incessant musket firing, while shells with lighted fuses were bounding in every direction in and about our lines." Bragg's men at the top, realizing that their cannon barrels could not be depressed far enough to fire into the advancing line, chose instead to light fuses and toss the lighted cannon balls down the mountain side. "It was an awful moment," Marcoot wrote, "enough to try the stronger hearts, but the boys were equal to the effort and continued manfully forward and upward, closing up the ranks as their comrades one after another fell."[47] As the blue wave drew closer, a man in the 36th Illinois recalled that the Rebels "defending the heights grew more and more desperate. . . . They shouted 'Chickamauga' as though the word itself were a weapon."[48]

Many regiments in that two-mile-wide charge years later would claim that they were the first into the trenches atop the ridge. From Orchard Knob a mile away, Granger's assistant adjutant general, with a clear view through his field glasses, counted the regimental flags closing in—six, nine, eleven, twelve flags were at the summit. The critical moment had arrived—"At six different points, and almost simultaneously, Sheridan's and Woods' divisions broke over the crest, Sheridan's first, near Bragg's headquarters."[49]

Coming in just in front of Bragg's headquarters were the 15th Missouri with their German comrades of the 2d Missouri. In line to their left were the 36th Illinois and the "preachers" of the 73d Illinois.[50] Confederate infantry in their front picked themselves up and turned to run, others scrambling out of trenches, a mass of gray flotsam now making a mad dash to the rear, the Northerners after them with cries that had taunted them earlier—"Chickamauga! Chickamauga!" Veterans of the 15th long after remembered: "At the top of the Ridge the fight was awful, fierce, desperate."[51]

A nineteen-year-old private from Ohio in Woods's division probably epitomized the temper of the Yanks; when a Mississippi captain refused to move after surrendering, the young Ohioan screamed "Chickamauga, God damn you!" spun the Southerner around, and proceeded to kick him down the hill. Others, trying to get away, were shot down in the back. "I saw many a poor fellow bayoneted, but it was all fair play."[52]

Union color-bearers vied for the honor of planting their regiments' flags atop the trenches. Some paid for it with their lives. A sergeant in the 74th Illinois, originally in line with the 15th Missouri, was hit twenty feet from the crest, a corporal seizing the staff just before he himself was killed, a private then snatching the falling flag before it hit the ground and finally jamming the staff into the breastwork. A moment later, Sgt. Michael Kick planted the colors of the 15th Missouri into the same works.[53]

The 24th Wisconsin, a regiment that started out two lines ahead of the 15th Missouri but now finishing behind the Missourians in the race to the crest, had seen their color-bearer shot before getting halfway up the slope, the next man taking the flag bayoneted in the Confederate trenches midway up, and the third decapitated by a shell. The eighteen-year-old adjutant, Lt. Arthur MacArthur Jr., supposedly grabbed the flagstaff, shouting "On Wisconsin," took the colors from there. As his son, Gen. Douglas MacArthur, was fond of boasting, Sheridan saw the whole thing, dismounted and embraced his father, telling troops nearby, "Take care of him. He has just won the Medal of Honor."

It likely did not happen that way; only enlisted men were awarded the medal during the course of the war. MacArthur did get his medal, but it took twenty-seven years after the event to get it, political connections probably having no small part. As one historian wrote, "MacArthur's act was no more intrepid than that of the dozens of long-forgotten soldiers who lost their lives carrying their unit colors to the crest."[54]

For the 15th Missouri, Captain Rexinger simply wrote, "Our colors were the second ones inside of the intrenchments at the summit of the hill."[55]

From Sheridan's vantage point, Sherman's brigade of Illinois and Missouri regiments, with the lone Wisconsin unit in trail, along with some of Harker's Ohioans, had indeed gotten to the top first. "The right and right centre gained the summit first," the general himself said—he being among the first of the generals on the crest to see it all.[56]

But for the intercession of Col. Joseph Conrad of the 15th Missouri there at the top, Sheridan might have become a dead general. "When I crossed the rifle-pits on the top, the Confederates were still holding fast at Bragg's headquarters and a battery located there opened fire along the crest, making things most uncomfortably hot. Seeing the danger to which I was exposed, for I was mounted, Colonel Joseph Conrad, of the Fifteenth Missouri, ran up and begged me to dismount. I accepted his excellent advice, and it probably saved my life, but poor Conrad was punished for his solicitude by being seriously wounded in the thigh at the moment he was contributing to my safety."[57] Conrad was sent to the rear, and "I took command," Rexinger reported, "and formed in line of battle at the summit of the hill."[58]

"After a short sharp struggle," Marcoot wrote, "the Ridge was ours and we had the exultant pleasure of witnessing Gen. Bragg, together with Generals Breckinridge and Buckner, spurring their horse . . . down the eastern slope of the Ridge, in their haste to prevent their capture." Sheridan's orderly remembered an "old log hut standing just to the left where our division went over. It was occupied by Genl. Bragg and his staff. They had barely time to mount and ride away. Some of the rebel guns were turned upon their retreating ranks and shots sent after them."[59]

With the enemy now in flight down the other side of the ridge, men stopped to rest and catch their breath. Exhaustion soon gave way to exhilaration—they had beaten the mountain, and the Rebels, and through it all, they were still alive. Cheer after cheer rose through the brigade and rippled along the summit.

The thought of food then came to mind. "We were after something to eat," said a sergeant in the 24th Wisconsin, "and we got it too. The first thing I did after the rebels skedaddled was to grab a full haversack and jerk it off a wounded rebel captain's neck. He was shot in the shoulder and his hand lay on the mouth of the haversack on the down-hill side. I opened it and divided its contents with my comrades in the immediate vicinity. It was saturated with the rebel captain's blood, but we ate it all the same."[60]

Hunger appeased, a thirst for vengeance took over. A captain in the 36th Illinois noticed a private with a bayonet prodding a Confederate captain from behind a log. The Southerner was hopping from side to side to dodge the thrusts, all the while snapping, "Call an officer!" "I'm officer enough for you," barked the private, "surrender, or I will put the bayonet through you." His company captain intervened. The Rebel bristled, "You Yankees are rough on prisoners." To that the Union officer shot back, "The soldier should have bayoneted you." "Why, sir, what do you mean, I have had prisoners in my charge and never treated them in this way." "Then take off that overcoat you have stripped from some of our shivering, wounded comrades on Chickamauga."[61]

Others continued the pursuit after the fleeing Confederates. "With Hurrah," the German captain of the 31st Missouri wrote, "we pursued them until their flight got entangled in a fearful crowd,—their guns being brought through,—blocked one another on the road, so that their troops were not able to get through. We,—close on their heels,—crack, crack,—a new volley at them, whole Brigades now surrendered."[62]

The young Confederate from Florida recalled his mad dash with a companion to get away down the steep east side of the ridge:

We dashed out to try to make our escape. . . . I certainly was running faster than a young deer before the hounds. . . . I ran into an old road . . . about a hundred yards farther on I came to some thick Brush . . . [and] as I rounded this little point of timber I heard the German command ["Achtung! Achtung!"]. . . . I looked and saw what I took to be two or three German regiments right together [They were the 2d and 15th Missouri, the only German regiments in this part of the Union line]. . . . I heard further orders given in German. Right then flashed across my mind: "We are fighting the world! Here on this battlefield are foreigners who do not speak English and yet are fighting for the American flag. . . . I looked over to the right of where I was and saw a little hut. In this Livingstone and myself took shelter. I peeked through the cracks at these same Germans, and I saw them shoot several men with their hands up.[63]

There are few recorded incidents of captors shooting prisoners during the Civil War. Probably the most infamous was the Fort Pillow massacre in Tennessee by Confederate cavalry under Nathan Bedford Forest. For those in the German regiments from Missouri, if the shootings did occur, perhaps they had something to do with memory—to be sure, the all-too-fresh reports of stripped comrades lying dead and wounded and left to freeze on the slope at Chickamauga, the evident taunts as they charged up the ridge. Longer back, the memories of scalped bodies at Pea Ridge, and longer back still, the business of the German-haters in St. Louis, the snipers, the rock throwings, and the taunts there too. It has been said that democracies "can produce the most murderous of armies from the most unlikely of men." Having resisted fighting even those judged to be their moral enemies, there can come a time when such men resist no longer. Driven to fight because they can see no other way, they then become the most savage of warriors.[64] Eighty-odd years later, an American GI fighting in the Ardennes may have explained the battle ethos of all armies, for all the ages, stripped of any pretense: "I used to wonder what I was doing in the army. I didn't have anything personal against the [enemy], even if they were making me live in a freezing, frigging foxhole. But I learned something. . . . I want to kill every goddam Kraut in the world. You know why? To save my own ass." In war, John Toland concluded in his book on the Battle of the Bulge, one eventually learns, out of vengeance and sometimes hate, to "kill without remorse or pity."[65]

Fortunately, for the young Confederate Floridian and his companion, there was another present in a blue uniform. With no other Union regiments in the vicinity, he too was likely a German.

I saw a man coming towards us. . . . He was a Union soldier and was making directly for the cabin door. . . . He was a handsome fellow and looked to be about twenty-two. . . . I knew I could kill him as soon as he got close enough . . . [but] I said to myself, "I cannot kill that boy!" I thought of his mother at once; a strange thing that she came into my mind; but that is just as it happened.

When he got to the door, he sang out a violent oath and told us to come out. I am sure I surprised him more than he ever before was surprised in his life, for with my gun pointed at his breast, I was within five feet of him in a moment and shouted, "Throw up your arms!" They went up, and his gun went down.

Was meinst du?—"What do you mean? You are surrounded and cannot get away."

I answered, "I want to be treated as a soldier and not murdered, as your men have murdered all around us in the last few moments. Promise me that and I will surrender."

He said, "I will protect you."

For the young man from Florida, now a prisoner, the war was over, and he would live to see the end of it.[66]

Marcoot remembered, "As night had already cast her shadows around us and we were all worn out, pursuit was postponed until the following morning."[67] Behind them, on the top of the ridge, down the slope, and out on the plain, lay the comrades who had not made it up the ridge. Among them was Lt. Friedrich Lipps, one of the heroes of Chickamauga, now lying with a severe wound in the right thigh. Lipps would return to action in a few months, but back on duty, he would hobble with his disabled leg. It would remain as a grim reminder of the war for the rest of his life.[68]

Of the six thousand who began the assault, Sheridan's division lost 123 officers and 1,181 men in killed and wounded in little more than an hour, more than Sherman had lost in all of his three divisions over two days of fruitless assaults on Tunnel Hill. In exchange for their own casualties, Sheridan's men took 1,762 prisoners. The Confederate division defending the ridge in Sheridan's front reported a loss of 288 in killed and wounded and another 591 missing, most of the latter among the prisoners.[69]

Except for the terrible price Wagner's men had to pay for the generalship back on Orchard Knob, the rest of Sheridan's regiments shared about equally in the casualties. The 15th Missouri lost twenty-seven of about two hundred officers and men, almost 14 percent, about the same as the rest of the brigade. Being in the last line of the assault made no difference; the 15th suffered more or the same number of casualties as two of the three regiments in the first line, and just two fewer than the other. It probably never occurred to these Germans from Missouri that one of the places they would find the equality they sought would be on the battlefield.

. . .

Twenty-two years later, Grant intimated in his memoirs that he had issued the order "to carry the ridge."[70] Among veterans of the old Army of the Cumberland, the assertion resurrected the old seeds of bad feelings for Grant. To them, both officers and men, an attempt had been made to take from them what they knew to be rightfully theirs, a legacy that was to grow into legend. It was they who had taken it upon themselves to storm the top of that mountain, and their officers with them, and not any general.

With the publication of his memoirs, Grant's claim stirred a tempest among senior officers who had witnessed and took part in the charge. Was it Grant's plan for the Army of the Cumberland to deliver the final blow by taking the ridge? William Tecumseh Sherman said it was.[71] Coming from Sherman, that was to be expected.

A colonel who took part in the assault, a future governor of Kansas, wrote twenty-three years later, "The principal point, which, in my judgment, should always be made prominent, is the fact that Missionary Ridge was fought without orders from the commander-in-chief." Sheridan concluded in his memoirs that the charge up the ridge was "not premeditated by Grant, he directing only the line at its base to be carried."[72]

Not the least of those to contradict Grant was his own chief of engineers, the one officer who needed to know every detail of the plan, if there was one. General William "Baldy" Smith some twenty years after the war wrote, as if to wish to hear nothing further on the subject, "The assault on the center before either flank was turned was never seriously contemplated, and was made without plan, without orders."[73]

The tempest also stirred the teapots of historians deep into the twentieth century. In the 1960s, a popular historian wrote that Grant had ordered Thomas on the day of the charge for the Army of the Cumberland to assault Bragg's entrenchments, giving him the option to attack those at the base, and if circumstances offered themselves, to go for the summit. The date of that order to Thomas is November 18, a week before the assault.[74] There is no evidence that Grant repeated that order on the afternoon of the assault. In point of fact, Grant made it clear that afternoon that Thomas's men were not to move until he, Grant, gave the order.[75]

The same historian also asserted that Sheridan and Woods gave the orders to attack the summit. A single source is cited.[76] The source was Charles Dana, assistant secretary of war, who at the time of the battle was on Orchard Knob. Dana was hardly an eyewitness to what Sheridan and Woods were doing or saying more than a mile away. But Dana was within earshot of Grant on Orchard Knob. In the same dispatch, Dana reported,

"Neither Grant nor Thomas intended [the assault to the top]. Their orders were to carry the rifle-pits along the base of the ridge . . . when this was accomplished the unaccountable spirit of the troops bore them bodily up those impracticable steeps." Why this historian and Grant biographer, after citing this Dana report to support his contention, chose to ignore this last statement by Dana is impossible to understand.

Modern historians have also contested the supposed order, notably, James Lee McDonough in *Chattanooga—A Death Grip on the Confederacy* and Peter Cozzens in *The Shipwreck of Their Hopes*. If it was indeed Grant's intention for the Army of the Cumberland to storm the top of Missionary Ridge, for those on Orchard Knob that afternoon, there had been many a slip between the cup and the lip.

For his part, Grant was proclaimed a national hero. A joint resolution by the Senate and the House of Representatives ordered a specially struck gold medal "with suitable emblems, devices, and inscriptions, to be presented to Major-General Grant." Then, in language with all the ring of an afterthought, the resolution included "the thanks of Congress . . . to the officers and soldiers who have fought under [Grant's] command during this rebellion, for their gallantry and good conduct in the battles in which they have been engaged."[77]

There was no mention of a charge without orders.

14

Two Ears of Corn

On the morning of the assault on Missionary Ridge, Grant received a telegram from the president: "Your dispatches as to fighting on Monday and Tuesday are here." (Lincoln was referring to the taking of Orchard Knob and Lookout Mountain.) "Well done," the president said. "Many thanks to all. Remember Burnside."[1] Lincoln had his mind on Eastern Tennessee.

Grant got the message. "On the 28th of November, only three days after the great battle of Mission Ridge," Marcoot wrote,

> we were supplied with three days' rations and ordered out on a forced march of one hundred and fifty miles to Knoxville, to relieve our force there, besieged by Gen. Longstreet.
>
> We left camp with our tents standing and all our baggage except a single woolen or rubber blanket, as we expected to return in a few days. We crossed the Chickamauga River near its mouth at the Tennessee River. . . .
>
> The country through which we passed was exceptionally fine, but at this time there was nothing for us to forage and as our rations were uncomfortably short we would really have appreciated it had it been otherwise. . . . I paid a teamster a quarter for an ear of corn—he stole it from one of his mules—and shelling it placed it in a quart cup with water. In my haversack I had a hunk of thick—originally white but now very black—pork, which I could not eat even with my crackers before they were gone, although I had on several occasions swallowed a number of pieces of it that I had cut off, about the size of a pill. This piece of

black pork I now cut up into very small pieces and mixed it with the corn in the cup and set it on the campfire to boil. It proved a dainty dish and before it was thoroughly cooked I discovered that it had all disappeared from frequent tasting on my part. I was considerably disappointed at this, but consoled myself with the belief that I had had a pretty fair meal after all.

We next crossed the Little Tennessee River and passed through Marysville and Rockford, reaching Knoxville on the 6th of December, a day or two after the siege had been raised.

On the 11th, we again received marching orders. We proceeded up along the Holston [Holstein] River and finally camped at a small mill on a small stream near the Tennessee River and the North Carolina line. Here we were detailed to forage, but found nothing. Our sick had accumulated until we were compelled to erect a field hospital, and it was not long until it was filled. . . . We remained here until the 15th, when we received orders to return to Knoxville. It now began to rain day and night—a cold disagreeable rain, and as we had left our tents behind us we had no shelter whatever and but very little clothing.[2]

On arriving in Knoxville, Sheridan's inspection of his troops "showed that the shoes of many of the men were entirely worn out, the poor fellows having been obliged to protect their feet with a sort of moccasin, made from their blankets or from such other material as they could procure. . . . Mid-winter was now upon us . . . snow often falling to the depth of several inches. The thin and scant clothing of the men afforded little protection, and while in bivouac their only shelter was the ponchos with which they had been provided before leaving Chattanooga; there was not a tent in the command. Hence great suffering resulted."[3]

The 15th continued its march to Blaine's Crossroads, arriving on December 17. "We passed through Strawberry Plain," Marcoot recorded,

where it was reported the enemy had made a stand and would offer battle, but this proved a mistake. Here we lay in midwinter, and the coldest winter that had been known in this section for years, with no tents, no blankets, no change of clothing, no cooking utensils, and no salt even, while our entire bodies were actually raw from the bites of the famous "Gray-backs" [fleas]. At first we received half a pint of cornmeal every morning with the assurance that it was for breakfast only, but it was the last that we would get that day. This corn was foraged, the wagons sometimes going as far as 60 miles into the country before they got it and even then they would frequently come back empty. The corn thus foraged was ground at a small water mill in the vicinity of the camp and issued to us as rations at one pint per day, while the only means we had of preparing it was as a mush, boiled without even a dressing of salt. But this luxury was too good to last long, for the mill was too small or the army too large. At least they soon informed us that the mill had to be run day and night to supply the wants of Burnside's army, then in the front and so we soon became the recipients of one ear of corn on the cob a day for our rations.

The corn, as it was foraged, was put in strong pens and a heavy guard placed over it. Every morning as each company would fall in for roll call, they would be marched up to the corn crib, when each soldier would be permitted to take one ear of corn. They were all of an average size as the smaller ears or nubbins were sorted out to be fed to the mules and there was no trouble as to "first choice." On one occasion, and only one, I attempted to slip in both hands and take out two ears, but the guard detected me and I slung the extra ear outside the crowd and offered a prompt denial. But my protests were in vain and I was compelled to put the other ear back in the crib. When I went to look for the discarded it too had disappeared and I was compelled to fast that day.

We parched the corn by our campfires as we could eat it better in this manner than in meal. But how did we live that cold winter? We had no axes to cut our fuel and were compelled to use our sword bayonets for this purpose. We built houses of brush wood but they let in the wind and rain upon us. Our hair and beards—those who had them—had grown long and bushy. All the combs in the company had been broken and we had no scissors or razors to cut or shave with, so we had to let them grow in tangles. One cold night I raked out the warm ashes from the fire and scattering them about our hovel near the fire, bunked upon them. During the night as usual I rolled from one side to the other so as to alternate before the fire, and keep both [sides] warm. But in the night it commenced to snow, and as it fell the fire would melt it, and my long hair got wet and as I rolled about I mopped up the loose ashes. Before I got up the next morning it began freezing hard and soon froze the mass, hair, ashes and all, into long ice sickles so that when I moved they would jingle like "sleigh bells."

Pets in the shape of gray-backs were now becoming unendurable, but we had one boy [Chris Reber] who claimed to be bug proof. But alas, one morning about this time, while we were standing around the fire vigorously campaigning against them, we detected them upon him.

They were crawling out at the bottom holes of his clothes to enjoy, as it were, a little of the warmth of the fire. This raised the laugh and it was a long time before poor Reber heard the last of it.

Gambling among the boys was still their main occupation. The officers strenuously endeavored to break it up, but the boys would scatter and congregate on a high hill near the camp. We called it "chuck-luck hill," and who does not remember it? On the warm days this hill would be fairly covered with groups of boys at play and the guards seemed almost powerless to check them. The boys would station their own sentinels and were invariably informed of approaching danger in time to remove all evidence of the game.

On Christmas Day we received two ears of corn each, as rations, instead of one, a sort of Christmas gift you know, and we lived high I can assure you.

During the last few days of 1863, it rained continuously—a bitterly raw, cold rain and our clothing etc. became thoroughly soaked. We didn't have a dry thread about us. This continued until twelve o'clock on New Year's eve night [when] the wind . . . turned suddenly bitter cold and our wet clothes froze stiff on our very bodies.[4]

1864

Long, too long, America.

—Walt Whitman, "Drum Taps"

15

A New Kind of War

Too much blood. Too much of the nation's treasury. Opinion in the North was ever turning against the war on both counts. Winter added to the grim outlook. The armies faced each other but went dormant as the cold, snow, and frozen mud began to settle in. The outcome would have to wait until spring at the earliest, while the strength of the Union armies continued to dwindle, earlier by the battle casualties of the fall and now, by desertions. And there were virtually no incoming volunteers.[1]

The men in the 15th were tending to more immediate things. "On the first day of January, 1864, we received our mail," Marcoot wrote, "and as this feature had become such a scarcity of late, it was highly enjoyed." It was "noised around," Marcoot added, "that it was the desire of the authorities that the old veterans of '61 should re-enlist for three more years, or for the duration of the war. On the 3rd, Gen. Sheridan made us a speech on this subject."[2]

Two days later, men willing to reenlist stood huddled and shivering in long lines as they waited to sign the papers. "The army was virtually on the point of starvation, each soldier subsisting on one ear of corn on the cob per day, was poorly clad, badly sheltered and exposed to the cold wintery blasts. In fact it was so cold that the ink actually froze on our pens as we were signing our names to the roll."[3] Of the seven hundred or so who had volunteered in 1861, 168 were all that remained of the regiment in January 1864. Only one of four had survived, yet 138 of the survivors chose to reenlist, better than 80 percent.[4]

The regiment was ordered to return to Chattanooga to receive their
veteran's furlough. On January 22, they moved again, crossing the Tennessee River at Chattanooga, settling into the old camp they had left after the
Battle of Missionary Ridge.

> We found our old camp just as we had left it, for . . . each company had
> left a guard behind them who remained to look after our tents, etc. Our
> tents were still standing and our knapsacks and clothing were just as we
> had left them.
>
> Upon getting settled again more comfortably, my first move was to
> procure a pair of scissors and persuade Engelbert Dreher to clip my
> long neglected flowing locks. He was something of a barber, but was out
> of the business, and only reluctantly consented to perform the favor.
>
> He first cut off the locks, for they were [inseparably] linked together,
> until he could use a comb, and then attempted to even up on his job,
> resulting in a pretty close cut. . . . I had the consolation however to know
> that several weeks would, in all probability, elapse before I should be
> able to reach home, giving it time to grow somewhat and present a more
> respectable appearance.
>
> We tried our very best to prevent our blankets and clean clothing
> from being contaminated with the pests that had become almost unen-
> durable, and as the weather had materially moderated we took to the
> river, stripped for the fray and started our old clothing down the Ten-
> nessee. Entering the river for a bath we were horrified to discover our
> enemies had preceded us and were swimming about in droves. The boys
> above us had preceded us to the water and had succeeded in starting
> their surplus stock down upon us. But we made the best of a bad job, and
> getting into our clean clothes felt much better and enjoyed the comforts
> of good quarters and full rations hugely.
>
> On the 5th of February we were mustered out and also into the ser-
> vice again [regulations at the time required men to be discharged before
> they could be reenlisted], and there was not much time lost between the
> two acts. . . . On the 10th we left Chattanooga via rail for Nashville.[5]

After almost two years since crossing over the river at Cape Girardeau into
the hell of Kentucky, Mississippi, and Tennessee, the men of the 15th Missouri were about to see home again.

More than just hard times had come to Missouri. Business was not just
bad; for many there simply was none. Farming had been devastated; whole
sections of the state had been abandoned to the depravations of raiding

guerilla bands. Bankers floated worthless paper money, and postage stamps often did the job of coins.

For soldier families in St. Louis, the business of daily living was desperate. With the men away, there was little if any money. Soldiers had difficulty sending their pay home, at least on a predictable basis. Just getting food was a serious problem. Free staples were being distributed for soldiers' families, but many women with children, living far from the distribution location with no means of travel, found it impossible to acquire any of it. One wife of a German soldier begged her husband to try to send army blankets. That was illegal, of course; he tried, nevertheless, but was stopped.[6] Charitable and church organizations were, for most, the only means of survival.

The 15th Missouri reached East St. Louis by train on the afternoon of February 15, four hours late, the delay caused by a rail accident. "East St. Louis was handsomely decorated in our honor," Marcoot recalled, "and the streets were thronged with people, as they had been informed of our re-enlistment for the war and our return. . . . When the train containing our regiment reached the depot we were received by a committee on reception, a delegation from the common council and a large number of people."

Marcoot recalled that "Mr. Gottschalk, of the council of St. Louis, welcomed us home in a neat and appropriate speech, and we were tendered cheer after cheer by the multitude and shaken by the hands by numerous relatives and friends." A railroad bridge as yet had not been built across the Mississippi, and so

a ferry boat had been chartered to convey us across the river, and when it reached the shore we were again greeted by throngs of people. A company of the 1st Mo. cavalry, parts of eight companies of the National guards, the Swiss committee with the native flag of Switzerland, and delegations from several local societies were in waiting to receive us.

We were thus escorted to Turner's Hall which had been especially decorated and were there tendered a sumptuous banquet. When we came in sight of that table, how eager we were to get a place and I fear our actions betrayed our thoughts. But when we were seated and had just began "the feast" we found, to our great sorrow, the lusting of eyes and the craving of our hearts could not induce our poor contracted stomachs that had been accustomed to one ear of corn on the cob per day, to do the occasion justice. . . . As we sat around that board and received with grateful feelings the grand reception tendered us, we could not help—many of us—from recalling to mind those of our comrades who were

Colonel Joseph Conrad sat for this portrait on the 15th Missouri's return to St. Louis in February 1864. The loss of more
than half his men the previous year may explain the evident
melancholy. (United States Army Military History Institute,
Roger Hunt Collection)

missing. Those who marched off to the war as buoyant as any . . . but
who fell in the line of duty and now slept in their silent tombs all along
our line of march. Of the nine hundred men [the number was probably
closer to eight hundred] who went out with us three years before, only
one hundred and sixty-seven were left to tell the story of our trials and
triumphs, our joys and sorrows. . . .

We brought home with us four flags, one a plain American flag bearing the inscription, "the first flag of the regiment." Another, a mere
remnant, tattered and torn, with "Pea Ridge" inscribed upon it, the
third contained the names of "Stone River, Chickamauga and Mission
Ridge" upon its folds, while the fourth was the Swiss flag which the
ladies of Highland had presented to us by Major Landreth while we

were stationed at Springfield, Mo., early in 1862. . . . At this time also Mr. Bernhard Suppiger also handed him [the major] a fine gold watch with the request that he present it to the first Highland boy who displayed conspicuous bravery in battle. But it appeared that no such event ever followed as he remained the sole proprietor of the watch. But the flag we had carried faithfully through every battle, I can assure the ladies of Highland that that flag was one of the very first flags of all Sheridan's division to be planted on the crest of Mission Ridge. It was now—upon our return—tattered and torn, and it showed marks of the many bullets it had encountered in honest battle. It had Pea Ridge inscribed on its folds before we received it."

Marcoot remembered, "After the banquet at Turner's Hall was over, the ladies of St. Louis presented us with another flag." A Colonel Fletcher, probably from the Department of Missouri headquarters, was selected to make the presentation speech. It was a lengthy tribute delivered in the lofty language of the time for such occasions, including a description of the new flag: "Upon its folds are emblazoned the names of the glorious fields on which the gallant Fifteenth Missouri Volunteer Infantry has won distinction for valor and reflected honor on our state," citing in particular Stones River, "where many of your gallant comrades laid down their lives in the defense of the cause of liberty and the government of our fathers" that "the names and heroic deeds of the soldiers of Stones River will live in story and in song as long as language shall endure or liberty shall find a home on this green earth . . . the heroes who clung to the shrine of freedom, defying the storm, they trod the dark valley of terror and blood, but victorious at last in their majesty stood." Concluding finally, the colonel made the presentation: "Take then this flag . . . let it kiss the breeze with the flag of the Union, one and inseparable, let them be in fair fight, and never will they go down."[7]

Rising to receive the flag, Colonel Conrad responded, "In the name of the regiment, I tender you our most heartfelt thanks. . . . Many thanks for all the honors the citizens of St. Louis have shown us today . . . we will always endeavor to uphold the honor of our state and the national government under which we live." His four lines took less than a minute to utter.[8]

Marcoot took note of the occasion: "Our Colonel was no speaker and was not prepared for such an experience." The men had learned that their colonel was no orator months before when Conrad was introduced to the regiment upon taking command: the presenting officer declared, "Gentleman and Comrades, here is a man, who, like General Grant, cannot make a speech for you, but he is a man that can fight for you."

A 15th Missouri battle flag. Women in St. Louis presented this flag, the Missouri state seal on a blue field, to the 15th Missouri upon the regiment's return in February 1864. It was intended to replace the battle-torn flag with the Swiss white cross on a red field, first presented to the regiment's Swiss volunteers in 1861. This 1864 flag may not have seen battle; the apparent damage is not typical of battle action. Another 15th Missouri battle flag showing the familiar federal eagle on a dark blue field is furled and hermetically encased in the museum in the state capital. (State Historical Society of Missouri, Columbia)

The day following the feast and presentation, February 16,

Uncle Sam gallantly came forward and settled our accounts. . . . We were also to receive one hundred dollars as a bounty for our first three years' service, as was promised in 1861, but when we figured it out as to its actual value, we found that it only represented about $60 in gold. . . . We had no sooner received our pay than . . . many of our boys not only possessed a new suit of clothes but found themselves handsomely fleeced.

I was more fortunate here than some of my comrades. My brother John then resided in St. Louis. He accompanied me to the clothing store where we purchased the necessary clothing, carried it to a barber shop where I enjoyed an old fashioned shampoo—I did not need a shave or a hair cut, for my beard did not then bother me much and my hair had not recovered from the shock it received at the hands of comrade

Dreher at Chattanooga, and afterwards a splendid bath. After a thorough scrubbing here I donned my new suit and left the old regimentals to walk off by themselves.

After this we felt that we could go and see our civilized friends, but we soon concluded that St. Louis was not the best place for us to tarry long if we expected to retain money enough to reach our respective homes.[9]

On the 17th, the regiment received its furlough, and the men scattered to family and friends. Colonel Conrad joined the Highland group of thirty or so in hacks and wagons for the purpose of bringing home the remnant of the old Swiss regimental flag as he had promised. Upon reaching Highland, "we formed in line," Marcoot wrote, "and marched into and through the city . . . headed by a brass band." There followed another banquet, a concert and then a ball, the proceeds going to the widows and orphans of the men who would never return.[10]

Marcoot's father had long since recanted his opposition, even displaying a noticeable amount of pride at the record of his son's regiment and his safe return, "but not so with mother." She saw that her son had changed; for one thing, "he used words and expressions that he had not known before he first left the family circle."[11]

The thirty days of furlough were filled with more "balls, concerts and parties" that extended to farm houses and neighboring towns, some breaking up "only a little before daylight." One such affair involved the regiment's officers "amid music, wine and cigars" at a neighbor's substantial "residence on the hill." Living close by, Marcoot found himself included. "It was the first time that I had associated in such a manner with our officers, but I got along first rate until the wine began to flow. . . . I soon found out that I was no match for them." Returning the next day to visit the neighbors on the hill, Marcoot noted that all of the windows had been thrown open, in spite of it being February. "I learned that the scent of tobacco smoke was very disagreeable to them and they were trying to free the house from the fumes of the late party there."[12]

Their return had not been all pleasure. One member of the regiment had been bushwhacked and nearly killed by a gang of Southern sympathizers. Others had been "badly treated," apparently out of similar disrespect and opposition to the war.

As the furloughs wound down to their last week, the men prepared for the moment when they would have to say their good-byes. Marcoot said of his mother, "She could not be reconciled. . . . It was not my health or bodily danger that seemed to worry her most, but the certainty, as she feared, of my being eternally lost should death overtake me. . . . I was obliged to leave her almost heart-broken with fears . . . for her wayward son."

The time came on March 16 to return to St. Louis to rejoin the regiment. "A company of friends and neighbors, including a number of ladies, accompanied us. . . .We roamed about the city at leisure until the 18th, when we were ordered to assemble at the corner of Locust and 4th streets, from whence we were marched to Benton Barracks, where some of the comrades were locked up for misbehavior. It happened this way: We had received a number of recruits at Highland for our company and they had preceded us to St. Louis several days to complete their muster, and on account of the frequent bounty jumping that was practiced at this time, they were kept under heavy guard."[13]

Bounty-jumping was an outgrowth of the hated draft system, which Congress enacted and Lincoln signed the year before. One of its provisions permitted a man to legally avoid the draft by paying a substitute three hundred dollars to serve in his place. The result was outrage, mainly among poorer men who had no means of buying their way out.

But two could play the game. One would pay another the three hundred dollars, both duly signing the documents in the presence of a recruitment officer or draft official. As soon as the original draftee handed over the three hundred dollars, he was officially off the hook. His substitute had only to take the money and run. And run many did. Or "jump," in the vernacular of the time. Untold thousands jumped the bounty by simply never showing up for their mustering in. All were eventually declared deserters, but few were ever caught.[14]

Every new recruit was likely viewed by their new regiment as a potential "jumper" and literally locked up the moment he signed his muster papers. Startled to hear how their new comrades were being handled, Marcoot with his own youthful sense of justice sprang into action:

> As soon as we broke ranks and were assigned quarters, it was learned that our recruits were confined on the other side of the parade grounds . . . and three of us young boys . . . started on a run across the grounds. I was first to reach the guard, and was suddenly halted, next came Reber, and he was received in the same manner . . . but Jackson, who brought up the rear . . . thought he would go in any how, when the guard knocked him down with his gun. Reber . . . was also knocked down. All the guards having turned out and seeming desirous of getting a whack at us . . . but I was the only one who had a revolver, and quick as thought I attempted to use it in our defense. I was soon overpowered however and hustled off

to the guardhouse. I did not like it much as it was the first punishment I had received since I entered the service, and it looked then that it might become quite serious.

My two companions were soon relieved, but Capt. Walker, commander of the Barracks, preferred charges against me for attempting to shoot a commissioned officer. . . . I did not suffer much during my confinement . . . my comrades brought me little extras, and many a quart of beer was smuggled through with the supposition that it was coffee. . . . But when our regiment was ready to leave St. Louis, our Colonel went to headquarters and procured my release. . . . When he brought me out of the guard house, he laughed and told me that I should behave better next time, and that was the last time I heard of it. . . .

On the 25th we received our arms, not the old Enfield rifles, but brandnew Spring-field rifles, which pleased us very much.

The Springfield was a .58 caliber percussion, rifled, single-shot muzzle-loader. More than 4.5 feet long, it was smoothly finished with a deeply oiled walnut stock that extended almost the length of the arm. Its metal parts were finished bright so that its forty-inch barrel would catch the sunlight, setting off hundreds of sparkling flashes in time to the rhythmic cadence of a regiment on the march. With "our new guns glistening in the sunshine," Marcoot remembered, the 15th left Benton Barracks on March 26 and "proudly marched through the city with our new flag floating above us." Before long, they were "brought up on the levee, where, during the afternoon, we boarded the 'Silver Lake' steamer and proceeded down the Mississippi."[15]

There would be more changes than their new flag and muskets for the reenlisted regiment. Just about everything about the war would change—changes in how it would be fought in the months ahead, and changes in the men who would fight it.

The 15th Missouri had shrunk in "number of bayonets," the preferred term used by the officers when counting those in their ranks, to fewer than two hundred. The 15th suffered from the drought in new recruits throughout the North, adding only a sprinkling of replacements to begin the year. Those new to the regiment at the start of 1864 continued in the main to be volunteers. However, it would still be appropriate to refer to the regiment officially as the 15th Missouri *Volunteer* Infantry. Before the year was out, however, that descriptor would disappear.

The few new men who did arrive had Germanic names for the most part, such as Abel, Buengener, and Schmidt. There were also a handful of other newcomers, not volunteers but draftees, men with different-sounding names such as the Britannic Bush and the Gallic Courtois.[16] Still, the German volunteer remained dominant in the regiment. But that too would change.

Lincoln exploded when he learned that Longstreet's army had escaped from Tennessee to return to Lee without resistance from an eastern army. "If this Army of the Potomac was good for anything," the president proclaimed, "if the officers had anything in them, if the army had any legs, they could move thirty thousand men down to Lynchburg and catch Longstreet. Can anybody doubt if Grant were here in command that he would catch him?"[17] It was just a matter of time before Lincoln would appoint Grant as the general he felt was needed to win the war.

To replace himself in the West, Grant appointed a West Pointer and former military school superintendent in Louisiana whose last job before the war was president of a St. Louis trolley car company. William Tecumseh Sherman was in many ways a mirror image of Grant. For one, Sherman fostered a strategy that would change how the war would be fought. In the first years of the war, generals of both armies fought a battle for a day or two and then backed off to give their armies time to lick their wounds and replenish. These battles had been set pieces, disconnected by time and distance until the next battle piece. That would change. Grant and Sherman would employ a new set of battlefield strategies. These new strategies would require an emotional hardness that few generals during the Civil War could reach down and find within themselves a hardness that could turn aside casualties, day after day, month after month. No more would there be fight and let go, only to fight and let go once again. Now, the enemy once in their jaws, Grant and Sherman, like the big snapping turtles in the muddy rivers of the land where their armies would fight, would hang on and hang on some more.

Their main objective would still be Richmond and Lee's Army of Northern Virginia. Lincoln made that clear to his new commander. The president's directives in place, the plan evolved: while Grant was to push Lee back to the Confederate capital (and destroy Lee's army if at all possible), the other Union armies were to attack at the same time. Sherman, having the larger force of the armies of the Cumberland, the Ohio, and the Tennessee, was to move toward Atlanta against the Confederate Army of Tennessee, their old adversary, now under Gen. Joseph E. Johnston. For the first time in the war, all of the Union armies were to strike in concert with a single purpose—to attack the Rebel forces in their fronts, to be sure, but in the doing, cause as much widespread destruction as possible in the line of march. It was all to begin on May 4.

For Sherman, his job was, as Grant wrote, to "break up" the Confederate army in Georgia, prevent Johnston from sending troops to reinforce Lee in Virginia, and "to get into the interior of the enemy's country as far as you can, inflicting all the damage you can against their war resources."[18]

The 15th Missouri worked itself down the Mississippi aboard the "Silver Lake" paddlewheel steamboat. Marcoot recalled passing Cape Girardeau and "that day, where we had in 1862 taken to the boats in our travels." There was a brief stop for a leg stretch at Cairo, before boarding again and heading up the Ohio, passing the mouth of the Tennessee River at Paducah and finally reaching the Cumberland River.

"As we were not on a forced march," Marcoot wrote, "we were permitted to make our advance very leisurely, with an occasional day of rest . . . with letter writing, games and sports was the order of exercises. Leap-frog seemed to be the craze."

Marcoot continued, "It now rained incessantly for several days, but after two days rest, the 22nd found us "on the road" again. Crossing the Tennessee River at Bridgeport, and "reaching Whiteside's station where a huge trestle railroad bridge . . . no less than one hundred feet high had been destroyed and rebuilt so often by the two armies that it was in a terrible condition. Great long saplings strapped to one another five or six stories in height and braced only with ordinary planks gave it the appearance of a veritable spider web, and when trains would pass over it would rock to and fro as though it must surely fall. . . .

"On the 24th, after a fourteen mile tramp, we reached Chattanooga . . . a place we had surely not forgotten. We remained here three days, climbing over the mountains and scouting over our old battlefields in quest of lancel roots and soapstones from which to manufacture rude pipes, etc., as mementos."[19]

The last day of April, the 15th marched into camp of their new division near Cleveland, Tennessee. They learned here that they would remain in the Fourth Corps, a corps composed of what one authority has called the "fightingest" regiments in the western armies; among Union regiments that had sustained the greatest losses in battle, more of them were to be found in the Fourth Corps of the Army of the Cumberland than in any other corps.[20] The corps' commander was Gen. O. O. Howard, "a good, brave and sober minded officer," Marcoot wrote, "[who] had lost his right arm

. . . while connected with the army of the Potomac at the battle of Fair Oaks, Va. General J. Newton had also succeeded to the command of our division. . . . We grieved over the loss of our former commander . . . Phil Sheridan,"[21] whom Grant had since appointed commander of Union cavalry in the East.

In the reorganized Fourth Corps, the 15th Missouri remained in the brigade of nine regiments formed just before Missionary Ridge, the division now under Maj. Gen. John Newton, a transfer from the Army of the Potomac, where he had commanded a corps at Gettysburg. Most of the regiments had been in service for at least two years and by now reduced to less than half their normal size, many unable to muster even two hundred rifles. Continuing to double the number of regiments to a brigade consequently made sense. A long campaign was probably ahead, one intended to reach deep into enemy territory and likely incur heavy casualties. Replacements, if any were to be had, might be a long way from the battle lines.

The 15th's brigade commander continued to be Col. Francis T. Sherman. Remaining with the 15th were the remnants of the old Pea Ridge Brigade, the 2d Missouri and the Illinois 44th, 73d, and 36th, adding now the 74th and 88th Illinois, 28th Kentucky, and the 24th Wisconsin, the latter to be commanded by Lt. Col. Arthur MacArthur Jr., the future father of Gen. Douglas MacArthur.

"Discipline in our army had . . . become more stringent since its reorganization," Marcoot recorded, "not a few officers were dismissed from the service for drunkenness and other causes. . . . Privates for negligence while on duty and for desertion were punished without mercy. . . . It was reported that General Sherman had said when he first took command of this army, 'I will shortly come among you and hold a terrible inspection,' and it was evident that he intended to fulfill his promise."[22]

The army was about to move. Veterans somehow always knew. They knew how to gather up just their essentials: rifle, cartridge box, bayonet, and their accoutrements, canteen, haversack and knapsack, wool blanket, shelter half, a rubber sheet that could double as a poncho, maybe a hatchet that dangled from their belts, tin cup, possibly a small skillet, spare clothing (which might include a couple pairs of socks and maybe a change of underwear), writing paper, diary, letters from home, watch, money, and more often than not, a Bible. Standard headgear was the short-billed kepi, but in the West, many wore the black slouch hat with its wide brim for better protection against the sun and the rain. Then they waited for the moment when company sergeants rang out—"Fall in!"

16

"Come up from the fields, Father, there is a letter"

"In pursuance of orders, my regiment, as part of the First Brigade, Second Division, Fourth Army Corps, left Cleveland, Tenn., May 3." So began Colonel Conrad's report of actions of the 15th Missouri, a mere two pages for a campaign that was to last more than four months.[1] To say that the report is spare in detail would be a wild understatement; the colonel was indeed a man of few words.

Newton's division was but one column, a small part of about 98,000 men in Sherman's combined armies, on the march south. Somewhere up ahead were 65,000 "Johnnies" in their motley shades of butternut and gray and other colors, on the lookout for their coming.

After only one day on the march, Union cavalry began to tangle with small groups of Southern horsemen. "On the 4th of May our cavalry skirmished all day," Marcoot recorded. Crossing the border into Georgia, the 15th marched into Catoosa Springs, just east of Ringgold, and encamped. Two days later, the division picked up the march again and headed south toward Tunnel Hill on the Western & Atlantic Railroad. Here the division was posted in reserve, a couple of miles north of a sharp-edged ridge known as Rocky Face. A gap in the ridge to the south made way for the railroad and a wagon road. The locals referred to it as Buzzard's Roost.[2]

Confederate batteries commanded the length of the ridge. "On its north front, the enemy had a strong line of works behind Mill Creek," Sherman wrote, "so that my attention was at once directed to the south. . . . I found

Snake Creek Gap, affording me a good practicable way to reach Resaca,"
below Dalton. Accordingly, Sherman ordered Maj. Gen. James McPherson and his Army of the Tennessee to move "directly on Resaca . . . and
make a bold attack."[3] Thomas, meanwhile, "was to make a strong feint of
attack in front" of Rocky Face Ridge. On Sunday, May 8, Newton directed
a brigade to "ascend to the northern extremity of Rocky Face Ridge. The
summit was a sharp ridge," Newton reported, "never wider than the room
occupied by four men abreast, and oftentimes so narrow and obstructed
by boulders that men in single file could with difficulty climb over the
obstacles. The enemy . . . steadily resisted the advance of the brigade until
dark." The men nevertheless succeeded in gaining about three-fourths of
a mile of the crest. Marcoot recorded that the 15th Missouri in Col. F. T.
Sherman's brigade, in support, "marched eight miles to the top."[4]

Back in Ringgold, about six miles off to the northwest, William Tecumseh Sherman lay down around midnight for his customary three or four
hours of sleep. The day's developments had gone well. The highlight had
been a message from McPherson that afternoon—his army had met little
opposition in moving down Snake Creek Gap and was "within two miles of
Resaca." That was all Sherman wanted to hear. Those within earshot heard
the exclamation: "I've got Joe Johnston dead!"[5]

Sherman telegraphed Halleck outlining his next moves, adding, "I
believe McPherson has destroyed Resaca." But Sherman was to be sorely
disappointed; McPherson managed to report only that his division tore
down "a small portion of telegraph wire." In reply, Sherman could offer
little more than "I regret beyond measure you did not break the railroad."
Seeing McPherson four days later, Sherman would say, "Well, Mac, such
an opportunity comes but once in a lifetime."[6]

For the Missourians on top of Rocky Face Ridge, "It now began to rain
heavily," Marcoot wrote. "One who was not there can hardly realize how
cold and disagreeable it was on the top of the mountain at this time, although
in the month of May. The rain froze as it fell and the stones and earth were
soon covered with a solid sheet of ice." The day was spent nevertheless with
the men of the 15th building breastworks. With the night rose a series of
violent thunderstorms that raged till dawn, turning the two-man pup tents
into sieves that added pools of water to the crusty frozen ground inside.[7]

The next day, they "charged the enemy and experienced heavy fighting
all day," Marcoot recorded, "while the weather continued most disagreeably cold . . . in skirmish line fighting all day and night . . . for a full twenty-
four hours without relief."[8]

While the 15th Missouri and the rest of F. T. Sherman's brigade skirmished in the cold a couple miles away, Confederate general Joseph E. Johnston issued the order for his infantry around Dalton to pull out as soon as it was dark and march along the railroad to Resaca. That evening, Johnston boarded one of the last trains leaving Dalton.

Fires burning in the town gave proof that the Confederates were evacuating. At first light, May 13, Newton's division took up the march for Dalton. Heading into Buzzard Roost Gap, they found the Rebel trenches empty. In the gorge itself, boulders stuck up on every side, "like pointed monuments in a grave yard," an Illinois soldier wrote. It was indeed a graveyard, but without graves—corpses of their comrades who had been killed in the previous days' fighting lay about, "stripped of every vestige of clothing, their nude forms exposed to the hot blistering sun."[9] The destitute Johnny Reb continued to use the aftermath of battle to replenish his knapsack, if he still had one, down to the clothing on his back. The blue column continued on, marching through Dalton, "much surprised to behold the formidable works that had been erected," Marcoot recorded. The division set up camp in the Sugar Creek Valley south of town.[10]

"We could hear considerable fighting in the direction of Resaca," Conrad reported, "and were pressed toward [the town] as rapidly as possible. . . . After a hard march, we pushed on the confederate lines near that place. . . . When near Resaca my regiment, for the first time in this campaign, was actually engaged."[11] (*Fully* engaged would have been a better choice of words; a limited English vocabulary may have had something to do with it. To this point in the campaign, the 15th had been assigned only support positions or had skirmished with no more than a few companies in action at a time. It is worth noting again that Conrad's report was written more than four months later, covering all of the battles in the campaign in little more than two pages, a campaign that saw almost continual contact with the enemy. In that limited amount of space, some important facts about the regiment's actions undoubtedly got left out. Writing reports was not Conrad's favorite chore. In fact, Conrad's reports to the governor back in Missouri frequently begin with an apology for their tardiness, his excuse being that he had many more important responsibilities to deal with. Writing reports, he felt, clearly was not one of them.)

The 15th had been the last of Sherman's troops to arrive on the scene at Resaca. Johnston had concentrated his forces, entrenching in lines starting about three miles north of the town, his right pegged on the railroad and his left below Resaca on the banks of the Oostanaula River. To his front ran Camp Creek with steep, mud-slick banks lined with thickets so dense it was nearly impossible for even one man to push through.

Fighting had begun earlier that day with the Union forces pressing the Confederate lines from the north and west. The heaviest fighting had been at the north end near the headwaters of Camp Creek. Sherman's brigade took position on the wooded heights overlooking the valley where Harker's Third Brigade was attacking. At about 3 P.M., the 15th was ordered "to relieve part of the Third Brigade [Harker's] . . . at the time hotly engaged with the enemy." Harker's men had run out of ammunition, with no way to resupply it through the thickets. The decision was made to withdraw the Third Brigade and send in the 15th. "In doing so," Conrad wrote, the regiment "had to move across a large open field, exposed to a terrible fire of the enemy, who opened upon us with his artillery, first with shell, and as we came within range, with grape and canister, but still my men moved on in good order." Reaching Camp Creek and dropping into the water, the men found shelter from the withering fire by leaning low against the opposite bank, many standing in the water and hunkering down behind the ranks in front. "We stopped here for about ten minutes, when we, with the Thirty-sixth Illinois Volunteers . . . made a second charge on a small fort of the enemy in our front." Slipping and sliding to scramble out of the slithery banks, "again we had to cross an open field; again we were exposed to a murderous artillery fire and musketry. We came close to the enemy's works, drove the same away, and held our position until my men were entirely out of ammunition, when we fell back" to the creek. Ammunition having arrived, the Missourians, with their comrades from Illinois, using the muddy banks for a breastwork, "opened a brisk fire again, held our position, and stayed there until 9 P.M., when . . . we were relieved and went into bivouac. My regiment was that day for six hours under constant fire." "Our loss was considerable," Newton reported.[12]

Over the course of the two days of fighting around Resaca, almost 2,800, not quite 3 percent of Sherman's army, had been killed or wounded. Among the 15th, thirty-one men had been hit including six killed, more than 10 percent of the already thin regiment. Most of the wounded would rejoin the regiment; nevertheless, the 15th had taken more than its share of casualties. "Our company lost four men," Marcoot recorded, "among them Peter Beele, of Highland, who was shot through both ankles." Following five months in an army hospital, he was discharged for disability.[13]

The Fourth Corps began its pursuit at sunrise. About midmorning, dust clouds alerted the people around Calhoun, about seven miles south, that the

Yanks were coming. As the long columns approached, the men straightened up and shouldered their arms and the musicians lifted their instruments and began to play. Howard's corps of fifteen thousand men soon began to enter the "pretty little town" of about four hundred, as a *New York Tribune* correspondent reported it, most of whom had fled.

With the brigade in the lead, Conrad ordered the 15th to fan out in companies: "Company F was detailed as flankers to cover our left, Companies B and G to cover our right flank; Companies A and C to support the Eighty-Eighth [Illinois], which was deployed as skirmishers and had relieved the Thirty-Sixth Illinois; the rest of the regiment was held in reserve either to support the skirmish line or right flank wherever it was required." Every half mile or so after leaving Calhoun, the 15th ran into log barricades across the road, behind which dismounted Rebel cavalry took a stand. The brigade would then deploy into a heavy line of skirmishers, taking on the enemy in the front while others worked around their flanks, finally sending the gray horsemen scurrying for their mounts and retreating another half mile or so to do it all over again. "In this way we moved all day until about 4 o'clock."[14]

The brigade drew within sight of Adairsville but halted when heavy artillery and sniper fire drove it to cover. The day's encounters did not fail to leave an impression on Private Marcoot: "On the 17th [we had been] placed in the advance, skirmishing and charging all day, and pushed forward some eight miles—young Charles Weniger [Winnegar], a special friend and comrade of mine, fell badly wounded at my side." Winnegar, a twenty-year-old immigrant from Paris, France, actually suffered only a flesh wound in the left hip and was able eventually to rejoin the regiment.[15] Nevertheless, the 15th, skirmishing and charging throughout the day, suffered another of their own killed and four others wounded.

General Howard noted that "necessary supplies, at the hands of smiling quartermasters and commissaries, now found us. The dead were buried, the sick and wounded were made more comfortable, and everybody got his mail and wrote letters."[16] In his letter home, a Wisconsin soldier in the brigade with the 15th Missouri included his own observations: hundreds of men "are sick and dying from want of sleep."[17]

Sherman prepared for his "next grand move," as his Special Field Orders No. 9 put it. Sherman decided to strike out across country to the southwest, around the Confederate left flank and away from his railroad supply line. "The whole army must be ready to march by May 23," Sherman ordered, "stripped for battle, but equipped and provided for twenty days."

McPherson's Army of the Tennessee was to swing to the far right, with Thomas and the Army of the Cumberland taking the main road directly south toward Dallas, a crossroads village about fourteen miles south of the Etowah River.[18]

The next morning, we "continued our march 12 miles," Marcoot recorded, "amid a continuous heavy rain, toward Dallas."[19] Once across the Etowah, the country opened up to broad fields with acre upon acre planted in wheat and corn. Cattle, pigs, and chickens ambled about the farms and plantations, the owners for the most part having left ahead of the invading Yankees. Pillaging had become a problem for the Union commanders, which prompted Sherman to include in his order that "indiscriminate plunder must not be allowed." But then, the general had also stated that, beyond the two days' ration allowance *per week* that the supply wagons would carry, "all else must be gathered in the country." As it had been since the beginning of the war, "such is the general license given," a Wisconsin soldier wrote, "that few can save anything that a soldier can use. . . . Strict orders are issued against plunder and killing pigs, chickens and so forth but there are few company or regimental commanders who will report a man."[20]

Despair and panic were beginning to rule the hamlets north of Atlanta and the city itself. A growing flow of refugees was arriving every day as if the already crowded city could be counted on as a sure haven. More depressing was the continuous stream of Confederate wounded arriving from the front. Swelling to such gargantuan numbers that there was no longer a building to put them in, they lay in long rows in freight yards outside the large brick railroad station near Five Forks as they waited to be transported south of Atlanta, a scene made memorable seventy-five years later by the epic movie *Gone with the Wind*. "War," concluded a young Southern clerk, "is a terrible thing."[21]

Camping near Burnt Hickory on the night of May 24, the Fourth Corps entered a country "desolate in appearance," Howard wrote, "with few openings and very few farms . . . parts were covered with trees and dense underbrush, which the skirmishers had great difficulty in penetrating. Off the ordinary 'hog backs' one plunged into deep ravines or ascended abrupt, almost vertical slopes. There was much loose, shifting soil on the hills, and many lagoons and small streams bordered with treacherous quicksands."[22]

Marcoot recorded that the 15th Missouri traveled seven miles that day, not a long distance for a regiment on the march, but slowed a great deal no doubt by the country described by their corps commander. The brigade was now under the command of Brig. Gen. Nathan Kimball.

The next day turned rainy, which made the going even harder, the men barely able to slog through the muck of Georgia's red clay country. Five miles ahead of Kimball's brigade and the rest of Howard's corps was a division of Hooker's Twentieth Corps. They were headed for a crossroads where it was understood that a road led to Dallas, Georgia. Hooker's men began to run into stiff resistance from gray skirmishers, and in the process, took several prisoners. Confederate general John B. Hood's whole corps, the prisoners said, was up ahead at a little log Methodist church called New Hope.

This information came as a shock. Support in the form of Howard's corps was more than an hour's march away, and if Hood indeed had his full corps at New Hope and decided to attack, Hooker's lone division could be destroyed. A captain on Thomas's staff was instructed to ride hard to find Howard and urge him to hurry up his corps. But when he found the one-armed general at midafternoon, Howard replied that getting his men to march faster would only "use them up."

Howard's Fourth Corps men, as Marcoot had indicated, may already have been used up. Some of the regiments had new recruits not yet hardened to life on the march. Others among the veterans had not yet fully recovered, even with a rest a few days before; Howard's corps had been in the lead ever since Resaca pursuing the retreating Confederates, bearing the brunt of the constant skirmishing with Johnston's rear guard and now paying the price. General Newton, commanding one of Howard's divisions, referred in his report to the period as one of "unprecedented fatigue." Having served with distinction as a brigade commander at Fredericksburg and as a corps commander at Gettysburg, John Newton knew fatigue when he saw it.

Throughout the army, there was no love lost for "Fighting" Joe Hooker, which might have influenced Howard's reluctance to hurry his troops. Hooker, a transfer from the Army of the Potomac, as was Howard, who knew him well, was detested from Sherman on down to the ranks. Besides, even Sherman doubted that there was any sizeable force of Confederates in the vicinity, so why hurry up?

Howard's corps finally arrived late in the day. As Marcoot remembered it, with some disdain, a "battle was provoked by a charge from Hooker's corps. . . . Our division formed the second line, and although the confederates were driven from their position by Hooker, there were many stragglers from his command. We had never seen the like before. Two and three able-bodied men assisting one wounded soldier to the rear, and in many instances traveling at such a fast gait that the wounded many could not keep up." Hooker and many of his regiments, after all, had come from the "elite" Army of the Potomac, an impression men in the western armies had choked on for some time.

"We massed in column" Marcoot went on, "and prepared for a final charge that evening, but as it had become so dark in the woods where we were situated, it was abandoned and we were ordered to break ranks and get to work building breastworks."[23] In the twilight, the start of a downpour brought the cannonading to a halt. Twenty-five miles away, people in Atlanta heard the thunder of the cannons for the first time.[24]

"These were the hardest times which the army experienced," General Howard recalled years later. Strong words for one who had experienced Chattanooga barely six months back. "It rained continuously for seventeen days; the roads, becoming broad as fields, were a series of quagmires."[25] Rain and mud were nothing new to the men in Howard's corps, or to any other part of the army for that matter. It was the introduction of a new kind of warfare, experienced for the first time near a log church named New Hope, that would warrant men's recall even decades later.

The two armies settled in to face each other along a line that twisted and turned for about ten miles, dense timber and underbrush screening the entrenchments that were in some places fewer than a hundred yards apart. To guard against surprise assaults, skirmishers positioned themselves in the wooded no-man's-land to watch and fire at any position—or body—they could see. Added to that, sharpshooters took to the trees and other high points to snipe at any target that came into their sights, officers and cannoneers being their favorites. Poking a head above a breastwork even for a second or two was suicidal. The shooting began at dawn and did not die down till dusk, a constant rain of musket balls with an occasional thunder of cannonballs, which meant that men were in constant danger of being killed. Thousands of bullets and artillery shells went on to shatter acres of trees and mow down acres of brush.

It was a kind of warfare that men had not seen before, a prelude to what men would experience fifty years later in the trench warfare of World War I. An incessant rain fell, turning trenches into mud bottoms that sucked at men's shoes with every step. Cold nights followed with inevitable sleeplessness. The acrid haze of gun smoke hung over it all, mixed, as a colonel from Indiana put it, with "the smell of gore and decaying men." It added up to more than some men could take. White-hot anger moved some to fling picks and shovels whipping toward the trenches on the other side. A lieutenant colonel, loaded up with whiskey and in a "crazy fit," charged alone and was killed. Unable to stand the business any longer, others simply broke down and were sent to the rear. And always there were the skulkers, those who found their way to the rear much sooner than was warranted. Most simply hunkered down behind the head logs, feet in mud and water, and in the almost constant rain and drizzle, soaked to the skin.

The 15th was one of the regiments closest to the Rebel works fewer than a hundred yards away. The regiment consequently was "almost daily more or less engaged with the enemy," Colonel Conrad recorded. "Companies F, G, and I, especially, suffered severely on the 27th, a new skirmish line being established on that day, [these] companies being out as skirmishers." In Company F, Pvt. Cajetan Bernauer, a German immigrant from St. Louis, died in a field hospital "from gun shot wounds received in a skirmish" that day. Among the wounded were Jacob Steiger, twenty-three, a German immigrant from St. Louis, and John Sherman, a twenty-year-old farmer, also from Germany, shot in the right shoulder and hip. First Lt. John Droste, twenty-two years old, from St. Charles, and cited for gallantry in the charge up Missionary Ridge, was struck in the shoulder and moved by rail to the army's general hospital in Louisville.[26]

Men assigned to picket duty "constructed an additional line of works nearer to those of the enemy. . . . We would, during the night," Marcoot wrote, "station pickets in front of our works in such numbers that they would be only a few yards apart. Each picket during the night would dig himself a hole, using his bayonet to loosen the dirt and his tin cup to throw it out [the foxhole of World War II, seventy-eight years earlier]." This accomplished, they would take their picks and shovels and dig a trench from hole to hole, being perfectly safe from Rebel bullets after they had first dug their holes. Thus in the morning Confederate troops across the way would behold a complete new line of works and considerably nearer than the old ones of before, fully manned with a sufficient number of soldiers to hold it against their attacks.

"The two lines of works finally became so close together that it became very unhealthy for the boys on either side to expose themselves much above the level of the works, as there was some one always on the watch to lay him low, and it was thus that Comrade Seeling [Ernst Sieliger] of our company was killed on June 2d." Sieliger was a thirty-two-year-old German from St. Louis.

"We played several 'yankee tricks' on the rebs while we lay in these works," Marcoot wrote. "On the 3rd of June for instance, being within hearing distance, we unfurled our flags and one of the boys gave all the preliminary commands for a charge, when the yell was raised as if we were starting for them. But when the confederates raised up to see us coming we were in our works with our muskets nicely in line ready to fire a volley into them. What execution we did by it we did not know but they shouted over to us their utter disgust for such a d—d yankee trick." Fairness in the killing and compassion for the killed had long since disappeared.

"One of the most disagreeable duties during this time that we had to perform," Marcoot recalled,

> was when we were detailed to crawl out of our works after dark as a videt[te] to observe the movements of the enemy so as to prevent a surprise. One night I was ordered out and crawled cautiously a considerable distance forward. I removed everything in my way fearful of making a noise and scarcely dared to breathe. . . . I soon wanted to cough and only a great effort could I suppress it. I was sure I had crawled over half the distance between the two lines [when] I imagined I heard something . . . like the heavy breathing of some one right [in] front of me and came nearer and nearer. . . . I did not turn around but I soon found myself involuntarily sliding backwards, and when day dawned I had only five yards to go to get inside our works. I have thought since that it was all my imagination but if my hair had turned gray the next day I should not have been surprised.
>
> On the morning of June 4th all was suddenly quiet in the enemy's works and rumor began to float around that they had decamped. On such occasions some one of the boys would cover himself with green leaves and boughs like a horse in fly time and crawl cautiously toward their line while his companions would keep a sharp lookout towards their line so as to shoot the first one that might discover our crawler. If they were gone, he would reach their works in safety, while if they were not gone he would discover the act and reach his position sometimes even undiscovered. This morning it was true, the enemy had left our front.[27]

The skirmishing and sharpshooting around the little log church called New Hope had cost the 15th four men killed and twenty wounded, close to 15 percent of the 180 or so men remaining in the regiment.[28]

Sherman's army at the same time was going hungry. The root of the problem lay in his ordering the armies to strike out across country away from the railroad, his only sure source of supply, with little or no understanding of its roads or foraging possibilities.[29] That did not stop Sherman from asserting to Grant, "Thus far our supplies of food have been good, and forage moderate, and we have found growing wheat, rye, oats, &c."[30]

Therein lay the misjudgment. Men were expected to take their food from "the most God-forsaken country we ever saw," as one soldier put it. "Two whippoorwills could scarcely get a living on a mile square, and if a third one should come on a visit, he would have to bring his rations or all three would starve to death." Miles away, Maj. Gen. Frank Blair, coming from Alabama with his Seventeenth Corps to reinforce Sherman, had already learned from guides that "the country is poor and destitute" and therefore was coming with his own wagon trains of rations, ammunition, and forage.[31]

Further, Sherman's wagon supply trains faced a serious difficulty of getting rations to the front; it was twenty miles to Kingston, the army's base of supplies, yet even Sherman had said that there are "no roads of any consequence" in that part of the country. On a ridge overlooking the country, Howard observed, "No person can appreciate the difficulty in moving over this ground unless he can see it."[32]

Men in their muddy hellholes wondered at the sense of it all. Friends were getting killed where they had hunkered down. Death kept coming with no letup and no reward in ground gained or, as far as they could see, Johnnie Rebs killed as payback. The physical and emotional strain was getting to be too much. With the shrinking supply of rations, with no farm or plantation nearby to forage, men looked for the first opportunity to escape the trenches. Men heading for the rear gave the excuse that they were helping wounded find a field hospital, incidents like the ones that appalled Marcoot after witnessing Hooker's men scurrying to the rear. Others were found loafing behind the lines miles from their regiments.[33]

After almost two weeks in the trenches around New Hope, Howard's corps was ordered to move. "The troops of this corps will move to-morrow," the order to General Newton read, "and you will leave the smallest brigade of your division to cover the corps hospital at this place until all of the wounded can be transported to the railroad. It is supposed that it will take about two days to move them. By order of Major-General Howard."[34] The "smallest brigade" would be Kimball's; that meant the 15th Missouri with the other five brigade regiments would stay behind on guard duty, eventually to bring up the corps hospital to join the rest of the division.

On the morning of June 10, Sherman again ordered his army to move south. Newton's division pushed ahead in a downpour on the 11th, the advance regiments skirmishing constantly for four days in the rain and mud. The 15th followed in reserve with the rest of Kimball's brigade.[35]

"On the 14th the artillery of our corps . . . opened a great bombardment toward Pine mountain," Marcoot wrote, raising the prospect that they would soon be ordered to charge, uphill and against a dug-in enemy, a prospect that no veteran cared to think about. To their relief, the order never came.

"On the following morning we were again convinced that the enemy had 'moved on,'" and hope for the day began to flicker again. "But it was soon discovered that he had taken up his position on some rugged hills that connected Kenesay [Kennesaw] with Lost mountain." As night came on, the 15th and the rest of the division halted and encamped in front of Pine Mountain, about a third of a mile from the entrenched Confederate line. They had come to a halt on "a fine position on a high hill which we fortified strongly during the night . . . earthworks were again thrown up. . . . It had now commenced to rain." It had in fact rained, according to Sherman, for twelve straight days. To the dug-in Missourians, "Our earthworks thus were not a very inviting retreat and were soon filled with mud and water."[36]

Men on both sides were not about to repeat the hell of their mud holes of a couple weeks back. Both sides took it upon themselves to cut a deal with their adversaries across the way. Perhaps a couple of pickets, one in blue and one in gray, by chance or by intent, met halfway in the no-man's-land between the entrenchments. Or perhaps someone waved a white piece of cloth, out where an officer to the rear could not see it, but far enough in front where the line up ahead could. Whichever way it came about, "during this time," Marcoot wrote, "the boys in blue and boys in grey entered into an agreement not to shoot at one another unless ordered to do so, in which case due and timely warning should be given. By this compact, while we lay at ease we could move about freely, getting on top of our works and talking with each other, the Johnnies and the Yanks."

Yankee and Rebel also partnered at times in an entrepreneurship of sorts. "We would meet half way between the lines," Marcoot recalled, "exchange newspapers with them and swap our coffee for their tobacco." Sometimes trade negotiations reached an agreement only after an extended amount of tough bargaining:

During this time one of the 44th Ill. went out with a few pounds of coffee to meet his tobacco merchant but they could not agree. The "John-nie" wanted more coffee for his tobacco, while the "Yank" wanted more tobacco for his coffee. So they agreed to wrestle for it, with the under-standing that the one who threw the other [two] out of three times was to take the whole lot. The works on both sides were lined with soldiers and when the scuffle began they began to shout, hurrah for the 44th, hurrah for the Johnnie. It was a short affair, however, and the 44th was soon master of the field and came marching back proudly with his coffee and tobacco. The shouting then became tremendous and one would have believed to hear the "yell" that a great victory had been won.[37]

Marcoot makes no mention about how the regiment's officers regarded these activities. Lieutenants at least no doubt knew and likely even shared in the bartered trade, as they too had to endure the mud and water-filled trenches. For those higher up and to the rear, there was the other and all-to-common escape: "Our division commander, General Newton, frequently appeared to be under the influence of liquor from the way in which he at this time quarreled with our brigade commander, General Kimble [Kimball]. . . . The boys," Marcoot added, "were decidedly in sympathy with the latter."[38]

The 18th of June saw a flurry of messages, the usual wigwagging of signal flags from the surrounding hills and the scurrying back and forth of galloping couriers. Thomas's signalmen wigwagged to Sherman of an assault by Newton's men the night before and again of Howard's entire corps advancing nearly a mile and half just that morning, to which Sherman's aide responded, "I am directed by the general commanding to say it is satisfactory, and that it is probably impossible to do anything to-day during such a storm. Raining here a perfect torrent."[39]

Even so, Howard and Newton thought it was possible to do something. Just before sunset, "we again charged the enemy," Marcoot recorded, "and drove them out of two lines of their works." Newton's report stated that the whole division advanced during a violent rainstorm, "directly under the fire from the enemy's line of works. Portions of the division had to maintain an incessant fire . . . to keep down the enemy's infantry." Newton concluded his report with the simple sentence: "Our loss this day was very large." Sherman for his part wired a brief message that night to Halleck. It started with the declaration: "Nothing new to-day."[40]

Sherman's telegram did not reflect the facts. But the general had reason to be less than straightforward with Halleck in Washington. That same day, Sherman had sent a letter to Grant. It was a letter that Sherman had probably thought about for at least a few days before he finally put the words to paper. Now, with a pause in the fighting, for him at least, he found the time to finish and get it off. The trouble was, the day's successes of Thomas and his Army of the Cumberland, minor perhaps in the overall scheme of things, nevertheless contradicted what Sherman had written to Grant.

Any time now, Grant could be expected to question Sherman about why he had not made more progress. Why had he not been able to engage and make Johnston pay in a major battle? Because they both had launched their marches south at the same time, Grant had been able to cover more ground—and he had the casualties to show for it.

Sherman chose to pin the blame on his, and Grant's, favorite scapegoats: "My chief source of trouble is with the Army of the Cumberland which is

dreadfully slow. A fresh furrow in a plowed field will stop the whole column, and all begin to intrench. I have again and again tried to impress on
Thomas that we must assail and not defend . . . it seems the whole Army
of the Cumberland is so habituated to be on the defensive that, from its
commander down to the lowest private, I cannot get it out of their heads."
He complained that just that day he had ordered Thomas's men to move at
daylight for Marietta, but that it had required his personal attention to get
them started. ("I'm afraid I swore, and said what I should not.") Sherman
neglected to mention that he had effectively cancelled the order soon after
by directing his aide to tell Thomas that "it is probably impossible to do
anything to-day during such a storm."[41]

Thomas's men moved anyway. A heavy rain fell on June 19, as it had for
the last two weeks. "The command suffered great hardships," the 15th's
brigade commander recorded, "being constantly engaged in skirmishing
or fighting with the enemy, bivouacking without tents, and often in wet
and unhealthy conditions . . . skirmishing continually day and night."[42]

Three days earlier, bugler John Beisel, one of the three musician friends
who volunteered together back in St. Louis, was admitted to a field hospital, a victim of the "great hardships" that Kimball spoke about. Whatever
the cause, John Beisel would never return. "Dropped from the rolls" is all
his record has to say. Joseph Lixfeld was another who would not return.
At the foot of his hospital bed in Chattanooga, the medical descriptive list
read, "Chronic Diarrhoea [sic]." Treatment: "Cod liver oil and whiskey" and
"lead." The list ended: "Makes no complaint . . . life feebly flickering."[43]

After a charge on the 18th and driving the Confederates out of the two
lines of works, but not a third, Marcoot recorded that

> the boys in Gray again left our front during the darkness. We followed
> them up quickly, experienced considerable fighting on the 19th and suc-
> ceeded to gain another fine position almost directly south of the Kensaw
> [Kennesaw] mountains.
>
> The 20th we spent on the skirmish line, and the day proved an
> uneventful one until about 4 o'clock, when a general bombardment with
> over one hundred guns was inaugurated. . . . Along toward evening our
> company cook brought forward our coffee, and while in the act of drink-
> ing my comrade and "bunkie," Adolph Fa[e]ss, was struck by a bullet
> from the enemy, inflicting an ugly scalp wound. Although he was not
> dangerously injured he had to be taken to the hospital in the rear. . . .
> It still continued to rain day and night and we layed quiet in our earth-
> works, muddy as they were.

The bombardment "never ceasing. The noise . . . had little or no effect on us. We had become so accustomed to it that our sleep was as sound as if all was as still as death."[44]

The Confederate forces had contracted their lines from two of the ridge-top knobs and concentrated new entrenchments a bit farther to the south on the larger 691-foot Kennesaw Mountain—a stronghold more formidable than the one Sherman had avoided a month back when he took the army into the wilderness around New Hope Church. From here, Johnston and his Confederate army "could look down upon our camps and observe every movement." Sherman's official report stated, " his batteries thundered away, but did us but little harm on account of their extreme height, the shot and shell passing harmlessly over our heads." The weather was "villainously bad," Sherman recorded, "the rain falling now almost continually for three weeks."[45]

"The sun does shine this morning," wrote a captain in the 1st Michigan Light Artillery in his diary entry for June 22. For more than a month, soldiers in both armies had been marching, eating, and sleeping in the rain and mud, standing to fight in trenches foot-deep in water and mud, never able to take off and dry their soaked clothes. A battle could scarcely produce a greater loss, men thought, than the hundreds who had gone to the rear suffering from pneumonia, influenza, and rheumatism, not to mention the many who had broken down from the mental strain.[46]

Two days later, Sherman ordered an assault. The rain had stopped, the sun was out, and the roads were drying out. "An army to be efficient must not settle down to a single mode of offense," he said in his official report, "but must be prepared to execute any plan which promises success. I wanted, therefore, for the moral effect to make a successful assault against the enemy behind his breast-works."[47] Six months earlier, Sherman had written his sister that "wherever a result can be accomplished without Battle I prefer it."[48] One wonders whose "moral effect" needed addressing. Perhaps he was recalling when he first saw the horror and chaos of battle, "when for the first time in my life I saw cannonballs strike men and crash through the trees and saplings above and around us, and realized the always sickening confusion as one approaches a fight."[49] He may have revealed more about himself than he knew.

There was also the question of measuring his results with those of his mentor in the East. Gen. John A. Logan of the Fifteenth Corps had been at Sherman's headquarters the day before the orders were issued. Sherman, he said, had been reading a newspaper account of Grant's frontal assaults against Lee's entrenched positions; newspapers had been focusing on Grant's campaign, which, through Cold Harbor, had cost the Union 65,000 casualties, far in excess of the campaign in Georgia. "The whole attention of the country is fixed on the Army of the Potomac," Sherman said according to Logan, "and my army is entirely forgotten. Now it will fight." When McPherson offered that the same thing could be accomplished by a flanking movement, the general replied that "it was necessary to show that his men could fight as well as Grant's."[50]

After reading Sherman's assault order, Thomas had but one comment: "This is too bad." His adjutant asked him why he didn't protest. "I have protested so often against such things that if I protest again Sherman will think I don't want to fight . . . he knows my views."[51]

The order stood. The only choice now for Thomas was how to execute it. With a captain of his staff, Thomas made a reconnaissance of the Confederate line to his front, riding sometimes in sight of Rebel pickets. "During that entire search of almost half a day," the captain related years later, "I did not see one place that seemed to me to afford the slightest prospect of success. The place finally selected was chosen more because the lines were nearer each other than because the enemy's line seemed vulnerable."[52]

On the 26th, Thomas notified Howard that a division from his corps would cooperate in the attack, leaving it up to Howard to do the selection. Howard chose Newton's. Like the other division chosen for the assault, Newton's had not made a full-scale assault with all of its brigades at one time since the start of the campaign, which is probably why they were chosen.[53] That meant Kimball's brigade—and the 15th Missouri—would take part in the uphill charge against the entrenched Southerners.

Friendly staff officers or couriers possibly told some of Newton's men what they were going to do come tomorrow morning. Newton's men could not like what they heard. Privates who had made assaults like the one to come, and who now would have to do so again, could assess their prospects better than any general. If the men of the 15th found out, Marcoot gives no indication; he says only, "We were again sent out on the skirmish line."[54] Rumors are slower to get out to men on the skirmish line. Besides, June 26 was Pentecost Sunday. Back in the lines, men attended religious services, while in front of the entrenchments, informal truces, which had become common, had been quietly agreed to. Even the artillery batteries stopped their cannonading.

The Missourians' first indication of what lay ahead likely came with sunup. "[We] were relieved on the 27th by the 59th Ill., of the 1st division."[55]

The men of the 59th were not going to take part in the assault, but they knew who would.

The sun rose in a murky haze. "Awful hot," said a major from Ohio. The temperature would climb to more than 100 degrees. Marcoot and his comrades ate their breakfast, got up, and went back to Noyes Creek to rinse their tin cups and fill canteens. Drifting back from the creek, they were told to stack their knapsacks and haversacks and then pass alongside the ammunition wagons to fill their cartridge boxes. After that, they were to assemble with the rest of the division behind the outer works. The 15th "was posted on the left of the second line of our brigade."[56]

Sherman took a position on Signal Hill, a mile and a half north of where the main assault would take place. From this location, he had telegraph wire laid to his three army commanders. Messages now would come and go, for the time, with remarkable speed, delivering an immediacy not felt before. The first message began at eight o'clock: "The movement of my troops against the enemy's works has commenced. [From] Geo. H. Thomas, Major-General."

Not quite. Thomas's regiments were still filing into position in front of their works. Thomas's wire had jumped the gun; it was not until nine o'clock, according to Howard's adjutant general, that the prelude on his front began: two hundred Union cannon opened up on the Confederate works on the mountainsides—"Gun spoke to gun, Kennesaw smoked and blazed with fire, a volcano as grand as Etna. . . . It seemed as though the whole earth was upheaving." The Union bombardment lasted only fifteen minutes. With some of Newton's division still not in position, Thomas delayed the charge while the rest stood in line.[57]

"Our division was now formed into line," Marcoot wrote, "with fixed bayonets for a charge."[58] The division was five thousand strong, with Nathan Kimball's brigade on the left, George D. Wagner's in the center, and Charles Harker's to the right. They were formed into "close column of divisions,"[59] which means that Kimball's regiments were lined up in two columns of two companies each, about forty men wide in total (companies now being about half their full size), one regiment right behind the other. The nine regiments of the brigade therefore formed a long column with an overall front of forty or so men, forty-five ranks in all, one right behind the other, about seventeen hundred men.

The formation is the narrowest but deepest in the drill book. Howard expressly ordered it, "the ground being favorable for this." Ahead of them was a field of brambles and brush for about a quarter mile before the men would reach a skirt of woods. Once through the timber and out into the open, the regiments would then "deploy," spread out, and make a "sudden rush of numbers" for the enemy entrenchments.[60]

At last, possibly around 9:30 A.M., the order was given to advance. Wagner's and Harker's brigades moved up and scaled the outer line of works, two columns each for a total of four. Ahead of them was a strong line of skirmishers.[61] Kimball's brigade, which included the 15th Missouri, stayed put; they were to go in if the two brigades ahead failed or needed support, but not until they received the order.

The brigade first had to push their way through brush snarled by briars and snaky vines. "The obstructions in our path were so great that our progress was slow," Marcoot recalled, cannonballs and bullets screaming and whizzing at them from the hill in front. The brigade "lost heavily before we had covered one half the distance."[62]

At about 9:45 A.M., they reached the woods, pausing in the timber to deploy into line of battle. They then rushed forward at the double-quick, "unmindful of the terrific havoc in their ranks," running finally up the incline toward the entrenched Confederates just seventy yards away.[63]

"The enemy's works were almost impregnable," Marcoot wrote,

> on account of the obstructions placed in our way. They had two rows of . . . long logs bored through cross ways with three inch augurs, through which sharpened sticks were placed . . . two points of the sticks would rest on the ground while the other two stuck up about four feet. These sticks were only six or eight inches apart, while the logs were often sixty feet in length. They also had two lines of brush fences. All the brush from the timber cut was placed into rows with the tops cut off and the sharp points facing us. It was almost impossible to get through such barriers . . . in addition to this they had dug a broad and deep ditch. One could easily drop into it but to get out again was altogether different.[64]

Behind those obstructions were men commanded by Major Generals Patrick Cleburne and Benjamin Franklin Cheatham, Johnston's most determined commanders. Their troops were every bit as determined. Amid a fury of shot and shell, men in blue all around were hit and fell. Still, some of Wagner's and Harker's men made it through the entanglements. A color guard reached the trench and shot a Rebel captain. Almost immediately, the color guard was hit and fell dead, with twenty-four bullets in his body. The handful of others who made it were shot down, bayoneted, or taken prisoner.

Possibly at that same moment, Thomas received a reply from Sherman: "All well. Keep things moving." Sherman was referring to McPherson's assault to his front, about a mile to the left of Wagner's and Harker's men. McPherson's were driving back a brigade, the 1st Missouri, forcing them to fall back with heavy casualties.[65] These Missourians were from every corner of the state, and they were fighting for the Stars and Bars.

Farther to the right on the Union line, about a mile south, Wagner's assaults had fallen short: "After repeated efforts of both officers and men to get to the enemy's works . . . the command fell back for shelter to a ravine close to the enemy's works [probably the deep ditch that Marcoot referred to]."[66] Others were streaming to the rear in "an inglorious rush . . . like a herd of infuriated buffalo, running over and trampling each other under foot," Howard later wrote. Over on the right near what was to become known as Cheatham Hill, the brigades withdrew in good order, some men taking cover behind rocks and stumps. Thomas, his field glass focused on the scene, was overheard to mutter, "Too bad, too bad."

If there were "repeated efforts," they were made by only a few of the men who had started out. In less than fifteen minutes, by ten o'clock, it was over for Wagner's brigade. Nevertheless, Wagner received an order to charge again, this time with the division's other two brigades.[67] Harker's brigade had since withdrawn, and Wagner no longer had enough men left to make anything resembling a charge. The charge would have to be made by Kimball's men and Kimball's alone.

Kimball's regiments moved up and over the works and headed for the strip of woods and the clearing in front, now littered with both moaning and silent bodies of Wagner's devastated brigade. They moved out in two columns, the 15th Missouri in the middle of the left column. They were hardly over the top of their own works when they were hit with "a terrible artillery fire and musketry . . . as soon as we came outside of our breastworks and crossing an open field," the "field" of tangle-foot and snaky briars, some remembered as chest high. When the 15th reached and came to a halt in the strip of woods, Conrad deployed the regiment in line of battle to cover the brigade's left flank.[68]

The brigade was now formed into three successive lines of battle, two regiments abreast in each line. In the first line was the 44th Illinois on the right with the 74th Illinois on the left. The 15th was moved from its flanking position and "posted on the left of the second line of our brigade."[69] That meant that the 15th was now just behind the lead 74th.

It was now probably close to 10:15 A.M. While the other regiments remained in line in the woods, waiting their turn to make the assault, the

Kennesaw Mountain from Confederate entrenchments. An Illinois regiment was "swept away" by Confederate fire before a halt was called to the federal assault that spared the 15th Missouri from a similar fate. (Library of Congress)

men in the 74th and the 44th deployed. They were to be the first wave. The order was given and 160 men followed by 160 or so more rushed forward out of the woods and into the sunlight. For many, it is their last memory on earth.

Cannons belched fire at point-blank range, rifles flashed sheets of flame from beneath the head logs just seventy yards away. They could hardly miss. Heads of the blue-coated wave shattered like broken pumpkins, splattering brains and tissue on men all around. Moving bodies crumpled forward. Kimball watched as the 74th Illinois was "swept away."[70]

With a pause in the firing and the cannonading, the 88th Illinois was next in line with the 15th Missouri. They prepared to deploy, but then Kimball received an order: halt any further assaults. Kimball's regiments were to remain where they were: the 15th had been spared.

Fifteen minutes later, at 10:45 A.M., the telegraph clattered again on Signal Hill: message from General Thomas to General Sherman: "General Harkers' brigade advanced to within twenty paces of the enemy's breastworks and was repulsed with canister at that range, General Harker losing an arm. General Wagner's brigade, of Newton's division, supporting General Harker, was so severely handled that it is compelled to reorganize. . . . Colonel McCook wounded. The troops are all too much exhausted to advance," the message continues, "but we hold all we have gained."[71]

The firing continued through the afternoon, the Union wounded groaning and begging for help as they lay unattended in the glade between the Confederate works and the strip of woods. The day turned incredibly hot, at least a hundred degrees by more than one account, drying the brush to tinder. The constant firing of burning powder, wadding, and exploding shells soon set the brush to flame and blaze. The moans from the sprawled bodies in the open fields soon turned to screams as the flames crept closer.

Confederates behind their head logs could stand it no longer. A lieutenant colonel of the 1st Arkansas improvised a white flag with his handkerchief and tied it to a ramrod. He climbed on top of the parapet, all the while waving his improvised flag of truce, and shouted across the battlefield: "Come and get your wounded. They are burning to death. We won't fire until you get them away."

Maj. Luther M. Sabin of the 44th Illinois saw the flag and commanded a cease-fire from Kimball's men firing back from the cover of the woods. Groups of bluecoats emerged from the woods and began dragging the wounded off the field and into the safety of the timber while clusters of Confederates clamored from their trenches to help the Yankees, and in some cases, plunder the dead bodies. "Such is the effects of war," wrote an Alabama soldier to his mother a couple of days later. Grateful, nevertheless, for the humanity of the act, Major Sabin presented the Arkansas officer, Lt. Col. Will Martin, with a brace of Colt revolvers. The men on both sides returned to their positions in the woods and the trenches and resumed their firing and killing.[72]

Marcoot failed to mention this incident. Perhaps it ranked among the battle memories he said were too horrible to describe. The men of the 15th certainly had to be witnesses. They likely were willing participants in bringing back the wounded with Major Sabin and the 44th Illinois, who were lined up just ahead in the woods; the Illinoisans would have needed help to bring in the hundreds of wounded carpeting the burning field in front of them.

Sometime in the afternoon, the word finally came to withdraw. "I was ordered to fall back behind our works," Kimball reported, the movement "accomplished without confusion, under a most terrific fire from the enemy." Conrad recorded that the 15th was "compelled to withdraw" with the brigade, "to take our old position we had left in the morning," a third of a mile back from the disaster that had taken place that morning. "The order was carried out in good order."[73]

That night, the Union commanders began to tally up their dead and wounded. Overall, Sherman's losses totaled three thousand in the morning's attacks on the Kennesaw knobs. The 15th Missouri suffered relatively few casualties: Kimball's initial report listed one killed, eight wounded, and one missing for the 15th. A later authority reported the regiment's loss at Kennesaw Mountain as eight killed, nineteen wounded, and two missing.[74] But for the charge not made, there would have been more. Of the nineteen major battles in which they were engaged during the war, in only four did the 15th suffer a greater number of casualties. Other than at Pea Ridge, where they truly were bystanders, Kennesaw Mountain may have been the sole battle in which they were unable to fire a shot.

General Newton arrived early the next morning at Howard's headquarters. Newton's division had suffered the worst. The devastation of the battle must have been on his mind—two thousand killed and wounded, 40 percent of his men. There was the death of Colonel Harker, his—if not the army's—most courageous brigade commander. There were others as well. With all of this flooding his mind, he entered the tent. And he saw Sherman. Newton may have been fortified by whiskey, as Marcoot had seen him just days earlier. Second in his class at West Point, Newton possessed an intellect that was a match for anyone, and further, the general had already been recognized for his valor as a division commander at Fredericksburg and Chancellorsville and of a corps at Gettysburg. His reputation conspicuous to everyone in the headquarters tent that morning, Newton walked up and confronted the commanding general: "Well this is a damned appropriate culmination of one month's blundering." Sherman made no response. General Stanley, who despised Sherman, said he simply bit his lip.[75] Sherman would claim later that the attack could have been managed better, "With one-fourth more vigor, mathematically."[76]

In that, Sherman may have had a point. Eight brigades, fifteen thousand men, about the same number as Pickett had at Gettysburg, were to have made the assault. One difference was that Sherman's men went in piecemeal. Probably no more than half took part in the final assaults on the Confederate entrenchments. No more than half likely even fired their weapons. Instead of forming in one grand mass and attacking simultaneously, Howard insisted his corps attack in columns of regiments, one right behind the other. But the thick tangle of underbrush was also laced with fallen timber, no place, in Howard's judgment, to form a broad front of troops for the purpose of a rapid rush on the enemy works. Instead, narrow columns were to concentrate and move to penetrate what were considered to be the weakest spots of the enemy's line. But that also meant that the Confederates could concentrate their fire on the narrower target of the few leading regiments. Consequently, most Union riflemen could not fire because they would have shot into their own ranks in their front.

Both sides turned to the task of burying the federal dead. "We sent out a flag of truce and made an agreement," Marcoot wrote, "that each side should have the privilege of caring for its own dead and wounded as they lay between the two lines and neither could do so without the consent of the other."[77] Once again Marcoot perhaps could not bring himself to say more. A Confederate wrote about it years later: "I get sick now when I happen to think about it." The burial armistice took place "not for any respect either army had for the dead, but to get rid of the sickening stench." The Georgia heat had made handling the corpses an abhorrent task. He recalled the Yankee ingenuity for the situation: "Long and deep trenches were dug, and hooks made from bayonets crooked for the purpose, and all the dead were dragged and thrown pell mell into these trenches. Nothing was allowed to be taken off the dead, and finely dressed officers, with gold watch chains dangling over their vests, were thrown into the ditches."[78]

With both armies hard at work burying the federal dead, Yanks and Rebs mingled on friendly and even jolly terms. At the end of the day, the repugnant task complete, the men returned to their respective positions. As they were parting, a Confederate called to one of the Northerners: "I hope to miss you, Yank, if I happen to shoot in your direction." "May I," came the reply, "never hit you Johnny if we fight again."[79]

"After burying our dead and caring for our wounded," Marcoot recalled, "I think our company lost six—we remained quiet in our works. We were again on friendly terms with the enemy, and did not shoot at each other."[80]

On the last day of June, the 15th was put in the skirmish line, and Marcoot reported, "We exchanged papers with the boys in gray, thereby getting news from Dixie." The next day, "confederates came towards our line to exchange papers. We took them to be officers of considerable rank. They met us over half way and were anxious to view our lines. If we had St. Louis papers they would want New York. If we had them from New York they wanted them from Chicago and so kept us trotting back and forth to our lines to look for them. But soon the Major of the 24th Wisc. came forward and told them that if they did not go back to their lines he would order them fired upon. They went." The "major" was Lt. Col. Arthur MacArthur.

Marcoot recorded, "The artillery duel still continued vigorously but we did not shoot at each other on picket line until the 2nd of July when an order was given to keep up a steady picket fire for fifteen minutes. Before putting this order into execution however, we notified the 'Johnies' to keep low that we were ordered to shoot, and they all sought safe retreats. After the fifteen minutes were up our firing ceased and we notified them that it was all over. It took some time however to convince them that there was no 'yankee trick' in it, and it was late in the evening before our friendly traffic in papers, etc., was resumed."

"On the night of the 2d," Marcoot continued, "we received orders to move quietly." Along the way, "we picked up a number of letters that had been purposely dropped for us: 'Goodbye Yankees, the next time we will fight you nine miles on the other side of Atlanta and if you flank us out there, the next place will be on the other side of h-ll, where we are strongly fortified.' Another: 'Yankees, if I was in your place I would quit fighting for negro equality, for you will never succeed.'" Marcoot added, the regiment "marched through Marietta with our flags flying."[81] The 15th moved again on the 5th, camping on a high hill near the Chattahoochee River. Conrad noted, "We had a fine view of Atlanta in the distance."[82]

The failure at Kennesaw would not go away, and on the 9th, Sherman telegraphed a letter to Halleck seeking absolution: "Drop me a word now and then of advice and encouragement. I think I have done well to maintain such an army in such a country, fighting for sixty days. . . . The assault I made was no mistake; I had to do it." But then came the assignment of blame: "The enemy and our own army and officers," he said, "had settled down into the conviction that the assault of lines formed no part of my game, and the moment the enemy was found behind anything like a parapet, why everybody would . . . take it easy, leaving it to the 'old man' to turn the position."[83]

On that day too Sherman wrote a letter to his wife. Regarding Kennesaw, he repeated that he was "forced to make the effort." It would have succeeded, he said, had not his troops become "so used to my avoiding excessive danger and forcing back the enemy by strategy that they had to assault."[84] Days before in another letter to his wife, Sherman confessed to a hardening he felt within himself that seemed to bother him: "I began to regard the death and mangling of a couple thousand men as a small affair, a kind of morning dash."[85]

There were other letters from the regiments. "I tell you the men were mowed down like grass," a young man wrote home to his parents in Illinois.[86] Sometimes they were letters that arrived at a soldier's home from another soldier, the letter telling of the friend and comrade who would never write home again. Often, they were the only way a wife or family would learn of their son or husband. Letters that, in the words of Walt Whitman, the Civil War poet, changed lives and generations forever:

Come up from the fields, Father,
There is a letter. . . .

Adam Happ had recently arrived from Prussia when he volunteered in August 1861. Happ was in the assaulting column with the 15th Missouri at Kennesaw Mountain when he was shot in the left leg. The leg was soon amputated, probably in one of the hospital tents just behind the main line. He was put aboard a hospital train bound for the army hospital in Chattanooga. Three weeks later, on July 16, he died. "No personal effects," said the inventory of his possessions. Nor was there a notation indicating "nearest relative."[87] There would be no letter to someone back home for Adam Happ.

17

────────────

────────────

Fortwahrend Schlachten und Mord

A captured trooper from Johnston's Rebel army was asked what he thought of Sherman. "Sherman gits on a hill, flops his wings and crows, then yells out, 'Attention! Creation! By kingdoms right wheel! March!' And then we git!"[1]

Sherman wasted no time in calling his kingdoms together. At nine o'clock on the night of the Kennesaw disaster, Sherman telegraphed Thomas asking if he was "willing to risk" the move on Fulton, a rail town ten miles to the south. "When do you wish to start?" came the reply. Sherman answered, the "day after tomorrow."[2]

Along the march, Johnny Reb continued to leave a trail. Marcoot remembered, "When [the Confederates] evacuated Dallas they nailed a sign board upon a tree reading: 'Till here and no further.' After we had crossed the Chattahoocha [Chattahoochee] river we saw many more similar arranged messages saying."[3]

A week later, across the lines, Gen. Joseph E. Johnston received a message from President Jefferson Davis: "You are relieved." The next day, headlines blazed in Atlanta: "Hood Supplants Johnston."

Gen. John B. Hood, born in Kentucky and a graduate of the United States Military Academy—"bold even to rashness and courageous in the extreme," Sherman had learned from another general who had known Hood at West Point. Hood was all that and more. He had lost an arm at Gettysburg and a leg at Chickamauga. In the mornings, he now had to be strapped into his saddle. If anything, at thirty-three, he was fiercer than ever.

Hood lost little time in his new assignment. Sherman had sent the two armies under McPherson and Schofield toward the east, around the Confederate right near Decatur, six miles east of Atlanta. Thomas's Army of the Cumberland was to move against the center. The problem was that Sherman's plan created a gap nearly three miles wide between Thomas and his nearest support from Schofield's force. Hood spotted the opening and moved to attack.

On July 18, Newton's division marched seven miles down the main road toward Atlanta, meeting little resistance and camping that night near Buckhead. The next evening, they crossed Peach Tree Creek, Hooker's corps crossing first. "By the time we had reached the opposite shore," Marcoot recorded, "it had become quite dark. The works of the enemy were but a short distance back from the river, and we had already captured a number of persons."[4] These prisoners could have been ones who let Thomas know that most of Hood's army was in his front.

Late that night, Sherman's plan for the next day arrived for Thomas. Sherman intended to take the bulk of Howard's corps from Thomas, and, with McPherson's and Schofield's armies, move on Atlanta from the east and "fight the whole of Hood's army, leaving you [Thomas] to walk into Atlanta, capturing guns and everything." Only two divisions, Stanley's and Newton's, were necessary, Sherman said, for Thomas to take the main road into Atlanta to do the walking and the capturing.[5]

If most of Hood's army indeed was in Thomas's front, then Sherman was operating in the dark. Not completely sure what he was hearing, Howard went to Thomas early the next morning to make sure his assignment was correct. Yes, it was according to orders, Thomas said. Then, with a smile that was probably a little more than wry, Thomas added, "We must act independently." Saying goodbye to Howard, Thomas moved off to the east, leaving only Newton's division on the road to Atlanta.[6]

Newton's division moved out, away from the south bank of Peach Tree Creek, across open country of sedge grasses and rushes. Once in a while they crossed a soft ridge of thickets and woods cut by deep hollows. They had spread out in line of battle, Kimball's brigade in the lead, the 15th Missouri posted in the center of the second line. Late in the morning, the division advanced about a mile along the road and the adjacent fields when it began to run into gray skirmishers. Around noon, Thomas arrived on the scene. Skirmishing was also going on off to the right in front of Hooker's corps, he said. Hood could be loose somewhere in front, but where? Given this Confederate's reputation for rashness, Newton remarked that the situation to him had an "ugly look."[7]

Ahead on a low ridge about a third of a mile away, Thomas could make out a line of entrenchments. Turning to Newton, Thomas ordered a strong skirmish line to advance and take the works. Around noon, four Illinois regiments with Ohio and Kentucky regiments in support, about twelve hundred men in all, advanced up the rise toward the Confederate line, about six hundred yards away. The six regiments "charged upon them," Marcoot wrote, "and drove them out of their strong works and captured many prisoners. "It was in this engagement that Comrade Nicholas Kessler, of Highland, was killed." Kessler had been detached from the 15th to serve as a brigade sharpshooter.[8] He apparently advanced with the first wave of skirmishers when he was hit.

The six regiments took possession of the Confederate trench works on the first ridge when they discovered another, wooded and crowned with a number of cedars, about a quarter mile away. Pushing forward, they seized the second ridge without serious opposition, capturing a surgeon, two privates, and their ambulance and team in the process. With the ridge now in control, Newton moved the division forward to the new line and dug in among the cedars. Newton was no stranger to setting up a defense along a ridge, nor was Thomas, the former having been at the Union center at Gettysburg when Lee launched Pickett's charge. What might happen next may well have surged to the front of their respective memories of Gettysburg and Chickamauga.

Men immediately stacked arms and went to work with shovels while others with axes gathered timber and formed rails in front of the trenches. Four cannons were posted to straddle the road in the center of the line, each sighted to sweep a specific area to their front and side. Kimball's brigade took position to the right of the road with the Second Brigade on the left, part swung back to cover the division's left flank. Newton's right flank was unprotected, hanging in the air as it were. (Hooker's Twentieth Corps, ordered to move up from Peach Tree Creek to fill in the line, was late.) Newton's Third Brigade, Bradley's, formed along the road, "nearly perpendicular to the line of the other two brigades," as Newton described in his official report. "The formation was as near as possible that of a T, Bradley's brigade forming the tail of it."[9]

While this activity was going on, Kimball relieved the first skirmish line of six regiments. Assigned to take their place was the 15th Missouri, the 24th Wisconsin, commanded by Lt. Col. Arthur MacArthur Jr., and the 73d Illinois, the German-Missourians' old preacher friends. In command of the new skirmish line was Colonel Conrad.

Conrad had reason for worry. Off to the left, as well as up ahead, were woods. Who and what might be in them? Memories perhaps of what happened at Chickamauga assailed Conrad. "Having advanced about 400 yards, my right met the enemy's skirmishers in a hollow, where they had rifle-pits," Conrad recorded, adding in perfect German syntax, "out of which we drove them."[10]

The 15th rushed toward the top of the slope. "My regiment was nearly on the summit . . . when the Seventy-Third Illinois, with which we connected on our right, came to a halt." *Hahlt!*—Conrad bellowed in German when giving orders in the field—while at the same time ordering his left to draw back "to protect my left flank. I then ordered a few men to go on the top of the ridge to ascertain any enemy in force was near us."

Marcoot may have been one of those ordered to scout ahead. Marcoot remembered that the 15th had "advanced in skirmish line about a half a mile in advance of our main line. We had passed the hollow in which the confederates had dug their skirmish pits, while just on the hill beyond their main works had been erected. We thought these works were vacated from their appearances." Here his teenage brashness may have gotten the better of him. With the same recklessness that had gotten him in trouble back in February when he raced across the drill yard in an attempt to free jailed recruits in St. Louis, the nineteen-year-old Marcoot volunteered to go up the hill to see if there were any Rebels in those trenches. "At my request, I was permitted to crawl up the hill and ascertain, but was cautioned to be very careful, as we had no orders to go further forward than the hollow."[11]

Conrad no doubt ordered Marcoot and others up the hill to scout; it may have become an order only after Private Marcoot came up with the idea and the colonel concurred: "*Aber wacht aus!*"—but watch out! "And don't go any further than the hill. We have already gone farther than we're supposed to."

"Proceeding forward," Marcoot

soon gained a position where I commanded a view of the works, and vicinity beyond them and found that their troops were marching toward our left. . . . Soon [our] bugler in the center—far to our left—blew "retreat" but we were in no hurry [Conrad had ordered more than one up the hill] as we saw nothing to retreat from, and I still continued to watch the "Johnies." . . . Suddenly they came to a halt, then in quick succession came the command, "front, forward, double quick, march!" and over their works they jumped with a yell toward us. The fun was suddenly all over for me—for as soon as I started to run for my command, I was discovered and the way the bullets rattled around me for a few moments was not slow, and I could not make up my mind to heed their friendly intimation to "surrender, you d—d [Yankee]."

Conrad's scouts "came back in a few minutes" and reported "that the enemy was approaching in heavy columns on our left and also in our immediate front. Their reports proved to be true."[12] Marcoot and his buddies had stumbled onto half of Hood's army.

"A few minutes afterward," Conrad continued, "the enemy appeared in heavy force right in our front, on our left and right, firing and yelling, demanding to surrender, &c. Seeing the impossibility to hold my ground," Conrad ordered the men "to fall slowly back, which was done in good order, the men running from tree to tree, always keeping firing up, until we came near our works. . . . The First Battalion came in on the main Atlanta road. I posted it on the right of the Eighty-eighth Illinois Volunteers, near the First Ohio Battery."[13] That put part of the 15th with the rest of Kimball's brigade to the right of the road near the four cannons, the other landing behind the rails to the left of the road and mixing in with Blake's brigade, which is where Marcoot probably ended up.

Newton had been in position on the second ridge for a couple of hours, and, Marcoot recalled, "our troops had already thrown up considerable earthwork, not formidable at all, but something for the boys to stand by. As soon as we had returned from the skirmish line, our command opened fire, and I fear that Comrade Phister fell from a bullet from a musket of one of our own men, as I had passed him completely fagged some thirty yards from the line in my own wild race for life." Samuel Phister, thirty-five, a shoemaker originally from Switzerland, was hit in the shoulder and the left leg, which was soon amputated. Phister died six weeks later in a Chattanooga hospital.[14]

The dusky gray columns came over the hill so quickly that Kimball's brigade barely had time to throw aside their shovels and grab their rifles. Both sides opened fire. One of Newton's cannoneers said it sounded "something like the heavens and earth had suddenly come together."[15]

A gray column raced past Kimball's right. Another passed clear of the left through the woods headed for the rear of the brigade. To the center and the left, Confederate lines rushed forward "in echelon," one line after the other in a staggered formation, each succeeding line slightly farther to the right of the one ahead for the purpose of getting around the Union flank. All were aiming for the thin blue line—possibly as many as 15,000 of Hood's men setting their sights on Newton's 3,200 and another 15,000 striking Hooker's Twentieth Corps of 9,000 off to the right—half of Hood's army taking on about a tenth of Sherman's.

The attacks came fast and close together, "so rapid I could not keep account," Newton reported. "The only thing that troubled me was that I did not have half men enough to hold the ground." With only one line, regiments had to be moved out of line to meet an attack at another point. "The enemy passing around Kimball's right, he was compelled to take a regiment from his line of battle and form against them . . . firing into their flank, dispersing them and driving them off."[16]

Marcoot recalled a rifleman's view from behind the rail breastworks in Newton's front line:

> Our cannon . . . had been brought up quickly and took their position on our right [next to the Atlanta road] a little to the front of our line, so that they could shoot down in front and parallel with our lines. When our confederates had advanced so near us that our officers were firing upon them with their revolvers, it was the grape and canister fired by those two guns that saved the day. The carnage however was fearful. The enemy seemed determined to stay and were literally mowed down again and again before they would yield. . . . Hooker's men joined us on the right and as we watched them we feared lest they were compelled to give way, in which case we would have been flanked on the right as well as the left. At times they were actually mixed up with the rebels fighting hand in hand, but they never wavered.[17]

With the fighting still going on a little past six o'clock in the evening, two hours after the first Confederate assault, Thomas sent off a message to Sherman: "The enemy attacked me in full force at about 4 P.M., and has persisted . . . attacking very fiercely, but he was repulsed handsomely by the troops all along my line. Our loss has been heavy, but the loss inflicted upon the enemy has been very severe."[18]

Two hours later, Sherman sent a message of his own. But there was no acknowledgment of Thomas's 6:15 message. Had Sherman received it? Did he not know that Thomas had been, maybe even still was, heavily engaged with almost half of Hood's army? Sherman's message communicated little more than acknowledging the one Thomas had sent at midnight, twenty hours before.

Sherman concluded this latest message with, "In the morning you will find the forts on the Chattahoochee abandoned, and think you will have no difficulty in pushing your line up close to Atlanta."[19] Sherman was far behind in his staff work. The general was just now getting around to responding to a message that had been sent to him ten hours earlier. Amazingly, he apparently was going over the oldest messages first—missing in the process the latest information that would have told him Thomas was fighting a major battle!

. For the Union, the Peach Tree Creek battle was one-sided: Hood lost 4,800 to Thomas's 1,700, a far greater disparity in numbers than Sherman's debacle at Kennesaw. Newton's division lost only 102 officers and men, the bulk of the casualties falling on Hooker's corps. The 15th Missouri suffered just one killed and two wounded of the total thirty-six reported casualties for Kimball's brigade.

At seven o'clock on July 21, Howard sent a brief message to Sherman's chief of staff outlining his corps' new positions. He then made special note of Newton's division, their casualties of the day before and the number of enemy dead buried in Newton's front, concluding, "The division made a gallant fight and deserves unqualified praise."[20] From Sherman, the praise would never come.

Even though it was one of only two lopsided victories he could point to during the campaign south—the other handed to him by a glaring Confederate misjudgment—Sherman barely took note of the battle along Peach Tree Creek in his official report. "During the afternoon of the 20th, about 4 P.M., the enemy sallied from his works in force," he said, "and fell in line against our right center, composed of General Newton's division. . . . The blow was sudden and somewhat unexpected, but General Newton had hastily covered his front by a line of rail piles, which enabled him to meet and repulse the attack on him."[21] That was all he had to say about Newton and his division's stand against an enemy that had greatly outnumbered him. Perhaps Sherman could not forget Newton's tongue-lashing a month earlier.

But for the stand by Newton and his division, a stand brought on by Sherman and the gap his marching orders had created, the Union may well have suffered the "serious consequences" that Newton reflected on in his report,[22] consequences not unlike those created by another gap along another creek in Georgia. As at Chickamauga, one of those consequences could have marked the end of another commanding general's career.

The next day, Marcoot recorded that a large number of the regiment "were detailed to bury the dead." The men of the 15th had no way of knowing that they had lost another of their own that day a hundred miles away. Charles Delfs, a musician from Holstein, Germany, had been languishing almost three months in the army hospital at Chattanooga from wounds he had suffered at Resaca. Delfs had only joined the regiment in March. On July 21, he died. To Charles J. Richter, his "next friend," as he had designated on his volunteer papers, Charles Delfs left his silver watch. One month after he had died, the watch was delivered by the Adams Express Company to his friend on Franklin Street in St. Louis.[23]

After the bloody repulse at Peach Tree, Hood withdrew his army into Atlanta's inner defenses. The fox had failed to catch the quarry out in the open, and the quarry was now inside the hole.

Off to the west, the men of the 15th Missouri could only wonder at the sounds of battle that raged to the east. It would be referred to as the Battle of Atlanta. During the night, Hood withdrew again behind the city's defenses, leaving the Union line blunted but still intact. Hood had gotten the far worst of it, losing 8,500 men and Sherman 3,700, but the Union had lost a boy general, Maj. Gen. James McPherson, thirty-five, killed at the outset of the battle.

With McPherson's death, General Howard, the 15th's corps commander, assumed command of the Army of the Tennessee. Col. Emerson Opdycke of the 125th Ohio took over the First Brigade, the 15th's. "I can not say that we fully appreciated the change," Marcoot wrote.[24]

There was much more behind Marcoot's recollection than he was willing to reveal. Perhaps Marcoot preferred to be vague, for many of the principals involved in one of the 15th's most bizarre episodes were still alive at the time of his writing. That the 15th did not fully appreciate the change is an understatement; the incident brought the regiment to an uproar.

It began a day or two after the Peach Tree Creek battle. The 15th's quartermaster, Lt. Adolphus Erdmann, learned he was under investigation for supposedly having violated an order by General Newton's assistant adjutant, a captain. Erdmann was accused of withdrawing the regiment's supply train when it came under artillery fire, refusing the captain's order to remain. Newton, who was not present to witness the incident, asserted in his endorsement of the accusation that "Lt. Erdmann's conduct had in it the essence of mutiny."

In a highly unusual act for a subordinate, Colonel Conrad refused to endorse the general's charge, writing instead, "Lt. Erdmann has [conducted] himself always as a good and efficient officer, always obeyed his orders strictly. The matter of which he complains is known by me to be true and I respectfully wish that proper . . . reply may be made for the indignity so unjustly placed upon him." How Conrad concluded that the charge was untrue is not known; the record includes no other facts for the charge. When Newton demanded that Conrad change his endorsement, Conrad refused, and the general placed the 15th's colonel under arrest for "contempt and disrespect towards his superior officer."[25] So began one of the more curious and extraordinary episodes in the history of the 15th Missouri.

German officers from the beginning of the war made no secret of their contempt for American soldiery, and its officers in particular.[26] This German lieutenant was no exception. Erdmann fired off a countercharge—to Maj. Gen. O. O. Howard, Newton's superior no less—accusing Newton of "unjust and unofficerlike treatment" and demanding "redress."[27]

Newton was unprepared for the counterattack. Further, a major blow against Newton came when General Stanley, the new corps commander, informed both parties that Erdmann's charges against Newton could not be settled without a formal charge and specification notification—which logically would have to come from Lt. Erdmann, a document that would initiate a general court-martial proceeding—against General Newton.[28]

What happened next sent the regiment into the uproar. The reorganization brought about by McPherson's death created an opening for a new commander for the 15th's First Brigade. The post should have gone to Conrad but went instead to Col. Emerson Opdycke, an Ohio native. Conrad's date of rank, the basis for command promotions, predated Opdycke's by four months—but the post could not be assigned to Conrad because of his previous arrest. The controversy dragged on for more than a month, the regiment in a rage, perhaps even close to mutiny. In the regiment's view, not only had a gross injustice been perpetrated against their colonel but the appointment went to an officer considered an "outsider" by the Germans.[29]

Late in August, a conciliatory overture in the form of a note to Erdmann arrived from General Newton's aide. (A copy of the note apparently has not survived.) Erdmann responded with a note of his own dated August 23, in which he referred to the aide, a captain, and his communication: Erdmann's response began with, "Your kind note with enclosure of Genl. Newton."[30] Peace negotiations were underway. "I will avail myself of the General's offer," Erdmann continued; the German lieutenant would accept the general's offer "to give all ample reparation in [my] power."[31]

Erdmann then took the opportunity to attempt a deal on behalf of Conrad. In two letters written to the captain on the same day, Erdmann called attention to the fact that Conrad "was not restored" to command of the brigade (had Conrad received command of the brigade before his arrest?) and that his colonel's military honor had been "impaired." "By assigning him *again*" to command the brigade "would have the beneficial advantage, together with the proposed settlement of my case to promote cordial harmony . . . and restore the '*status quo*' in our Rgmt and in fact through the whole division." Erdmann concluded, now apparently feeling in command of the situation, that "a favorable decision would settle everything satisfactory to all parts interested." One can only wish to know of Newton's reaction. A lieutenant bargaining with a general!

Erdmann was not finished. That same day, he sent off another letter, to the general's adjutant, this time with a veiled threat. Not only did Erdmann invoke the names of General Stanley and his assistant adjutant, Colonel Fullerton, but he also implied that both had "great interest in [the] Col. C. case," adding that "there would be new trouble and dissatisfaction" if Conrad was not restored to command. Erdmann insisted that Conrad knew nothing of his "supplications" on his colonel's behalf.[32]

Pressure, apparently from an unknown source, brought the matter to a close. The charges against Erdmann and Conrad were dropped. But Erdmann did not get everything he wanted. Conrad was not restored to command of the brigade—if Conrad had in fact ever been given the command in the first place, and there is no record of that.

Was there a German-American conflict behind the scenes? The actions and behaviors that followed Conrad's arrest beg for another explanation. Erdmann's actions and the series of responses may have been motivated as much by ethnic animus as anything else. Anti-German feeling among Anglo officers was well established, and German officers made no secret of their scorn for their American counterparts.[33] Was the initial charge against Erdmann prompted by a disdain for Germans? It is impossible to know. The perpetrator may have been German. There is no mistaking that Erdmann brought with him the social prejudice and air of superiority that marked the German officer class. (This was the same Erdmann who two years earlier had written to express his personal disapproval of his regiment's commander, because, in Erdmann's words, his commanding officer did not possess "those high *military* and *social* qualities indispensable for a Commander of a Rgmt."[34])

There is evidence of an effort to mask the whole affair, adding weight to ethnic enmity as the cause, in the absence of any other hard evidence. The captain's charge never made it into Erdmann's record, and there is no arrest notation in Conrad's official record. (Were these removed?) No bill of charges and specifications apparently were filed against Newton. Newton made no mention of the extraordinary affair in any of his surviving communiqués; however, an official acknowledgment would do no favor for the reputation of anyone involved in such an episode.

What about Opdycke? Did he know of the affair? It is hard to believe he did not, considering his obviously close relationship with Newton. Did he harbor a bias against the 15th Missouri? An August 6 letter to his wife, written within days and likely before the charges against Erdmann and Conrad became public, told of his new command, taking note of the 15th Missouri among his new, "good body of reliable troops."[35] But ten days later, with the Erdmann-Newton affair now in full sway, and the uproar from the German-Missourians now heard throughout the division, Opdycke wrote again to his wife: an "inferior" regiment, he said, was to be transferred out of his command—the regiment was the German 15th Missouri (adding, interestingly, "I had nothing to do, or say about it, at any time").[36] Nothing in the regiment's performance throughout the campaign justifies Opdycke's "inferior" label. On the contrary, Conrad received brevet recommendations twice for his leadership during the campaign,[37] reflections too of the 15th Missouri's performance.

Opdycke added to his wife that the transfer of the regiment was "one way of getting rid of ranking officers,"[38] namely Conrad, who technically outranked him. For Conrad and his regiment to remain in Opdycke's brigade would have been awkward, potentially even disruptive. The transfer was, and is, the military way to avoid a technically senior officer reporting to a lower ranking officer, and everyone involved would have accepted it as such. Unfortunately for the 15th Missouri, the transfer would also remove them from a place in Civil War history that was to unfold three months later at Franklin, Tennessee.

As for Erdmann, although an effective officer, his personal character was more than a little questionable. On more than one occasion he was accused of dealing in army property. He was, nevertheless, honorably discharged after the war. A year later, now a civilian, the army accused him of selling an army mule during his quartermaster service; a request went out for his arrest. Once again, Erdmann managed to dodge the authorities with his reputation still intact; a year later, still at large, he was brevetted a captain for "efficient and meritorious service." There is no record that the army ever caught up with the irrepressible former lieutenant Erdmann.[39]

Near the end of August, the men of the 15th learned of the Confederate prison at Andersonville. "Many of my comrades will remember the two soldiers who reached our lines here," Marcoot noted,

having escaped the confederate prison at Andersonville, Georgia. None who saw or heard them relate their experiences will fail to remember them. It would melt a heart of stone to hear a recital of the horrible sufferings and wrongs they endured, and one would have supposed that inhuman-

ity itself would have grown abashed at the barbarous cruelties inflicted
upon these helpless men and their comrades who were confined within
that pen of death. These men described the prison as a field of sand and
swamp, about twenty-five acres . . . surrounded by a stockade. In this were
huddled ten or twelve thousand prisoners. . . . When it was first occupied
it contained some brush and trees, but these the prisoners had early consumed in constructing little huts, only to be soon torn down again for
fuel. If a soldier was captured without a coat he lived without one during
his stay. Very few of them had blankets, while many of them did not have
enough clothing to cover their nakedness . . . there was also a fatal line
which had attained the significant name of "Dead Line." It was simply a
little furrow some twenty steps from the stockade on each side, which, for
a person to pass, was death. At first there was nothing to mark its location
and many a poor fellow that thoughtlessly stepped beyond it paid the penalty with his life. Afterwards a wooden railing was built to mark it and if
even a hand was placed upon it, the guard fired upon the offender. "Many
a poor fellow[,]" said our comrades, "who when first brought into the
pen noting the clean vacant space beyond innocently stepped over onto
it, only to be instantly shot down by the guard." They informed us that
there was scarcely a well man in the prison. They would dig holes in the
ground and huddle into them at night for warmth and were then almost
literally burned by the hot sun during the day . . . together with starvation
almost staring them in the face daily should cause universal sickness. The
hospitals were inadequate. . . . It soon became the prevailing sentiment
among the prisoners according to these men that to be ill enough to get
into the hospital meant a hasty journey to the graveyard.[40]

Marcoot could not have known at the time, but there were more than a
few of his comrades from the 15th confined to Andersonville. Most had been
there since their capture at Chickamauga, as had Charles Neikirch, eighteen
years old, and Joseph Reiterman, nineteen years old. Just that week, on July
25, John Engler of the 15th Missouri died of starvation and exposure. Henry
Rutz, of Highland, Illinois, would survive after more than a year of captivity.
Three weeks after Lee's surrender, Rutz was paroled and returned home, as
was Phillip Schuh, also to return home when the war ended, only to die a
month later from the effects of exposure and starvation. There were others.
Peter Bischoff and Xavier Blum were both known to have been captured at
Chickamauga and likely taken to Andersonville. Neither returned.[41]

Two days before the battle along Peach Tree Creek, Marcoot's "bun-
key, Comrade Adolph Fass [Faess] . . . wounded some weeks ago, [had]
returned from the hospital. He had been proffered a furlough but refused

it, preferring to return to his regiment." A few days later, Faess received a letter from his sister, disappointed and even angry at his turning down a chance
to go home. On July 29, Faess found time to sit down and write his reply:

> Dear Sister R:—
>   With joy did I receive your dear letter of the 21st inst. to-day and see in
> it your displeasure at my not accepting a furlough and coming home. I am
> truly sorry that I gave you a vain cause for such a hope and joy, and as you
> ask, for an explanation and a reason why I longed to return to my regi-
> ment more than to my home. I will give you the following: As my wound
> was again healed, I considered [i]t my duty to return to the field where
> I was again able to perform my duty to my country. I could not content
> myself with the idea that my comrades in arms should stand in that field
> facing the enemy and fighting battle after battle while I should be sulking
> [skulking] in the rear. Had my wound been more serious, so that I would
> have been disabled for a longer time to perform my duty in the field, I
> should certainly have accepted the proffered furlough and returned home
> to see you all, for the Lord knows how I long to return home in peace.
> But as it is, let us be content with our correspondence for a little longer,
> as I believe, with the help of God this war will soon be over.[42]

· · ·

August had opened sultry hot, even for Georgia for that time of the year.
Men collapsed from heat prostration while digging new works or out on
the march. But "our position," as Sherman saw it, "was healthy, with ample
supply of wood, water, and provisions. The troops had become habituated
to the slow and steady progress of the siege; the skirmish-lines were held
close up to the enemy . . . and kept up a continuous clatter of musketry. The
main lines were held farther back . . . with muskets loaded and stacked for
instant use. . . . The men loitered about the trenches carelessly, or busied
themselves in constructing ingenious huts out of the abundant timber, and
seemed as snug, comfortable, and happy, as though they were at home."[43]

Even so, death was ever close. While the 15th was on picket duty, Marcoot recorded, "Two confederate officers had secured blue uniforms and
came within our lines. They were suspected, watched and soon placed under
arrest. They were immediately tried as spies, [judged] guilty and executed
without delay."[44]

More men in ragged gray were now finding their way into the Union
lines and laying down their arms, and Johnny Reb chewed the fat with Billy
Yank. "From conversation with our confederate prisoners," Marcoot wrote,
"we learned that their losses during the campaign were very heavy. They

were much dissatisfied with General Hood and seemed to have greatly preferred Johnston." Not many days back, Marcoot recalled, there had been a different kind of talk, messages left along the march by Johnny Reb indicating there was still a good deal of fight left in the Southern soldier. "After we had crossed the Chattahoocha [Chattahoochee] river we saw many more similar arranged messages." One of the latest read, "Thirteen miles to Atlanta, eleven miles from h-ll."[45]

The Southern writer was more correct than he knew. Hell had indeed come to Atlanta. Hood was struggling to feed the forty thousand or so troops manning entrenchments on the outskirts. Within the city, possibly ten thousand citizens and refugees refused to leave, digging "bombproofs," as they called them, in backyards and gardens. A man who lived through it recalled, "Shot and shell rained in every direction. Great volumes of sulphurous smoke rolled over the town, trailing down to the ground; and through this stifling gloom the sun glared like a great red eye peering through a bronze-colored cloud."[46]

From where they were entrenched north of the city, the men of the 15th could see most of it: "The bombardment of Atlanta continued vigorously and many were the fires that broke out in the city; so effective was the fire. We could not only plainly see the fires as they broke out but could often during the night hear the fire bells ring out the alarm. . . . At four o'clock on the morning of the 19th," Marcoot recalled, "we witnessed the greatest bombardment we had yet seen. It was even greater than at Kenesaw [*sic*] mountain. General Sherman had procured a number of large siege guns and was now testing them on doomed Atlanta, and the earth fairly trembled so great was the concussion."[47]

Marcoot remembered, "It was on the 25th of August and I had just been relieved from picket duty. It was a very dark night, uncomfortably warm, and the roads were in a frightful condition from the recent rains. Our pioneers had cut poles and laid them corduroy fashion across the worst places to enable the wagons to pull through, it made it very hard and disagreeable marching for us. We were warned on leaving our works to proceed as quietly as possible so that the enemy wouldn't detect our movement, but it was very trying upon such roads to do so for some one was constantly falling, pealing their shins, etc., and exclamations were in demand. We marched in the rear of our line towards our right, passing over our battle field of July 20th at Peach Tree Creek."[48]

Sherman had decided to attempt another maneuver. After twenty-four days of bombarding Atlanta, with no evidence that Hood would do anything but continue to hole up in the city, Sherman ordered his armies to move out of their trenches. Leaving a corps entrenched north of the city to guard his

railroad supply line over the Chattahoochee, Sherman sent the rest of his
army to wheel around to the southwest. Once again on the march, the Union
column stretched for six miles to the west of the city. The objective was to
destroy two railroad lines coming in from the west that were helping to keep
Hood and his Southerners alive inside the city. "When we first moved out,"
Marcoot said, "we were put on the double quick march and were compelled
to keep it up most of the time for some ten miles, or to Red Oak."[49]

Confederates could not help but know something was up. After more
than three weeks of almost constant bombardment, the shelling stopped.
Gray pickets crept out of their holes. Probing across the no-man's land, they
learned what could only be hoped for: the Union works were empty. Had
Sherman finally abandoned the effort to take the city? Had he turned around
to head back north? Hood and the Southerners thought so. A ball was even
prepared to celebrate the supposed victory, with women brought back to the
city after a sanctuary in Macon to the south. There would be a celebration.

But seventy thousand of Sherman's Yankees had come to a halt just west
of the city. Facing about, they presented a six-mile front toward the unsus-
pecting Hood and his men a handful of miles away. The Yankees once again
began to dig in: On "the 28th, we moved forward some fifty yards," Marcoot
said, "and succeeded in making another line of works. . . . We had all become
expert choppers and diggers by this time, and the boys seemed to delight in
fortifying themselves." That done, the men put their picks and shovels to
a different work. Levering up the rails and gathering the ties into gigantic
piles, Sherman's men soon had huge bonfires ablaze to heat the rails for
twisting the iron around trees, "Sherman hairpins," as they became known.

"Early on the morning of the first of September . . . [w]e struck the
Macon railroad at Rough and Ready station, and completely destroyed the
track for several miles towards Jonesboro." In a rare night attack for the
Civil War, the regiment was ordered to charge

> across an open field. The grass and weeds, fully knee high caused many
> of our boys to fall as if shot down. . . . There was a thick wood in our
> front in the edge of which we could see the flash of the enemy's rifles.
> From what we could see we supposed that it was merely a skirmish line
> and lunged headlong in upon them and were soon mixed up among
> them. As I and two other comrades came upon one of the pits a Johnnie
> threw his rifle out between us and fired, but as good luck would have it
> he injured no one. We grabbed him on the spot and made him a pris-
> oner. Some thought he ought to have been shot, and he seemed to fear
> some such action himself, as he begged manfully for his life.

The wood into which we had come was as thick as a cane break, all young saplings, and so close together that we could hardly get through them . . . we became scattered, lost our commands and in some instances got mixed up with the confederates. It was thus that a squad of confederates met a few of our regiment. Up went their rifles followed by those ominous sounds click, click [musket hammers being cocked for firing], with the query: "What regiment do you belong to?" Our boys answered promptly, "the 15th Mo.," and it so happened that they had a 15th Mo. Confederate regiment with them, and thought it was all right and their guns were lowered but it was too dark to see much. It was now our turn to interrogate and we immediately asked, "What regiment do you belong to?" and they answered the "3rd Florida." Click, click went our guns and they were made our prisoners. . . .

About two o'clock in the morning we were startled by the sound of a terrible explosion in the direction of Atlanta, some 25 miles distant, followed by other light reports. No one at that time knew just what it was, but we afterwards found out that the confederates had blown up their ammunition and destroyed other government property in Atlanta, prior to evacuating the city.

After driving the enemy through Jonesboro [on September 3] we pushed them as far as Lovejoy Station, where they made another stand. . . . We then made one desperate charge to carry their works but failed. It was not a general movement but a spurt of our brigade commander General Opdycke.

The editorial tone of Marcoot's remark reflects, no doubt, his feelings following the Erdmann affair that ended only a week before. "Our loss was considerable. Engelbert Dreher and Wm. Lorenz were both wounded; the former soon recovered and returned to the company, but the latter was discharged finally for disability."[50]

Sometime that day, Sherman learned that Hood had evacuated the city. He sent off a wire to Lincoln: "Atlanta is ours, and fairly won." One hundred and twenty days after breaking camp across the river from Chattanooga, Sherman's armies had at last won the great victory.

In Washington, with reelection or defeat looming just weeks ahead, the president's attention had been focused for the most part on the outcome of the happenings in the trenches around Petersburg, Virginia, for there, many thought, is where his future would be determined. Then came the news from Sherman.

For Mr. Lincoln, his salvation had come from the West.

In spite of the Opdycke-ordered charge that morning, September 3 "was a quiet day in the main" for the 15th, according to Marcoot. "A non-veteran of Co. 'C' whose time had been out [service expired] . . . and who had been staying with the company cook in the wagon train, at this time came forward to drink coffee with us. He had seated himself behind a large tree and was enjoying himself with us, when a stray bullet from the front struck and killed him instantly."

Marcoot continued, "The next morning when the confederates came to feel of our line we captured one hundred of them with very little fighting . . . the men could sense it was all but over. On the 7th all was again quiet."[51]

Hood's army was gone. Southwest of Atlanta, it took a turn and headed north, away from Sherman and his army. Although he had plucked the plum of the South, Sherman had failed in his assignment to "break up" the Confederate army in his front. Hood's army was, in spite of mass desertions, still very much intact with upward of forty thousand men, and they were heading north, into Sherman's rear.

Even so, Lincoln and the North celebrated. After months of grim silence that had followed failure upon failure, the mood now changed to jubilation. Bells rang, guns boomed, and the president requested that thanksgiving be offered in all churches on the following Sunday. For Lincoln's reelection chances, Republican politicians expressed delight that the fall of Atlanta had wiped out half of their opponent's platform.[52]

Near the end of September, the Army of the Cumberland held a dress parade. The purpose was to read to the troops General Order No. 134. The order read that the major general commanding, George Thomas, took pleasure in joining "such distinguished marks of appreciation from the President of the United States for the tenacity of purpose, unmurmuring endurance, cheerful obedience, brilliant heroism and all those high qualities which you have displayed in attacking and defeating the cohorts of treason." The order ended with an appeal to remain true to the "silent mounds" of their comrades that marked the march along the way. Along their courses through northern Georgia, the armies of the Cumberland, the Ohio, and the Tennessee had left almost thirty thousand in dead and wounded, almost a third of those who had started the march four months earlier.

A young German soldier from St. Louis in the 3d Missouri, resting now in camp on the outskirts of Atlanta, perhaps expressed in his *Tage Buch*, his diary, the feelings of thousands of others and what they had come to know firsthand: the war had become a *"fortwahrend Schlachten und Mord."*[53]

Those writing in another language probably wrote something similar: the war had indeed become a "continual slaughter and murder."

18

Second Best in America

Boarding a train in Richmond, Jefferson Davis made his way south to Macon, Georgia, stopping along the way to battle the despondency that was sweeping the South. But Davis's mission to Macon had another purpose. In three days of meetings with Hood that had ended the night before, the details for a battle plan were sharpened, in the president's words, "to plant our banners on the banks of the Ohio."

As Hood was to describe the meetings, "I conceived the plan of marching into Tennessee with the hope to establish our line eventually in Kentucky" and to destroy Sherman's communications along the Tennessee River and "move upon Thomas and Schofield, and attempt to rout and capture their army before it could reach Nashville. I was imbued with the belief that I could accomplish this feat, afterward march north-east . . . then move into Kentucky. . . . In this position I could threaten Cincinnati, and recruit the army from Kentucky and Tennessee; the former State was reported, at this juncture to be more aroused and embittered against the Federals than at any other period of the war."[1] If Sherman were to move south, Hood added, he would take his army into Kentucky, compelling Sherman "to return to confront my forces. . . . I hoped then to be in condition to offer battle; and, if blessed with victory, send reinforcements to General Lee, in Virginia, or to march through the gaps in the Cumberland Mountains and attack Grant in rear. . . . This move, I believed, would defeat Grant, and allow General Lee, in command of our combined armies, to march upon Washington."

Sherman was also beginning to nurture an idea. Asserting now that protecting his supply line from the North required too "many men to guard it," Sherman proposed a counter plan: march *away* from Hood and his Confederate army, and in the process "sweep the whole State of Georgia."[2]

Grant dodged the idea. With Sherman away, there would be just George Thomas and his Army of the Cumberland to deal with Hood, and Grant had already demonstrated his lack of confidence in both. If Hood were to defeat the Army of the Cumberland in Tennessee, or even just brush it aside, a Southern army loose behind federal lines, with the way open through Kentucky and into the North, Jefferson Davis's boast of planting Confederate banners on the banks of the Ohio could become all too real. Cities such as Cincinnati and Louisville could feel the torch. The war-weary public might even insist on negotiations to stop the war.

While Hood was conferring with Davis on his move north, changes were taking place for the men of the 15th Missouri. Friedrich Lipps, the young lieutenant who had been cited for gallantry at Chickamauga and severely wounded at Missionary Ridge, nevertheless hobbled along with the regiment through its battles to Atlanta. The campaign now over, Lipps decided that his army days were also now over. His wounded leg was no longer fit to carry him well ever again, certainly not through the rigors of more campaigning. He was also "compelled to go to Europe to settle up my family business." Perhaps his parents were now deceased and he was needed back home. In any event, on September 22, the crippled young officer handed in his resignation, which was duly accepted. (He later returned from Europe and apparently lived long enough to collect his Civil War veteran's pension that began twenty-five years later.)

John Droste, the twenty-four-year-old lieutenant who had been wounded in the shoulder around New Hope Church and transported by rail to a Louisville hospital, now returned to his regiment. He was cited for distinguished gallantry during the campaign, as was Colonel Conrad, who was also being recommended for promotion to brigadier general.

On September 23, Pvt. George Rau got his stripes back. Promoted to commissary sergeant,[3] Rau had proved his mettle once again, but his combatant days were essentially over, physical breakdowns apparently taking their toll. His reward was a place with the supply trains and the rear echelons, a place of comparative safety.

There were other changes in the 15th. Earlier in the month, they had been transferred out of Opdycke's First Brigade into the Third Brigade under Brig. Gen. Luther Bradley from Illinois. In addition, of the regiment's 220 or so men in the ranks who started out in May on the long march of skirmishes and battles to Atlanta, 26 had been killed. At least as many more had been mortally wounded or permanently disabled. That left possibly about 190 in the regiment. Now, "On the 21st our non-veterans were mustered out [about 30]," Marcoot wrote, "and on the 24th they left us." Even so, more than 80 percent had chosen to reenlist, placing the 15th among the highest, if not *the* highest, regiments in reenlistments.[4]

Other regiments did not fare as well. Some failed to retain enough men to continue as a unit, the remaining members reassigned to other regiments. Such was the case with three other Missouri regiments, the German 3d, the 12th, and the 17th, all organized in St. Louis. In addition to participating in the battles for Atlanta, all had served in the Vicksburg campaign. The handful of veterans from these three regiments who did decide to reenlist folded into the 15th. That said, there were still no more than 160 German volunteers remaining in the 15th Missouri after three years of war.

On September 21, Sherman detected signs that Hood was shifting his army to the west toward the Alabama line. Sherman guessed that Hood intended to circle west of Atlanta and head north to strike the railroad from Chattanooga to cut his federal supply line. Sherman ordered two divisions north from Atlanta, one being Newton's depleted command, now just half its original size as a result of the summer's campaigning and the host of veterans who chose to go home at the end of their three-year commitments. With the remnants of Newton's division went the similarly depleted 15th Missouri.[5]

Sherman and the rest of his army soon followed in pursuit of Hood. The Confederates had been striking repeatedly along the railroad as far north as Dalton, tearing up track and even capturing that town where, ironically, Sherman's campaign to Atlanta had begun. Union troops quickly repaired the rails, Sherman refused to be lured into traps and ambushes, and the footsore Confederates were finally forced to withdraw toward Alabama for supplies.[6]

Now in Chattanooga, the 15th Missouri was getting an infusion of new blood. Near the end of October, the regiment received, Marcoot wrote, "about one hundred recruits." Replacing the dead and disabled veterans were recruits with names like Bennett, Burns, and Warrington, draftees, and a few who were simply bounty-pluckers—men such as John Riley who deserted in less than a month.[7]

Although the bulk of the ranks was still made up of German immigrants, with a few of German descent mixed in, the 15th could no longer be considered a truly German regiment. It now numbered fewer than 250 men in the ranks, but about 40 percent were native-born with Anglo names. There were barely a hundred left from the original German boys of 1861.[8] More

than 80 percent of them were gone. Three years of fighting had taken the lives of or maimed almost a generation of young German immigrants.

Almost immediately after mustering in, the new recruits marched off with the old veterans to the Lee and Gordon mill on the old Chickamauga battlefield, fifteen miles to the southwest. There was no basic training for recruits during the Civil War. New soldiers, if they could even be thought of as "soldiers," had to learn on the fly—how to march, how to respond to commands, even how to fire their muskets. Chances are, most of the recruits—almost half of the regiment now—had never touched a weapon until they were handed their Springfields when they arrived in the regimental camp in Chattanooga. They knew nothing of military discipline. They were, in short, little more than a rabble with arms.

The command marched to Alpine, Georgia, some thirty-five miles south. Here they joined the division now in the command of Brig. Gen. George Wagner. Three days later, the 15th received orders to retrace its steps to Chattanooga. But once again, Marcoot would be left behind. "I had been quite ill of rheumatism and rheumatic fever since the 23rd and was now unable to walk." He was placed in the ambulance train, arriving finally in Chattanooga, where he was assigned to a tent in a hospital compound. "There were many German boys in the hospital," Marcoot said, and he soon found himself in the role of interpreter for the many who could not speak English.

During his days in the hospital encampment, which would stretch to four months, the Yank from Illinois would develop a close friendship with a wounded Confederate prisoner from Alabama, H. M. Meadors. The Southerner would come to call his new friend from the North "Dutchey," and the young Yank would refer to his new friend as "Mr. Meadors," for there was a significant age difference. Years later, their friendship would have a major influence on the preservation of the 15th Missouri's history.[9]

But for now, the regiment had lost its main eyewitness recorder. For the second time in their long partnership of maintaining their regimental log, the job fell once again to Marcoot's cryptic bunkie, Adolph Faess, when some of the regiment's most dramatic, and tragic, experiences lay just ahead.

The regiment arrived back in Chattanooga on the last day of October but immediately received orders to get back aboard the rail cars. A report had just been received that "the enemy has crossed the Tennessee River above Florence," Alabama, no more than fifteen miles from the Tennessee border. Maj. Gen. George Thomas promptly issued orders to "get between the enemy" to resist "the enemy's progress into Middle Tennessee."[10]

Thomas followed up that message with another to Sherman, advising him that the Confederates had crossed the river and that he "was unable to prevent it." Thomas ended with an anxious request: "Can you send me Schofield [a corps of ten thousand] . . . because the force at Chattanooga is not sufficiently large or well organized to do more than defend that place."[11] Meanwhile, the train carrying the 15th pulled out at two that morning for Athens, Alabama, almost a hundred miles west. A forty-mile march from there could put them face-to-face with a part or all of Hood's estimated forty thousand infantry and as many as ten thousand cavalry.

Sherman himself had given up on bagging Hood. While the 15th Missouri and other regiments were chugging along the rails for Athens, Sherman telegraphed Grant: "The enemy is now in the full tide of execution of his grand plan to destroy my communications and defeat this army. His infantry, about 30,000 [a likely underestimation] with . . . cavalry, from 7,000 to 10,000, are, now in the neighborhood of Tuscumbia and Florence . . . the water being low is able to cross at will. . . . General Thomas has near Athens and Pulaski . . . about 15,000 strong, and Schofield's corps, 10,000 corps, en route by rail, and has at least 20,000 to 25,000 men, with new regiments and conscripts arriving all the time."[12]

The last was a flagrant misstatement. Reinforcements were not even dribbling in. Just the day before, Thomas had telegraphed Sherman that he had heard "nothing of the troops [he was expecting] from Missouri . . . neither can I hear anything of the balance of the new regiments expected." With the force he could muster to confront Hood at the Tennessee border, Thomas was outnumbered possibly by as many as two to one. There were possibly another 31,000 at Nashville and surrounding hamlets,[13] many of provisional militia and quartermaster and medical units, and they were more than eighty miles away.

Further, Thomas's forces were as yet not concentrated. The threat of being defeated piecemeal was all too real. Nevertheless, all but ignoring Thomas's message of the day before, Sherman pushed forward with his case to Grant for relieving himself of the responsibility of taking on Hood, using the excuse that a chase would cost the loss of hard-won territory: "If I were to let go Atlanta and North Georgia and make for Hood, he would . . . retreat to the southwest . . . to occupy our conquests, and the work of last summer would be lost."

Sherman's suppositions would turn out to be gross miscalculations. Sherman finished his message to Grant with words that made it clear he intended to "move [to the sea] as soon as possible."[14]

That evening, Grant telegraphed: "Do you not think it advisable that Hood has gone so far north to entirely settle him before starting on your proposed campaign? . . . If you can see the chance for destroying Hood's army, attend to that first and make your other move secondary."[15]

Their two messages had crossed; the next day, Grant got Sherman's message of the day before: "Your dispatch of 9 A.M. yesterday is just received. . . . I do not really see that you can withdraw from where you are to follow Hood, without giving up all we have gained in territory"—Grant was abandoning the dictum of destroying the enemy's army in favor of conquering *territory*, a directive that Lincoln had taken pains to instill into his Eastern generals. Thomas, Grant added, "must be able to take care of Hood and destroy him." Sherman then read the words that he wanted to hear all along: "I say, then, go as you propose."[16] At another time, a Union general would have been chastised for turning his back on the enemy. Meade after Gettysburg and McClellan after Antietam both paid a stiff price for not following up to destroy Lee's retreating army. McClellan was relieved of command of the Army of the Potomac largely for not aggressively pursuing Lee, and Lincoln came close to handing Meade a stiff reprimand. But now, Lincoln, having been handed the plum of Atlanta that allowed him to sense victory in the upcoming election, was in no position politically to question Sherman. Indeed, Lincoln would later write to Sherman that at the time, he and others, presumably the president's cabinet, could only "acquiesce" on the decision to march to the sea, that in "leaving Atlanta for the Atlantic coast," Sherman was "the better judge."

Getting down out of the rail cars later that morning, the troops of the 15th marched out of Athens, Georgia, setting up camp in a grove of woods. "It rained steadily the whole day and was disagreeably cold. . . . On the 4th, they marched eighteen miles and were compelled to wade" the frigid water of the Elk River, Marcoot wrote, "no pleasant job I can assure you at that season of the year. . . . They passed thru Pulaska [Pulaski] the next day and camped on a fine hill a mile or so beyond where they were put to work building breastworks in anticipation of the approach of the enemy. . . . [It] rained almost incessantly."[17]

Early in November, mail caught up with the men as they began to dig into the rain-soaked hill near the Tennessee town. At least one letter arrived at the tent of Lt. Col. John Weber: "Since the death last April of the last of your three children, your wife is getting worse day to day. . . . The physician attending to her has given his opinion, that her life can only be saved with your return home." On November 4, Weber submitted his resignation so that he could return to his home in St. Louis to be with his ailing wife. Twelve days later, November 16, his resignation was officially accepted.[18] Weber, the determined drillmaster and intrepid commander of Stones River and countless other engagements, was free to go home. More important, with him would go a level of leadership at a time the 15th could least afford to lose it.

That same day, after telling the townspeople to evacuate, Sherman burned Atlanta.

Sherman was headed east, away from Hood, on his march of destruction to the sea. With him Sherman would take his Army of the Tennessee, "the best men in America," he had said at the outset of the Atlanta campaign. With Sherman's "best," he would also take what he considered two select corps of the Army of the Cumberland. Sherman, in other words, would take with him his pick of the lot, about sixty thousand of the best troops in the West, leaving Thomas the remainder—the units that had been shrunken through casualties, disease, and expirations of service, their ranks replaced by recruits who knew little of soldiering.[19]

With Sherman shaking himself free of Hood, the problem of following the Southern general fell to George Thomas. The two were not strangers. Thomas had been an instructor at West Point when Hood was a cadet. During academy days, the pupil could probably recall how the austere instructor had earned a nickname that was to dog him the rest of his army life. When cadets on cavalry exercise would gallop ahead, Thomas, their portly instructor, would ring out the command, "Slow Trot, Slow Trot," so that he might, the cadets would say, catch up. Four years later, in the 1850s in the West, Thomas would be Hood's senior officer in the Indian-fighting Second Cavalry.[20] Now, the rash and even reckless Hood versus the deliberate but unflinching Thomas would be adversaries in the war in the West.

Sherman had left behind the remnants of the armies of the Cumberland and the Ohio, the two now reduced to barely two corps. To fill the gaps, many of the old regiments like the 15th Missouri had been handed, in addition, little more than a motley collection of civilians who up till now had been able to dodge the war, with few among them ever having fired a gun at more than a squirrel, if that. Further, Conrad had only eight line officers for duty in the 15th—less than a third of the normal complement to command the regiment's ten companies—which meant at least two companies were commanded by sergeants.[21]

Thomas's army truly was now no better than the second best in America, if that. That had been Sherman's oblique assessment back in Chattanooga before the battle of Missionary Ridge, the Cumberlanders' best days as a fighting army. A shadow of its former self—just one corps now, the Fourth, joined by another Sherman reject, the Twenty-third Corps from the Army of the Ohio—to this body of men and boys Sherman would leave the job of tracking down and bagging Hood and his hardened Southerners.

On October 21, Marcoot wrote that it began to snow.[22]

19

An Act of Providence

Having crossed the Tennessee River north of Florence, Hood stopped and appeared content to stay put. Perhaps the flooded streams and mud-choked roads were the reason. But a telegram on the morning of November 21 to Thomas's headquarters in Nashville brought a very different message. The commander of the cavalry patrols reported Hood was moving. Just about his entire Army of Tennessee had crossed the night before into Tennessee. "There is no doubt of their advance."[1]

Thomas promptly ordered Maj. Gen. John M. Schofield, in command in the southern part of the state, "to move back gradually from Pulaski and concentrate in the vicinity of Columbia, so as to reach that place before Hood could, if he should really move against that place." Orders followed for Wagner's division to march with the Twenty-third Corps' ten thousand men to Lynnville, fifteen miles to the north, about half the distance to Columbia. Included in the march would be the 15th Missouri. The division was to march at eight the next morning.[2]

The 15th broke camp in time to be on the road at eight. The day turned intensely cold. Hunching their shoulders into icy winds, the regiment covered fifteen miles in six hours, arriving at Lynnville in Wagner's division at two in the afternoon. Quickly setting up camp, they formed in line of battle anticipating an attack. But there was no sign of Hood.

Reveille sounded at 1:45 A.M., and the march resumed at four, moving north again on the Nashville turnpike. Around midmorning, hearing "the reports of three cannons apparently west of that city," Marcoot wrote, the 15th was "hastily put on the 'double-quick,'" arriving in Columbia, Tennessee, where they were again placed in line of battle and "commenced fortifying." Patrols of Forrest's cavalry "had come within reach of our artillery and were being held at bay by [artillery] but in the evening all became quiet again," the men returning to shivering around campfires before turning in under their single blankets.[3] The 15th likely took little note of the presidential proclamation that declared it a day of national thanksgiving.

Hood's infantry was still more than thirty miles away. The 15th, in Luther Bradley's brigade, had spent the day digging entrenchments when word came to move to the west side of town. They "built a line works" for the second time in two days. Marcoot's bunkie recorded in the log: "rains source of much discomfort."[4]

In Nashville, Thomas was feeling pressure from Grant to take the offensive. Thomas may have felt that Grant, a thousand miles away, did not understand his predicament in Tennessee. Their relations were not now and never had been on the positive side, the "Old Slow Trot" reputation possibly having no small part in Grant's urging. Those things notwithstanding, Thomas responded on November 25 with a message stating no more than the facts:

> Your dispatch of 4 P.M. yesterday just received. Hood's entire army is in front of Columbia, and so greatly outnumbers mine at this time that I am compelled to act on the defensive. None of General Smith's troops have arrived. . . . All of my cavalry was dismounted to furnish horses [for cavalry] which went with General Sherman. My dismounted cavalry is now detained at Louisville awaiting arms and horses—horses . . . and arms have been detained somewhere en route for more than a month. . . . Since being placed in charge of affairs in Tennessee I have lost nearly 15,000 men, discharged by expiration of service and permitted to go home to vote. My gain is probably 12,000 of perfectly raw troops, therefore, as the enemy so greatly outnumbers me both in infantry and cavalry, I am compelled for the present to act on the defense.

Probably not wanting to appear insubordinate, Thomas concluded, "The moment I can get my cavalry I will march against Hood, and if Forrest can be reached he will be punished."[5]

Two days later, Grant telegraphed a report with vague information that, "if true, will give you a chance to take the offensive against Hood," the message read, "and to cut the railroads up into Virginia with a small cavalry force."[6] One may wonder how severing rail lines "up into Virginia" could help Thomas defeat Hood in Tennessee.

That same day, Sunday, November 27, amid more rain throughout the day, Hood's army approached Columbia and took up positions along the south bank of the Duck River across from the city. A chaplain with the Rebel army observed in his diary that the people of Columbia were in "the wildest enthusiasm" over the thought that Hood had the Yankees on the run. But for the new arrivals in ragged gray and whatever else they had found to wear, the thought of provisions so close at hand in the town, now clearly in view, was too much to resist. Before daylight, many among the impoverished Southern troops, led in fact by two regiments from Tennessee, rushed into the town, breaking into stores and swilling down liquor wherever they found it. Some carried off bedding, while others hauled off school desks to fuel campfires. Hood issued orders against the plundering, but no punishments followed.[7]

Hood had no intention of remaining in Columbia. The goal was to cut off and defeat Schofield's small army before it could get to Nashville to join up with Thomas. Further, getting behind Schofield would give the Confederate commander the option of attacking Thomas first, before Schofield or other reinforcements could concentrate at Nashville. Hood would then have the opportunity to defeat Thomas in detail and capture the city with its large supply base, all of which meant first getting around the bluecoats now blocking the way.

On the 28th, word reached Schofield that Confederates were crossing the river in force east of Columbia. Schofield was in a quandary. Having no idea of Hood's intentions, and given orders to maintain his position to buy time for reinforcements to reach Nashville, Schofield decided to stay put in his entrenchments north of Columbia. But could these latest movements be a try to outflank him, to get behind him to cut him off from Nashville? Maybe even to make a dash for that place? Not sure which, Schofield ordered Maj. Gen. U. S. Stanley to take two divisions north as soon as possible. The first to go would be George Wagner's division. That included the 15th Missouri among the nineteen regiments—about four thousand men. With them would go most of the artillery and eight hundred wagons of commissary rations and ammunition. Their goal was to get to a small village on the map called Spring Hill.

About the same time, Hood had indeed decided to cross the Duck River and march north as rapidly as possible. Early on the morning of the 29th, gray infantry, probably close to thirty thousand (about eight thousand having been left behind to distract the Union general), began to make their

way down the riverbank. By 7:30 A.M., Hood's leading division had crossed
the river. Six other divisions were across in the next couple of hours and
starting to stretch out along country roads paralleling the Nashville pike to
Spring Hill.

They would have to cover about seventeen miles in back roads to get to
the pike, whereas Stanley would have a comparatively straight ten-mile line
to reach the village. By midmorning, Hood's infantry was about abreast of
the Union entrenchments three or so miles away. They were beginning to
get clear of the bluecoats with each marching step.

Being closer to the destination, Stanley's troops should have had a head
start. But for some unexplained reason, the first division did not move
out until eight in the morning. Wagner's division was even slower getting
underway, not reaching the Nashville pike until nine, about the same time
that the head of Hood's column was abreast of the Union line, only three
miles away to the east.[8]

Stanley did not know it, but a race was underway. Perhaps the weather
had something to do with it. After days of rain sometimes mixed with snow,
this day began with a soft breeze and mild temperatures for November,
signs of at least one more round of Indian summer. With the weather as
idyllic as the Tennessee countryside, Luther Bradley's brigade began the
march, bringing up the rear of Wagner's division. Behind them, about forty
pieces of artillery and the supply train of eight hundred wagons curled
lazily over the rolling road, moving at about two miles an hour. Riding
aboard one of the wagons carrying the rations for the 15th, Commissary
Sergeant Rau may have thought it looked like a good day to be taking a
ride in the country.

Near noon, a rider was seen galloping toward the column. Drawing up
to Stanley at the head of the column, a badly scared cavalry soldier, as Stanley described him, clattered to a halt: Rebel cavalry was ahead and almost
to Spring Hill. Stanley ordered the column to push on. Hearing the crackle
of firing up ahead east of town, the men were ordered to step out at the
double-quick. Coming in to Spring Hill, "General Wagner was ordered
to deploy his division at once; Opdycke's and Lane's brigades [were] to
cover as much space about the village" as possible to park the wagon train;
"General Bradley's brigade was sent to occupy a wooded knoll about three-
quarters of a mile" east of town.[9]

Around 1 P.M., Bradley was still about two miles away when he got the
order. Before he had a chance to up the pace to get to the knoll, he was
directed to move his brigade off the road "to let two batteries of artillery
pass." Losing possibly as much as another half-hour in getting off the road

and waiting for the artillery pieces to pass before getting back on, the brigade "then moved on again and reached Spring Hill about 2 P.M., and went into position on the east side of the village."[10]

While Bradley's brigade was still coming up, Opdycke's men arrived on the run and sprinted past the village a short distance when they ran into a line of dismounted gray cavalry that had advanced to within range of the parked wagon train. After a quick exchange of gunfire, the skirmishers gave way and disappeared. East of town, Lane's brigade, detecting a line of Confederates on a low hill a half-mile east, rushed the gray line, and after a half-hour of fighting, forced more of Forrest's dismounted cavalry to mount up and withdraw.[11] It appeared that at least two of Wagner's brigades had won the race for possession of Spring Hill.

Luther Bradley's brigade arrived at last about 2:00 P.M., delayed by their move off the road for passing artillery. They took up position on a wooded knoll east of the Columbia-Franklin pike. Bradley "immediately threw out the 64th Ohio as skirmishers," while four other regiments were directed to form into line of battle facing east. To the right went the 65th Ohio, followed by the 15th Missouri, then the 51st Illinois, and finally, the 79th Illinois to the far left. The 42d Illinois was held in reserve.[12] All were veteran regiments, but, as with the 15th, almost half of their ranks were now filled with recruits who probably had never shot a gun.

Back in Columbia, Schofield learned that a heavy column of Confederate infantry had moved north. The risk of being cut off was mounting, but the enemy force was putting up a good front, their artillery dueling across the river with his. Continuing to feel the pressure from across the river, Schofield decided to hold his position through the day and then withdraw all of his forces, beginning with Jacob Cox's division, as soon as it got dark. But around three in the afternoon, word came that more gray infantry was on the move toward the north. Grabbing two brigades to escort him, Schofield lit out up the road to see things for himself. In the distance, a rumble of artillery fire could be heard coming from the direction of Spring Hill.

It was now close to five o'clock, and the sun was behind the bare trees. The two Wagner brigades had been sparring with the dismounted cavalry off and on for more than two hours. Back on the main line, Bradley was having his men carry fence rails to build up a barricade. Suddenly, the "skirmish line was attacked by superior numbers and driven back to within 300 yards of my line of battle," Bradley reported. "I immediately got my men in line ready for an attack and rode down the skirmish line," where officers reported that "the enemy was massing troops in front of our right. I immediately rode back to my line, and as I had no connection [with other Union units on my right or left], I was fearful that my flank would be turned." To cover the flank, Bradley moved the reserve 42d Illinois about 150 yards to the right to form a 45 degree angle to the main line. The 64th Ohioans had come back in from skirmishing. After refilling their pouches and pockets with cartridges, they joined the 42d Illinois to cover the right flank. No sooner were they in position when "a heavy column of infantry was seen approaching."[13] The "heavy column" was Hood and his infantry arriving finally from the banks of the Duck River.

Minutes went by as Bradley's troops watched the gray columns form into battle lines across from the 15th Missouri and the 65th Ohio. For many of the Midwesterners, this was about to be their first test under fire.

Bradley was "soon furiously attacked in front. . . . We gave them a very destructive fire and somewhat staggered them." The Confederates withdrew. On the ridge overlooking the scene, the Confederate commander saw "cheering and waving of hats" along Bradley's main line.[14] The Missourians and the Ohioans had held, and they were feeling awfully good about it. Some no doubt were taking deep breaths and perhaps silently congratulating themselves for having passed at least the first test.

A hundred and fifty yards to the right, the commanding officer of the 42d Illinois was not congratulating anybody. Maj. Frederick Atwater had been ordered to hold the line "as long as possible, but having 350 entirely new recruits, who had no drill at all and never were under fire, I did not expect to hold such a line very long."[15]

Atwater had another reason to be concerned. He did not know it at the time, but the troops he and his new men were facing about a half-mile away were the division of Maj. Gen. Patrick Cleburne, possibly the best division commander, and the best division, that the South had in the West. Now in three successive lines, their battle flags rippling softly in the breeze, they began to move forward in the direction of Atwater's green regiment.

Another Confederate division virtually duplicated the scene across from the 15th Missouri and their companions waiting behind the rail barricade. Having beaten them back on their first attempt, the 15th Missouri and the Ohioans watched as the gray mass across the way re-formed for a second try. Once in line, the long files appeared to stand almost still, a quiet for a long moment hovering over both sides. Finally, there was a movement forward, walking first and then into a trot. The familiar high, shrill yell could be heard rising from the gray lines, now running. The blue line with the floppy black hats, common to the federal troops from the West, waited for the mass to come into range. As the order came, more than a thousand federal muskets fired at the body of troops running toward them, clusters of men falling, others stopping to fire volleys, reload, then run on toward them once again.

On the right, a crashing volley from Cleburne's charging lines could be heard above the base roar as another gray line swung around to the right and the rear of the two regiments trying to hold the right flank. The zip-zip of the first missiles swelled to a continuous noise like heavy rain, the bullets now a hail of lead ripping through the blue ranks from the front, the right, and the rear.

After ten minutes or so, the 42d Illinois recruits rose up from behind their barricade, turned, and began to run. The 64th Ohio joined in. (Atwater later reported that he gave the order to retreat.) Down went the color guard, all shot dead, the flag falling into oncoming hands of bodies now crashing over the barricade. The terrified recruits fell in bunches, some shot in the back; others tossed away knapsacks and muskets in a mad dash to get away from the yelling, shooting, stabbing, clubbing horror. More than a hundred of the 42d's recruits were killed or wounded in less than fifteen minutes.[16]

On the left, seeing their right giving way—men streaming away behind them and gray ranks on their heels shooting and clubbing down the blue as they ran—the three regiments from Illinois and Ohio and the one from Missouri turned as well and broke for the rear. After about a quarter mile, they came to a halt near the village, where officers and sergeants were able to bring them to a stop. Behind them, Confederates were crossing a wide cornfield when eight federal cannons on a knoll opened up, exploding spherical shot across the field, scattering the gray swarm and forcing their withdrawal.[17]

Almost two hundred of the brigade's fifteen hundred or so had been killed, wounded, or were reported missing, more than half of the casualties having fallen in the 42d Illinois. Bradley himself had been shot in the shoulder and carried off the field. The wound compelled him to relinquish command of the brigade to the colonel of the 15th Missouri, the next officer senior in line. Conrad got his brigade at last, but not under the circumstances he would have wanted.

With the regiment's officer staff so depleted, with not even a major to back him up, Conrad could only resort to a captain, George Ernst, to take over command of the 15th. Fortunately, the regiment remained in good hands, for Ernst was a superb officer. He had survived Stones River with a shoulder wound and returned to fight on, from Chickamauga, Missionary Ridge, and all the battles of the Atlanta campaign.[18]

Except for the 42d, the other five regiments shared about equally in the number of casualties. In spite of the high number of recruits in their ranks, the 15th suffered only three killed, eleven wounded, and three missing, a short list of casualties under the circumstances. Only one recruit is known to have been taken prisoner, and he may have been captured later under different circumstances.[19]

The recruits had likely been the first to break, because the veterans bore the brunt of the battle and the collapse. It was an observation that evidently did not escape the attention of George Wagner, the division's commander. In the next twenty-four hours, it would have a tragic effect on the regiment and the rest of the brigade.

The number of the 15th's German boys of 1861 continued to shrink. Gotthardt Ruebsam, a twenty-seven-year-old company sergeant, who literally stood out in a crowd—his record took special note that he was six feet tall—was shot in the right thigh. Permanently crippled, he would walk with a cane the rest of his life. Lt. William Eisermann took a bullet in the right shoulder, fracturing his collarbone and a shoulder blade, but luckily missing vital organs. Twenty-two-year-old Frederick Eberle was shot in the head, a ball entering the left side of his neck two inches below his left ear and then traveling up his skull and across his forehead before exiting above his right eyebrow. His medical treatment consisted solely of "cold water dressing, laudanum [tincture of opiate], and stimulants." Miraculously, Eberle survived, though with the permanent loss of hearing in his left ear. All would recover, but their army days were over.[20]

Late in the afternoon, orders went out from Hood's headquarters tent for Cheatham to renew the attack. At the same time, Stewart's corps was to go north beyond Spring Hill to cut off a possible federal retreat. But dark came without the sound of any firing. Benjamin Franklin Cheatham, the newest corps commander to the Army of Tennessee, had never been called on to conduct a battle with more than a division. Confronting Cheatham, Hood stormed at the general: Why had he not attacked? Cheatham replied that an enemy force outflanked his right, and he had needed help. Hood acquiesced. In the morning, trapping Schofield's army would not be much of a problem, he said. With that, Hood got up from the headquarters tent and disappeared into the fine antebellum home of Absalom Thompson.

A "big feast" followed for the general and his staff, which featured considerable toasting. By nine o'clock, having been up since three that morning, Hood went up to a guest bedroom, which he would share with his staff officers, unstrapped his artificial leg, possibly swallowed some laudanum, and went to bed.[21]

About an hour after dark, about the time the toasts were making their rounds at the Thompson mansion, Schofield was attempting to slip into

Spring Hill. A mile or so outside of town, the lead brigade was spreading out across the road when a picket near some haystacks in a meadow called out a challenge. "It's all right, my boy," the brigade's colonel called back, "I want to put my brigade in position here." A bluecoat in the line quickly warned the colonel that the voice was probably from "a damned Rebel," whereupon the colonel dashed back ahead of a rifle shot from near the haystack. Schofield's column, with the battle line out front, hurried on, skirmishing with pickets as they went.[22]

Getting into the village finally around seven that night, Schofield hurried into the brick McKissack house on Main Street, which was serving as Stanley's headquarters. Schofield immediately conferred with Stanley. He had seen for himself, by the immense ring of Confederate campfires circling the town, that Stanley's men, holding on to the village, appeared to be surrounded—with two-thirds of the rest of his army still strung out for ten miles to the south, hardly concentrated and desperately vulnerable to an attack.

That was far from the only worry. If they had to fight their way out, could the wagon train be saved? The train was ponderously slow for a rapid movement. There was talk of burning the wagons. But even if they attempted a quick movement, would the men fight if they had to? Many had hardly slept for the last three nights. If they sensed that all escape routes might be cut off anyway, Stanley thought that many might chose to "surrender their way out."[23]

Schofield himself thought about surrendering the army. Told that her house might be used "unpleasantly" that night, Mrs. McKissack asked if that meant burning it. "No madam," Schofield was said to have replied, "we will not burn the house, but here we will have to surrender this army to the Rebels." Stanley's chief of staff jotted in the corps journal that evening: "Take it all together, we are in a very bad situation."[24]

In the midst of the discussion, a report came in stating that a withdrawal north, if it were to be made, was now blocked at Thompson's Station a few miles up the pike. Setting aside the question of surrendering, for the moment at least, the two Union commanders took on "the anxious question . . . whether we could force our way through to Franklin."[25]

Schofield determined to find out for himself and clear the road if necessary. Taking along a full division, he set out around nine o'clock.[26] As he rode at the head of the column, "the anxious question" had to be burning in his mind: what would he do if he found the road blocked and could not get through? Was surrender his only choice? No other Union commander throughout the war, East or West, faced the possibility of surrendering a force nearly as large as his.

An hour later, Schofield's aide telegraphed Thomas with the information that all the "troops are pushing for Franklin as rapidly as possible" but that they probably would not get any farther that night than Spring Hill. The aide capped it off with one of the understatements of the war: General Schofield, the message read, "regards his situation as extremely perilous."[27]

Meanwhile, confusion reigned throughout Hood's command. Inexplicably, Stewart's Corps, ordered north earlier that evening, had failed to move. The corps finally got underway, but in spite of even having a local guide, it got lost. Looking for directions, Stewart accidentally stumbled upon Nathan Forrest's headquarters cabin, only to find that the cavalry commander, instead of planning to join an attack, had ordered his troops, after fighting all day and nearly out of ammunition, to pull back to rest. About that time, an officer drew up as Stewart was about to mount and ride off. By orders of General Hood, the officer said, he was to pull back to help Cleburne southwest of the village. What made the orders "strange," Stewart later wrote, was that the officer was not from Hood's own staff. Stunned and skeptical, Stewart directed his men to stay put while he went back to find Hood to confirm the order.[28]

Stewart's men had been standing in the road awaiting orders for almost six hours. It was probably close to eleven o'clock when they were allowed to move off the pike and bivouac. Campfires were lit, coffee heated—possibly with some fatback and a cracker if it could be found in a pocket or a knapsack—pickets were set out, and the rest of the command of more than ten thousand rolled up in their blankets for the night along the side of a road leading to Franklin and on to Nashville.

About the time the Confederates were rolling into their blankets, Gen. Jacob Cox with his two-division Twenty-third Corps was attempting to slip undetected into Spring Hill past Hood's line, hardly a mile away off the pike. Despite the pleadings of officers for no noise, the 40th Missouri, formed with draftees just two months earlier in St. Louis and having arrived only the day before, could not find a way to keep quiet. Clattering tin cups, frying pans, and the other "necessaries" that green recruits seemed to have to carry, set up a constant rattle. Gray pickets soon began shooting into the darkness in the direction of the clinking and the clattering, sending federal troops up and down the column ducking and scurrying for cover. When the firing died down, the order was whispered once more to get up and move on. But the frightened recruits continued to lie frozen in the road. A commander of a veteran unit just to the rear, not about to be stopped, ordered his men to march over the prostrate bodies, which the veterans proceeded to do amid considerable whispered cursing and swearing. The

Missourians finally got up and resumed the march. Thereafter, they would be dubbed the "Fortieth Misery." (The regiment would finish the war with sixty-eight dead—fifty-eight by disease—in less than a year of service.)[29]

Getting into the village finally, Cox got the good news: Schofield had returned—the pike past Spring Hill was open. No force other than skirmishing gray cavalry had been sighted. Orders to march went out immediately; Cox was to take the lead, and Ruger's division would pick up and escort the wagon train. Stanley and the two divisions of Wagner and Kimball would be the last to leave to cover the withdrawal. Schofield was about to attempt the Great Escape of the Civil War.[30]

In the pitch dark of a moonless night, the columns of infantry filed onto the road. A wind had come up to muffle the sounds of shuffling feet. As the long column began their silent walk (a shuffle really, for the bone-weary troops had not slept for almost two days), Confederates could be made out walking about campfires, some no more than a quarter mile away. Commands for no noise were passed down the line.[31]

At the Thompson farm, about two miles to the southeast, Hood was awakened. Stewart, commander of the corps now bivouacked along the road, had come in to ask why he had been redirected to support divisions south of the Spring Hill village; that would, of course, place his corps *away* from the turnpike he had ordered to block. It was not of importance, Hood responded. Let the men rest. They will find Yankees in the morning. Others followed into the bedroom, each asking for clarifications, only Forrest getting permission to send a division north toward Thompson's Station to attack traffic that might come that way. All got about the same message: "You'll find the Yankees in the morning," Hood going so far as to say to one, "In the morning we will have a surrender without a fight."[32]

Long after midnight, Hood was awakened again, this time, by a private. No one was awake in the house, so the private looked around until he found a general. The turnpike was full of Yankees, he said, wagons and cannons, all going somewhere, and somebody needed to know so something could be done about it. Hood, not getting out of bed, directed a staff officer to send a message to the corps commander *south* of town to attack if any Yankees came up the pike. Hood then went back to sleep.[33]

The 15th Missouri was among the last to leave the barricades south of the village. Not until four in the morning did Conrad receive orders "to commence withdrawing [the brigade]. I moved my command immediately and took up the line of march on the Nashville turnpike."[34] Almost as quickly, the 15th and the rest of column were forced to come to a halt. The lead wagon of the five-mile-long train had to cross a single-lane bridge.

The result: a massive traffic jam in the pitch darkness. Four hours passed before the column got straightened out and again underway.[35]

Daylight was still more than an hour off when gunfire a mile or two up ahead brought the entire train and the shuffling column to a halt once again. A ride in the wagons was hardly turning out to be a ride in the country for George Rau. As the first wagons passed Thompson's Station, with a yell, dismounted Confederate cavalry burst out of the dark. A staff officer wrote that "for a while there was great consternation." Three regiments of a Texas brigade had gotten within a hundred yards of the wagons before they were discovered. Firing "a well-directed volley, killing several Yankees and mules," the Texan commander reported, his men "rushed forward with a yell, producing among the teamsters and wagon guards a perfect stampede." The Confederates took control of the train and began setting fire to the wagons. About a half-hour went by when federal infantry could be seen quick-stepping up the pike. Outlined against the burning wagons and making good targets, the Texans scurried for their mounts and galloped off, shots chasing after them. Thirty-nine wagons were left burning.[36] Miles back, George Rau's wagon, among those in the tail of the column, was spared.

Once again, the column began to move. A "cloud of the enemy's cavalry [made] frequent dashes" at the rear guard as the long column continued on. It was still dark when the lead brigade of Cox's division reached the outskirts of Franklin.[37] It was about that time, with an hour still to go before daylight, when the 15th Missouri, more than ten miles back, finally crossed the single-lane bridge just south of the soon-to-be-abandoned village. Just behind them was Opdycke's brigade, assigned as rear guard, the only element standing between them and possible captivity or worse.

Stragglers were soon "filling the road, mostly new men with immense knapsacks," Opdycke reported. "They were so worried as to seem indifferent to capture." Ordering his men "to bring along every man at the point of the bayonet," Opdycke had the knapsacks cut off to get the new recruits to move along faster. "These orders were obeyed rigidly. . . . I am sure that we saved 500 men from capture." Opdycke ventured that "probably less than twenty men escaped our vigilance and were captured."[38] Perhaps the lone recruit in the 15th taken prisoner at Spring Hill was among them.

At sun up, Hood discovered that Schofield's army was gone. About all that remained were five hundred or so knapsacks of the straggling recruits strewn along the road.[39] Hood appeared thunderstruck. He called for a conference of his generals immediately after breakfast, those who were not involved in pursuing the retreating Yankees. A torrent of fault poured down on each corps and division commander, on those present and others who were not. A staff officer said the commanding general was as "wrathful as a rattlesnake, striking out in every direction."[40]

Luther Bradley, writing three weeks later while recovering from his wound, considered the escape an act of Providence.[41]

For Alexander P. Stewart, whose corps the morning before Hood had ordered south, away from the pike, the lost opportunity at Spring Hill was especially hard to explain, even to himself. Had he not gotten lost, even with a local guide, had he not stumbled upon Forrest's headquarters cabin, had he not encountered the "strange" staff officer—had he instead rode on with his corps to block the way north—the enemy may not have gotten away. Writing years later, Stewart could explain the mystery to no one possibly but himself: "If in the next life we are permitted an insight into the events of this life and their causes, we shall be surprised to find how much Providence, and how very little human agency and planning have to do with all really noble and grand achievements."[42]

20

Every Man a Commander

The sun had been up less than an hour when, at about eight in the morning, the 15th Missouri with the last of the column trudged down a long decline known locally as Breezy Hill. Before them about two miles away to the north lay the picturesque village of Franklin, with its brick and wood-framed houses along pleasant lanes, clusters of buildings gracing the town center, and church spires here and there rising above it all. Broad fields spread two miles away from the village. The fields also spanned east to west for about two miles, bordered on the east by the Lewisburg pike running alongside the Central Alabama Railroad tracks and the river. Down the center into town ran the Franklin & Columbia Turnpike. Angling in from the west ran a creek and another road. Sweeping behind it all curled an arc of the Harpeth River.

In front of the village, the two divisions of the Twenty-third Corps under Brig. Gen. Jacob Cox had arrived just before sun up and had begun to form a line now curving two miles around to the northwest. Two days before, in Columbia, Schofield had gotten a message from Thomas asking him to hold Hood for three more days if at all possible before withdrawing to Nashville. Thomas had only been able to collect a ragtag garrison to defend the capitol city. Quartermaster and railroad department staff had been given arms. There was even a detachment of five thousand walking-wounded that Sherman had sent back to Chattanooga; they, with "a brigade of colored troops," were that morning on their way by rail from Chattanooga. Fortunately, the first of the reinforcements from St. Louis had

242

arrived, enabling Thomas to report, "My infantry force was now nearly equal to that of the enemy."[1]

As Schofield's columns trooped up the pike toward Franklin, they filed off to the left and right to extend and fill out the line. Both flanks would be pinned on the banks of the river northwest and east of the town.

Ever since the first of the columns had arrived, men had been digging entrenchments and building up barricades with the familiar head logs that allowed troops to fire from small spaces in between. Openings were constructed through which artillerymen could point their cannon barrels. Off to the west of the turnpike, a sizable grove of locust trees in front of the works was cut down for the head logs, their branches gathered to form a barrier against a possible charge.

To the left, with no timber near, men pulled down planks and even joist timbers from a cotton gin, a barnlike structure that stood about a hundred yards to the east of the Columbia-Franklin pike. In some places, parapets were built five feet high and as wide as four feet thick at the base with the dug-out dirt. A hedge of Osage orange was chopped down to form a thorny barrier in front of part of the line.[2]

Conrad, when within "about two miles of Franklin," received an order to form into "two lines of battle on the east side of the turnpike, fronting south, and to allow the men to make coffee."[3] As with other regiments, very few had any coffee to cook. The time had long passed for rations to be handed out, and from the looks of things, it would be longer still; the wagons had long passed this way in the effort to get across the river and away from the pursuing Rebels. The new Commissary Sergeant George Rau was likely coming in for some strong language, just as other commissary sergeants in other regiments. While some of the men rustled up dry brush to make cook fires, others with no coffee to cook and dead on their feet, lay down to go to sleep.

After about an hour and half, Conrad received orders to move his six regiments of thirteen hundred about a quarter mile farther north toward Franklin. Some of the men had to be shaken from sleep before being told to get up and grab their muskets and fall in. Amid no small amount of grumbling, no doubt, they stumbled into line and before long shuffled off for another quarter mile, only to be halted again and reformed into another battle line. Hardly were they into position for the third time in less than three hours when they were ordered to move yet again. This time, they were to go about a mile farther to a slight rise in the open and otherwise flat field.

All the while, occasional musket and artillery fire could be heard coming from the other side of the small hills to the south. A staff officer from General Stanley galloped up to Wagner: the officer told Wagner to turn his

division around and march back to the hills and "hold them unless too severely pressed." At about the same time, word came from Opdycke's brigade, still the rear guard back on the hills: "the enemy was moving two heavy columns of infantry . . . one by each of the two pikes leading into Franklin." One column was beginning to push back Opdycke's left flank. "I thereupon again withdrew my command and retired toward the main line."[4]

To cover the withdrawal, Wagner directed Lane's brigade with some artillery to remain on a small hill to the right of the pike to hold off advancing gray skirmishers. Left of the pike, Captain Ernst got an order to move the 15th Missouri forward to support Lane's left. Back they went toward the low hills to the south.

The rest of Conrad's men continued on. At about eleven o'clock, the other five regiments reached the rise and moved off the Columbia-Franklin pike to the east. They were ordered to form into line of battle—in the open with fields all around—from a veteran's experience, fully exposed. And they were not happy about it. To make matters worse, their only route to safety, if the need came to that, was about a half-mile to the main line. Conrad placed "the Fifty-first Illinois on the left [east] of the turnpike, leaving a space the width of the turnpike . . . in that space was a section of . . . First Ohio Light Artillery." Next to the artillery, from west to east, the 79th Illinois moved into line followed by the 42d Illinois, the 64th Ohio, and finally, on the left flank, the 65th Ohio.[5]

After about two hours of skirmishing, around two o'clock, the 15th Missouri and Lane's brigade were ordered to fall back to the small rise where the rest of Conrad's brigade had formed their battle line. As Lane's men came up, Wagner ordered them to move off the road to the left, toward the west, and form in line with Conrad's.[6]

Next along the pike came the 15th Missouri, probably in four columns, as were Opdycke's men coming up behind.[7] Opdycke's brigade had been the rear guard and the very last to escape from Spring Hill. Among his seven regiments were the 36th, 44th, and 73d Illinois, regimental comrades of the 15th going back as far as the days of the old Pea Ridge brigade. The veterans of the 15th were well acquainted with Col. Emerson Opdycke

Facing page: The view looks north toward the main federal line and the town of Franklin, from a photograph after the war. The two trees in the mid-ground approximate the 15th Missouri's advanced position with Conrad's brigade across the Columbia Pike. The mile-and-a-half wide Confederate assault of 20,000 troops across this field ended in over 7,000 Southern casualties. (State Historical Society of Missouri, Columbia; from *Battles and Leaders of the Civil War*)

from the Erdmann affair. Opdycke was known as a fiery and keenly intelligent leader, a reputation that had been well earned at Chickamauga and Missionary Ridge.

He was also known to have a short fuse to light a hot temper.[8] The men at the tail end of the 15th's column, just in front of Opdycke riding ahead of his brigade, may well have been within earshot of yet one more of his famous explosions. A captain in the 64th Ohio wrote about it years later, attributing the words to Opdycke: "As I was moving on the Columbia pike, I came to where Lane's and Conrad's brigades were in position, in perfect exposure, on the plain. Wagner rode to me, and ordered me into line with them. I energetically objected to having troops out there where they were in serious exposure, and where they could aid the enemy and nobody else. Wagner rode on with me as I was urging my objections (for I did not even halt)."

The confrontation was very likely more explosive than Opdycke's words indicate. The Ohio captain, who may have witnessed some of it, wrote that Opdycke "strenuously objected" to placing his troops in the advanced line with Conrad's and Lane's men. "He also pleaded that his brigade was worn out, having been marching for several hours during the morning while covering the rear . . . climbing over fences and passing through woods, thickets and muddy cornfields," all the while "in sight of the enemy."[9]

Opdycke continued on with his brigade shambling along behind him, Wagner all the while riding beside his fuming subordinate. Finally, losing what had turned into a running battle of wills, Wagner bellowed, possibly slurring the words, for he may well have been drinking: "Well then, Opdycke, fight when and where you damn please, we all know you'll fight."[10] With that, Wagner drew in his reins, wheeled about, and trotted off back to the small rise where he had posted Conrad's and Lane's brigades.

The 15th Missouri had been ordered into line just west of the road next to Lane's. They were the last of the twelve regiments, about 2,700 men in all, to be posted in the forward line that now stretched a half-mile across the open field. The pike divided the line, with five of Conrad's regiments east of the road, and his sixth, the 15th, just west of the pike. Next to the 15th were Lane's six regiments. No woods or friendly troops were near to give cover or support. They were at sea in a flat field that reached out in every direction. The nearest haven was the main federal line, with the Carter house visible on a direct line along the pike almost a half-mile away.[11]

Conrad could see "the enemy maneuvering" in heavy columns a mile and a half away. "I sent word to the general commanding the division to ask him if it was expected that I should hold the line I was on."[12] To Conrad, and to the veterans in his brigade, holding the line against the gray columns they could see massing would be impossible.

Before Conrad could send off a staff officer with the message, Wagner rode up. The orders for Conrad were clear: "Hold the line as long as possible." Then, perhaps remembering how this brigade, with its large share of recruits, had broken and run back the day before at Spring Hill, Wagner issued one more order, an order that would have serious repercussions, for the brigade, for the 15th Missouri, and for Wagner: "Have the sergeants to fix their bayonets and to keep the men to their places."[13] With that, Wagner turned about and trotted back to the Carter house and the main line behind them.

Conrad relayed the instructions to his regimental commanders. The veteran soldiers in the line were shocked: "We never before had received any such orders on going into battle." Most rationalized that "our harsh orders were given for effect upon those drafted men," which were prevalent in four of Conrad's six regiments, one of them the 15th Missouri.[14]

At least one commander followed through on the bayonet order; how many of the others did are not known. Captain Ernst made no mention of the order in his report on the 15th Missouri's actions.[15] Lt. Col. Robert C. Brown of the 64th Ohio made it clear in his report that he did not.[16]

Opdycke's brigade, meanwhile, moved along the pike and through the main line, passing the Carter house and coming to a halt about three hundred yards in the rear. It was now about three o'clock. Here, Opdycke's seven regiments of about seventeen hundred men stacked arms while a detail of twenty men went for rations at the supply wagons across the river. A captain in the 73d Illinois remembered that permission was given to "cook coffee," but "very few had any *coffee to cook*." Here and there, men worked to start up small cook fires or simply settled down to rest and nap. The Southerners probably had no more interest in fighting that day than they had.

Schofield apparently felt the same way. After seeing to it that his wagon trains got across the river, Schofield adjourned to a house about a half-mile beyond the river north of town. Stanley, leaving Brig. Gen. Jacob Cox in command at the Carter house, went with him. Writing his report much later, Stanley said that "in view of the strong position we held, and reasoning from the course of the rebels during this campaign, nothing appeared so improbable as that they would assault."[17]

Conrad had a much better view. Conrad ordered his commanders to build a line of works and with the gray lines in view, to *mach schnell* (be quick about it)! "During the morning my men had provided themselves

with a large number of spades and shovels from one of the wagons, which
had been cut down by the way."[18] "These spades were the only tools we had
to work with," the captain in the 64th Ohio recalled.

> The ground we occupied had been frequently camped on by other troops
> who had destroyed all the fences and other materials ordinarily found . . .
> so that on this occasion our only resource was the earth thrown with the
> few spades we had. Under the stimulus afforded by the sight of the enemy
> in our front preparing for attack the men eagerly relieved each other in
> handling the spades. As soon as a man working showed the least sign of
> fatigue a comrade would grab the spade out of his hands and ply it with
> desperate energy, but in spite of our utmost exertions . . . we had only suc-
> ceeded in throwing up a slight embankment which was high enough to
> give good protection against musket balls to the men squatting down in
> the ditch [but] it was so low that a battle line could march over it without
> halting. . . .
>
> It was a pleasant, hazy, Indian summer day, so warm that I was carry-
> ing my overcoat on my arm. When the line squatted down I folded the
> coat into a compact bundle and placing it on the edge of the bank in rear
> of my company and sitting on it, with my feet in the shallow ditch, by
> craning my neck, could look over our low parapet.[19]

Sitting on top of the piled-up dirt, the Ohio captain could see better than
most.

> We could see all their movements so plainly while they were adjusting
> their lines that there was not a particle of doubt in the mind . . . as to
> what was coming, and . . . that a big blunder was being committed in
> compelling us to fight with our flank fully exposed in the midst of a wide
> field, while in plain sight in our rear was a good line of breastworks with
> its flank protected by the river. The indignation of the men grew almost
> into a mutiny and the swearing of those gifted in profanity exceeded
> all their previous efforts in that line. Even the green drafted men could
> see the folly of our position, for one of them said to me, "What can our
> generals be thinking about in keeping us out here. . . . Why don't they
> take us back? . . .
>
> The regiment contained a number of men who had not re-enlisted
> when the regiment had veteranized and whose time had already expired.
> They were to be mustered out as soon as we got back to Nashville and

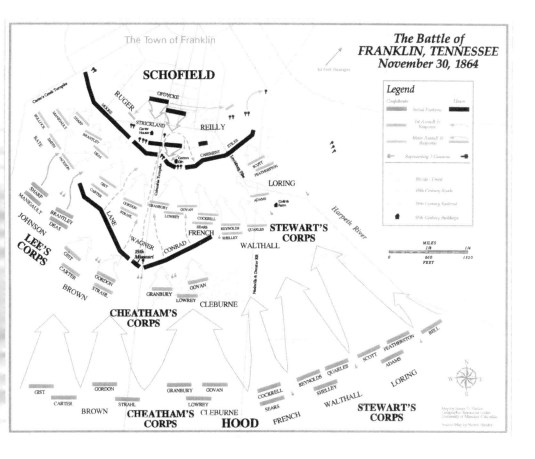

with home so nearly in sight after more than three years of hard service these men were especially rebellious.[20]

All the while, as Conrad's men made the dirt fly, they could glance up and see the Confederates forming up a mile and a half away. "It took two hours, from two till four o'clock," for the columns "to come up and get into position." Their bands could be heard playing "Dixie" as the gray columns quick-stepped into line. The playing stopped, and after a moment of silence, a shout was heard. In town, sitting in a tree along one of the pleasant lanes, a teenager overlooked the scene and heard a federal band down by the cotton gin playing "Hail Columbia," "and the Federals replied with a vigorous shout of defiance."[21]

The gray lines began to move. "They advanced very slowly and steadily, and in three lines of battle." Conrad was now looking at a line a mile and a half wide, close to twenty thousand men, advancing on a wider front and with more men than the Army of the Potomac had to face the final day at Gettysburg.[22]

Along Conrad's line, the men "kept the spades flying." A sergeant in the 64th Ohio on the left flank rose up and started for the breastworks to the rear, "vehemently declaring that he would not submit to having his life thrown away, after his time was out, by such a stupid blunder." Some of the new recruits also got up and started to go but returned at "the profane order of their captain, 'God damn you, come back here.'"[23] The skirmish line too "came scurrying back, the men, with a very serious look on their faces, settling down like a covey of flushed birds dropping into cover." A captain jumping in with them said he had just been "face to face with the whole rebel army."[24]

Close to where the 15th was posted, an Ohio soldier, crouched in the ditch behind the thrown-out dirt, said, "The suspense and the nervous strain became greater and greater . . . the lines of grey came nearer and nearer. . . . We stood up a part of the time, and part of the time we sat down with our guns resting" on the mounds in front. "Nearer the Confederates approached with the precision of dress parade, and our hearts beat rapidly . . . swords glistening and bayonets flashing. . . . Every man carefully examines his gun . . . 'for God's sake, let us get in behind the works.' . . . But the captain . . . all that he can say is, 'Sergeant, keep your place, sir, and not another word.'"[25]

A cannon ball "flew a little high directly over" where the captain was sitting. "The second shot dropped short, and I was thinking with a good deal of discomfort that the third shot would get the exact range . . . but before it came our line had opened fire on the approaching rebel line."[26]

Conrad, as well as Lane, sent word to General Wagner, "telling him that they could see the enemy advancing, in close column even without skirmishers."[27] The intent of their messages was clear: to get approval to withdraw.

"Just as the enemy got within good musket-range," Conrad reported, "a staff officer of the general commanding the division [Wagner] rode up to me and said that the general ordered that if the enemy came on me too strong, and in such force as to overpower me, that I should retire my line to the rear of the main line of works." But by then, "the enemy was too close." Conrad rang out the order: "Make ready, fire at will!"[28]

In the middle of Conrad's line, the 79th Illinois held its fire "until their solid lines were within 150 yards of the front. . . . Though we mowed them down in a terrible manner they seemed to pay but little attention and kept rushing on."[29]

The blue line poured "a very destructive fire into their line," Conrad reported, "and it staggered them very much . . . at the second volley . . . the enemy fell back under the crest of a small hill in our front, but they quickly reformed and advanced on us again. My men were very cool and steady, and loaded and fired very rapidly." That they fired fast and furiously, there can be no doubt. "There is now a wall of blazing guns all along our front," an Ohio private wrote, "loading and firing till the gun-barrels burn our hands." All the while, "Men are dropping all along the line."[30]

Perhaps it was at this point that the 15th Missouri's captain, William Hark, of Company H, was struck. Mortally wounded, Hark continued to encourage his men and called out, according to Captain Ernst, recording the incident later and perhaps employing a bit more of the melodramatic, "Boys, I die, but give them of your bullets and they will not go farther and our country is saved." Ernst had seen men killed before. Whatever Hark called out to his men, Ernst clearly was moved beyond the ordinary. In his report, Ernst reserved special mention for Hark as "a hero and a patriot."[31]

Conrad stated that "my men were very cool and steady, and loaded and fired very rapidly" for "fifteen minutes." That would have meant his veterans would have fired up to forty-five rounds—fire, reload, ram home the cartridge, and fire again, all in about twenty seconds, about three rounds per minute—the expected rate of a well-drilled veteran but not a recruit.

Others had different recollections. The captain in the 64th Ohio recalled that his company had "fired only five or six rounds" when he and his men started heading for the rear. The 79th Illinois had "kept up the fire until the enemy was within ten yards." The gray mass now running at the line could easily have covered the 150 yards in less than twenty seconds, barely giving the Illinoisans time to get off another volley before the Confederates were on top of them. All became "terrible confusion."[32]

Somewhere, above the din, the order was heard—"Fall back!" When Conrad saw that Lane's brigade on his right was "falling back, and that the enemy was flanking me on the right, I then gave the order for the Fifteenth Missouri to retire and they did so, and before I could get to the next regiment on the left [the 51st Illinois] I found that they had already commenced retiring, and about the same time all the rest of my regiments fell back, but so close were the enemy . . . that some of the men of the Fifty-first Illinois clubbed muskets with them." The Illinoisans had waited too long, paying with the most casualties of the brigade.[33] Bayonets, rifle butts, and bodies now collided, with fists and arms jabbing and swinging.

With the noise, the yelling, and the shooting, it would have been impossible for everyone to hear the order. Conrad was standing next to the 15th

Missouri along the pike and in the middle of his line. His far left, where the 64th Ohio was posted, was about a quarter mile away. An orderly would have needed more than a minute or two, even on horseback, to deliver the order down the line.

"We [were] all mixed up in hand to hand conflict," an Ohio private remembered. "The line breaks into a mad rush for the works behind us . . . I grasped my ramrod and gun in one hand, and as my hat was knocked off at this instant, I seized it with the other, and broke for the rear." Another Ohioan "got ten yards from the ditch [when] a Rebel officer jerked his sword in front of me, told me to throw down my gun and go to the rear."[34]

About one in five of Conrad's men were taken prisoner, most probably before they even had a chance to break for the rear. In the 15th Missouri, Corporals Engelbert and Dreher, Pvt. Charles Winnegar, and draftee Francis Raffel were captured and sent to a prison camp at Meridian, Mississippi. Thirty-four, almost 20 percent of the regiment all told, were taken prisoner.[35] The bayonet order for sergeants to hold the men in their places likely had much to do with so many being captured; some of Conrad's recruits no doubt were taken because they held to the ditch, intimidated by their sergeants' bayonets, until it was too late.

Veterans knew better. Experience had told them when to break for the rear, and no sergeant's bayonet was going to stop them. It was no coincidence that the 64th Ohio, whose commander had refused to give the bayonet order to his sergeants, escaped with the fewest number of casualties in Conrad's brigade. The captain in the 64th Ohio did not wait for the order to fall back. "I had been glancing uneasily along our line, watching for a break as a pretext for getting out of there, and was looking towards the pike when the break first started. It ran along the line so rapidly that it reminded me of a train of powder burning." What followed for him bespoke the same raw impulses and flights for life of hundreds of others.

I instantly sprang to my feet and looked to the front. They were coming on the run, emitting the shrill rebel charging yell, and so close that my first impulse was to throw myself flat on the ground and let them charge over us. But the rear was open and a sense of duty, as well as a thought of the horrors I had heard of rebel prisons, constrained me to take what I believed to be the very dangerous risk of trying to escape. I shouted to my company, "Fall back! Fall back!" and gave an example of how to do it by turning and running for the breastworks. As the men were rising to go the rebels fired, but so hastily and with such poor aim that their fire did not prove nearly so destructive as I had feared. . . . The range was so close that it seemed bullets had never before hissed with such a diabolical venom, and every one that passed close by made a noise like it was big enough to tear your body in two if it should hit you.

The captain remembered his new overcoat. He looked back with the intention of returning to get it,

but the rebels then appeared to be as close to the coat as I was and very reluctantly . . . I let them have it. After running a few rods farther I again looked back. They were then standing on the low embankment we had left, loading and firing at will, but just as I looked some [of] their officers waved their swords and sprang forward. The fire then slackened as they started in hot pursuit to get to the breastworks with us.

Our men were all running with their guns in the hands which was good evidence that there was no panic. . . . While knapsacks or blanket rolls were frequently thrown away I did not see a single man drop his gun unless hit. The cry of some of our wounded who went down in that wild race, knowing they would have to lie there exposed to all the fire of our own line, had a pathetic note of despair in it, I had never heard before.

A shell exploded over the captain's head just as he collided with another man, knocking both to the ground.

I caught a glimpse of his face . . . and its horrified look read his belief that it was the shell that had hit him. The idea was so comical that I had to laugh, but my laugh was a very brief duration. . . .

Our men were nearly all drifting towards the pike as if with the intention of entering the breastworks through the gap at the pike. . . . With panting lungs and trembling legs I toiled along, straining every nerve to reach the breastwork . . . towards the pike the ground was thickly covered with [men], extending from the breastworks nearly a hundred yards along the pike, and in some places so densely massed as to interfere with each other's movements. The fleetest footed had already crossed the breastwork and all those outside were so thoroughly winded that none of them could go any faster than a slow, labored trot. . . . The rebel ranks were almost as badly demoralized by pursuit as ours by retreat. Their foremost men had already overtaken our rear most stragglers and were grabbing hold of them to detain them.

A Confederate came at a trot within fifty yards of the Ohio captain when he stopped, withdrew his ramrod, primed, loaded, and then aimed.

> I thought I was looking at the man who would shoot me . . . [but] much to my relief . . . [he] fired at a little squad of our men close on my right. . . .
>
> I then noticed that there was a ditch on the outside [of the breast-works]. . . . With the fervent prayer . . . "O, God, give me strength to reach that ditch," I turned and staggered forward. I fell headlong into the ditch just as our line there opened fire. The roar of their guns was sweeter than music. . . . I lay as I fell panting for breath. . . . I happened to raise my head and was astounded by the sight of the rebels coming into the ditch between me and the pike, the nearest of them only a few yards away. They were so tired that they seemed scarcely able to put one foot before the other . . . with amazement I watched them until the thought flashed into my mind that in an instant some of their com-rades would come in on top of me and I would be pinned down with a bayonet. The thought . . . was so terrifying that it spurred me into a last effort. . . . I sprang on top of the breastwork . . . then followed a brief period of oblivion. . . . I found myself lying . . . inside of the breastworks, trampled under the feet of the men, and with no knowledge whatever of how I got there. . . . I was lying across the body of a wounded man who had been hit by a bullet. . . . He was unconscious, but still breathing and the breast of my coat was smeared with the blood from his wound. . . . In a desperate attempt to avoid being trampled to death [I] managed in some way to crawl out between the legs of the men to the bank of the ditch, where I lay utterly helpless with burning lungs still panting.[36]

For Conrad and the 15th Missouri, positioned just to the right of the road, the shortest way to the main line was straight back along the Columbia Pike. Dead ahead, a half-mile away on a straight line, the men of the 50th Ohio, entrenched in the main line, watched. It probably took no more than five minutes or so for the first of the Missourians to sprint the distance and pile into the entrenchments on top of the Ohioans, some on the run, some staggering and collapsing into the trenches, the Confederates right behind.

A lieutenant had ordered the Ohioans to fix bayonets. As the grays stumbled into the trench—they were exhausted from the run as much as the Missourians—they were met by the 50th Ohio, bayonet to bayonet and hand to hand. A lieutenant "glanced to the left to see how the balance of the Regiment was faring, and to my horror, the regiment was gone. . . . Rebs were pouring over the works all the way along." A corporal remembered the lieutenant shouting, "Boys, we have got to get out of here!" Seeing the regiment's flag going back, the corporal was about to jump the parapet when he came face-to-face with "a big Johnnie Reb with a musket pointed at me." He surrendered, as did others of the 50th, when his captor and other Southerners were shot down as the terrified corporal cowered in the ditch with the 50th and the 15th Missouri. Lying in the ditch with others piled on top of him, the corporal remembered blood from above staining and soaking through his uniform to the skin.[37]

Cox's soldiers manning the entrenchments had held their fire for fear of shooting into their own men. Up and down the federal line for about three hundred yards, Confederates and the crowd in blue were now in the ditches together, all mixed up. Others fought across the breastworks, "both sides lying low and putting their guns under the head logs that were on the earthworks, firing nervously, rapidly."[38]

"On our right the artillery teamsters stampeded," another Ohioan recalled.

> The ammunition went with the teams and caissons, and the gunners took picks, shovels or anything at hand and . . . defended their guns. . . . One of the guns was loaded but in the confusion caused by the stampede of the teamsters was not fired. The enemy, thinking the battery silenced, made for the embrasure and a large crowd [was] rushing to the muzzle of that gun. The man with the lanyard . . . held his fire until the first rebel in the rush placed his hands upon the muzzle of the cannon to spring over, when he let her go. Like a huge thunder bolt that awful roar and flash went blasting through that crowd of men. . . . Arms, legs and mangled trunks were torn and thrown in every direction.[39]

How long they clubbed, stabbed, and slashed at each other in the trenches no one could say. "At some point a break started and then it spread rapidly until it reached the men who were too busily occupied in firing on the rebels to become affected by panic."[40]

One of Cox's commanders reported that Conrad's and Lane's brigades' dash into the entrenchments caused "a slight confusion" in his own ranks. Panic would have been a more accurate description. After flinging himself into the trench after his long run, the captain of the 64th Ohio, one of Conrad's regiments, saw that "[Cox's men] were all gone from the ditch to within a few feet of where I was lying. . . . This break in our line was . . . occasioned by the panic and confusion created by [our] men crossing the breastworks. Cox's men, along this part of our line, seem to have lost their nerve at the sight of the rebel army coming and on account of their own helpless condition. They could not fire a single shot while our men were between themselves and the rebels." The stampede was underway. Men from Conrad's brigade, how many no one knows, joined in.[41]

Others stayed to fight. Conrad wrote about it twenty-five years later. He kept a *Tage Buch*, a diary, so he had more than his memory to go on when he wrote years later to the captain in the 64th Ohio: "No doubt men of all Regts. belonging to our Brigade went with the crowd, which became demoralized when they came into the line closely followed by the Rebels and run to the town instead [of] remaining as they should have done, but the great part of the Brigade was stationed between the gin house and Columbia Pike." The colonel added that all of his regiments did "some good fighting" that day.[42] First out of the entrenchments in panic were Cox's two brigades, which led a mad dash toward town, with many of Conrad's and Lane's men in tow—all told, possibly as many as two thousand of the four brigades, recruits in new blue uniforms and veterans in their worn and faded ones, on the run with the gray mob after them. A captain on Cox's staff saw "General Wagner . . . on his horse directly in front of the Carter house . . . backing against his will . . . by the surging mass of his own soldiers. . . . With terrible oaths he called them cowards, and shook his broken stick at them; but . . . nothing could stop them," and the general "drifted out of sight with his own men toward the town."[43]

A woman with a home near the town square saw the "stampede. Many Federals ran by my house. Several wounded came by. Some of them asked for water. One was very weak from loss of blood, and I gave him some whiskey. Another was badly shot, and I tore one of my lace curtains for a bandage." She then took her children and servants to the cellar.[44]

Schofield and Stanley had been north of town at the Truett house, which they had commandeered for their headquarters. Stanley had been sleeping when the alarm came in. Schofield had not thought Hood would attack, so formidable were the Union entrenchments. "For a moment my heart sank within me," he later wrote. Mounting their horses, they galloped off together toward the growing sounds of the battle.

Crossing the river into town, Stanley galloped into chaos—terrified horses pulling wagons and caissons at breakneck speed through the streets, dazed and frightened men mixed in, running, trying to get out of the way. It got worse as he neared the hill where the Carter House stood. Men everywhere, many without weapons, the pike too crowded, they dashed through yards and over fences, desperate to escape. Officers were trying to rally their troops but none could hope to be heard in the roar. Up ahead, Stanley could see through the swirling smoke troops in blue—and gray—spilling over the log barricades and pouring out of the trenches. "The moment was critical beyond any I have known in any battle," Stanley later wrote. Disaster was staring him in the face, and there was nothing he could do about it.[45]

Fortunately for Stanley, and Schofield and Cox, and possibly for the Union itself, Opdycke had stopped his men to rest in exactly the right place. They were the only Union troops in the path of the breakthrough that was occurring almost a quarter mile ahead. The stampede of blue-coats, with their gray drovers close behind, was heading their way. The command of this brigade of Union troops might have been Conrad's but for his arrest back in July over the Erdmann affair. And for what was about to happen, fate would have handed the 15th Missouri a special place in the annals of the Civil War. One may wonder if the restrained Conrad instead of the explosive Opdycke would have made any difference in the command of the brigade. On this November day, it would have made no difference. In spite of impressions the official reports may leave, no officer had any control over what was to follow. One more of the great moments of the Army of the Cumberland was about to be added to its history, for as at Missionary Ridge, men in the ranks were once again about to take charge. This time it would be around the Carter House and the cotton gin.

The 73d Illinois had filed off the road west of the pike and "stacked arms about one hundred yards to rear and north of the breastworks, just north of the Carter house and outbuildings, gardens, yards, etc." The other five regiments did the same, spreading out on both sides of the pike for about another three hundred yards.[46]

Opdycke's men had settled down in little groups around their cook fires along the pike. About an hour had gone by, most of it spent in the age-old army custom of complaining about everything in sight as they boiled their coffee—and the men of the 73d Illinois had plenty of reasons that afternoon—when the "Preacher Regiment" from Illinois "was started from its coffee and cursing"—a mob was pouring out of the entrenchments and pounding down upon them, "a stampede of our own men." Mounted officers "deployed across the pike and flourishing their swords and revolvers, swore terribly that they would shoot the first man [who] undertook to pass, but all to no avail. . . . The gathering flood-tide . . . gathered sufficient strength, shoving horses and riders and everything irresistibly forwards."[47]

The dying light and the growing blanket of smoke added to the great confusion about what really happened next. Visibility beyond more than a few yards was impossible. After-action reports consequently often conflict.

Even firsthand accounts are suspicious for their detail when describing what regiment was where at a given moment. There was no longer any command organization. "Without one command," an officer in the 73d recalled, "and but very little excitement—by mutual consent, and almost as one man—the regiment went to their guns, took them out of the stacks. . . . Here they seemed to stop and consider a moment, and for a moment only."[48]

If commands were given, and other officers in the brigade, including Opdycke, reported that they were, few men would have heard them over the tremendous noise. Further, the Confederates were coming on in such a sudden rush that some men had only time to get up and grab whatever could be used as a weapon—axes, hatchets, picks, whatever was at hand. Shot of every kind was now falling around them "in goodly numbers. To go to the rear was only folly, and would result in drowning [in attempting to get across the Harpeth River] or capture."[49]

What happened next no official report could hope to describe. Every man was fighting on his own hook. Capt. George W. Patten of the 73d wrote years later that "every man was his own commander, and he was a major-general at that."[50]

Ahead,

> between us and the works, were two paling fences, the most formidable of which was heavy oak-paling to heavy oak stringers with large nails. . . . Beyond this was what every man in the regiment knew was the safest place on that field—the main line with its breastworks. Without hesitating one moment, and as . . . every man in the regiment, with a yell and bound they went for the works. By the time they reached the oak-paling fence the balls of the enemy were striking very fast, and reminded one of a boy rattling a stick on a picket-fence. . . . The getting over or through that fence in the face of that fire was *one* of the most, if not *the most* terrible experiences the 73rd Regiment ever had. . . . It was too high to climb over . . . so thick they could not be broken with the butt of a gun. . . . After what seemed an age, a breach was made.[51]

Opdyke's brigade "crowded and bayoneted their way to the front." Seeing Opdycke's men charging into the oncoming Confederates, others in blue broke off from the stampede, turned about, and rallied. "It is true," the captain in the 64th Ohio wrote years later, "that hundreds of brave men from the four broken brigades of Conrad, Lane, Reilly and Strickland, who were falling back, [as] they met Opdycke's advancing line . . . faced about and fought as gallantly as any of Opdycke's men."[52]

One man said it reminded him "of two enormous ocean waves crashing together." They collided in yet one more hand-to-hand horror. Thirteen hundred of Opdycke's brigade and possibly double that number from the four rallying brigades—four thousand or so Union troops—collided with at least that number and likely more of the seven Confederate brigades that had funneled toward the breakthrough along the pike. A Michigan soldier wrote that the "horror of that collision . . . was beyond description. . . . I surely do not want to ever witness the like again." A captain in 73d Illinois recalled "cursing, yelling men, flailing with clubbed muskets and jabbing with bayonets, were as demons possessed. It was the pandemonium of hell turned loose." In the Carter yard, on the porch, around the house, through the garden, and around the smokehouse, so dense was the scene crowded with grappling, clubbing, and stabbing bodies that a Union regiment across the road from the Carter house could not find room to join in.[53]

Individual battles were repeated thousands of times. "We used bayonets, butts of guns, axes, picks, shovels . . . and even a hatchet," a man in the 88th Illinois recalled. The colonel of the 64th Ohio saw a Confederate "thrust one of our men through with the bayonet, and before he could draw his weapon from the ghastly wound his brains were scattered on all of us that stood near, by the butt of a musket swung with terrific force by some big fellow whom I could not recognize in the grim dirt and smoke that enveloped us . . . as I glanced hurriedly around and heard the dull thuds, I turned from the sickening sight and was glad to hide the vision in work with a hatchet."[54]

Some said the wild melee around the Carter house lasted only a few minutes. Others said it lasted longer. Who could tell? Who could possibly remember for certain? Likely no greater scene of violent hand-to-hand fighting—on this scale certainly—was equaled in the Civil War.

The blue wave gradually drove back the gray. Around the Carter smokehouse, Opdycke's men, mixed in with rallying fugitives from the stampeding brigades, fought their way into a second entrenchment sixty yards behind the main line. Many of Opdycke's men, now mixed in with rallying troops of Conrad's, Lane's, and the returning ranks of Cox's regiments, crowded four and five deep into the retrenched line near the Carter smokehouse. From here, they fired the first of volley after volley into the Confederates. Men in the front ranks fired, passed their muskets to the rear to be reloaded and passed them back to the front. The firing was so rapid it sounded as "one continuous roar," said one man. With Hood's men crumpling to the ground all around, some in butternut and gray ducked and turned and made for the main line of entrenchments sixty yards away, back across the Carter garden. Others simply dropped their muskets and yelled out in surrender.[55]

A Union veteran wrote that the horror of the collision at the Carter house at Franklin "was beyond description. . . . Cursing, yelling men, flailing with clubbed muskets and jabbing with bayonets, were as demons possessed. It was the pandemonium of hell turned loose." So dense was the scene with grappling, clubbing, and stabbing bodies that a Union regiment across a road could not find room to join in. (from the author's collection)

The way was now cleared to the Carter house, past the interior line, and now up to the main entrenchments, and General Stanley found his way up to the main line. One of the officers he encountered was Colonel Conrad. "When Stanley made his appearance," Conrad wrote, "I met him inside of the works [the main line]. At that time I was with part of the Brigade east of the Columbia Pike. Stanley ordered me to take all the troops I could get together and move to the left near the Cotton gin."[56]

East of the cotton gin ran a hedgerow of Osage orange for almost three hundred yards. To the west, the Union entrenchments continued on, across the Columbia pike, for another three hundred yards or so to a sawed-off grove of locust trees and beyond. It would be along these six hundred yards, a quarter mile or so along the Osage hedge to the locust trees, with the cotton gin in the center, that the outcome of the climactic battle in the West would be determined.

Along those six hundred yards, Conrad, unknown numbers of the 15th Missouri, and unknown numbers of the rest of his regiments, with remnants of possibly as many as two dozen others, crammed into the main trench line. They were "all mixed up together," Conrad later wrote, "perhaps there was not a perfect Regt. organization in [any] respect." In the process of moving men into the line across the pike, "Stanley as well as I were wounded, my wound being only a slight flesh wound did not keep me from my men." Stanley's was more serious, a bullet slicing across his neck and inflicting a shallow wound as it traveled down his back and exited near the spine. The general trotted off, eventually getting medical help back in town, as Conrad moved on to the new firing zone by the cotton gin.[57]

It was now dark. Whatever light the night sky may have offered was blocked by a blanket of smoke. "It was so dark," Conrad wrote, "that it was impossible to see where all the different Regts were."[58] The only light was coming from the thunderstorm of rifle fire glowing like summer lightning through the clouds of smoke against a constant roar of rifle and cannon fire.

A soldier in the 88th Illinois remembered, "We formed at the works [near the cotton gin], and were no sooner formed than another [Confederate] line charged. They came to the works and settled down in front of it." Sheets of flame from the long line of federal muskets flashed from below the head logs. The Confederates "disappeared just like melting away. Then another line charged." One line was Brig. Gen. Francis Cockrell's Missouri Brigade.[59] It would be the one time, for certain, that men of the 15th Missouri fighting for the North fired on Missourians fighting for the South. They had come close to facing each other once before, at Kennesaw Mountain. This time, there in front of the cotton gin, the Northerners would not miss.

Cockrell's Missourians were one of seven Confederate brigades that were now funneling toward what had been the break in the federal line. A Virginia-born farmer from Jackson County, Missouri, remembered how they had stepped off that evening; the brigade's small brass band "went up with us, starting off with *The Bonnie Blue Flag*," then changing to "Dixie" "as we reached the deadly point." The "deadly point" was about a quarter mile away when they first came under artillery fire. One Missourian in gray believed that "more than 50 percent of our men had fallen" there before they reached the blazing line of Northerners.[60] Others were shot down by musketry within yards of the Union line. Those that did reach the parapet near the cotton gin went over swinging their muskets or jabbing bayonets, but most would never leave, overwhelmed in the trenches by the swarming Federals.[61]

For four more hours, until sometime around ten that night, the firing wore down to a trickle of shots, then they stopped altogether. Above the quiet, about the only sound that could be heard, was the moaning of thousands of Southern wounded and dying who were lying out in the dark.

Muskets flashed along a quarter of a mile of the federal line at Franklin, Tennessee, the cotton gin building in the center, and "the Confederates disappeared just like melting away." It would be one time for certain that the 15th Missouri, fighting for the North, fired on Missourians fighting for the South. (State Historical Society of Missouri, Columbia; from *Battles and Leaders of the Civil War*)

"About half past ten," Conrad wrote, "we were ordered to leave the trenches and fall back towards Nashville. I remember we, that is the Brigade, made a respectable show when we left the breastworks, near the bridge [across the Harpeth River north of town] we were joined by [a] good many of our men, some wounded, some on duty and perhaps [a] few demoralized. I always conten[d]ed that our Brigade did as much fighting on that glorious day as any other organization, especially when you take in consideration the terrible position we had been placed in before the real fighting commenced. . . . I know personally that all the Regts. of the Brigade were represented and done some good fighting and remained here until the end of the battle."[62]

The Union columns formed outside the entrenchments and made their way in the dark through the town and across the Harpeth River bridges, leaving their dead and the wounded who could not walk, behind. They had eighteen miles to go to join up at last with Thomas at Nashville.

With the morning light, the townspeople awoke to a horror on their fields south of town never before seen on a battleground in America. Along what had been the Union trenches and breastworks, the Confederate dead lay five and more deep, one piled on top of the other. Some of the dead were still standing, their ranks packed in so tight that their bodies had no place to fall.

A Confederate account "stated that the next morning they found some of their dead with their thumbs chewed to a pulp. They had fallen with disabling wounds and the agony of their helpless exposure to the murderous fire from the federal breastworks, which swept the bare ground where they were lying, had been so great that they had stuck their thumbs in their mouths and bit on them to keep from bleating like calves. Many of the bodies thus exposed were hit so frequently they were literally riddled with bullet holes." The bodies of five Confederate generals were found on the field, some still mounted on their dead horses.[63] By the end of the day, four thousand wounded would be brought in to choke every hospital, church, and home in Franklin.

Hood's report stated his losses at 4,500 in killed, wounded, and taken prisoner. The number is a gross underestimate. Federal figures number 6,252 in Confederate casualties. That number too is low; for one, it does not include the uncounted wounded who were able to return to Hood's lines or were helped or carried back by their comrades, many to die or never return to the ranks. As one authority concluded, even "7,000 Confederate soldiers lost in five hours of fighting seems quite conservative."[64] That number would be more than the 6,500 Robert E. Lee lost with Pickett's charge at Gettysburg.

Even that comparison makes the number appear too low. Hood sent almost double the number of men that Lee sent in that almost mythical charge. Hood's charge covered two miles, Pickett's, one mile. The charge and the fighting that followed at Franklin lasted more than five hours, compared to the two that final day at Gettysburg. The estimated seven thousand Confederate casualties at Franklin indeed appear conservative.

The Union lost 1,368 men, a small number in comparison. Conrad's and Lane's brigades suffered the highest casualties, most occurring when they were left isolated in advance of the main line.[65]

For the third time in their history, the 15th Missouri suffered 40 percent in casualties. They had been in the center of the line of the two brigades where the casualties were the highest. Only at Chickamauga did the 15th endure a greater loss.

Among those killed at Franklin was Christian Heyer, George Rau's friend, who, together back in 1862, had gone home for a visit to St. Louis, when Heyer would see home for the last time.[66]

. . .

For the Union, a number of officers had a lot of explaining to do. The debacle of the advanced line to start the battle had almost cost the Union the victory. Schofield, Wagner, and Cox, who had been given overall charge of the units in front of Franklin, had been in the army long enough to know that it could turn out to be a career-ending event. The finger pointing by the federal generals began almost immediately after the battle. All three attempted to distance themselves from the fact that Conrad's and Lane's brigades had been positioned and allowed to remain too long in their exposed location.

Conrad was the first to issue his battle report. He attempted to justify his decision not to withdraw when given the choice: "One-half my men were recruits and drafted men," he wrote, "and knowing that if I then retired my lines my men would become very unsteady and confused, and perhaps panic-stricken, I concluded to fight the enemy on the line I then was."[67] They "retired" in panic anyway. The surprising fact is that his command suffered no greater number of casualties than it did in the sprint for the main line.

It likely was for another reason that Conrad was the first to deliver his report: Wagner's order to hold his troops in line with the bayonet. It was for this reason that Conrad submitted his after-action report on December 1, the *morning after* the battle—Conrad did not wait to receive the reports from his regimental commanders, the standard procedure. He probably wrote his report even as the army was retreating into Nashville. There is even evidence that the copies were distributed to the generals *before noon*—as his brigade was arriving in Nashville—for by early afternoon, Wagner was in Cox's tent trying, according to Cox, to soften the implications of Conrad's report.[68] No battle report in the Civil War could have been submitted quicker. Conrad had seen brutality practiced before in his former homeland, and he had rebelled against it then. Perhaps he was reminded of that in Wagner's bayonet order. If so, he was having none of it now.

Conrad's report started a flurry of defensive writing. Cox wrote a "preliminary report" just one day later—that too was spectacular for its quickness. Cox's report shifted blame on both Conrad and Lane, stating that the two brigades "fell leisurely back"—in spite of his having witnessed the wild retreat himself while viewing it from a knoll east of the main line. Cox's personal defense went beyond his first writing. Judging by a much more detailed and craftily written report more than a month later, one wonders just how much of the battle Cox did see. He even claimed credit for placing Opdycke's brigade in the critical location behind the main line, a claim Opdycke refuted.[69]

Wagner in his report—it too was written a day after Conrad's—tried a different tack. Wagner had little choice but to accept responsibility for placing the two brigades in the advanced line but, in so doing, claimed he directed Lane and Conrad "to hold their position . . . but not attempt to fight if threatened by the enemy in too strong a force." It was not quite in agreement with Conrad's report. Wagner also attempted a patronizingly magnanimous if not diabolical approach. Conrad's "men fought gallantly," he added, "refusing to retire till completely flanked and driven out of their hastily thrown up barricades." Implicit in that statement was the assertion, as in Cox's report, that Conrad waited too long before deciding to withdraw.[70]

Wagner's report was clearly at odds with the facts as they started to stream in to General Thomas's headquarters. Further, Wagner left out in his report any mention of the other order he gave to Conrad—the order for "sergeants to fix their bayonets and to keep the men to their places." Cox said it was the "equivalent to preferring charges."[71]

The bayonet order: Conrad may have suspected, maybe even hoped, that the mention of it would catch Thomas's attention immediately. What else would explain Conrad's unusually rapid delivery of his report? If so, Conrad had calculated correctly. Thomas took but two days to relieve Wagner of his command. Wagner, fearing an official inquiry or even a court-martial, asked to be relieved from further duty with the Army of the Cumberland. The request was granted. Four days later, Wagner left for Indianapolis, his army career effectively over.[72]

21

A Cry of Victory

The 15th Missouri left Franklin in the black of the morning. Two hours after midnight, "we departed in peace from our late battle field,"[1] the 15th among the last to leave.

Schofield's army had marched and fought for two days with little food or sleep. They were now beginning the third with no promise of things getting any better. Men who fell out of ranks or collapsed were shaken awake and roused by their sergeants or officers and told to keep moving. An Ohio soldier remembered that the column, several miles long heading north for Nashville, "staggered rather than marched."[2]

Hood decided to follow. Casualties and desertions had reduced his infantry from the forty thousand or so that started the campaign north to little more than thirty thousand, many regiments now no larger than the size of companies. Leaving Franklin, a demoralized and no longer proud army,[3] they passed acres of their dead lying south of the now-empty federal entrenchments around Franklin.

Ahead by several miles, the federal column crested rise after rise, a "seemingly endless series of hills and ridges." Finally, on the horizon, they saw Nashville. The air rang "with our cheers and shouts," one soldier recalled.[4] The 15th Missouri arrived "shortly before noon," Marcoot wrote.[5]

Officers guided the incoming columns off the roads into positions to form a seven-mile cordon south of the state capitol. Cook fires were quickly set, rations cooked, camps set up, most of the men soon collapsing into sleep. Now with an army of 60,000, Maj. Gen. George Thomas waited for the trailing Confederate Army of Tennessee.[6]

Grant, five hundred miles east, was nervous. Part of it was due to his longtime low opinion of "Old Slow Trot." That opinion apparently also poisoned the air for Thomas around Washington. Even the president seemed afflicted. Grant had barely got off a telegram to Thomas urging him to take the offensive before Stanton fired one off to Grant relaying Lincoln's anxiety: "The President feels solicitous about the disposition of General Thomas to lay in fortifications. . . . This looks like the McClellan and Rosecrans strategy of do nothing. . . . The President wishes you to consider the matter." Thomas's reply to Grant said that only now was he getting the reinforcements he had been promised, and, mincing no words, asserted that "it must be remembered that my command was made up of the two weakest corps of General Sherman's army and all the dismounted cavalry."[7]

Six days after his last message, Grant telegraphed Thomas again: "Attack at once and wait no longer. . . . There is great danger of delay resulting in a campaign back to the Ohio River."[8] That night the weather suddenly turned colder. A cold rain soon turned to sleet. By morning, the trees were sheathed in ice and the ground froze rock hard. Men and horses trying to ambulate along the roads slipped and skidded and crashed to the icy pavements in clattering heaps, men breaking elbows and kneecaps. That night, Thomas received the fourth prodding telegram from Grant in three days: "Why not attack at once?" "The next day, Faess recorded, "we were greeted with a heavy snow."[9]

Grant had worked himself into believing that Hood was about to make good on his plan to "elude Thomas and manage to get north of the Cumberland River. If he did this," Grant was to write, "I apprehended most serious results from [a] campaign in the North and was afraid we might even have to send troops from the East to head him off."[10]

With no sign that Thomas was about to attack, Grant's fears took control. Picking up his gear in Virginia, Grant headed for Washington with the intent of boarding a train to go to Nashville and relieve Thomas. But before Grant's train could get to Nashville, the weather changed. "On the 14th of December . . . it began to thaw out with a warm rain," Marcoot wrote. With that, Conrad received orders to have his command ready to move the next morning at daylight. "The cannonading became more earnest, and we were given orders to be constantly in readiness to march."[11]

December 15 dawned with a dense fog. Long lines of blue-coated troops moved out of their entrenchments and formed into lines of battle. Thomas's plan was to hold the Confederates in place with his left while he reinforced his right to swing around the dug-in Confederate left flank. With the fog veiling their movements, a massive diversionary attack at about eight o'clock struck the Confederate right, causing the gray troops to fall back. Two miles to the right, Thomas's main force slammed into the Confederate left, but Alexander Stewart's corps fought off the Union men until they were flanked. The fighting continued until dark when Hood decided to withdraw his battered army two miles to a shorter line. That night, the Confederate commander patched together a thin line several miles south of the capitol building, stretching for about three miles from Shy's Hill to Overton Hill on the right, his army now on the verge of collapse.

The 15th, in the left center of the Union line, had been held in reserve with the rest of the brigade. The regiment's commander, Capt. George Ernst, reported that the 15th advanced all day but "was not very much exposed to the fire of the enemy," adding that the 15th had "lost not a man killed nor wounded. During the night we camped in an open field, [throwing] up light earth-works for defense."[12]

The next morning, December 16, the Missourians moved into line of battle once again. They formed the left wing of the first line of Conrad's brigade, stretching three-fourths of a mile. They were to assault Hood's works on Overton Hill. "About 11 A.M. a general forward movement was made," Conrad reported, "driving the enemy's skirmishers rapidly. Upon entering the woods the double-quick was ordered, and the command was thrown forward rapidly assaulting the enemy's works, carrying a strongly fortified skirmish line." "Our boys advanced bravely under a steady storm of bullets," Marcoot wrote, "until they reached the enemy's works." But the attack was repulsed all along the line, and Ernst reported that "the regiment fell [back] in good order and took position behind small earth-works."[13]

At 3:30 P.M., the entire Union line charged again, "rushing forward and pouring a deadly volley of solid lead into them, the dead and wounded falling thick and fast, so terrible was the slaughter. In an instant almost a galling fire was opened [on] their right and left" when the men of the 15th "heard the cry of victory over to our right [which we returned] on our charge . . . the works with their artillery and troops fell into our hands and they were compelled to withdraw, leaving many dead and wounded in the deep and almost impassable trenches."[14]

The assault along a three-mile front sent the remnants of the Confederate Army of Tennessee streaming south. It was, according to Conrad, a "complete and utter rout. . . . Here my brigade captured two pieces of artillery, a great number of small-arms, and a large number of prisoners; it is impossible to tell how many, as they were sent to the rear immediately in squads, and no account kept of them. The command moved forward rapidly, crossed to the left of the Franklin pike, and pursued the enemy to the vicinity of Brentwood," seven miles to the south, before bivouacking for the night.[15]

The lone fatality among the 15th's nine casualties was Pvt. Joseph Mohr. He was the last identified soldier of the 15th Missouri to be killed in battle. Originally from Bingen, Germany, Mohr was wounded in the left thigh. Following amputation of his leg, Mohr died later that day. Three days later, another member of the 15th was killed in a skirmish near Columbia, Tennessee. Unfortunately, his name apparently was not recorded, truly an unknown soldier of the 15th Missouri.[16]

For the next two weeks, disheartened Confederates streamed south. Others deserted by the thousands or simply surrendered. Thomas stated that during the campaign, his army "captured 13,194 prisoners of war" and "during the same period, over 2000 deserters from the enemy were received."[17] Most were likely taken following the collapse of the army at Nashville.

It had been one of the most one-sided battles of the Civil War. The Fourth and Twenty-third corps joined at Nashville by a division of the Army of the Tennessee, with provisional detachments of disparate units—including quartermaster and railroad personnel entering the trenches, even walking wounded from the hospitals had been handed rifles—had done what Sherman with twice the number of men had failed to do. The Confederate Army of Tennessee had been effectively destroyed. Now no more than 21,000, many without shoes or weapons, recrossed the Tennessee River into Alabama in late December, retreating finally to Tupelo, Mississippi, an army no longer.

The final humiliation came in early January. Hood was directed to send east "whatever troops you can spare."[18] Two weeks later, on Friday the 13th, Hood submitted his resignation. The war in the West was over.

For another four months, Lee and his Army of Northern Virginia hunkered in their trenches before Grant and the Army of the Potomac around Petersburg, both armies remaining motionless. Sherman and his men meanwhile continued their march to pillage and burn northward along the eastern seaboard. Come April, Lee and his army would attempt a hopeless escape. It would end several days later around a small table in the Appomattox, Virginia, Court House.

Outnumbered more than two to one, with no provisions, and many without shoes, some without arms, the Confederate Army of Tennessee's defeat at Nashville was all but inevitable. Had Hood prevented the Union forces' escape at Spring Hill or defeated Schofield's army at Franklin, the outcome at Nashville, and even of the war itself, might have been different. Hood later wrote that his next move would have been a march to Louisville and then to Cincinnati, with the threat of putting the torch to either or both.[19] With that, the North suing for peace, or at least an armistice, would have become a distinct possibility.

On more than one occasion, before and long after the battle at Nashville, Grant wrote of his worry that Hood might defeat or elude federal forces in Tennessee.[20] He apparently was among the few in Washington who could see the danger. "I was never so anxious during the war as at that time," he would later write. Had Hood been able to "elude Thomas and manage to get north of the Cumberland River, I apprehended most serious results."[21] But for the failures at Spring Hill and Franklin, Hood would have had in reach what Lee had failed to accomplish with his invasion of the North a year earlier. For the Union, a defeat at Spring Hill or Franklin could have been what Gettysburg had become for the Confederacy. And American history could have traveled down another road.

News of the great victory at Nashville reverberated throughout the country. The next morning, Washington awoke to bands blaring, crowds cheering, and the firing of one hundred guns. Grant ordered another hundred fired at City Point headquarters, as did Meade commanding the Army of the Potomac, and Sheridan in the Shenandoah followed with especially warm congratulations for his old comrades. The sentiments most appreciated by Thomas came from Secretary of the Treasury Salmon Chase: "We all feel profoundly gratified to you and your gallant Army for the great success over Hood. I rejoice that you were in command."[22]

Others followed: from Grant, a cryptic note, and from Sherman, a self-preoccupied, almost apologetic letter for possibly "leaving you too weak to cope with Hood." It was a letter that Thomas, after showing it to an aide, reportedly cast aside.[23]

From the president, there had even been an admonition: "Please accept for yourself, officers, and men the Nation's thanks for your good work of yesterday. You made a magnificent beginning. A grand consummation is within your easy reach; do not let it slip."[24] The memory of Meade's dilatory pursuit after Gettysburg was not far off.

The morning after the battle, Thomas's army took to the muddy roads before daylight in pursuit of Hood. Leading the advance slugged the cavalry, harassed all the while by Hood's rear guard of Nathan Bedford Forrest's cavalry. The first day of the chase, December 18, the 15th Missouri "marched fifteen miles in the pouring rain, passing through Spring Hill, and on the 19th continued forward some four miles . . . when we encountered the enemy again; they had undertaken to entrench themselves. We formed our line."[25]

Southward flowed the retreating flotsam of gray fugitives. Even the best commanders could not get their men to turn around and face the enemy. "It was like trying to stop the current of Duck River with a fish net," one man said. An officer hailed a mud-spattered infantryman intent on heading south and ordered him to halt and face about. "You go to hell," came the reply, "I've been there."[26]

The 15th and the Fourth Corps trudged on. The 15th Missouri, Marcoot wrote, "went into camp on Duck River . . . [it] continued to rain steadily and turning decidedly colder, and the rain was soon followed by sleet . . . snow fell almost all day . . . laid a pontoon bridge across Duck River and crossed over upon it during the night . . . advanced six miles, the rear guard of the enemy, Forest's cavalry, withdrawing slowly as we advanced. . . . On the 25th, Christmas day, we marched fully fourteen miles, passing through Pulaski . . . commenced to rain again. . . . On the 28th, after marching twelve miles, we camped near Lexington, Alabama."[27] It was also on the 28th that Thomas learned that Hood's rear guard had crossed over the Tennessee River in Alabama. Hood's remnants had made good their escape.

That night, Thomas telegraphed Halleck that bad weather, a countryside ravaged of provisions, and the exhaustion of his troops and animals would force him to halt and refit. Thomas had also learned a week earlier that the long march over bad roads in the rain, the snow, and the mud had chewed up so many shoes of his pursuing Fourth Corps that many of the men would be disabled "in a very few days."[28] Thomas added that he would go into quarters to refit and rest his army until spring.

Two days later, Thomas received a wire from Halleck relaying an order from Grant. With his own Army of the Potomac bogged down around Petersburg, Grant disagreed with Thomas's winter plan, summed up in the wire's last sentences: "Please give us the earliest possible notice of Hood's line of retreat, so that orders may be given for a continuance of the campaign. General Grant does not intend that your army shall go into winter quarters; it must be ready for active operations in the field."[29]

Thomas recounted his reasons for going into camp while proceeding to carry out his new orders. In the field, his cavalry a few days earlier had to give up the pursuit for lack of ammunition and rations. Fourth Corps infantry, short of provisions and awaiting a supply train, scoured cornfields already gleaned for every stray ear.[30]

On the last day of the year, Marcoot recorded, "Our provisions by this time were becoming very scant, and we were again put on half rations."[31]

1865

Hush'd be the camps, to-day
. . . let us drape our war-worn weapons

—Walt Whitman, "Drum Taps"

22

...orm passed over us"

...the 15th marched south eight miles from
...ear Lexington, Alabama, and camped on
... weather was very fine," Adolph Faess
...ng while Marcoot remained in the hos-

...lay of the year building a bridge across
...over and made five miles before night."
The corps was on its way to carry out Grant's orders to continue the pursuit, but first with a stopover in Huntsville to replenish their desperately short provisions. On the 6th, they and the rest of Conrad's brigade boarded train cars for Decatur. Two days later, "we laid out a regular camp near that city. . . . We were now arranging our quarters as best we could for the winter."[1] They were not in fact disobeying Grant's orders—with barely a week past since ordering Thomas to continue the offensive, Grant had rethought and changed his mind.

Seven hundred miles away in Washington, perhaps Grant had come to realize what the 15th and the rest of Thomas's men were witnessing firsthand; there no longer was much of a Confederate army to worry about in the West. Adolph Faess's log meticulously testified to the fact: almost daily, through February and March, "another squad of Johnies came into our camp" and surrendered.[2]

In Chattanooga, "Dutchey," the young Yank from Illinois and the older Reb from Alabama prepared to say their goodbyes. A deep friendship had grown between Maurice Marcoot and H. Meadors after four months together in the Chattanooga hospital tents. The camp was being dismantled, and the two would now go their separate ways. Maurice Marcoot and the other recovered Union troops were to rejoin their regiments. The Confederate convalescents were to be sent to prison camps. "Mr. Meadors," as Marcoot came to call his older friend, had survived a leg amputation so close to his hip that he would never be able to make use of an artificial limb. Now he was headed for a military prison. "On the 20th [February], Mr. Meadors and I exchanged addresses . . . and he took his departure." They believed they would never see each other again.

Three weeks later, the Union men packed their kits, drew rations, and pulled down the tents. "We received orders to leave at one o'clock . . . [and] marched down to the depot." Two days later, March 14, Marcoot arrived at Huntsville, Alabama, to rejoin the 15th. "The meadows were becoming green and the peach trees were in full blossom."[3]

Rumors were beginning to circulate that "we would soon be getting orders to march." Decisions in the East were reaching every Union army east of the Mississippi; Grant at last was getting ready for the final move against Lee. The 15th Missouri and the Fourth Corps were to have a role, although a small one. As part of a vast movement of federal armies, north, east, south, and now even west, Thomas and his men were to move north into eastern Tennessee to block Lee if he should escape from Grant and emerge from the Appalachians out of West Virginia.

The 15th Missouri was "ordered to be ready to march on the morning of April 1st. We were promptly in line by seven o'clock" but were kept in position "loaded like a lot of pack mules, until fully one o'clock . . . before the gun boat 'Thomas' ferried us across the river. Here we took the cars and were soon speeding along."

"Early the next morning," Marcoot continued, "we came to sudden halt . . . between Lookout Mountain and Chattanooga. The train just ahead of us had been thrown from the track by obstructions placed there by unfriendly hands. . . . After traveling some sixty five miles from Knoxville we reached Bulls Gap. . . . It was at this time we first experienced, in all our army service, the pleasure of drawing pickles, potatoes, sourkraut, turnips, etc. and we felt exceedingly joyful."[4]

On the morning of April 5, Conrad's brigade was ordered to move forward. As the men went into camp, dispatches began to arrive signaling victories in the East. Their old commander, Phil Sheridan, had routed George Pickett's men at Five Forks, Virginia, southwest of Petersburg, with many of the gray taken prisoner while others fled into the pine forests to escape. More telegraphed messages followed, with the news that Petersburg and Richmond had fallen and "that the enemy had thus been driven out of their stronghold." That evening, "we selected a fine position on a hill near by, nicely shaded by beautiful trees, with numerous gushing springs of water surrounding us."[5]

Three days later, April 9, the men of the 15th took their turn standing picket duty in a steady rain. Some seven hundred miles to the east in Virginia, Lee was surrendering at Appomattox Court House. Now, on the final day of the war, "in the evening," Marcoot wrote,

a terrific storm passed over us. . . .

It continued to rain on the 10th, but in the afternoon of that day, regardless of the mud, we were ordered out on dress parade. When thus in line a dispatch was read to us stating that General Lee had surrendered all his forces to General Grant at Appomattox. The cheering in the ranks at this good news was simply tremendous and was kept up some time, while the cannonading and musket firing in honor of the event was as fierce and rapid as if in battle, and lasting until long after nightfall while in the excitement incident thereto, two comrades were accidentally killed and many others wounded.

Nor was such a scene to be wondered at. We had been in ranks in the front for over four long, weary, bloody years, and now it seemed as if by one stroke the end was at hand.

The next day, Marcoot wrote, "we had an abundance of brightness in our hearts and the latest news was all the talk, while many walked about with sore heads—too much joy and 'Tennessee mountain dew.'"

Marcoot continued, "The 14th was Good Friday, and General Stanley ordered that it be made the occasion of Thanksgiving . . . it was a most beautiful day. The stars and stripes were to be replanted on and over Ft. Sumter, a salute of one hundred guns were fired and religious services were held among the various commands."[6]

Four hundred miles east of Bulls Gap, Tennessee, where the men of the 15th were celebrating or attending religious services, a young man in Washington, having just attended a play at Ford's Theatre, wrote home to his parents, "I first heard the report of a pistol & immediately after a man jumped from Mr. Lincoln's box."[7]

The 15th brought more rain. . . . Later in the day . . . rumors were circulated, but not believed, that Lincoln was dead, that he had been assassinated at Ford's Theatre the evening before, and that his son, [Secretary of State] Seward, and other prominent members of the Cabinet had been fatally assaulted. We could not dare believe it, but were fearful lest it might be true and our joy turned to sadness. . . . The official dispatches on the 16th confirmed the rumors . . . and a heavy pall, a dense gloom fell over and upon us . . . the news was terrible and crushing . . . silence and sorrow reigned supreme. . . .

On the 22nd we . . . marched to the depot and boarded a train about midnight. . . . [Sometime before daylight,] our train jumped the track, and three cars were overturned and others seriously damaged. It was a fearful wreck . . . one man being killed and 10 seriously wounded. It was night when we finally reached Knoxville . . . Nashville was reached the next evening. . . . We were all worn out, being so crowded . . . fifty men to each box car. . . .

Orders were received to drill three times a day . . . now when we thought the war was over and that we would be mustered out, we were [treated] as new recruits . . . why should we drill now? . . . On the 9th of May . . . a grand review was had and large numbers of citizen spectators were present and when General Thomas appeared he was greeted with cheer after cheer by the troops. . . . The 10th was a very lonesome day, and the boys were becoming terribly homesick."[8]

"Jos. Baden, of our company, who had been wounded and captured at Franklin, returned at this time in good health." Perhaps Marcoot was mistaken, for the official records tell a different story. Baden had indeed been wounded and taken prisoner at Franklin, as was another man in Marcoot's Company B, twenty-three-year-old Frank Raffle, originally from Bavaria. Both had spent the last five months in a Deep South prison stockade. They, with other former captives, were now free and getting ready to crowd aboard a sidewheel steamboat, the *Sultana*, one of the largest on the Mississippi. They were destined for passage home. In a virtual mob at Vicksburg, possibly as many as nineteen hundred other freed captives, almost five times the steamer's authorized capacity, crowded the landing, all anxious and some even desperate to board and not to be left behind.

Also present was Pvt. Jerrie Dresser of the 15th Missouri, but his record is too incomplete to know more about him. Undoubtedly there were others from the regiment attempting to board, for there were more than sixty who had been taken prisoner since Chickamauga. Those who had survived the prison camps were now being funneled to the landings along the Mississippi, some ticketed for the *Sultana*.

Aboard at last, they now were going home. Or so they thought. Nine miles up the river from Memphis, the boilers exploded, blowing the steamer apart. Men not killed outright dove through the flames into the dark and frigid water. Most would drown. The official figure totaled 1,585 dead, although the actual number was probably higher. It was the greatest maritime disaster, with more fatalities than the *Titanic*. The *Sultana* explosion and sinking killed more than the total number killed on both sides at the first battles of the war at Bull Run and Wilson's Creek in Missouri.[9] Baden, Raffle, and Dresser were listed among the dead.[10]

Phillip Schuh, originally from Baden, Germany, and another of Marcoot's company comrades who had been a captive, got as far as the army hospital in Nashville. Schuh was one of the "old men" of the regiment, having volunteered back in 1861 at the age of thirty-nine. Now forty-three, he too had been freed after a year and a half at Andersonville following his capture at Chickamauga. Schuh would not see home again. He would die in the Nashville hospital, "starvation and exposure" listed as his cause of death.[11]

"May 24th was the day set apart for the grand review of the army at Washington," Marcoot remembered, "and, although we had borne a full share of the duty in the field, as aided as best we could to secure victory, we were excluded from that pleasure, and in all our service of nearly five years were never fortunate enough to visit Washington or see the White House. But on the grand review day we had our usual brigade drill dress parade and Company drill in camp, near Nashville, all to ourselves, although we did not fully appreciate the pleasure."[12]

Marcoot and his comrades of the Fourth Corps of the Army of the Cumberland had been handed many reasons to be bitter over the past months. Now those in Washington had given them yet another: men who had charged without orders up Missionary Ridge to rout an entire Confederate army, who were instrumental in taking Atlanta, thereby winning a presidential election, who bore the brunt of the largest Confederate charge of the war and then turned the fields of Franklin into a massive death ground for those who had begun the rebellion, who twice in head-on attacks drove entire Confederate armies from entrenched positions in total rout—the only Union army to do so in all the war—for the North's grandest celebration, the Union's most victorious were left out of the Grand Review.

23

Pull for the Shore

It was ordered "that all those whose term would expire on or before the 31st of October, should be mustered out forthwith. This . . . opened our eyes . . . of those of us whose time would not expire." Since the veterans of the 15th Missouri had reenlisted back in 1864 with no expiration date—"it meant a later date for our contemplated journey home."[1]

Commissary Sgt. George Rau submitted a request for a furlough. "My wife and child are sick at home for the last three months, and this makes it almost utterly necessary that I should personally look to their welfare for a short time at least."[2] The request was denied.

On June 15th, "we fell into line, marched to the depot and took the train for Johnstonville" where "we were immediately transferred to the steamer 'Indiana.' . . . On the morning of the 17th we started down the Tennessee and reached Paducah." The regiment learned that they were not going home. They were headed for Texas. "The boys did not relish the supposed Texas jaunt, and considerable dissatisfaction was manifested."[3]

The steamboat anchored on the Illinois side of the river. "This was done ostensibly to prevent any of the boys from getting away, as the banks here were low and the country terribly swampy. Notwithstanding this precaution, our drummer, John Vandeventer, [an eighteen-year-old Hollander from Weston, Missouri] made his escape although he sank into the mud knee deep when he left the boat."[4]

The next day, "I had another severe attack of rheumatism and fever, and was lying in the cabin when the boat reached Cairo, Ill. The order was given to anchor in the middle of the stream here [the Ohio River], and some of our officers were making preparations to go to Cairo in a skiff. This was a little more than the boys would stand, and a squad of them, fixing bayonets, marched up to the pilot and ordered him to 'pull for the shore.' It is unnecessary to say that he obeyed," for obey he did.[5]

There had been near-rebellions by regiments on both sides during the war. Union troops had rebelled over all manner of complaints including bad food and barracking with black soldiers. The 43d Missouri once threatened to rebel at being ordered to cross ice on the Missouri River when they thought it was too dangerous. But as far as actual mutiny was concerned, it had never happened aboard any vessel, naval or civilian, during the Civil War. It was happening now—by an entire brigade.

"Our officers took in the situation . . . and hastily detailed a strong guard to prevent the boys from leaving the boat as soon as the shore was reached. But the guards threw down their guns and shouted for their comrades to come on as they themselves started for the city. The officers then formed a line among themselves and with drawn swords tried to prevent the boys from leaving. It was no use however. . . . One officer was knocked down with a piece of coal, while Fred White of our company [another eighteen-year-old, from St. Joseph, Missouri] hastily rammed a cartridge into his gun. When asked by his lieutenant as to his intentions, he answered that if there was to be any blood shed he would have a hand in it."

Another of the mutineers was "our color bearer of Company 'C,'" Sgt. Michael Kicks [Kicke?], of Trenton, Missouri, originally from Wurtzburg, Germany, and one of the heroes in the charge up Missionary Ridge. Kicks, "a young, slenderly built boy," according to Marcoot,

> who had bravely snatched our colors from the grasp of its mortally wounded bearer at the battle of Stone River, and saved it from falling into the enemy's hands, and had so gallantly carried it from that time on through every engagement . . . now grasped his colors in his left hand, and shouting to the boys, exclaimed: "I have carried this flag through all our battles with the enemy and now that the war is over I will carry it home for you if you will follow me," and threatened to shoot any one that opposed him. Our old Colonel [Conrad] now the commander of our Brigade, loved and respected our brave color bearer and calling to him reasoned with him calmly, telling him not to act too hastily, nor to tarnish the noble record he had made not to undertake to carry away the regimental flag, nor place himself in such a position as this act might bring to him. The kindly words of our Colonel were not for naught, for

our color bearer hesitated, wavered, and then laid aside the flag . . . but left the boat with the boys.

This was now not only mutiny but desertion as well, either of which could get a man shot.

"Although two hundred men had been detailed as guards and the entire number of officers had formed a line themselves, almost every man of the brigade went up to Cairo . . . some of whom had no intention of returning to their commands at the boat or making the trip to Texas with us as their absence afterwards disclosed, among whom were eleven of our company"[6]— a majority of the company, given the reduced size now of the regiment.

That "most of the brigade"—five regiments in all that were on board— "went up to Cairo"—deserted—appears to have been no exaggeration on Marcoot's part. The record shows that ten of Company B were indeed marked down for deserting on June 15, 1865, at Cairo.[7] The regimental number corroborates Marcoot's number. A hundred or more of the 15th, possibly as much as half of the regiment at the time, with likely an equal share of the other four regiments—upwards of five hundred men—literally jumped ship at Cairo.

Officially, the affair apparently went unnoticed or at least unrecorded. The *Official Records of the Rebellion*, in reports, dispatches, or official correspondence, makes no mention of a mutiny in or around Cairo, Illinois, at that or any other time. Desertions throughout the Union army were again becoming commonplace, approaching the epidemic proportions experienced earlier in the war. Perhaps, with the fighting now over and men simply going home at the first chance, without waiting to be told, few officers were bothering to do anything more than record the missing names. The *Compiled Service Records* of the 15th show a growing rash of desertions the weeks following the surrender at Appomattox and through the following summer months.[8]

Not surprising, most of the 15th's deserters were draftees and substitutes taken into the ranks in 1864, conscripts who had a reputation for skipping out at the first opportunity. With many of them now in the brigade's ranks, it perhaps explains why the steamboat was anchored in the middle of the river at Cairo, a practice that had not been followed before their influx.

"When the boat left Cairo that evening, Fred White . . . was aboard, and Lieut C. Muri, who was in command of our company and who was an intimate friend of mine, informed me that he intended to prefer charges against him for threatening to shoot a commanding officer, as soon as we arrived at New Orleans, in fact he had already prepared the charges and read them over to me. He also requested me to keep a watch on him, as he wanted to make an example of him. Of course he had no idea of his confidence being misplaced in me, as I had been such a 'good boy' at Cairo, I was so sick that I could not raise my head, but I could not resist the temptation and it was not long before White was informed of what was brewing, with the advice to 'skip' at the first opportunity." Five days later, Fred White did indeed leave. When the steamboat hauled in at Vicksburg for the night, White went over the side and disappeared, never to return.[9]

"On the 23rd we reached New Orleans. . . . July is a very hot month usually at New Orleans and 1865 was no exception. We had no water that was fit for use." The men bought vinegar to mix with the water to kill the foul taste. "Many . . . sickened and died."

Marcoot records, "It was now known definitely that we were booked for Texas, and the necessity for such a movement was also soon very apparent to us."[10] France was sending an armed force to Mexico to establish a monarchy with an Austrian, Maximilian, as emperor, ostensibly, to protect French citizens still living there. The U.S. government saw the move as an effort to establish a European foothold on the American continent and was prepared to send in troops to see that it did not happen. Mexicans themselves put an end to the affair, rising up to overthrow their governing tormentors. Maximilian was eventually brought before a Mexican firing squad and executed.

For now, however, a number of steamers lay at anchor in the Mississippi, ready to take the 15th and the rest of the corps along the gulf coast to Texas. Troops of other divisions began loading. On the morning of July 17, the 15th Missouri with two other regiments began boarding the *Daniel Webster.* At eleven o'clock, the steamer weighed anchor and headed down the river. The journey to Texas had begun.

Four days later, the steamer dropped anchor off Matagorda, Texas. About a mile offshore before Powderhorn, Texas,

we were transferred to a small schooner which conveyed us twelve miles further up the bay passing Indianola and finally landing us at the wharf at Port Lavaca . . . that afternoon our adventure across the plains was commenced.

Our first march of twelve miles was made without finding a drop of water or a single tree or shrub fit for shade or shelter from the terrible sun. . . . The heat was very oppressive . . . and we [were] loaded down with baggage. . . . Boys became prostrated and sank down under the strain . . . some suffered sunstrokes. . . .

Late in the evening . . . we struck camp on the banks of a small creek . . . of which were scattered a few live oak trees, covered with grape vines and moss, the latter hanging in shreds from the shaggy limbs. . . .

After refreshing ourselves with a draught of this warm creek water we dropped down in our tracks . . . soon the air became thick with mosquitoes, the ground alive with snakes, scorpions, tarantulas, horned frogs . . . while the prairie surrounding us seemed to be alive with wolves.

The next morning, "a squad of us started out early to capture a wild beef. . . . We would scatter our men and by this means surround a herd and in that way one or the other would almost invariably get a good shot and bring one down."

After the regiment's arrival, "we received an order that we were to be sent out to build a railroad from Indianola to Victoria. This was a stunner . . . the war over, and we are shipped into Texas in the middle of summer to build a railroad. Who was it for?"[11] Nor was building a railroad their only occupation. "Desperadoes," Conrad reported, were committing depredations "of every kind" on the inhabitants in and about the town of Texana. Conrad ordered a squad of mounted officers and men to ride out "to ascertain the facts." Two days later, a dispatch arrived from the commanding general directing him to send a regiment to "capture all jayhawkers and other lawless persons . . . seize for the government all property belonging to the late so-called Confederate Army or Government . . . establish justice . . . encourage former slaves to contract [for] labor . . . at just wages." In short, they were to be the local police, magistrates, labor organizers, and whatever else the situation called for when they got there.[12] There is no record of further orders or a report from Conrad about a regiment in "desperado country."

The 15th continued to watch as other regiments got the "glad tidings" and marched off to go home. In late September, the men of the 15th stood by and watched the 44th Illinois receive the news that now they were to go home. "We did not begrudge them their good fortune," Marcoot wrote—the two regiments had been together ever since Pea Ridge in 1861, with many German-born among the 44th—"but we could not help feeling that it would have been pleasant for us to be treated likewise."[13] The 15th was now the last of the old brigade.

During the weeks that followed, a few who jumped ship at Cairo began to drift into camp. Most who had jumped into the mud and water that day would never return. Their service records eventually labeled them as deserters. The government apparently never attempted to track them down or bring them to any kind of a trial. But they or their widows would nevertheless pay. Twenty-five years later, Congress would get around to expressing the nation's gratitude to old soldiers by granting them pensions. Those, that is, who could claim faithful and honorable service on the government's terms.

The few of those who jumped to freedom that day three months ago and did decide to return found their way back by tracking their old regiments downriver from Illinois to New Orleans and then across the Texas plains— because, as Marcoot put it, "they would not tarnish the good record they and their regiments had made."[14]

Among those returning was "our . . . brave color bearer, John Rick [Michael Kicks or Kicke]. He was, as might be expected, however, arrested immediately" and tried by court martial. Kicks was convicted, but the court recommended that his sentence be "disregarded" and reduced from thirty days of hard labor to fatigue duty in camp. Since Kicks was "a brave and so good a soldier to be an honor to the army," the justification read, "having earned the esteem and respect of every officer of the Regiment," the full sentence would "destroy the 'esprit de rigor' and dishearten . . . every Volunteer Soldier." The reduced sentence was endorsed by another cited for gallantry at Missionary Ridge, brigade adjutant and now major, John W. Droste. Conrad approved the recommendation.[15]

In October, a Kentucky regiment and three more from Ohio departed for home. There was still no word for the Missourians. They took some comfort a day later when a tremendous wind and rain storm "demolished all the large wall tents of our officers, while we quietly lay in our little 'pup' tents and witnessed them" amid the flash of lightning and rumbling thunder "chasing about for their valuables."[16]

"On the 26th while we were enjoying a spirited game of base ball, we received orders to prepare to take 'the road' . . . one o'clock the following morning the drum beat called all forth into line for reveille, and at three o'clock we were ordered to move forward. We marched across the prairie towards Victoria arriving there at noon . . . and went into camp for the night. It was only a twenty-mile march, but we were pretty well 'done for.'"[17]

Almost a month later, on November 21, a special order arrived at the regiment's headquarters—"the following regiments are to be mustered out of service." Near midway down the column of listed regiments appeared "15th Missouri Volunteer Infantry."[18] More than seven months after the war had ended, their turn at last had come.

But the day they could go home was still days away. "December came and went . . . as other regiments passed by and departed for home, sweet home. While we were daily sent out to work on the road. We were beginning to lose heart and become careless. . . . We neglected every duty we could consistently and began to enjoy ourselves as best we could with newly made friends in Victoria and among the farming people round about . . . we attended a number of private parties and frequently met Confederate soldiers and joined with them in merry making."

On the fourth day of the new year, 1866, they were ordered to pack their kits, fall in, and march to the railroad depot. They boarded railroad cars for Port Lavaca, where they embarked aboard a steamer. Six days later, they arrived at New Orleans. Boarding a steamboat, the men watched as the paddlewheels began to churn the way up the Mississippi. Passing Memphis, they began to note a change in climate. "While the peach trees were in bloom at New Orleans we here began to encounter drift ice, as the ice had broken at St. Louis." Here too, Marcoot wrote, they could sense a change, a "keeness of the air."[19] A growing nearness to home.

The drift ice grew thicker as they headed north. It was soon too dangerous to continue on by boat. When the steamer arrived at Cairo the next evening, the men disembarked for rail cars. At seven the next morning, the cars slowly began to move on the final leg of their journey home. A day later, barely a hundred officers and men, if that many, stepped off the train in East St. Louis. A ferry took them across the Mississippi to St. Louis. By late morning, they crossed over the gangplank and onto Missouri soil.

Marcoot and his bunkie, Adolph Faess, could now close the book on their log of the 15th Missouri Volunteer Infantry. By their reckoning, they and the German boys of 1861 had fought in twenty-five battles, marched 3,290 miles, traveled 2,334 by rail, and 4,550 by water, a grand total of 10,154 miles. Of the 904 who had served in the regiment, more than half had been killed, died of disease, or would bear a wound or the memory of one for the rest of their lives.[20]

Down on the levee, the small band fell in and dressed their pitiful ranks one last time—each company now had fewer than ten men—shadows now of the more than eight hundred who had marched off to war back in 1861. Their march this time would end at a large hall on Second Street. Here "the citizens had prepared a fine feast." The ritual over, the men were on their own, waiting for "Uncle Sam to pay us off and award us our discharge papers." This would take another five days.

On January 24, 1866, four years and eight months after the war for them had begun, the day at last came. "I will not attempt to describe my feelings upon this memorable occasion," Marcoot wrote twenty-four years later.

"Thus it was that [a] few hours elapsed after our muster out was completed before the old gallant 15th—those that remained of them—companions closer than brothers for years, were scattered, each eager to reach his own home and greet his own family and friends. . . .

"It was enough to know that we were soldiers no longer . . . the cruel war was over."[21]

Epilogue

Joseph Conrad went on to a career in the regular army, attaining the rank of brevet brigadier general and command of the 18th U.S. Infantry, retiring finally after twenty years of service. He lived another fifteen years and died in 1897 at the age of sixty-nine in Atlantic City, New Jersey. He is buried in Arlington National Cemetery.

George Rau returned home to St. Louis. He tried his hand again as a carpenter, but the war had taken its toll. A growing illness, perhaps the residue of the years spent in the rain, the sleet and snow, and the mud, made it hard for him to work. Eventually, on the verge of poverty, George and his wife and three children received clothing and other support from the Masonic Lodge. An ungrateful nation waited twenty-five years to grant pensions for Civil War veterans or their widows, eleven years after Rau had died at the age of forty-four of kidney failure. It was said that in his last years he sometimes had a hard time sleeping indoors and would take his bedroll outside to sleep under the stars.

John Droste returned to St. Charles, where he was referred to as "the Major" until his death, and even so today. He is buried in a Lutheran cemetery on the top of a hill.

As it was for Maurice Marcoot, who had seen and experienced more in those five years than most men do in a lifetime (before he even became eligible to vote), so it was for most of those who had served, probably for all of them—their years in the 15th Missouri defined their lives for the rest of their years.

Sometime in 1886, a letter arrived in Highland, Illinois, for Maurice Marcoot. "H. Meadors," the return said. "A thunderbolt from a clear sky could not have overtaken me with more astonishment." Marcoot had tried to communicate with his old Confederate tent mate immediately after the war, but his letters were returned as undeliverable.

Maurice Marcoot as he appeared in 1890. (Missouri Historical Society, St. Louis)

Stunned now to hear from his old friend whom he had given up for
dead, Marcoot quickly responded. Less than two months later, Meadors
arrived at Marcoot's doorstep, a crutch now serving for the missing leg lost
twenty-two years ago. "I will not attempt to describe our meeting after so
many years of doubts and fears."[1]

The following year, Marcoot traveled to his friend's home in Alabama.
"It was during this trip that I first decided to collect my data together for
my reminiscences, as I had an opportunity to revisit many of our old battle
fields." Four years later, his reminiscences were printed under the title *Five
Years in the Sunny South*. The small booklet was offered to the public for the
price of one dollar.

"It was seldom that the soldier voluntarily referred to his life in the ranks,"
wrote Maurice Marcoot. For all he had seen and for all he had experienced,

it would remain within, the uninvited, yet, paradoxically, the profoundly cherished. It would be impossible to bring even some of it into the light without bringing forth the rush of feelings that would have to flow too. For an old soldier, that would have been an unseemly thing to do.

Now, a quarter of a century later, he spoke at last of what had mattered most to him when the war had ended, and still so now. Recalling those years, he spoke no doubt not only for himself but for the others as well. "Sad as the thoughts were within us for the loss of comrades and friends, whose bodies were strewn along the long line of our march during those fated years, and while we sincerely mourned our depleted ranks, we were joyous at the thought of being permitted to see home."

As he closed his manuscript, it appears he felt in reflection an obligation to write something about why he and his comrades had chosen to fight. He possibly needed to find some kind of justification, an accountability for the terrible price that had been paid, a fact to which he had been both witness and willing participant. And so he ended: "Our cause, thank God, just as it was, had prevailed, and that, regardless of the great sacrifice made, the great loss of life sustained, and the horrible suffering endured . . . America was saved and the government still lived."[2]

In November 1894, on the thirty-first anniversary of the great charge up Missionary Ridge, they gathered at a hall on South Broadway in South St. Louis, an area at the time of predominantly German neighborhoods. The Association of the 15th Regiment, Missouri Infantry, Veteran Volunteers, had been formed eight years before at Highland, Illinois, there having been one company of Highland men in the regiment. Marcoot no doubt had much to do with the forming of the association.

This gathering was a special one. They would have been in their Sunday best, woolen suits and vests, starched collars and ties, watch fobs, looking more like bankers than carpenters, farmers, shoemakers, mechanics. Some had not seen each other since the war. A reporter attending for the *St. Louis Globe Democrat* wrote, "There were tears of joy and fond embraces, an unusual warmth and fraternity . . . seldom witnessed, even at a gathering of old comrades and friends who [had] fought side by side."[3]

Here and there would have been an empty coat sleeve or pant leg, yet another reminder of a time once shared, of terrible times remembered in the profound and inexplicable way that bring men together as no other.

There was the routine business meeting. Gustav Baare of St. Louis was elected president for the coming year; Emil Dosenbach of Clayton, who had been wounded in that great charge up Missionary Ridge, was elected vice-president, and August Reimens, then of Davenport, Iowa, as secretary and treasurer. They then got up from their chairs, some slower than others perhaps, and adjourned to a large adjoining room. Here they sat down to a meal, a "plain, but substantial collation spread upon clean, unpretentious tables in the center of the hall . . . one common family," the reporter wrote, "the blind, the lame, the halt, the aged and infirm, together with those whose faces time [had not yet] written his sign in deep furrows and wrinkled brows. . . .

"An orchestra of several pieces discoursed the national airs, interspersed with the more spirited martial music of the regimental drum and fife corps, and speeches commemorative of the deeds of valor and bravery of the boys in blue."

They continued to meet down the years, singing the songs, reviving the tales, and no doubt enlarging on them a bit . . . remembering . . . their numbers dwindling, inexorably, with each gathering. Until there were too few of them, too tired and worn to do any of those things.

And then they were gone.

In his Annual Report of 1863, the adjutant general of Missouri saw fit to include a citation for one regiment of the state's volunteers. With the end of the war still nowhere in sight—it would have more than a year to go—the citation read nonetheless: "No Regiment of the patriotic army of the United States is entitled to more honor than the 15th Infantry, Missouri Volunteers . . . in the history of the war it will hold a distinguished place for its devotion, perseverance and undeviating bravery."

. . .

> Their seed shall remain for ever
> And their glory shall not be blotted out
> Their bodies are buried in peace
> And their name shall live forever.
> —Ecclesiasticus XLIV

Appendix

A Statistical Portrait of the 15th Missouri Soldier

The National Archives' *Compiled Service Records* is the basic source for descriptive data of this Civil War soldier. At the least, a soldier's record will contain a bimonthly muster card showing his name, rank, regiment, and company. Some records include a "muster-in" card or one labeled "descriptive identity" that lists enlistment date. Enlistment papers may show height, eye and hair color, occupation, birthplace, and "nearest relative." If these records are not included, the data can sometimes be found on additional documents such as hospital registrations and disability certificates.

Records for the 15th Missouri suffer greatly for lack of these descriptive data and supporting documents. Many do not include a muster-in card. Few include initial enlistment papers and, consequently, vital data for physical descriptions, occupations, and birthplace or origin are often lacking. Some documents apparently never were included among those sent to national record-keeping sources; a handful of initial enlistment papers, for instance, can be found in the Missouri state archives rather than in the *Compiled Service Records*. No *initial* enlistment papers, which show birthplace and other vital data, are in these records for 1861 volunteers from the St. Louis area.

Human intervention may explain why some records are fairly complete and others, the majority in fact, list no more than name and enlistment date. It may be significant that the 15th Missouri records for volunteers of Swiss origin, those from the Highland, Illinois area, are more complete than those from the St. Louis area. Firsthand sources cite a "crowded arsenal" in St. Louis where volunteers went to enlist during the war's first summer in 1861. Perhaps only the most basic information was taken to keep the many volunteers moving through the enlistment process and the rush to get them into a regiment. The much more complete records of the Illinois group, which organized and drilled before the 15th Missouri was organized in St. Louis, were possibly prepared beforehand and submitted as a group during their enrollment at the arsenal. Volunteers from the St. Louis area arrived individually to be processed by possibly overloaded clerks who recorded only the most essential data. It is significant that records of all 15th Missouri volunteers enrolling at the arsenal months later are substantially more complete. For those first St. Louis volunteers in 1861, only when one examines their *reenlistment* papers of 1864, which are complete in most cases, will the vital data of age and birthplace be found.

METHODOLOGY

One hundred and eight individual records were randomly selected from a base of about eight hundred enlisted men. The sample size assures a 95 percent confidence level for birthplace/origin and the age factor with an error of less than 1.83 years, calculated by the Statistical Services Center of the University of Missouri-Columbia. Data for other categories should be considered directional, since these data appear in only a few records.

Twelve microfilm reels, each containing approximately eighty records in alphabetical order, make up the *Compiled Service Records* for the 15th Missouri. For this sample, two criteria were required for sample selection: (1) enlisted men only (no officers) and (2) the enlistment date had to be July or August 1861, when the regiment was formed. These make up about seven hundred of the total eight hundred men in the ranks, excluding officers, representing those who were with the regiment from beginning to end.

One record for each company and noncommissioned staff was selected from each reel. The first encountered on a reel was selected. Where none for a company was encountered, two were taken from the next reel.

CONCLUSIONS AND INTERPRETATIONS

The "typical" soldier in the 15th Missouri was a German immigrant, in his mid-twenties (median age was twenty-six, the same as his American-born Union counterpart), 5'5" tall, with blue or gray eyes and brown hair. The German volunteer would likely have been a tradesman or laborer in civilian life, which suggests a significant difference from American-born Union soldiers, half of whom were farmers in civilian life (source for data of American-born Union soldiers: McPherson, *For Cause & Comrades*). Of course, there are many variations to this portrait:

Origin

Seventy-four percent of the first volunteers in the 15th Missouri during the summer of 1861 were of German birth or of German parents:

	Sample	Share
Germany; states, e.g., Bavaria, Prussia	32	30.0%
Germanic surnames, birthplace unidentified	45	41.7%
St. Louis, native-born, Germanic surnames	3	2.8%
Switzerland (Highland, Illinois, contingent)	15	13.9%
France	2	1.9%
Australia, Canada, Holland, Luxemburg, Indiana, and Louisiana, each 1% or less	6	5.6%
Unidentified, Anglo surnames	5	4.6%
Total	108	100.5%

The median age was twenty-six:

Age range	Sample	Share
50–56	1 (56 years)	0.9%
40–49	9	8.3%
30–39	31	28.7%
20–29	42	38.9%
16–19	25	23.1%
Total	108	99.9%

The median height was 5'5" (typical for all Union soldiers):

Height	Sample	Share
6'0"	1	3.8%
5'9–11"	4	15.4%
5'6–8"	7	26.9%
5'3–5"	9	34.6%
5'0–2"	2	7.7%
4'9–11"	3**	11.5%
Total	26	99.9%*

*Rounding effect
**Two sixteen-year-old drummer boys

Eye and hair color:

	Eyes			Hair	
	Gray	9		Brown	14
	Blue	10		Light	7
	Brown	5		Gray	2
				Black	1

Occupation:

Farmer	1
Laborer	8*
Merchant	1
Musician	3
Tradesman**	8

*Could be misleading, as many German immigrants resorted to work as laborers when they could not get jobs in their original occupations because of anti-German sentiment in St. Louis. Original occupations or professions in Germany are not known.

**Butcher, carpenter, clockmaker, mechanic, shoemaker (4)

Notes

ABBREVIATIONS

CCNMP   Chickamauga-Chattanooga National Military Park, Fort Oglethorpe, Georgia
LC   Library of Congress, Washington, D.C.
MHR   *Missouri Historical Review*
MHS   Missouri Historical Society, St. Louis
MSIC   Missouri State Information Center, Jefferson City
NA   National Archives, Washington, D.C.
OR   *Official Records of the Rebellion*
SHSM   State Historical Society of Missouri, Columbia, Missouri
SRNB   Stones River National Battlefield, Murfreesboro, Tennessee
USAMHI   U.S. Army Military Institute, Carlisle Barracks, Pennsylvania
WHMC   Western Historical Manuscript Collection, University of Missouri-Columbia and University of Missouri-St. Louis

INTRODUCTION

1. Craig, *The Germans*, 21–34, 83–94.
2. Wellbery and Ryan, *A New History of German Literature*, 561–67.
3. Gatzke, *Germany and the United States*, 30.
4. Boatner, *Civil War Dictionary*, 612.
5. "Seeing the elephant" was an expression of the time for experiencing something new, an adventure. It probably had its origin in one going to see the circuses that traveled from town to town.
6. Fox, *Regimental Losses in the American Civil War*.
7. Cutler, *North Reports the War*, 35.
8. Dyer, *Compendium of the War of the Rebellion*, 2:582.
9. Gallagher and Nolan, *Myth of the Lost Cause*.
10. Kaufmann, *Germans in the American Civil War*, 287; "Battles and Leaders of the Civil War," *Century Magazine*, 1:13.
11. Burton, *Melting Pot Soldiers*, 50.
12. Ibid., 216.
13. Ibid., 111.
14. "Woechelicher Anzeiger des Westens," Jan. 10, 1863.

15. Lonn, *Foreigners in the Union Army and Navy*, 573–79; Kaufmann, *Germans in the American Civil War*, 1; Dyer, *Compendium of the War of the Rebellion*, 1:11. Applying that percentage to Missouri's 109,000 Union soldiers produces a conservative 10,000 Germans in blue. Given Missouri's great influx of these new arrivals in the 1840s and 1850s, added to the fact that the state contributed more men to the Union military as a share of population than any Northern state, the actual number is probably much higher.

16. McPherson, *For Cause and Comrades*, ix.

17. Wiley, *Life of Billy Yank*, 273.

18. McPherson, *Battle Cry of Freedom*, 606–7; SHSM, Compiled Service Records, 15th Missouri; Goebel, "Laenger als ein Menschenleben in Missouri," chap. 27, pt. 1.

19. See Appendix, "A Statistical Portrait of the 15th Missouri Soldier," this volume.

20. Burton, *Melting Pot Soldiers*, 48.

21. Craig, *The Germans*, 15.

22. Herriott, *Conference in the Deutches Haus*, 89.

23. Krause, "German Americans in the St. Louis Region, 1840–1860," 301.

24. Burton, *Melting Pot Soldiers*, 210.

1. Black Dutch

1. Marcoot, *Five Years in the Sunny South*, 5.

2. Rowan and Primm, *Germans for a Free Missouri*, 4–13; Rombauer, *Union Cause in St. Louis in 1861*, 127.

3. Goebel, "Laenger als ein Menschenleben in Missouri," chap. 28, p. 2.

4. Ibid., chap. 27, pp. 6–7.

5. Phillips, *Missouri's Confederate*, 235.

6. Rowan and Primm, *Germans for a Free Missouri*, 13; Rombauer, *Union Cause in St. Louis in 1861*, 131.

7. Dunson, "Notes on the Missouri Germans on Slavery," 355–66.

8. Krause, "German Americans in the St. Louis Region, 1840–1860," 302.

9. Gatzke, *Germany and the United States*, 31–32.

10. SHSM, Compiled Service Records, 15th Missouri.

11. *Daily Missouri Republican*, Sept. 4, 1854.

12. Krause, "German Americans in the St. Louis Region, 1840–1860," 308.

13. Donald, *Lincoln*, 239.

14. Meyer, *Moving Frontiers*, 234–35.

15. *Daily Missouri Republican*, Sept. 4, 1854.

16. Herriott, *Conference in the Deutches Haus*, 58–95.

17. Rowan and Primm, *Germans for a Free Missouri*, 15.

18. Ibid., 16.

19. Marcoot, *Five Years in the Sunny South*, 5.

20. WHMC, Buegel, diary, 1.

21. WHMC, Buegel, diary, 1

22. *OR*, vol. 3, 1:82–83.

23. Burton, *Melting Pot Soldiers*, 52.

24. Kargau and Tolzmann, *German Element in St. Louis*, 38; Rombauer, *Union Cause in St. Louis in 1861*, 128.

25. Burton, *Melting Pot Soldiers*, 53.

26. Buegel, diary, 1.

27. Buegel, diary, 2–3.

28. Sherman, *Memoirs*, 1:174.

29. Ibid.

30. Goodrich, "Civil War Letters of Bethiah Pyatt McKown," 237–39.

31. Marcoot, *Five Years in the Sunny South*, 5–7.

32. Cole Camp, Missouri, *Hier Snackt Wi Plattduetsch; Here We Speak (Low) German*, 187–92; Boernstein, *Memoirs of a Nobody*, 343–44.

33. Dyer, *Compendium of the War of the Rebellion*, vol. 2, *Battles, Campaigns, in Missouri*.

34. Rowan and Primm, *Germans for a Free Missouri*, 275n.

2. A CROWDED ARSENAL

1. Marcoot, *Five Years in the Sunny South*, 6–8.

2. Dyer, *Compendium of the War of the Rebellion*, vol. 3, *Regimental Histories*, 1301–29.

3. Appendix, "A Statistical Portrait of the 15th Missouri Soldier"; Wiley, *Life of Billy Yank*, 303; McPherson, *For Cause and Comrades*, viii.

4. Appendix: "A Statistical Portrait of the 15th Missouri Soldier."

5. Marcoot, *Five Years in the Sunny South*.

6. Buegel, diary, 9.

7. Goodrich, "Civil War Letters of Bethiah Pyatt McKown," 239.

8. Dyer, *Compendium of the War of the Rebellion*, vol. 2, *Battles, Campaigns, in Missouri*.

9. Marcoot, *Five Years in the Sunny South*, 8.

10. SHSM, Compiled Service Records, 15th Missouri.

11. Appendix, "A Statistical Portrait of the 15th Missouri Soldier."

12. Anders, "Preserving Our Civil War Battle Flags," 10.

13. SHSM, Compiled Service Records, 15th Missouri.

14 Marcoot, *Five Years in the Sunny South*, 8.

15. *OR*, vol. 3:16.

16. Ibid., p. 38.

17. Buegel, diary.

18. Buegel, diary.

19. Buegel, diary.

20. Wiley, *Life of Billy Yank*, 109–23.

21. Rowan and Primm, *Germans for a Free Missouri*, 309–10; *Anzeiger des Westens*, Mar. 3, 1862.

22. Rowan and Primm, *Germans for a Free Missouri*, 309–10.

3. We Are to Meet the Enemy

1. Burton, *Melting Pot Soldiers*, 46–51.

2. Ibid., 46.

3. Ibid., 50.

4. Ibid., 105.

5. SHSM, Compiled Service Records, 15th Infantry, roll 502, Francis J. Joliat.

6. Marcoot, *Five Years in the Sunny South*, 9–10.

7. MSIC, 15th Missouri Volunteer Infantry, Miscellaneous correspondence, box 407, folder 21.

8. Marcoot, *Five Years in the Sunny South*.

9. Ibid.

10. SHSM, Compiled Service Records, 15th Missouri, roll 502, Francis Mohrhardt.

11. Sheridan, *Personal Memoirs*, 1:73.

12. Marcoot, *Five Years in the Sunny South*.

13. Wiley, *Life of Billy Yank*, 55; Marcoot, *Five Years in the Sunny South*, 11.

14. Wiley, *Life of Billy Yank*, 55.

15. Ibid., 24.

16. MSIC, 15th Missouri, correspondence, Miscellaneous file, letter, Lt. Col. Weber to adjutant general of Missouri, Nov. 1862.

17. Warner, *Generals in Blue*, 196.

18. Catton, *Glory Road*, 175; Donald, *Lincoln*, 476.

19. National Archives, report of Inspection, Dept. of the Missouri, Van Rennsalaer, inspector general to Thomas, adjutant general, Washington, D.C., Feb. 10, 1862, M619, roll 108.

20. *OR*, vol. 8, Halleck to McClellan, Jan. 14, 1862; Sandburg, *Abraham Lincoln*, 1:418.

21. Dyer, *Compendium of the War of the Rebellion*, vol. 3, *Regimental Histories*, 1312.

22. Wiley, *Life of Johnny Reb*, 43–48; Wiley, *Life of Billy Yank*, 233–36.

23. Report of Inspection, Dept. of the Missouri, Washington, D.C., Feb. 10, 1862.

24. *OR*, vol. 8, Schofield to Prentiss, Jan. 3, 1862.

25. Goebel, *Laenger als ein Menschenleben in Missouri*, translation, chap. 28, pp. 2–4.

26. Ibid.

27. Fellman, *Inside War*, 185.

28. Marcoot, *Five Years in the Sunny South*.

29. SHSM, 15th Missouri, Compiled Service Records, roll 504, Rexinger.

4. A Home Not Made with Hands

1. SHSM, Compiled Service Records, 15th Infantry, roll 502, Joliat.

2. SHSM, Compiled Service Records, 15th Infantry, roll 502, Joliat.

3. Bennett and Haigh, *History of the Thirty-sixth*.

4. SHSM, Compiled Service Records, 15th Missouri, roll 502, Joliat.

5. *OR*, vol. 8, Curtis to Kelton, Jan. 9, 1862.

6. Ibid., Halleck to Curtis, Jan. 21, 1862.

7. Ibid., Yeatman to Halleck, Jan. 3, 1862.

8. NA, report of Inspection, Dept. of the Missouri, Van Rennsalaer, Washington, D.C., Feb. 10, 1862. Microfilm Publication, M619, roll 108.

9. Marcoot, *Five Years in the Sunny South*, 10.

10. SHSM, Compiled Service Records, 15th Missouri.

11. *OR*, vol. 8, Abstract from return of the Southwestern District of Missouri for Jan. 1862.

12. Ibid., Halleck to Curtis, Jan. 23, 1862; Donald, *Lincoln*, 329.

13. *OR*, vol. 8, Curtis to Sigel, Jan. 25, 1862.

14. Marcoot, *Five Years in the Sunny South*, 11–12.

15. Ibid.

16. Ibid.

17. *OR*, vol. 8, Curtis to Sigel, Mar. 3, 1862; Curtis to Sigel, Mar. 5, 1862.

18. Ibid., Asboth's after-action report, Mar. 16, 1862.

19. Ibid.

20. Marcoot, *Five Years in the Sunny South*, 13.

21. *Anzeiger des Westens*, Mar. 26, 1862, translation; Rowan and Primm, *Germans for a Free Missouri*, 312.

22. Donald, *Lincoln*, 336–37.

23. Kennedy, *Civil War Battlefield Guide*, 37.

24. Marcoot, *Five Years in the Sunny South*, 13.

25. Bennett and Haigh, *History of the Thirty-sixth*, 196.

26. Ibid., 197.

27. Marcoot, *Five Years in the Sunny South*, 13; Bennett and Haigh, *History of the Thirty-sixth*, 197.

28. Marcoot, 13–14.

29. Bennett and Haigh, *History of the Thirty-sixth*, 199.

30. Ibid., 201.

31. Ibid., 203.

32. Marcoot, *Five Years in the Sunny South*, 14.

33. Bennett and Haigh, *History of the Thirty-sixth*, 204.

34. Ibid.

35. Marcoot, *Five Years in the Sunny South*, 14.

36. Adams, *Doctors in Blue*, 20–21.

37. Wiley, *Life of Billy Yank*, 126–31.

38. Ibid., 126.

39. Marcoot, *Five Years in the Sunny South*, 14.

40. Ibid.; SHSM, Compiled Service Records, 15th Missouri.

41. SHSM, Compiled Service Records, 15th Missouri, roll 502, Joliat.

42. SHSM, Compiled Service Records, 15th Missouri, roll 501, Heyer.

43. SHSM, Compiled Service Records, 15th Missouri, roll 506, Rau.

5. Generals, Slavery, and Slurs

1. *OR*, vol. 25, Rosecrans et al. to Halleck, telegram, July 30, 1862, 3:05 P.M.

2. Sheridan, *Personal Memoirs*, 1:99.

3. Ibid., 1:98.

4. Marcoot, *Five Years in the Sunny South*, 14–15.

5. Wiley, *Life of Billy Yank*, 126–28.

6. SHSM, Compiled Service Records, 15th Missouri, roll 502, Joliat.

7. Marcoot, *Five Years in the Sunny South*, 15.

8. Bennett and Haigh, *History of the Thirty-sixth*, 233.

9. Marcoot, *Five Years in the Sunny South*, 15–16.

10. SHSM, Compiled Service Records, 15th Missouri.

11. Sheridan, *Personal Memoirs*, 1:99.

12. *OR*, vol. 23, Wright and Granger to Halleck, Sept. 12, 1862.

13. Ibid., Halleck to Wright, Sept. 13, 1862.

14. Donald, *Lincoln*, 497.

15. Ibid., 379.

16. Burton, *Melting Pot Soldiers*, 127.

17. Klingaman, *Abraham Lincoln and the Road to Emancipation*, 195–201; Sandburg, *Abraham Lincoln*, 2:14.

18. Donald, *Lincoln*, 377, 385.

19. Burton, *Melting Pot Soldiers*, 201.

20. Ibid., 202–3.

21. Ibid., 204

22. Ibid., 252n2.

23. Bennett and Haigh, *History of the Thirty-sixth*, 252n12.

24. Dyer, *Compendium of the War of the Rebellion*, vol. 3, *Regimental Histories*.

25. Cozzens, *This Terrible Sound*, 379.

6. War Means Killing

1. Sheridan, *Personal Memoirs*, 1:104.

2. Marcoot, *Five Years in the Sunny South*, 16.

3. Sheridan, *Personal Memoirs*, 1:105.

4. Marcoot, *Five Years in the Sunny South*, 16.

5. Sheridan, *Personal Memoirs*, 1:105.

6. Newlin, *History of the Seventy-third*, 98.

7. Marcoot, *Five Years in the Sunny South*, 16.

8. Sheridan, *Personal Memoirs*, 1:105, and *OR*, series 1, vol. 16, report of Brig. Gen. Philip H. Sheridan, Oct. 23, 1862.

9. Sheridan, *Personal Memoirs*, 1:105; *OR*, series 1, vol. 16, Sheridan, Oct. 23, 1862.

10. Newlin, *History of the Seventy-third*, 98.

11. Bennett and Haigh, *History of the Thirty-sixth*, 250–52.

12. Fox, *Regimental Losses in the American Civil War*, chap. 10, 2d Missouri Infantry.

13. Sheridan, *Personal Memoirs*, 1:106.

14. Newlin, *History of the Seventy-third*, 98.

15. Sheridan, *Personal Memoirs,* 1:107; *OR,* series 1, vol. 16, report of Brig. Gen. Philip H. Sheridan, Oct. 23, 1862.

16. Marcoot, *Five Years in the Sunny South,* 17; Newlin, *History of the Seventy-third,* 101.

17. Sheridan, *Personal Memoirs,* 1:107.

18. Watkins, *Co. Aytch,* 63.

19. Marcoot, *Five Years in the Sunny South,* 17.

20. Watkins, *Co. Aytch,* 64.

21. Fox, *Regimental Losses in the American Civil War,* chap. 10, 15th Missouri Infantry; SHSM, Compiled Service Records, 15th Missouri, roll 507, Seiss.

22. Newlin, *History of the Seventy-third,* 101.

23. Cooper and Worley, "Letters from a Veteran of Pea Ridge," 469.

24. Adams, *Doctors in Blue,* 83; Sheridan, *Personal Memoirs,* 1:110.

25 Marcoot, *Five Years in the Sunny South,* 18.

26. Sheridan, *Personal Memoirs,* 1:109.

27. Marcoot, *Five Years in the Sunny South,* 18–21.

28. Sheridan, *Personal Memoirs,* 1:110.

7. A NEW COLONEL

1. SHSM, Compiled Service Records, 15th Missouri, roll 502, Joliat.

2. MSIC, 15th Missouri regimental file, Miscellaneous correspondence, box 407, folder 27.

3. MSIC, 15th Missouri regimental file, Miscellaneous correspondence, box 407, folder 27.

4. MSIC, 15th Missouri regimental file, Miscellaneous correspondence, box 407, folder 27, and letters, Col. Fr. Schaefer to Governor Gamble, Nov. 8, 1862, and 15th Missouri officers, Nov. 10, 1862, folder 26.

5. Society of the Army of the Cumberland, 27th Reunion, Cincinnati, Ohio, 1898.

6. MSIC, 15th Missouri Infantry, correspondence, Miscellaneous file, box 407, folder 26, Erdmann to Curtis.

7. Sheridan, *Personal Memoirs,* 1:112–13.

8. Ibid., 1:114.

9. Marcoot, *Five Years in the Sunny South,* 21–22.

10. Ibid.

11. Ibid.

12. Minutes of the Twentieth Annual Reunion of the Survivors of the Seventy-third Regiment Illinois Volunteer Infantry, Oct. 2, 1906, paper presented by Henry A. Castle, 11–12.

13. Castle, 11–12

14. MSIC, 15th Missouri, correspondence, Miscellaneous file, box 407, folder 27.

15. MSIC, 15th Missouri, correspondence, Miscellaneous file, box 407, folder 27.

16. National Archives, Old Military Records, John Weber file.

17. *OR,* series 2, vol. 20, Rosecrans to McCook, Dec. 24, 1862.

18. Ibid., Garesche to McCook and Thomas, Dec. 24, 1862.

19. Marcoot, *Five Years in the Sunny South*, 22.
20. Catton, *Never Call Retreat*, 38–39.
21. Sheridan, *Personal Memoirs*, 1:115.

8. Fighting Retreat, Bloodiest Day

1. Marcoot, *Five Years in the Sunny South*, 22.
2. Logsdon, *Eyewitnesses at the Battle of Stones River*, 8.
3. Sheridan, *Personal Memoirs*, 1:116–17.
4. Logsdon, *Eyewitnesses at the Battle of Stones River*, 10.
5. Marcoot, *Five Years in the Sunny South*, 22.
6. Logsdon, *Eyewitnesses at the Battle of Stones River*, 13.
7. Sheridan, *Personal Memoirs*, 1:120.
8. Bennett and Haigh, *History of the Thirty-sixth*, 341–47.
9. Sheridan, *Personal Memoirs*, 1:120.
10. Catton, *Never Call Retreat*, 41; *OR*, series 1, vol. 20, report of Lt. Col. Bernard Laiboldt, Jan. 7, 1863.
11. *OR*, series 1, vol. 20, Laiboldt report; SRNB, "Troop Movement Maps," 7:00 to 8:00 A.M. positions.
12. Bennett and Haigh, *History of the Thirty-sixth*, 341–47.
13. *OR*, series 1, vol. 20, report of Brig. Gen. Philip H. Sheridan, Jan. 9, 1863; Sheridan, *Personal Memoirs*, 1:121; Bennett and Haigh, *History of the Thirty-sixth*, 347.
14. Watkins, *Co. Aytch*, 77.
15. *OR*, series 1, vol. 20, reports of Laiboldt, Jan. 7, 1863, and Sheridan, Jan. 9, 1863; Sheridan, *Personal Memoirs*, 1:121; SRNB, "Troop Movement Maps," 7:00 to 8:00 A.M. positions.
16. Beaudot, *24th Wisconsin Infantry in the Civil War*, 157.
17. *OR*, series 1, vol. 20, report of Brig. Gen. Philip H. Sheridan, Jan. 9, 1863; Sheridan, *Personal Memoirs*, 1:121; *OR*, series 1, vol. 20, report of Lt. Col. Bernard Laiboldt, Jan. 7, 1863; Bennett and Haigh, *History of the Thirty-sixth*, 341.
18. *OR*, series 1, vol. 20, report of Brig. Gen. Philip H. Sheridan, Jan. 9, 1863; Cozzens, *No Better Place to Die*, 116; SRNB, "Troop Movement Maps," position prior to 10:00 A.M.; Sheridan, *Personal Memoirs*, 1:121; Bennett and Haigh, *History of the Thirty-sixth*, 341.
19. Bennett and Haigh, *History of the Thirty-sixth*, 341.
20. *OR*, series 1, vol. 20, report of Lt. Col. Bernard Laiboldt, Jan. 7, 1863; SRNB, "Troop Movement Maps," prior to 10:00 to 11:00 A.M. positions.
21. *OR*, series 1, vol. 20, report of Lt. Col. Bernard Laiboldt, Jan. 7, 1863.
22. Ibid.
23. Sheridan, *Personal Memoirs*, 1:123; *OR*, series 1, vol. 20, reports of Lt. Col. Bernard Laiboldt, Jan. 7, 1863, and Brig. Gen. Philip H. Sheridan, Jan. 9, 1863.
24. Bennett and Haigh, *History of the Thirty-sixth*, 341, 392.
25. *OR*, series 1, vol. 20, reports Brig. Gen. Philip H. Sheridan, Jan. 9, 1863, and Lt. Col. Bernard Laiboldt, Jan. 7, 1863.
26. Watkins, *Co. Aytch*, 78.
27. SHSM, Compiled Service Records, 15th Missouri.
28. Watkins, *Co. Aytch*, 78.

29. SRNB, "Troop Movement Maps," 10:00 to 11:00 A.M.; Sheridan, *Personal Memoirs*, 1:123; *OR*, series 1, vol. 20, Laiboldt report.

30. Newlin, *History of the Seventy-third*, 131–32.

31. Ibid.

32. SRNB, "Troop Movement Maps," 10:00 to 11:00 A.M.; Sheridan, *Personal Memoirs*, 1:123.

33. Sheridan, *Personal Memoirs*, 1:123–24.

34. Sandburg, *Abraham Lincoln*, 2:6.

35. Sheridan, *Personal Memoirs*, 1:124; *OR*, series 1, vol. 20, report of Brig. Gen. Philip H. Sheridan, Jan. 9, 1862.

36. Sheridan, *Personal Memoirs*, 1:124.

37. *OR*, series 1, vol. 20, reports of Brig. Gen. Philip H. Sheridan, Jan. 9, 1863, and Lt. Col. Bernard Laiboldt, Jan. 7, 1863.

38. Sheridan, *Personal Memoirs*, 1:124.

39. Sandburg, *Abraham Lincoln*, 2:6.

40. Sheridan, *Personal Memoirs*, 1:125.

41. Logsdon, *Eyewitnesses at the Battle of Stones River*, 27.

42. O'Connor, *Sheridan*, 94.

43. McDonough, *Stones River*, 118; Cozzens, *No Better Place to Die*, 127.

44. *OR*, series 1, vol. 20, reports of Brig. Gen. Philip H. Sheridan, Jan. 9, 1863, and Lt. Col. Bernard Laiboldt, Jan. 7, 1863.

45. Sheridan, *Personal Memoirs*, 1:126; *OR*, series 1, vol. 20, reports of Sheridan, Jan. 9, 1863, and Laiboldt, Jan. 7, 1863.

46. MHS, Buechel Papers, letter of Charles Fuelle, 2d Missouri.

47. *OR*, series 1, vol. 20, report of Brig. Gen. Philip H. Sheridan, Jan. 9, 1862.

48. Sheridan, *Personal Memoirs*, 1:126.

49. Sandburg, *Abraham Lincoln*, 2:6.

50. Sheridan, *Personal Memoirs*, 1:126.

51. *OR*, series 1, vol. 20, report of Brig. Gen. Philip H. Sheridan, Jan. 9, 1862.

52. Logsdon, *Eyewitnesses at the Battle of Stones River*, 49.

53. *Missouri Republican*, Jan. 8, 1863.

54. Sheridan, *Personal Memoirs*, 1:131.

55. SHSM, Compiled Service Records, 15th Missouri; MSIC, 15th Missouri Infantry, correspondence, Miscellaneous file, box 407, folder 26.

56. Marcoot, *Five Years in the Sunny South*, 24.

57. *OR*, series 1, vol. 20, 201, 674.

58. *OR*, series 1, vol. 21, Lincoln to Rosecrans, Jan. 5, 1863; Sandburg, *Abraham Lincoln*, 2:6.

59. Sheridan, *Personal Memoirs*, 1:131.

60. Pollard, *Southern History of the War*, 566.

61. SRNB, Fuelle Papers, 1863, certificate, copy.

62. SRNB, Fuelle Papers, 1863, letter dated Jan. 18, 1863.

63. Warner, *Generals in Blue*, 253–54.

64. SRNB, Fuelle Papers, 1863, letter.

65. Kennedy, "Stones River," *Civil War Battlefield Guide*, 154.

9. "Those cowardly Dutch"

1. Marcoot, *Five Years in the Sunny South*, 24.
2. NA, Old Military Records, Joseph Conrad file.
3. Sheridan, *Personal Memoirs*, 1:129.
4. Wiley, *Life of Billy Yank*, 213.
5. Sheridan, *Personal Memoirs*, 1:129.
6. MSIC, 15th Missouri Regimental Correspondence, Miscellaneous, box 407, folder 26.
7. Sheridan, *Personal Memoirs*, 1:133.
8. Marcoot, *Five Years in the Sunny South*, 27.
9. Wiley, *Life of Billy Yank*, 49.
10. Sheridan, *Personal Memoirs*, 1:136–37.
11. Ibid.
12. Marcoot, *Five Years in the Sunny South*, 27.
13. Ibid.
14. Wiley, *Life of Billy Yank*, 282.
15. *OR*, series 3, vol. 3, Tod to Stanton, Mar. 5, 1863.
16. Ibid., Lincoln to Tod, Mar. 9, 1863.
17. Ibid., "A Proclamation. Respecting Soldiers without Leave," Mar. 10, 1863.
18. Marcoot, *Five Years in the Sunny South*, 27.
19. Ibid.
20. SHSM, Compiled Service Records, 15th Missouri, Joseph Conrad file, muster card for April 1863.
21. Marcoot, *Five Years in the Sunny South*, 27.
22. Sheridan, *Personal Memoirs*, 1:137–38.
23. Marcoot, *Five Years in the Sunny South*, 28–30.
24. Donald, *Lincoln*, 435–36.
25. Burton, *Melting Pot Soldiers*, index, regiments identified as German in the line of battle.
26. Ibid., 100.
27. Ibid., index, regiments identified as German in the line of battle.
28. Catton, *Glory Road*, 172–76; Sears, *Gettysburg*, 28.
29. Schurz, *Reminiscences*, 2:432–43.
30. Catton, *Glory Road*, 175.
31. Ibid., 172–76; Sears, *Gettysburg*, 28.
32. Burton, *Melting Pot Soldiers*, 100.
33. MSIC, 1863 Annual Report of the Adjutant General of the State of Missouri, 403.
34. Burton, *Melting Pot Soldiers*, 100.
35. SHSM, Compiled Service Records, 15th Missouri, roll 499, Ernst.

10. A Question of Will

1. Marcoot, *Five Years in the Sunny South*, 30.
2. Wiley, *Life of Billy Yank*, 206–7.
3. LC, James A. Garfield Papers, letter, Garfield to Salmon P. Chase, June 11, 1863.

4. Donald, *Lincoln*, 437.

5. Marcoot, *Five Years in the Sunny South*, 30.

6. Ibid., 31.

7. Sheridan, *Personal Memoirs*, 1:147.

8. *OR*, series 2, vol. 23, Stanton to Rosecrans, July 7, 1863.

9. Ibid., Rosecrans to Stanton, July 7, 1863.

10. Ibid., Sheridan to Rosecrans, and Thomas to Rosecrans, July 7, 1863.

11. Marcoot, *Five Years in the Sunny South*, 31–32.

12. *OR*, series 2, vol. 23, Halleck to Rosecrans, July 25, 1863.

13. Ibid., Rosecrans to Halleck, Aug. 1, 1863.

14. Ibid., Halleck to Rosecrans, Aug. 9, 1863.

15. Sheridan, *Personal Memoirs*, 1:147–48.

16. *OR*, series 1, vol. 30, Halleck to Burnside, Sept. 13, 1863.

17. Ibid., series 3, vol. 30, Thurston to Sheridan, Sept. 9, 1863—8:15 P.M.

18. Newlin, *History of the Seventy-third*, 215

19. Ibid.

20. Marcoot, *Five Years in the Sunny South*, 32.

21. Sheridan, *Personal Memoirs*, 1:148.

22. *OR*, series 1, vol. 30, report of Rosecrans, Oct. 10, 1863.

23. Sheridan, *Personal Memoirs*, 1:149.

24. *OR*, series 1, vol. 30, Halleck to Rosecrans, Sept. 11, 1863, 1:35 P.M.

25. Ibid., Halleck report to Stanton, Nov. 15, 1863.

26. Ibid., Halleck to Foster, Sept. 14, 1863, 1 P.M.

27. Woodward, *Mary Chesnut's Civil War*, 470.

11. The River of Death

1. Kennedy, *Civil War Battlefield Guide*, 227.

2. Sheridan, *Personal Memoirs*, 1:149.

3. Newlin, *History of the Seventy-third*, 217–21.

4. *OR*, series 1, vol. 30, Conrad to Governor Gamble, Sept. 30, 1863.

5. Ibid., report of Colonel Laiboldt, Sept. 29, 1863; McCook to Garfield, Sept. 18, 1863, 6:30 A.M.

6. Conrad to Gamble, Sept. 30, 1863.

7. Marcoot, *Five Years in the Sunny South*, 35.

8. Newlin, *History of the Seventy-third*, 231.

9. Ibid.

10. *OR*, series 1, vol. 30, report of Rosecrans, Oct. —, 1863.

11. Newlin, *History of the Seventy-third*, 231.

12. Marcoot, *Five Years in the Sunny South*, 35.

13. Watkins, *Co. Aytch*, 107.

14. Sheridan, *Personal Memoirs*, 1:152.

15. Marcoot, *Five Years in the Sunny South*, 36.

16. Griffith, *Battle Tactics of the Civil War*, 131.

17. *OR*, series 1, vol. 30, report of Sheridan, Sept. 30, 1863.

18. Marcoot, *Five Years in the Sunny South*, 36.

19. *OR*, series 2, vol. 30, report of Col. J. G. Coltart, no date.

20. CCNMP, 50th Alabama file, letter of Lt. James Fraser, Sept. 26, 1863.

21. *OR*, series 1, vol. 30, report of Brig. Gen. Jefferson C. Davis, undated.

22. *OR*, series 1, vol. 30, Davis report.

23. Fisher, *Personal Experiences*, 66.

24. *OR*, series 1, vol. 38, report of Col. Bernard Laiboldt, Aug. 18, 1864.

25. Cozzens, *This Terrible Sound*, 10.

26. *OR*, series 1, vol. 30, report of B. Laiboldt, Sept. 29, 1863.

27. Association of Survivors Seventy-third Regiment Illinois Volunteer Infantry, *Minutes of the Twentieth Annual Reunion*.

28. *OR*, series 1, vol. 30, report of Col. Joseph Conrad, Sept. 30, 1863; Marcoot, *Five Years in the Sunny South*, 36–37.

29. Gen. W. P. Carlin, published within a few years after the war in the *National Tribune*, quoted in Newlin, *History of the Seventy-third*, 234.

30. *OR*, series 1, vol. 30, report of Maj. Arnold Beck, 2d Missouri, Oct. 7, 1863.

31. Carlin, *National Tribune*, quoted in Newlin, *History of the Seventy-third*, 234.

32. Marcoot, *Five Years in the Sunny South*, 37.

33. *OR*, series 1, vol. 30, report of Conrad, Sept. 30, 1863.

34. Marcoot, *Five Years in the Sunny South*, 37. "Leather Breeches" was Capt. Hubert Dilger, known throughout the army for his daring as well as for his doe-skin pants. Dilger, a German immigrant, was awarded the Medal of Honor for heroism at Chancellorsville and recognized as one of the North's best field officers as a battery commander in the 1st Ohio Artillery, not the 1st Illinois Artillery as Marcoot implies. Dilger had survived the Confederate assaults against the 11th Corps at Gettysburg and Chancellorsville, where his was the only battery to put up serious resistance to Stonewall Jackson's massive flank attack. There may be a question whether he was at Chickamauga since he may not have as yet transferred to the western theater, where he eventually finished the war. In spite of recognition throughout the army and receiving the nation's highest commendation, Dilger wrote years later, "My war experiences were so unenjoyable in their results that they swell up in the form of memories that only irritate me." One can only speculate as to the reason. His memoir manuscript was destroyed in a fire. Kaufmann, *Germans in the American Civil War*, 285.

35. Sheridan, *Personal Memoirs*, 1:152; Association of Survivors Seventy-third Regiment Illinois Volunteer Infantry, *Minutes of the Twentieth Annual Reunion*, 16.

36. Bennett and Haigh, *History of the Thirty-sixth*, 469; Sheridan, *Personal Memoirs*, 1:152.

37. Marcoot, *Five Years in the Sunny South*, 37.

38. Sheridan, *Personal Memoirs*, 1:152.

39. Johnson and Buell, *Battles and Leaders of the Civil War*, 663.

40. Sheridan, *Personal Memoirs*, 1:153.

41. *OR*, series 1, vol. 30, Rosecrans to Halleck, Sept. 20, 1863, 5:00 P.M.

42. The passing years may have taken their toll on Marcoot's memory in this case, for it was the other way around: it was the company's sergeant who had lost a leg and an arm.

43. Marcoot, *Five Years in the Sunny South*, 37–38.

44. *OR*, series 1, vol. 30, reports of Col. Bernard Laiboldt and Col. Joseph Conrad, Sept. 30, 1863.

45. *OR*, series 4, vol. 30, September inspection report, Porter to Headquarters, Twentieth Army Corps, Oct. 6, 1863.

46. Warner, *Generals in Blue*, 294.

47. *OR*, series 1, vol. 30, Lincoln to Rosecrans, Sept. 21, 1863, 12:35 A.M.

48. Sheridan, *Personal Memoirs*, 155–56.

49. *OR*, series 1, vol. 30, report of Col. Joseph Conrad, Sept. 30, 1863.

50. Warner, *Generals in Blue*.

51. SHSM, Compiled Service Records, 15th Missouri, roll 506, John Weber.

52. *OR*, series 1, vol. 30, Conrad report.

53. *OR*, series 1, vol. 30, report of Col. Bernard Laiboldt, in trenches before Chattanooga, Sept. 29, 1863.

54. *OR*, series 1, vol. 30, report of Maj. Gen. Philip H. Sheridan, Sept. 30, 1863.

55. Ibid.

56. Marcoot, *Five Years in the Sunny South*, 46–47.

57. SHSM, Compiled Service Records, 15th Missouri, roll 506, Gustav Roehm.

12. The Buzzards Hold All the Cards

1. *OR*, series 1, vol. 30, Lincoln to Rosecrans, Sept. 21, 1863, 12:35 A.M.; Hay, *Inside Lincoln's White House*, 85.

2. *OR*, series 4, vol. 30, Halleck to Grant, Oct. 16, 1863.

3. *OR*, series 4, vol. 30, Halleck to Grant, 9:00 P.M., Oct. 16, 1863; Grant, *Memoirs*, 403–4.

4. *OR*, series 4, vol. 30, Thomas to Grant, Oct. 19, 1863.

5. Grant, *Memoirs*, 2:406.

6. Ibid.; Catton, *Grant Takes Command*, 38.

7. Grant, *Memoirs*, 2:403–4.

8. Sheridan, *Personal Memoirs*, 1:160.

9. Marcoot, *Five Years in the Sunny South*, 38–39.

10. Ibid., 39.

11. Sheridan, *Personal Memoirs*, 1:161.

12. SHSM, Compiled Service Records, 15th Missouri, roll 500, Conrad Herrman.

13. Catton, *Grant Takes Command*, 55.

14. *OR*, series 2, vol. 31, reports of Maj. Gen. Ulysses S. Grant, Dec. 23, 1863.

15. Grant, *Memoirs*, 2:418.

16. *OR*, series 2, vol. 31, Meigs to Stanton, Nov. 16, 1863.

17. Marcoot, *Five Years in the Sunny South*, 40.

18. Sheridan, *Personal Memoirs*, 1:163–64.

19. Marcoot, *Five Years in the Sunny South*, 40.

13. "Chickamauga, God damn you!"

1. Marcoot, *Five Years in the Sunny South*, 40.

2. Sheridan, *Personal Memoirs*, 1:163.

3. *OR*, series 2, vol. 31, report of Maj. Gen. Ulysses S. Grant, Dec. 23, 1863.

4. Cozzens, *Shipwreck of Their Hopes*, 96–97.

5. Account of Brig. Gen. Fullerton, asst. adj.-gen. to Granger, in Johnson and Buell, *Battles and Leaders of the Civil War*, 3:719.

6. *OR*, series 3, vol. 31, Asmussen to Howard, Nov. 7, 1863 (received Nov. 8).

7. Donald, *Lincoln*, 397.

8. Ibid., *OR*, series 2, vol. 31, report of Maj. Gen. Ulysses S. Grant, Dec. 23, 1863.

9. Account of Brig. Gen. Fullerton; Johnson and Buell, *Battles and Leaders of the Civil War*, 3:720.

10. *OR*, series 2, vol. 31, Grant to Thomas, Nov. 18, 1863.

11. Ibid.

12. Fullerton, quoted in Johnson and Buell, *Battles and Leaders of the Civil War*, 3:721.

13. Sheridan, *Personal Memoirs*, 1:166.

14. Fullerton, quoted in Johnson and Buell, *Battles and Leaders of the Civil War*, 3:723.

15. MHS, Osterhorn Papers, letter, Dec. 8, 1863.

16. Marcoot, *Five Years in the Sunny South*, 40–41.

17. *OR*, series 2, vol. 31, Grant to Thomas, Nov. 24, 1863.

18. Grant, *Memoirs*, 2:443.

19. Ibid.

20. Marcoot, *Five Years in the Sunny South*, 40.

21. Fullerton, quoted in Johnson and Buell, *Battles and Leaders of the Civil War*, 3:724.

22. Ibid.; Grant, *Memoirs*, 2:445.

23. *OR*, series 2, vol. 31, report of Maj. Gen. Ulysses S. Grant, Dec. 23, 1863.

24. Ibid., dispatches of Mr. Charles A. Dana to Stanton, Oct. 30–Dec. 12, 1863.

25. *OR*, series 2, vol. 31; see Thomas's official report, as well as Granger's and other corps commanders' reports, all of whom were present.

26. Ibid., Grant to Thomas, Nov. 18, 1863.

27. Sheridan, *Personal Memoirs*, 1:168.

28. Ibid.

29. Marcoot, *Five Years in the Sunny South*, 41; *OR*, series 2, vol. 31, report of Capt. Samuel Rexinger, 15th Missouri Infantry, Nov. 27, 1863.

30. Fullerton, quoted in Johnson and Buell, *Battles and Leaders of the Civil War*, 3:724–25.

31. Hemming, "Confederate Odyssey," 70.

32. Fullerton, quoted in Johnson and Buell, *Battles and Leaders of the Civil War*, 3:725.

33. Sheridan, *Personal Memoirs*, 1:168.

34. Fullerton, quoted in Johnson and Buell, *Battles and Leaders of the Civil War*, 3:725.

35. Sheridan, *Personal Memoirs*, 1:168.

36. Ibid.

37. Fullerton, quoted in Johnson and Buell, *Battles and Leaders of the Civil War*, 3:725.

38. Ibid.

39. Sheridan, *Personal Memoirs*, 1:168; Fullerton, quoted in Johnson and Buell, *Battles and Leaders of the Civil War*, 3:725.

40. Editors of Time-Life Books, *Voices of the Civil War—Chattanooga*, 132.

41. *OR*, series 2, vol. 31, report of Capt. Samuel Rexinger, 15th Missouri Infantry, Nov. 27, 1863.

42. Hemming, "A Confederate Odyssey," 70.

43. SHSM, Compiled Service Records, 15th Missouri; *OR*, series 2, vol. 31, report of Capt. Samuel Rexinger, 15th Missouri Infantry, Nov. 27, 1863.

44. Bennett and Haigh, *History of the Thirty-sixth*, 529.

45. Marcoot, *Five Years in the Sunny South*, 42.

46. Fullerton, quoted in Johnson and Buell, *Battles and Leaders of the Civil War*, 3:725.

47. Marcoot, *Five Years in the Sunny South*, 42.

48. Bennett and Haigh, *History of the Thirty-sixth*, 529.

49. Fullerton, quoted in Johnson and Buell, *Battles and Leaders of the Civil War*, 3:726.

50. CCNMP, monuments to the Missouri and Illinois regiments, posted for their positions at the crest of the assault by the veterans themselves.

51. *St. Louis Globe-Democrat*, Nov. 26, 1894.

52. Cozzens, *Shipwreck of Their Hopes*, 294; Hannaford, "The Story of a Regiment, a History of the Campaigns and Associations in the Field of the Sixth Regiment, Ohio Volunteer Infantry," 1868.

53. Cozzens, *Shipwreck of Their Hopes*, 308; *OR*, series 2, vol. 31, report of Capt. Samuel Rexinger, 15th Missouri Infantry, Nov. 27, 1863.

54. Cozzens, *Shipwreck of Their Hopes*, 308.

55. *OR*, series 2, vol. 31, Rexinger.

56. Sheridan, *Personal Memoirs*, 1:169.

57. Ibid.

58. *OR*, series 2, vol. 31, Rexinger.

59. Marcoot, *Five Years in the Sunny South*, 42; Editors of Time-Life Books, *Voices of the Civil War—Chattanooga*, 132.

60. Cozzens, *Shipwreck of Their Hopes*, 309–10.

61. Bennett and Haigh, *History of the Thirty-sixth*, 531–32.

62. Osterhorn Papers, letter, Dec. 8, 1863.

63. Hemming, "Confederate Odyssey," 70–72.

64. Hanson, *Soul of Battle*, 5.

65. Toland, *Battle*, 337–39.

66. Hemming, "Confederate Odyssey," 72–73.

67. Marcoot, *Five Years in the Sunny South*, 42.

68. SHSM, Compiled Service Records, 15th Missouri, roll 502, Lipps.

69. Johnson and Buell, *Battles and Leaders of the Civil War*, 3:730.

70. Grant, *Memoirs*, 2:445–46.

71. Sherman, *Memoirs*, 1:162.

72. Johnson and Buell, *Battles and Leaders of the Civil War*, 3:726n; Sheridan, *Personal Memoirs*, 1:173.

73. Johnson and Buell, *Battles and Leaders of the Civil War*, 3:717.

74. Catton, *Grant Takes Command*, 79; *OR*, series 2, vol. 31, Grant to Thomas, Nov. 18, 1863.

75. Grant, *Memoirs*, 2:443.

76. Catton, *Grant Takes Command*, 81n19, referencing *OR*, series 2, vol. 31, dispatch of Mr. Charles A. Dana to Secretary of War Stanton, 10 A.M., Nov. 26, 1863.

77. *OR*, series 2, vol. 31, General Orders, No. 398, War Dept., Adjt. General's Office, Dec. 21, 1863.

14. Two Ears of Corn

1. *OR*, series 2, vol. 31, Lincoln to Grant, Nov. 25, 1863, 8:40 A.M.

2. Marcoot, *Five Years in the Sunny South*, 42–43.

3. Sheridan, *Personal Memoirs*, 1:178–79.

4. Marcoot, *Five Years in the Sunny South*, 43–45.

15. A New Kind of War

1. Donald, *Lincoln*, 488–89.

2. Marcoot, *Five Years in the Sunny South*, 45.

3. Ibid.

4. SHSM, Compiled Service Records, 15th Missouri; *OR*, series 5, vol. 28, Cist to Sawyer, Aug. 12, 1864.

5. Marcoot, *Five Years in the Sunny South*, 47–48.

6. WHMC, Kueck Papers.

7. Marcoot, *Five Years in the Sunny South*, 49–50.

8. Ibid., 50–51.

9. Ibid., 52–53.

10. Ibid.

11. Ibid., 54.

12. Ibid.

13. Ibid., 55.

14. Donald, *Lincoln*, 417, 450; Wiley, *Life of Billy Yank*, 281–82.

15. Marcoot, *Five Years in the Sunny South*, 55–56.

16. SHSM, Compiled Service Records, 15th Missouri.

17. Donald, *Lincoln*, 490.

18. Grant, *Memories*, 2:479.

19. Marcoot, *Five Years in the Sunny South*, 57–59.

20. Fox, *Regimental Losses in the American Civil War*, chap. 8, Fourth Corps, Army of the Cumberland.

21. Marcoot, *Five Years in the Sunny South*, 60.

22. Ibid.

16. "COME UP FROM THE FIELDS, FATHER, THERE IS A LETTER"

1. *OR*, series 1, vol. 38, report of Col. Joseph Conrad, 15th Missouri Volunteer Infantry, Sept. 12, 1864.

2. Marcoot, *Five Years in the Sunny South*, 60; *OR*, series 1, vol. 38, report of Brig. Gen. John Newton, Sept. —, 1864.

3. *OR*, series 1, vol. 38, reports of Maj. Gen. William T. Sherman, Sept. 8, 1864.

4. Ibid., report of Maj. Gen. William T. Sherman, Sept. 8, 1864, report of Brig. Gen. John Newton, Sept. —, 1864; Marcoot, *Five Years in the Sunny South*, 60.

5. Castel, *Decision in the West*, 141.

6. Ibid., 142–43.

7. Marcoot, *Five Years in the Sunny South*, 60–61.

8. Ibid., 61.

9. Castel, *Decision in the West*, 150–51.

10. Marcoot, *Five Years in the Sunny South*, 61.

11. *OR*, series 1, vol. 38, Conrad report.

12. *OR*, series 1, vol. 38, reports of Brig. Gen. John Newton, Sept. —, 1864; and Col. Joseph Conrad, Sept. 12, 1864.

13. Marcoot, *Five Years in the Sunny South*, 61; SHSM, Compiled Service Records, 15th Missouri, roll 497, Beele.

14. Marcoot, *Five Years in the Sunny South*, 61; Castel, *Decision in the West*, 193.

15. Marcoot, *Five Years in the Sunny South*, 61; SHSM, Compiled Service Records, 15th Missouri, roll 508, Winnegar.

16. Johnson and Buell, *Battles and Leaders of the Civil War*, 4:305.

17. Castel, *Decision in the West*, 214.

18. *OR*, series 4, vol. 38; Special Field Orders No. 9, headquarters, Military Division of the Mississippi, May 20, 1864.

19. Marcoot, *Five Years in the Sunny South*, 62.

20. Castel, *Decision in the West*, 218.

21. Ibid., 213.

22. Johnson and Buell, *Battles and Leaders of the Civil War*, 4:306.

23. Marcoot, *Five Years in the Sunny South*, 62.

24. Castel, *Decision in the West*, 226.

25. Johnson and Buell, *Battles and Leaders of the Civil War*, 4:306.

26. *OR*, series 1, vol. 38, Conrad report; SHSM, Compiled Service Records, 15th Missouri.

27. Marcoot, *Five Years in the Sunny South*, 62.

28. Fox, *Regimental Losses in the American Civil War*, 15th Missouri.

29. Castel, *Decision in the West*, 242–50.

30. *OR*, series 4, vol. 38, Sherman to Grant, June 18, 1864.

31. Castel, *Decision in the West*, 251; *OR*, series 4, vol. 38, Blair to McPherson, May 24, 1864.

32. Castel, *Decision in the West*, 242; *OR*, series 4, vol. 38, Howard to Thomas, May 27, 1864.

33. Castel, *Decision in the West*, 259–64.

34. *OR*, series 4, vol. 38, Fullerton to Newton, June 5, 1864.

35. *OR*, series 1, vol. 38, report of Brig. Gen. Nathan Kimball, Aug. 4, 1864, reports of Brig. Gen. John Newton, Sept. 1864.

36. Ibid., Sherman to Halleck, June 18, 1864; Marcoot, *Five Years in the Sunny South*, 65.

37. Marcoot, *Five Years in the Sunny South*, 64–65.

38. Ibid., 65.

39. *OR*, series 4, vol. 38, Sherman to Halleck, June 18, 1864, Dayton, aide-de-camp, to Thomas, June 18, 1864.

40. *OR*, series 1, vol. 38, reports of Brig. Gen. Nathan Kimball, Aug. 4, 1864, and Brig. Gen. John Newton, Sept. 1864; Sherman to Halleck, June 18, 1864, 7:30 A.M.

41. *OR*, series 4, vol. 38, Sherman to Grant, June 18, 1864, Dayton, aide-de-camp, to Thomas, June 18, 1864.

42. *OR*, series 4, vol. 38, Thomas to Howard, June 18, 1864, report of Brig. Gen. Nathan Kimball, Aug. 4, 1864.

43. SHSM, Compiled Service Records, 15th Missouri, roll 497, Beisel and Lixfeld, 502.

44. Marcoot, *Five Years in the Sunny South*, 65–66.

45. *OR*, series 1, vol. 38, reports of Maj. Gen. William T. Sherman, May 1–Sept. 8, 1864.

46. Castel, *Decision in the West*, 290.

47. *OR*, series 1, vol. 38, Sherman reports, May 1–Sept. 8, 1864.

48. Castel, *Decision in the West*, 628n.

49. Sherman, *Memoirs*, 1:186.

50. Cleaves, *Rock of Chickamauga*, 221.

51. Ibid.

52. Ibid., 221–22.

53. Castel, *Decision in the West*, 305.

54. Marcoot, *Five Years in the Sunny South*, 66.

55. Ibid.

56. Castel, *Decision in the West*, 307; Marcoot, *Five Years in the Sunny South*, 66.

57. Cleaves, *Rock of Chickamauga*, 222; *OR*, series 1, vol. 38, report of Col. Joseph Conrad, 15th Missouri Infantry, Sept. 12, 1864; *OR*, series 4, vol. 38, Thomas to Sherman, June 27, 1864, 8 A.M.

58. Marcoot, *Five Years in the Sunny South*, 66.

59. *OR*, series 1, vol. 38, report of Brig. Gen. Nathan Kimball, Aug. 4, 1864.

60. Castel, *Decision in the West*, 307.

61. *OR*, series 4, vol. 38, Thomas to Sherman, 9:30 A.M., report of Brig. Gen. George D. Wagner, Aug. 4, 1864.

62. Marcoot, *Five Years in the Sunny South*, 66.

63. Castel, *Decision in the West*, 242–50.

64. Marcoot, *Five Years in the Sunny South*, 66–67.

65. *OR*, series 4, vol. 38, Sherman to Thomas, 9:50 A.M., June 27, 1864, and part 3, report of Brig. Gen. Francis M. Cockrell, C.S.A. army, June 27, 1864.

66. *OR*, series 1, vol. 38, report of Brig. Gen. George D. Wagner, Aug. 4, 1864.

67. Ibid.

68. *OR*, series 1, vol. 38, report of Col. Joseph Conrad, 15th Missouri Infantry, Sept. 12, 1864.

69. Ibid., Part 1, report of Brig. Gen. Nathan Kimball, Aug. 4, 1864, report of Col. Joseph Conrad, 15th Missouri Infantry, Sept. 12, 1864.

70. *OR*, series 1, vol. 38, report of Brig. Gen. Nathan Kimball, Aug. 4, 1864.

71. Ibid., Thomas to Sherman, June 27, 1864, 10:45 A.M.

72. *OR*, series 1, vol. 38, report of Brig. Gen. Nathan Kimball, Aug. 4, 1864. Kimball reported that this occurred the next day, the 28th; he likely confused this incident with a similar truce to remove wounded on the 28th. See Miles, *Fields of Glory*, 108, and Castel, *Decision in the West*, 316.

73. *OR*, series 1, vol. 38, reports of Kimball, Aug. 4, 1864, and Conrad, Sept. 12, 1864.

74. Fox, *Regimental Losses in the American Civil War*, chap. 10, 15th Missouri Infantry.

75. Castel, *Decision in the West*, 321.

76. *OR*, series 1, vol. 38, Sherman to Halleck, July 9, 1864.

77. Marcoot, *Five Years in the Sunny South*, 67.

78. Castel, *Decision in the West*, 323; Foote, *Civil War*, 3:400.

79. Castel, *Decision in the West*, 323.

80. Marcoot, *Five Years in the Sunny South*, 67.

81. Ibid., 67–68.

82. *OR*, series 1, vol. 38, Conrad reports, Sept. 12, 1864.

83. *OR*, series 5, vol. 38, Sherman to Halleck, July 9, 1864.

84. Castel, *Decision in the West*, 320.

85. Ibid.

86. Ibid., 319.

87. SHSM, Compiled Service Records, 15th Missouri, roll 501, Happ.

17. FORTWÄHREND SCHLACHTEN UND MORD

1. Sandburg, *Abraham Lincoln*, 3:155.

2. *OR*, series 5, vol. 38, Sherman to Thomas, June 27, 1864, 9:00 P.M.; Thomas to Sherman, June 27, 1864; Sherman to Thomas, June 27, 1864, 9:30 P.M.

3. Marcoot, *Five Years in the Sunny South*, 69.

4. Ibid., 69–70.

5. *OR*, series 5, vol. 38, Sherman to Thomas, July 19, 1864, 8:10 P.M.

6. Cleaves, *Rock of Chickamauga*, 229.

7. *OR*, series 5, vol. 38, Fullerton to Newton, July 20, 1864, 6:00 A.M., part 1, report of Col. Joseph Conrad, Sept. 8, 1864, part 1, reports of Newton and Kimball, Sept. 1864.

8. Marcoot, *Five Years in the Sunny South*, 70; SHSM, Compiled Service Records, 15th Missouri, roll 502, Kessler.

9. *OR*, series 1, vol. 38, reports of Newton and Kimball, Sept. 1864.

10. *OR*, series 1, vol. 38, Conrad report, Sept. 8, 1864.

11. Marcoot, *Five Years in the Sunny South*, 70.

12. Marcoot, *Five Years in the Sunny South* 70; *OR*, series 1, vol. 38, report of Colonel Joseph Conrad, Sept. 8, 1864.

13. *OR*, series 1, vol. 38, report of Colonel Joseph Conrad, Sept. 8, 1864.

14. Marcoot, *Five Years in the Sunny South*, 70; SHSM, Compiled Service Records, 15th Missouri, roll 506, Phister.

15. Castel, *Decision in the West*, 376.

16. *OR*, series 1, vol. 38, report of Newton, Sept. 1864.

17. Marcoot, *Five Years in the Sunny South*, 71.

18. *OR*, part 5, vol. 38, Thomas to Sherman, July 20, 1864, 6:15 P.M.

19. Ibid., Sherman to Thomas, July 20, 1864, 8:00 P.M.

20. Ibid., Howard to Whipple, July 21, 1864, 7:00 P.M.

21. Ibid., the Atlanta (Georgia) Campaign, reports of Maj. Gen. William T. Sherman, May 1–Sept. 8, 1864.

22. Ibid., reports of Brig. Gen. John Newton, Sept. —, 1864.

23. SHSM, Compiled Service Records, 15th Missouri, roll 498, Delfs.

24. Marcoot, *Five Years in the Sunny South*, 71.

25. SHSM, Compiled Service Records, 15th Missouri, roll 499, Erdmann; MSIC, 15th Missouri, correspondence, Miscellaneous file, box 407, folder 26.

26. Burton, *Melting Pot Soldiers*, 205–6.

27. SHSM, Compiled Service Records, 15th Missouri, roll 499, Erdmann.

28. SHSM, Compiled Service Records, 15th Missouri, roll 499, Erdmann.

29. NA, Old Military Records, Conrad file, Erdmann letters dated Aug. 23, 1864.

30. NA, Old Military Records, Conrad file, Erdmann letters dated Aug. 23, 1864.

31. NA, Old Military Records, Conrad file, Erdmann letters dated Aug. 23, 1864.

32. NA, Old Military Records, Conrad file, Erdmann letters dated Aug. 23, 1864 (emphasis mine).

33. Burton, *Melting Pot Soldiers*, 210.

34. SHSM, Compiled Service Records, 15th Missouri, roll 499, Erdmann.

35. Longacre and Haas, *To Battle for God and the Right*, 210.

36. Ibid., 214.

37. NA, Old Military Records, Joseph Conrad file.

38. Longacre and Haas, *To Battle for God and the Right*, 214–15.

39. SHSM, Compiled Service Records, 15th Missouri, roll 499, Erdmann.

40. Marcoot, *Five Years in the Sunny South*, 71–72.

41. SHSM, Compiled Service Records, 15th Missouri.

42. Marcoot, *Five Years in the Sunny South*, 69.

43. Sherman, *Memoirs*, 2:96.

44. Marcoot, *Five Years in the Sunny South*, 73.

45. Ibid., 73–74.

46. Miles, *Fields of Glory*, 150–51.

47. Marcoot, *Five Years in the Sunny South*, 73.

48. Ibid., 74.

49. Ibid.

50. Ibid., 75–76.

51. Ibid.

52. Sandburg, *Abraham Lincoln*, 3:229–30.

53. WHMC, Buegel, diary, 43.

18. Second Best in America

1. Hood, *Advance and Retreat*, 266–69.

2. *OR*, series 2, vol. 39, Sherman to Grant, Sept. 10, 1864, Grant to Sherman, Sept. 12, 1864; Donald, *Lincoln*, 553.

3. SHSM, Compiled Service Records, 15th Missouri, roll 503, Lipps; roll 500, Droste; roll 507, Rau.

4. Fox, *Regimental Losses in the American Civil War*, chap. 10, 15th Missouri Infantry; Marcoot, *Five Years in the Sunny South*, 77; SHSM, Compiled Service Records, 15th Missouri.

5. Sherman, *Memoirs*, 2:140; Castel, *Decision in the West*, 536.

6. Castel, *Decision in the West*, 552–53.

7. Marcoot, *Five Years in the Sunny South*, 77; SHSM, Compiled Service Records, 15th Missouri, roll 507, Riley.

8. SHSM, Compiled Service Records, 15th Missouri.

9. Marcoot, *Five Years in the Sunny South*, 79–80.

10. *OR*, series 2, vol. 39, Thomas to Hatch, Oct. 31, 1864.

11. Ibid., Thomas to Sherman, Oct. 31, 1864, 9:30 A.M.

12. Ibid., Sherman to Grant, Nov. 1, 1864, 9:00 A.M.

13. Cleave, *Rock of Chickamauga*, 247.

14. *OR*, series 2, vol. 39, Sherman to Grant, Nov. 1, 1864, 9:00 A.M.

15. Ibid., Grant to Sherman, Nov. 1, 1864, 6:00 P.M.

16. Ibid., Grant to Sherman, Nov. 2, 1864, 11:30 A.M.

17. Marcoot, *Five Years in the Sunny South*, 84.

18. SHSM, Compiled Service Records, 15th Missouri, roll 508, Weber.

19. Cleave, *Rock of Chickamauga*, 245–47.

20. Ibid., 49 and 55.

21. SHSM, Compiled Service Records, 15th Missouri, roll 499, Erdmann.

22. Marcoot, *Five Years in the Sunny South*, 84.

19. An Act of Providence

1. *OR*, series 1, vol. 45, Hatch to Thomas, Nov. 21, 1864, 8:00 A.M.

2. *OR*, series 1, vol. 45, Fourth Army Corps, Orders for tomorrow, Nov. 23, 1864, 7:45 P.M., and Nov. 24, 1864, 1:45 A.M.; Marcoot, *Five Years in the Sunny South*, 84.

3. *OR*, report of Brig. Gen. Luther P. Bradley, Dec. 5, 1864; Marcoot, *Five Years in the Sunny South*, 84.

4. Marcoot, *Five Years in the Sunny South*, 84.

5. *OR*, series 1, vol. 45, Thomas to Grant, Nov. 25, 1864, 11:00 A.M.

6. Ibid., Grant to Thomas, Nov. 27, 1864, 9:00 P.M.

7. Sword, *Confederacy's Last Hurrah*, 96–97.

8. *OR*, series 1, vol. 45, report of Maj. Gen. U. S. Stanley, Feb. 25, 1865, and report of Brig. Gen. George D. Wagner, Dec. 2, 1864; Sword, *Confederacy's Last Hurrah*, 104.

9. *OR*, report of Maj. Gen. U. S. Stanley, Feb. 25, 1865.

10. *OR*, series 1, vol. 45, report of Brig. Gen. Luther P. Bradley, Dec. 5, 1864.

11. Ibid.; Sword, *Confederacy's Last Hurrah*, 121.

12. *OR*, series 1, vol. 45, report of Brig. Gen. Luther P. Bradley, Dec. 5, 1864.

13. Ibid.; Sword, *Confederacy's Last Hurrah*, 121–22.

14. *OR*, series 1, vol. 45, report of Brig. Gen. Luther P. Bradley, Dec. 5, 1864.

15. Ibid., report of Maj. Frederick A. Atwater, Dec. 5, 1864.

16. *OR*, series 1, vol. 45, reports of Maj. Frederick A. Atwater, Dec. 5, 1864, and Brig. Gen. Luther P. Bradley, Dec. 5, 1864; Sword, *Confederacy's Last Hurrah*, 128–29.

17. *OR*, series 1, vol. 45, reports of Brig. Gen. George D. Wagner, Dec. 2, 1864.

18. SHSM, Compiled Service Records, 15th Missouri, roll 498, Ernst.

19. Fox, *Regimental Losses in the American Civil War*, chap. 10, 15th Missouri Infantry; *OR*, series 1, vol. 45, reports of Brig. Gen. Luther P. Bradley and Maj. Frederick A. Atwater, Dec. 5, 1864; SHSM, Compiled Service Records, 15th Missouri.

20. SHSM, Compiled Service Records, 15th Missouri, roll 498, Eisermann and Eberle.

21. Sword, *Confederacy's Last Hurrah*, 133–39.

22. Ibid., 143.

23. Ibid., 144.

24. Ibid., 144–45; *OR*, series 1, vol. 45, reports of Maj. Gen. John M. Schofield, Dec. 31, 1864, and Maj. Gen. U. S. Stanley, Feb. 25, 1865; Journal of the Fourth Army Corps, Nov. 14, 1864–Jan. 23, 1865; Campaign in North Alabama and Middle Tennessee, no. 11.

25. Sword, *Confederacy's Last Hurrah*, 144–45.

26. *OR*, series 1, vol. 45, reports of Maj. Gen. U. S. Stanley, Feb. 25, 1865.

27. Ibid., Twining to Thomas, Nov. 29, 1864, 10:00 P.M.

28. Sword, *Confederacy's Last Hurrah*, 133–39; *OR*, series 1, vol. 45, reports of Lt. Gen. Alexander P. Stewart, C.S.A. army, Apr. 3, 1864.

29. Sword, *Confederacy's Last Hurrah*, 149; Dyer, *Compendium of the War of the Rebellion*, 3:1337.

30. *OR*, series 1, vol. 45, report of Maj. Gen. John M. Schofield, Dec. 31, 1864.

31. Johnson and Buell, *Battles and Leaders of the Civil War*, 4:448; Sword, *Confederacy's Last Hurrah*, 142.

32. *OR*, series 1, vol. 45, reports of Lt. Gen. Alexander P. Stewart, C.S.A. army, Apr. 3, 1864; Sword, *Confederacy's Last Hurrah*, 147.

33. Sword, *Confederacy's Last Hurrah*, 148.

34. *OR*, series 1, vol. 45, reports of Col. Joseph Conrad, Dec. 1, 1864.

35. Johnson and Buell, *Battles and Leaders of the Civil War*, 4:448.

36. Ibid.; *OR*, series 1, vol. 45, report of Brig. Gen. Lawrence S. Ross, C.S.A. army, Jan. 12, 1865.

37. Johnson and Buell, *Battles and Leaders of the Civil War*, 4:449.

38. *OR*, series 1, vol. 45, reports of Col. Emerson Opdycke, Dec. 5, 1864.

39. Johnson and Buell, *Battles and Leaders of the Civil War*, 4:449.

40. Sword, *Confederacy's Last Hurrah*, 156.

41. Ibid., 152.

42. Ibid., 155.

20. EVERY MAN A COMMANDER

1. *OR*, series 1, vol. 45, report of Maj. Gen. George H. Thomas, Jan. 20, 1865.

2. Ibid., reports of Brig. Gen. D. Cox, Jan. 10, 1865.

3. Ibid., reports of Col. Joseph Conrad, Dec. 1, 1864; Bennett and Haigh, *History of the Thirty-sixth*, 459.

4. *OR*, series 1, vol. 45, report of Col. Emerson Opdycke, Dec. 8, 1864.

5. Ibid., reports of Brig. Gen. George D. Wagner, Dec. 2, 1864.

6. Ibid., reports of Col. Joseph Conrad, Dec. 1, 1864.

7. Ibid., reports of Capt. George Ernst, 15th Missouri Infantry, Dec. 8, 1864, and report of Maj. Gen. George D. Wagner, Dec. 2, 1864.

8. Sword, *Confederacy's Last Hurrah*, 174.

9. Bennett and Haigh, *History of the Thirty-sixth*, 466–67; Shellenberger, *Battle of Franklin*, 2.

10. Bennett and Haigh, *History of the Thirty-sixth*, 466–67.

11. *OR*, series 1, vol. 45, reports of Col. Joseph Conrad, Dec. 1, 1864, and report of Capt. George Ernst, 15th Missouri Infantry, Dec. 8, 1864.

12. Ibid., reports of Col. Joseph Conrad, Dec. 1, 1864.

13. Ibid.

14. Shellenberger, *Battle of Franklin*, 2–3.

15. *OR*, series 1, vol. 45, reports of Conrad's regimental commanders and one of Lane's: Capt. George Ernst, 15th Missouri Infantry, Dec. 8, 1864; Capt. Merritt B. Atwater, 51st Illinois Infantry, Dec. 5, 1864; Col. Allen Buckner, 79th Illinois Infantry, Dec. 5, 1864; Maj. Frederick A. Atwater, 42d Illinois Infantry, Dec. 5, 1864; Lt. Col. Robert C. Brown, 64th Ohio Infantry, Dec. 6, 1864; Maj. Orlow Smith, 65th Ohio Infantry, Dec. 5, 1864; Lane's brigade, Lt. Col. Milton Barnes, 97th Ohio Infantry, Dec. 5, 1864. No other regimental reports of these two brigades apparently exist.

16. Ibid., reports of Lt. Col. Robert C. Brown, Dec. 6, 1864.

17. Ibid., report of Maj. Gen. U. S. Stanley, Feb. 25, 1865.

18. Ibid., reports of Col. Joseph Conrad, Dec. 1, 1864.

19. Shellenberger, *Battle of Franklin*, 7.

20. Ibid.

21. Ibid., 5–6; Logsdon, *Eyewitnesses at the Battle of Franklin*, 8.

22. *OR*, series 1, vol. 45, reports of Col. Joseph Conrad, Dec. 1, 1864; Kennedy, *Civil War Battlefield Guide*, 395.

23. Shellenberger, *Battle of Franklin*, 6.

24. Ibid.; Logsdon, *Eyewitnesses at the Battle of Franklin*, 14.

25. Logsdon, *Eyewitnesses at the Battle of Franklin*, 13–16.

26. Shellenberger, *Battle of Franklin*, 8.

27. LC, Shellenberger Papers, Conrad to Shellenberger, May 24, 1889.

28. *OR*, series 1, vol. 45, reports of Col. Joseph Conrad, Dec. 1, 1864; Logsdon, *Eyewitnesses at the Battle of Franklin*, 17.

29. *OR*, series 1, vol. 45, reports of Col. Allen Buckner, Dec. 5, 1864.

30. Ibid., reports of Col. Joseph Conrad, Dec. 1, 1864; Logsdon, *Eyewitnesses at the Battle of Franklin*, 13–17.

31. *OR*, series 1, vol. 45, report of Capt. George Ernst, 15th Missouri Infantry, Dec. 8, 1864.

32. Ibid., reports of Col. Allen Buckner, 79th Illinois, and Lt. Col. Milton Barnes, 97th Ohio, Dec. 5, 1864.

33. *OR*, series 1, vol. 45, reports of Col. Joseph Conrad, Dec. 1, 1864, and Capt. Merritt B. Atwater, Dec. 5, 1864; Logsdon, *Eyewitnesses at the Battle of Franklin*, 17–18.

34. Logsdon, *Eyewitnesses at the Battle of Franklin*, 17–18.

35. SHSM, Compiled Service Records, 15th Missouri; Fox, *Regimental Losses in the American Civil War*, chap. 10, 15th Missouri Infantry.

36. Shellenberger, *Battle of Franklin*, 8–13.

37. Logsdon, *Eyewitnesses at the Battle of Franklin*, 24; Sword, *Confederacy's Last Hurrah*, 195.

38. Logsdon, *Eyewitnesses at the Battle of Franklin*, 26.

39. Ibid.

40. Shellenberger, *Battle of Franklin*, 14.

41. *OR*, series 1, vol. 45, report of Col. Silas S. Strickland, Dec. 7, 1864; Shellenberger, *Battle of Franklin*, 13–14.

42. LC, Shellenberger Papers, Conrad to Shellenberger, May 24, 1889.

43. Logsdon, *Eyewitnesses at the Battle of Franklin*, 26–27.

44. Ibid., 27–28.

45. Sword, *Confederacy's Last Hurrah*, 198–99.

46. Quoted in Bennett and Haigh, *History of the Thirty-sixth*, 459.

47. Ibid., 461; Logsdon, *Eyewitnesses at the Battle of Franklin*, 26–27.

48. Quoted in Bennett and Haigh, *History of the Thirty-sixth*, 461.

49. Ibid., 462.

50. Ibid., 463.

51. Ibid., 461–62.

52. Ibid.; Shellenberger, *Battle of Franklin*, 14.

53. Sword, *Confederacy's Last Hurrah*, 202–3.

54. Logsdon, *Eyewitnesses at the Battle of Franklin*, 28–29.

55. Sword, *Confederacy's Last Hurrah*, 205.

56. LC, Shellenberger Papers, Conrad to Shellenberger, May 24, 1889.

57. LC, Shellenberger Papers, Conrad to Shellenberger, May 24, 1889; Sword, *Confederacy's Last Hurrah*, 206.

58. LC, Shellenberger Papers, Conrad to Shellenberger, May 24, 1889.

59. Logsdon, *Eyewitnesses at the Battle of Franklin*, 35; Sword, *Confederacy's Last Hurrah*, 205, 207, and 225; Gottschalk, *In Deadly Earnest*, 467.

60. Gottschalk, *In Deadly Earnest*, 468–69.

61. Ibid.

62. LC, Shellenberger Papers, Conrad to Shellenberger, May 24, 1889.

63. Shellenberger, *Battle of Franklin*, 9.

64. Johnson and Buell, *Battles and Leaders of the Civil War*, 4:474; Sword, *Confederacy's Last Hurrah*, 268.

65. *OR*, series 1, vol. 45, reports of Maj. Gen. U. S. Stanley, Feb. 25, 1865; Col. Joseph Conrad, Dec. 1, 1864; Capt. George Ernst, 15th Missouri Infantry, Dec. 8, 1864; Capt. Merritt B. Atwater, 51st Illinois Infantry, Dec. 5, 1864; Col. Allen Buckner, 79th Illinois Infantry, Dec. 5, 1864; Maj. Frederick A. Atwater, 42d Illinois

Infantry, Dec. 5, 1864; Lt. Col. Robert C. Brown, 64th Ohio Infantry, Dec. 6, 1864; Maj. Orlow Smith, 65th Ohio Infantry, Dec. 5, 1864; Lane's brigade, Lt. Col. Milton Barnes, 97th Ohio Infantry, Dec. 5, 1864.

66. *OR*, series 1, vol. 45, reports of Col. Joseph Conrad, Dec. 1, 1864; SHSM, Compiled Service Records, 15th Missouri, Heyer.

67. *OR*, series 1, vol. 45, reports of Col. Joseph Conrad, Dec. 1, 1864; Capt. George Ernst, 15th Missouri Infantry, Dec. 8, 1864; Capt. Merritt B. Atwater, 51st Illinois Infantry, Dec. 5, 1864; Col. Allen Buckner, 79th Illinois Infantry, Dec. 5, 1864; Maj. Frederick A. Atwater, 42d Illinois Infantry, Dec. 5, 1864; Lt. Col. Robert C. Brown, 64th Ohio Infantry, Dec. 6, 1864; Maj. Orlow Smith, 65th Ohio Infantry, Dec. 5, 1864; Lane's brigade, Lt. Col. Milton Barnes, 97th Ohio Infantry, Dec. 5, 1864; Cox, *Battle of Franklin*, 79, 222–23.

68. Cox, *Battle of Franklin*, 222–23.

69. *OR*, series 1, vol. 45, reports of Brig. Gen. Jacob D. Cox, Dec. 2, 1864; Cox, *Battle of Franklin*, 99–100; *OR*, series 1, vol. 45, reports of Col. Emerson Opdycke, Dec. 5, 1864.

70. *OR*, series 1, vol. 45, reports of Brig. Gen. George D. Wagner, Dec. 2, 1864.

71. Cox, *Battle of Franklin*, 79n.

72. *OR*, series 2, vol. 45, Special Field Orders No. 337, Hdqrs. Dept. of the Cumberland, Dec. 9, 1864.

21. A CRY OF VICTORY

1. Marcoot, *Five Years in the Sunny South*, 86.

2. Brennan, "Last Stand in the Heartland," 21.

3. Ibid., 23.

4. Ibid.

5. Marcoot, *Five Years in the Sunny South*, 86.

6. Johnson and Buell, *Battles and Leaders of the Civil War*, 4:474.

7. *OR*, series 2, vol. 45, Grant and Thomas messages, Dec. 2, 1864.

8. *OR*, series 2, vol. 45, Grant to Thomas, Dec. 8, 1864, 8:30 P.M.

9. Marcoot, *Five Years in the Sunny South*, 87.

10. Grant, *Memoirs*, 2:655–59.

11. *OR*, series 2, vol. 45, reports of Col. Joseph Conrad, Jan. 8, 1865; Marcoot, *Five Years in the Sunny South*, 87.

12. *OR*, series 2, vol. 45, reports of Col. Joseph Conrad, Jan. 8, 1865, reports of Capt. George Ernst, 15th Missouri Infantry, Jan. 2, 1865.

13. *OR*, series 2, vol. 45, reports of Capt. George Ernst, Dec. 8, 1865; Marcoot, *Five Years in the Sunny South*, 87–88.

14. Marcoot, *Five Years in the Sunny South*, 87–88.

15. *OR*, series 2, vol. 45, reports of Col. Joseph Conrad, Jan. 8, 1865.

16. SHSM, Compiled Service Records, 15th Missouri, roll 504, Mohr; *OR*, series 2, vol. 45, reports of Capt. George Ernst, 15th Missouri Infantry, Jan. 2, 1865.

17. Johnson and Buell, *Battles and Leaders of the Civil War*, 4:474.

18. Hood, *Advance and Retreat*, 307–11; Sword, *Confederacy's Last Hurrah*, 431.

19. Johnson and Buell, *Battles and Leaders of the Civil War*, 4:426–27.

20. *OR*, series 2, vol. 45, Grant to Thomas, Dec. 8, 1864.

21. Grant, *Memoirs*, 2:655–56.

22. Cleaves, *Rock of Chickamauga*, 269.

23. Ibid.

24. *OR*, series 2, vol. 45, Lincoln to Thomas, Dec. 16, 1864, 11:30 A.M.

25. Marcoot, *Five Years in the Sunny South*, 89.

26. Foote, *Civil War*, 3:705–6.

27. Marcoot, *Five Years in the Sunny South*, 89.

28. Sword, *Confederacy's Last Hurrah*, 411–12.

29. *OR*, series 2, vol. 45, Halleck to Thomas, Dec. 31, 1864, 11:30 A.M.

30. Sword, *Confederacy's Last Hurrah*, 419–20.

31. Marcoot, *Five Years in the Sunny South*, 89.

22. "A TERRIFIC STORM PASSED OVER US"

1. Marcoot, *Five Years in the Sunny South*, 89–91.

2. Ibid., 91–94.

3. Ibid., 91.

4. Ibid., 91–93.

5. Ibid., 93–94.

6. Ibid.

7. Bruun and Crosby, *Our Nation's Archives*, 381.

8. Marcoot, *Five Years in the Sunny South*, 94–95.

9. Foote, *Civil War*, 3:1026–27.

10. SHSM, Compiled Service Records, 15th Missouri, rolls 497, 499, and 505, Baden, Dresser, and Raffle.

11. SHSM, Compiled Service Records, 15th Missouri, roll 507, Schuh.

12. Marcoot, *Five Years in the Sunny South*, 96.

23. PULL FOR THE SHORE

1. Marcoot, *Five Years in the Sunny South*, 96.

2. George Rau, June 1, 1865, letter, copy.

3. Marcoot, *Five Years in the Sunny South*, 96.

4. Ibid., 97.

5. Ibid.

6. Ibid., 97–98.

7. SHSM, Compiled Service Records, 15th Missouri, rolls 497–508. Although Marcoot indicates the mutiny took place on June 18, official records date the desertions as June 15.

8. SHSM, Compiled Service Records, 15th Missouri, rolls 497–508.

9. Marcoot, *Five Years in the Sunny South*, 98; SHSM, Compiled Service Records, 15th Missouri, roll 508, White.

10. Marcoot, *Five Years in the Sunny South*, 99.

11. Ibid., 100–103.

12. *OR*, series 2, vol. 48, Conrad to Stewart, Assistant Adjutant-General, Aug. 19, 1865, Stewart to Conrad, Aug. 21, 1865.

13. Marcoot, *Five Years in the Sunny South*, 103–4.

14. Ibid., 104.

15. Ibid.; SHSM, Compiled Service Records, 15th Missouri, roll 505, Michael Kicks, also shown as "Kicke," likely an error.

16. Marcoot, *Five Years in the Sunny South*, 105.

17. Ibid.

18. MSIC, Military Records, 15th Missouri Infantry, Box 407, Correspondence, Miscellaneous folder.

19. Marcoot, *Five Years in the Sunny South*, 106–9.

20. Ibid., "Publisher's Preface."

21. Ibid.,109.

Epilogue

1. Marcoot, *Five Years in the Sunny South*, 80.

2. Ibid., 109.

3. *St. Louis Globe Democrat*, Nov. 26, 1894.

Bibliography

Unpublished Papers

Charles Frederick Fuelle Papers. Stones River National Battlefield. Murfreesboro, Tennessee.

John T. Beugel. Civil War Diary, 1861–1864. Western Historical Manuscript Collection. Columbia, Missouri.

Julius A. Buechel Papers. Missouri Historical Society. St. Louis, Missouri.

Hiffman Family Papers. Missouri Historical Society. St. Louis, Missouri.

Goebel, Gert. "Laenger als ein Menschenleben in Missouri." Manuscript. Trans. M. Heinrichsmeyer, [1956], Missouri Historical Society, St. Louis.

Henry Kueck Letters. Western Historical Manuscript Collection. State Historical Society of Missouri. University of Missouri-St. Louis.

Theodore Augustus Meysenburg Papers. Missouri Historical Society. St. Louis, Missouri.

Johann Wilhelm Osterhorn Papers. Missouri Historical Society. St. Louis, Missouri.

Muench Family Papers. Missouri Historical Society. St. Louis, Missouri.

William Augustus Renken Letters. Missouri Historical Society. St. Louis, Missouri.

Julius Seidel Papers. Missouri Historical Society. St. Louis, Missouri.

George Daniel Shuster Papers. Missouri Historical Society. St. Louis, Missouri.

Primary and Secondary Sources

15th Missouri Infantry. *Combined Service Records.* Microfilm rolls 497–508. State Historical Society of Missouri, Columbia.

15th Missouri Infantry. Regimental Correspondence. Miscellaneous. Box 407. Missouri State Information Center, Jefferson City.

Adams, George Worthington. *Doctors in Blue: The Medical History of the Union Army in the Civil War.* Baton Rouge: Louisiana State University Press, 1952.

Ambrose, Stephen E. *Halleck: Lincoln's Chief of Staff.* Baton Rouge: Louisiana State University Press, 1962.

Anders, Leslie, "Preserving Our Civil War Battle Flags." *Missouri Historical Review* 37, no. 1 (1992): 10–11.

Andrews, J. Cutler. *The North Reports the War.* Pittsburgh, Pa.: University of Pittsburgh, 1955.

Angle, Paul M., and Earl Schenck Miers, eds. *The Living Lincoln: The Man, His Mind, His Times, and the War He Fought, Reconstructed from His Own Writings.* New York: Barnes & Noble, 1992.

Annual Report of 1863, the Adjutant General of Missouri. Missouri State Information Center.

Anzeiger des Westens. As translated in Rowan and Primm, *Germans for a Free Missouri.* Columbia: University of Missouri Press, 1983.

———. 1863: January, September, October, and December editions; 1864: November and December additions.

Association of Survivors Seventy-Third Regiment Illinois Volunteer Infantry. *Minutes of the Twentieth Annual Reunion.* 1906.

Barnard, George N. *Photographic Views of Sherman's Campaign.* New York: Barnard. 1866. Rpt., New York: Dover, 1977.

Barton, Michael, and Larry M. Logue, eds. *The Civil War Soldier.* New York: New York University Press, 2002.

Bates, David Homer. *Lincoln in the Telegraph Office: Recollections of the United States Military Telegraph Corps during the Civil War.* 1907. Rpt., Lincoln: University of Nebraska Press, 1995.

Beale, Howard K., ed. *The Diary of Edward Bates, 1859–1866.* Washington, D.C.: G.P.O., 1933. Rpt., New York: Da Capo, 1971.

Beaudot, William J. K. *The 24th Wisconsin Infantry in the Civil War: The Biography of a Regiment.* Mechanicsburg, Pa.: Stackpole, 2003.

Bennett, Lyman G., and William M. Haigh. *History of the Thirty-sixth Regiment Illinois Volunteers, during the War of the Rebellion.* Aurora, Ill.: Knickerbocker and Hodder, 1876.

Boatner, Mark M., III. *The Civil War Dictionary.* Rev. ed. New York: Vintage, 1991.

Boernstein, Henry. *Memoirs of a Nobody: The Missouri Years of an Austrian Radical, 1849–1866.* Trans. and ed. Steven Rowan. St. Louis: Missouri Historical Society Press, 1997.

Brennan, Patrick, "Last Stand in the Heartland: The Fight for Nashville," *North & South Magazine* (May 2005).

Bruun, Erik, and Jay Crosby, eds. *Our Nation's Archives: The History of the United States in Documents.* New York: Black Dog & Leventhal, 1999.

Burton, William L. *Melting Pot Soldiers.* 2d ed. New York: Fordham University Press, 1998.

Castel, Albert. *Decision in the West: The Atlanta Campaign of 1864.* Lawrence: University Press of Kansas, 1992.

Catton, Bruce. *Glory Road: The Army of the Potomac.* Garden City, N.Y.: Doubleday, 1952.

———. *Grant Takes Command.* New York: Little, Brown, 1968.

———. *Never Call Retreat.* Garden City, N.Y.: Doubleday, 1965.

Chattanooga-Chickamauga National Military Park. 50th Alabama file, letter of Lt. James Fraser, September 26, 1863.

Christensen, Lawrence O. "A Survey of Historical Writing in Missouri from 1860." *Missouri Historical Review* 80, no. 3 (1988).

Cist, Henry M. *The Army of the Cumberland.* New York: Charles Scribner's Sons, 1882.

Cleaves, Freeman. *Rock of Chickamauga: The Life of General George H. Thomas.* Norman: University of Oklahoma Press, 1948.

Cole Camp, Missouri. *Hier Snackt Wi Plattduetsch: Here We Speak (Low) German.* Cole Camp, Mo.: City of Cole Camp, 1989.

Connelly, Thomas L. *Autumn of Glory: The Army of Tennessee, 1862–1865.* Baton Rouge: Louisiana State University Press, 1971.

Conrad, Joseph. Joseph Conrad file. Old Military Records. National Archives.

———. Letter, Shellenberger Collection. Manuscripts. Library of Congress.

Cooper, Paul., and Ted R. Worley, eds., "Letters from a Veteran of Pea Ridge." *Arkansas Historical Quarterly* 6 (1947).

Cowley, Robert, ed. *With My Face to the Enemy: Perspectives on the Civil War.* New York: Berkley, 2001.

Cox, Jacob D. *The Battle of Franklin, Tennessee, November 30, 1864.* 1897. Rpt., Dayton, Ohio: Morningside Bookshop, 2003.

———. *The March to the Sea: Franklin and Nashville.* New York: Charles Scribner's & Sons, 1882.

———. *Sherman's Battle for Atlanta.* 1882. Rpt., New York: Da Capo, 1992.

Cozzens, Peter. *No Better Place to Die.* Urbana: University of Illinois Press, 1990.

———. *The Shipwreck of Their Hopes.* Urbana: University of Illinois Press, 1994.

———. *This Terrible Sound.* Urbana: University of Illinois Press, 1992.

Craig, Gordon A. *The Germans.* New York: G. P. Putnam's & Sons, 1982.

Current, Richard. N. *The Lincoln Nobody Knows.* American Century Series. New York: Hill and Wang, 1999.

Daily Missouri Republican. Sept. 4, 1854.

Daniel, Larry J. *Days of Glory: The Army of the Cumberland, 1861–1865.* Baton Rouge: Louisiana State University Press, 2004.

Donald, David Herbert. *Lincoln.* New York: Touchstone, 1996.

Duden, Gottfied. *Report on a Journey to the Western States of North America and a Stay of Several Years along the Missouri (During the years 1824, '25, '26, and 1827).* Trans. James W. Goodrich et. al. Columbia: University of Missouri Press, 1980.

Dunson, A. A. "Notes on the Missouri Germans on Slavery." *Missouri Historical Review* (April 1965).

Dyer, Frederick H. *A Compendium of the War of the Rebellion.* 3 Vols. 1908. Rpt., New York: Yoseloff, 1959.

Echoes of Glory: Illustrated Atlas of the Civil War. Alexandria, Va.: Time-Life Books, 1991.

Edwards, William B. *Civil War Guns.* Harrisburg, Pa.: Stackpole, 1962.

Elliott, Sam Davis. *Soldier of Tennessee: General Alexander P. Stewart and the Civil War in the West.* Baton Rouge: Louisiana State University Press, 1999.

Enderle, Ray L. "Harper's Weekly Coverage of the Civil War." Master's thesis, University of Missouri, 1961.

Fehrenbacher, Don E., ed. *Lincoln: Speeches and Writings, 1859–1865.* New York: Library of America, 1989.

Fellman, Michael. "Emancipation in Missouri." *Missouri Historical Society* 83, no. 1 (1988).

———. *Inside War: The Guerrilla Conflict in Missouri during the American Civil War.* New York: Oxford University Press, 1989.

Fisher, Horace Cecil. *The Personal Experiences of Colonel Horace Newton Fisher: A Staff Officer's Story.* Boston: n.p., 1960.

Flayderman, Norm. *Flayderman's Guide to Antique American Firearms.* 6th ed. Northbrook, Ill.: DBI, 1994.

Foote, Shelby. *The Civil War: A Narrative.* 3 vols. New York: Vintage, 1986.

Fox, William F. *Regimental Losses in the American Civil War.* Albany, N.Y.: Civil War CD-ROM Guild Press of Indiana, 1997.

Gallagher, Gary, and Alan T. Nolan, eds. *The Myth of the Lost Cause and Civil War History.* Bloomington: Indiana University Press, 2000.

Gatzke, Hans W. *Germany and the United States: A Special Relationship?* Cambridge, Mass.: Harvard University Press, 1980.

Gerling, Robert. *Highland: An Illinois Community in the American Civil War.* Highland Historical Association, 1978.

Gerteis, Louis. *Civil War St. Louis.* Lawrence: University Press of Kansas, 2001.

Goodrich, James W. "The Civil War Letters of Bethiah Pyatt McKown." *Missouri Historical Review* 67, nos. 2 and 3 (Jan. 1973), Part 1, and (Apr. 1973), Part 2.

Gottschalk, Phil. *In Deadly Earnest: The History of the First Missouri Brigade, CSA.* Columbia: Missouri River Press, 1991.

Grant, Ulysses S. *Memoirs and Selected Letters. Personal Memoirs of U. S. Grant: Selected Letters 1839–1865.* New York: Library of America, 1990.

Greenspan, David. *American Heritage Battle Maps of the Civil War.* New York: Smithmark, 1992.

Griffith, Paddy. *Battle Tactics of the Civil War.* New Haven, Conn.: Yale University Press, 1989.

Groom, Winston. *Shrouds of Glory. From Atlanta to Nashville: The Last Great Campaign of the Civil War.* New York: Grove, 1995.

Hanson, Victor Davis. *The Soul of Battle. From Ancient Times to the Present Day: How Three Great Liberators Vanquished Tyranny.* New York: Free Press, 1999.

Harvey, Charles M. "Missouri from 1849 to 1861." *Missouri Historical Review* 92, no. 2 (1998).

Hay, John. *Inside Lincoln's White House: The Complete Civil War Diary of John Hay.* Ed. Michael Burlingame and John R. Turner. Carbondale: Southern Illinois University Press, 1997.

Hemming, Charles. "A Confederate Odyssey." *American Heritage Magazine* (Dec. 1984).

Herriott, Frank I. *Conference in the Deutches Haus, Chicago, May 14–15, 1860.* Transactions from Illinois State Historical Society of 1928. Reprint.

Hood, John Bell. *Advance and Retreat: Personal Experiences in the United States and Confederate Armies.* New Orleans, La.: For Hood Orphan Memorial Fund, 1880.

Horn, Stanley F. *Civil War Tennessee, 1861–1865. Described by Participants.* Nashville: Tennessee Civil War Centennial Commission, 1965.

Hunt, John Gabriel. *The Essential Abraham Lincoln*. Avenel, N.J.: Portland House, 1993.

Ingenthron, Elmo. *Borderland Rebellion: A History of the Civil War on the Missouri-Arkansas Border*. Branson, Mo.: Ozarks Mountaineer, 1980.

Johnson, Paul. *A History of the American People*. New York: HarperCollins, 1997.

Johnson, Robert U., and Clarence C. Buell, eds. *Battles and Leaders of the Civil War*. 4 vols. New York: Century, 1884–88. Rpt., New York: Castle Books, 1956.

Jones, Howard. *Union in Peril: The Crisis over British Intervention in the Civil War*. Chapel Hill: University of North Carolina Press, 1992.

Kargau, Ernst D., and Don Heinrich Tolzmann, eds. *The German Element in St. Louis. St. Louis in Former Years: A Commemorative History of the German Element*. Translation. Baltimore, Md.: Clearfield, 2000.

Kaufmann, Wilhelm. *The Germans in the American Civil War*. Translation. Carlisle, Pa.: John Kallmann, 1999.

Kennedy, Frances. H. *The Civil War Battlefield Guide*. 2d ed. Boston: Houghton-Mifflin, 1998.

Klingaman, William K. *Abraham Lincoln and the Road to Emancipation, 1861–1865*. New York: Viking, 2001.

Krause, Bonnie J., "German Americans in the St. Louis Region 1840-1860." *Missouri Historical Review* 83 (April 1989).

Leech, Margaret. *Reveille in Washington, 1860–1865*. Alexandria, Va.: Time-Life Books, 1980.

Logsdon, David R., ed. *Eyewitnesses at the Battle of Franklin*. Nashville: Kettle Mills, 1996.

———. *Eyewitnesses at the Battle of Stones River*. Nashville: David R. Logsdon, 1989.

Longacre, Glenn V., and John E. Haas, eds. *To Battle for God and the Right: The Civil War Letterbooks of Emerson Opdycke*. Urbana: University of Illinois Press, 2003.

Lonn, Ella. *Foreigners in the Union Army and Navy*. Baton Rouge: Louisiana State University, 1951.

Lord, Francis A. *Civil War Collector's Encyclopedia*. New York: Castle, 1965.

Marcoot, Maurice. *Five Years in the Sunny South*. St. Louis: Missouri Historical Society, 1890.

McDonough, James Lee. *Chattanooga: A Death Grip on the Confederacy*. Knoxville: University of Tennessee Press, 1984.

———. *Stones River: Bloody Winter in Tennessee*. Knoxville: University of Tennessee Press, 1980.

McDonough, James Lee, and Thomas L. Connelly. *Five Tragic Hours. The Battle of Franklin*. Knoxville: University of Tennessee Press, 1983.

McPherson, James M. *Battle Cry of Freedom: The Civil War Era*. New York: Oxford University Press, 1988.

———. *For Cause and Comrades: Why Men Fought in the Civil War*. New York: Oxford University of Press, 1997.

Meyer, Carl Stamm, ed. *Moving Frontiers: Readings in the History of the Lutheran Church–Missouri Synod*. St. Louis: Concordia, 1964.

Miles, Jim. *Fields of Glory: A History and Tour Guide of the Atlanta Campaign*. Nashville: Rutledge Hill, 1989.

Missouri Republican. 1863 and 1864 editions.

Mitchell, Reid. *Civil War Soldiers*. New York: Viking, 1988.

Moe, Richard. *The Last Full Measure: The Life and Death of the First Minnesota Volunteers*. New York: Henry Holt, 1993.

Morison, Samuel Eliot. *The Oxford History of the American People*. New York: Oxford University Press, 1965.

Nagel, Paul C. *Missouri: A History*. Lawrence: University Press of Kansas, 1977.

Newlin, William H. *A History of the Seventy-third Regiment of Illinois Infantry Volunteers, Its Services and Experiences in Camp, on the March, on the Picket and Skirmish Lines, and in Many Battles of the War, 1861–1865*. Springfield, Ill.: Regimental Reunion Association, 1890.

O'Connor, Richard. *Sheridan*. New York: Konecky and Konecky, 1953.

The Official Military Atlas of the Civil War: To Accompany the Official Records of the Union and Confederate Armies. Washington, D.C.: G.P.O., 1891–95. Rpt., New York: Barnes & Noble, 2003.

Parish, Peter J. *The American Civil War*. New York: Holmes & Meir, 1975.

Parrish, William E., Charles T. Jones Jr., and Lawrence O. Christensen. *Missouri: The Heart of the Nation*. 2d ed. Arlington Heights, Ill.: Harlan Davidson, 1982.

———. *A History of Missouri*. Vol. 3, *1860 to 1875*. Columbia: University of Missouri Press, 1973.

Perret, Geoffrey. *Lincoln's War: The Untold Story of America's Greatest President as Commander in Chief*. New York: Random House, 2004.

Peterson, Norma Lois. *Freedom and Franchise: The Political Career of B. Gratz Brown*. Columbia: University of Missouri Press, 1965.

Phillips, Christopher. *Damned Yankee: The Life of General Nathaniel Lyon*. Columbia: University of Missouri Press, 1990.

———. *Missouri's Confederate: Claiborne Fox Jackson and the Creation of the Southern Identity in the Border West*. Columbia: University of Missouri Press, 2000.

Pollard, Edward A. *Southern History of the War*. New York: Fairfax, 1866. Rpt., New York: Crown, 1977.

Raeuber, Charles F. "A Swiss Regiment in the American Civil War." *Swiss Review of World Affairs* (Oct. 1963).

Raymond, Henry J. *The Life and Public Services of Abraham Lincoln, Sixteenth President of the United States, Together with His State Papers, Including His Speeches, Addresses, Messages, Letters, and Proclamations, and the Closing Scenes Connected with His Life and Death*. New York: Derby and Miller, 1865.

Report of Inspection, Dept. of the Missouri, Van Rennsalaer, Washington, Feb. 10, 1862. Microfilm Publication, M619, roll 108. National Archives.

Rombauer, Robert J. *The Union Cause in St. Louis in 1861*. St. Louis: Nixon-Jones, 1909.

Rorvig, Paul. *The Significant Skirmish: The Battle of Boonville, June 17, 1861*. *Missouri Historical Review* 86, no. 2 (1992).

Rowan, Steven, and James Neal Primm. *Germans for a Free Missouri.* Columbia: University of Missouri Press, 1983.

Sandburg, Carl. *Abraham Lincoln: The War Years.* 4 vols. New York: Harcourt, Brace, 1939.

Schofield, John M. *Forty-six Years in the Army.* New York: Century Co., 1897

Schurz, Carl. *The Reminiscences of Carl Schurz.* Vols. 2 and 3. New York: McClure, 1907.

Sears, Steven W. *Chancellorsville.* Boston: Houghton Mifflin, 1996.

———. *Gettysburg.* Boston: Houghton Mifflin, 2003.

Shellenberger, John K. *The Battle of Franklin.* N.p., 1916.

———. *The Battle of Spring Hill, Tennessee.* N.p.: Military Order of the Loyal Legion of the United States, 1907.

Sheridan, Philip H. *Personal Memoirs.* Vol. 1. New York: De Capo Press, 1992.

Sherman, William T. *Memoirs of General William T. Sherman.* Vols. 1 and 2. New York: Da Capo, 1984.

Society of the Army of the Cumberland, 27th Reunion, Columbus, Ohio. Cincinnati, Ohio: Robert Clark, 1898.

Spruill, Matt. *Guide to the Battle of Chickamauga.* Lawrence: University Press of Kansas, 1993.

Stanley, Steven. Map. *Battle of Franklin, TN.* Washington, D.C.: Civil War Preservation Trust, 2005.

St. Louis Board of Common Council. *Resolutions Expressing the Thanks of the City to the Officers and Soldiers in the Late Battle of Murfreesboro.* January 23, 1863. Stones River National Battlefield.

St. Louis City Directory. 1860–66. St. Louis: R. V. Kennedy.

St. Louis Globe Democrat. November 26, 1894.

Stones River National Battlefield. *Troop Movement Maps: A Regiment-by-Regiment Guide.* 1997.

Sword, Wiley. *Mountains Touched with Fire: Chattanooga Besieged, 1863.* New York: St. Martin's, 1995.

———. *The Confederacy's Last Hurrah: Spring Hill, Franklin, and Nashville.* Lawrence: University Press of Kansas, 1992.

Tasher, Lucy Lucille. *The Missouri Democrat and the Civil War.* Ph.D. diss., Chicago: University of Chicago Libraries, 1936.

Toland, John. *Battle: The Story of the Bulge.* Lincoln: University of Nebraska Press, 1999.

Van Ness, Capt. W. W. *The National School for the Soldier.* New York: Carleton, 1862.

Voices of the Civil War: Chattanooga. Alexandria, Va.: Time-Life Books, 1998.

Voices of the Civil War: Chickamauga. Alexandria, Va.: Time-Life Books, 1997.

War of the Rebellion: A Compilation of the Official Records of the Union and Confederate Armies, 1861–1865. The Civil War CD-ROM. Guild Press of Indiana, 1997.

War of the Rebellion: A Compilation of the Official Records of the Union and Confederate Armies, 1861-1865. Washington, D.C.: G.P.O., 1880–1902.

Warner, Ezra J. *Generals in Blue.* Baton Rouge: Louisiana State University Press, 1964.

————. *Generals in Gray.* Baton Rouge: Louisiana State University Press, 1959.

Watkins, Sam R. *Co. Aytch: A Side Show of the Big Show.* New York: Collier, 1962.

Weber, John. File, Old Military Records, National Archives.

Weigley, Russell F. *A Great Civil War: A Military and Political History, 1861–1865.* Bloomington: Indiana University Press, 2000.

Wellberry, David E., and Judith Ryan, eds. *A New History of German Literature.* Cambridge, Mass.: The Belknap Press of Harvard University Press, 2004.

Whitman, Walt. *The Civil War Poems.* New York: Barnes & Noble, 1994.

Wiley Bell, I. *The Life of Billy Yank.* New York: Bobbs-Merrill, 1951.

————. *The Life of Johnny Reb.* New York: Bobbs-Merrill, 1943.

Williams, T. Harry, and Editors of *LIFE. The LIFE History of the United States: The Union Restored.* Vol. 6. New York: Time, 1963.

Winter, William C. *The Civil War in St. Louis.* St. Louis: Missouri Historical Society Press, 1994.

Woodward, C. Vann, ed. *Mary Chesnut's Civil War.* New Haven, Conn.: Yale University Press, 1981.

Wynn, Ken. *History of Missouri.* Lectures, University of Missouri-Columbia, 1996.

HISTORICAL SOCIETIES AND LIBRARIES

Highland Historical Society

Highland Illinois Public Library

St. Charles County Historical Society Archives

St. Louis Mercantile Library, University of Missouri-St. Louis

St. Louis Public Library

U.S. Army Military History Institute

Index

Illinois Central Railroad, 50
Indiana (steamer), 280
Indianapolis, Indiana, 132, 265
Indianola, Texas, 283, 284
Iowa, 9

Jackson, Claiborne, 3, 10–11, 12, 18
Jackson, Gen. Thomas (Stonewall), xvi, 105
Jackson County, Missouri, 261
James River, 43
Jefferson City, Missouri, 4, 9, 10, 25
John Warner (steamer), 25
Johnson, Brig. Gen. Richard W., 91
Johnson's Cove, 116
Johnston, Gen. Albert Sidney, 43
Johnston, Gen. Joseph E., 176, 177, 180, 181, 185, 191, 204; at Kennesaw Mountain, 193
Johnstonville, 280
Joliat, Col, Francis J., 32, 50, 69, 72; absent without leave, 50, 56; arrested, 36; commands 15th Missouri, 23; illness of, 47; dismissal of Maj. Landry, 35; and F. Mohrhardt, 26, 27; neglect of 15th Missouri, 50; officers bring charges against, 64, 65; resignation of, 64, 66; sells rations, 25, 35
Jonesboro, Georgia, 218, 219

Kansas, 9
Kansas-Nebraska Act, 6; Germans oppose, 9
Keetsville, Missouri, 41, 43
Kelly Farm (Chickamauga), 117
Kennesaw Mountain, 193–203, 204, 210, 217, 261
Kentucky, 50, 53, 91, 112, 222
Kimball, Brig. Gen. Nathan, 184, 191, 205, 206, 208, 239; Kennesaw Mountain, 189, 191, 194, 195, 196, 197, 198, 199, 200
Kingston, Georgia, 189
Know-Nothings, 8, 9, 106
Knoxville, Tennessee, 141, 161, 162, 276, 278
Koerner, Gustav, 6, 7, 8
Kreuznach, Germany, 17
Kyger, Captain: on march to Lookout Mountain, 115–16

Lafayette, Georgia, 113
LaFayette Road, 118, 127

Laiboldt, Col. Bernard, 70, 108; and Battle of Chickamauga, 118, 121–30; and Chaplin Heights, 57, 58; commands demi-brigade, 139, 146; in German Army, 55, 109; and march to Lookout Mountain, 112, 115; and Stones River, 82, 87
Landreth, Major, 170
Landry, Major: dismissed by Joliat, 35
Lane's brigade, 233; Battle of Franklin, 245, 246, 250, 251, 255, 256, 258, 263, 264, 265; casualties, 263
Latin Farmers. *See* Germans, German immigrants
Lebanon, Missouri, 40
Lee, Gen. Robert E., xv, 104, 194, 221, 226, 270, 276; Bragg reinforces, 114; Longstreet rejoins, 176; Petersburg, 269; Pickett's charge, 206; surrenders, 277; defeat at Vicksburg, 109
Leesville, Missouri, 41
Lewisburg Pike, 242
Lexington, Alabama, 275
Lexington, Missouri, 25, 56
Liberty Gap, Tennessee, 108
Life of Billy Yank, The (Wiley): and education of immigrant soldiers, xviii
Lincoln, Abraham, 3, 6, 8, 100–101, 104, 161, 220, 270; on amnesty for deserters, 101; assassination, 277–78; commissions requested, 23; on conquering territory, 226; and draft, 174; and Frémont, 26; on German immigration and troops, 30, 106, 130, 132; and Halleck, 38, 108, 128; and Koerner, 7; on Longstreet's escape, 176; Sheridan's promotion, 52, 53; on Stones River, 89, 91; activates state militias, 10, 11; concern over Tennessee, 141; death of son William, 42
Lincoln, Mary Todd, 42
Lincoln, William: death, 42
Lipps, Lt. Friedrick, 128, 130; wounded, 158, 222
Little Tennessee River, 162
Logan, Gen. John A., 193, 194
London *Times*, 53
Longstreet, Gen. James, 114, 161, 176; at Chickamauga, xiv, 119, 121, 122, 123, 125, 126, 131; at Missionary Ridge, 139, 140, 141, 142

Lookout Creek, 113

Lookout Mountain, Georgia, 113, 115, 135, 140, 141, 161, 276; assault on, 145; Confederate evacuation of, 144

Lookout Station, 25

Lookout Valley, 115, 139

Louisiana, 3, 133

Louisville, Kentucky, 49, 51, 52, 62, 63, 98, 132, 222, 270; base at, 71, 99, 111; hospital at, 187

Lovejoy Station, Georgia, 219

Lucerne, Switzerland, 38

Lutheran Church, Lutherans: clergy on abolition, 9; generally pro-Confederate, 19–20; Missouri Synod, 5

Lynchburg, Virginia, 176

Lynnville, Tennessee, 229

MacArthur, Gen. Douglas, 155, 178

MacArthur, Lt. Col. Arthur, 155, 178, 201, 206

Macon, Georgia, 218, 221

Mainz, Germany, 8

Marcoot, Catherine, 18, 62

Marcoot, John, 172

Marcoot, Maurice, 3, 10, 53, 102, 152, 195, 197, 199, 206, 220, 228, 278, 282, 284–86; on 73d Illinois, 71; on Andersonville, 213–14; on march through Appalachians, 276; in Arkansas, 44; and march on Atlanta, 217, 218; and Battle of Chickamauga, 118, 119, 120, 123, 124–25, 127, 129; on Battle of New Hope, 185–86, 187–88; Battle of Pea Ridge, 41, 42, 43; Battle at Peach Tree Creek, 207–8; leave Benton Barracks, 175; Blaine's Crossing, 162–63; on burial detail, 210–11; on Camp Halleck, 40; on camps, 103; and Confederate troops, 190, 201, 204, 217; on changes in command, 26, 177–78, 211; and Chaplin Heights, 59, 60, 61; and Chattanooga, 110, 134, 135, 137, 168; and Cincinnati, 51; on march to Cleveland, Tennessee, 177; on Co. B of 15th Missouri, 16, 17; on Conrad's speech, 171; march to Corinth, 50; march toward Dallas, Georgia, 184; description of battles, 57; on discipline, 178; camp at Duck River, 271; enlistment of, 13–14, 15; on execution of deserters, 107–37;

on final day of war, 277; on first march and winter camp, 24 32; on pursuit of Forrest's cavalry, 271; on gambling, 147; move through Georgia, 179, 183, 184, 226; on Gen. Howard, 177–78; return to Illinois, 50; illness of, 47, 52, 56, 62, 101, 224, 275; at Kennesaw Mountain, 189, 190, 191, 192, 195, 196, 201; on leave of, 169–71, 172, 173–74; on Lookout Mountain, 113, 145; and Lost Mountain, 190; and H. Meadors, 224, 276, 287, 288; on memoir, 289; on Missionary Ridge, 149–51, 153–54, 155, 158, 161–62; on Murfreesboro, 74, 75, 76, 89, 109; at Nashville, 266, 267, 268; on Gen. Newton, 191; nonveterans muster-out, 223; move to Paducah, 45; on payday, 99; crosses Peach Tree Creek, 205; chasing Price, 39–40; treatment of recruits, 174–75; on reenlistments, 167; reinforcements, 223; and Resaca, 180, 182; at Rienzi, 47, 47; at Rocky Face, 180; on Roehm and patriotism, 131; at Rolla, 27, 28, 37; on spies, 103–4, 216; and Stones River, 97, 100; and sutler, 70–71; move to Texas, 283–84; on Weber, 68

Marcoot, Mrs., 62

Marietta, Georgia, 192, 202

Marine Hospital, St. Louis, 16, 17

Marshall, Missouri, 13

Martin, Lt. Col. Will, 199

Maryland, 13, 53

Marysville, Tennessee, 162

Matagorda, Texas, 283

Maximilian von Hapsburg, Emperor of Mexico, 283

McClellan, Gen. George, 42, 226, 267

McCook, Colonel, 198

McCook, Maj.Gen. Alexander McD., 73, 108, 112, 113, 138; Stones River, 75, 66; Chickamauga, 117, 118, 122, 123, 125, 126, 128, 129

McDonough, James Lee, 160

McKissick farm (Arkansas), 237; and search for Price, 41

McKown, Bethiah Pyatt, 13, 16

McLemore's Cove, 116

McPherson, James, xvii

McPherson, Maj. Gen. James, 184; death of, 211, 212; moves on Resaca, 180

p9 48 : re George Rau ... 3nd ppq.